John Dryden

Tercentenary Essays

John Dryden

Tercentenary Essays

EDITED BY

Paul Hammond

AND

David Hopkins

CLARENDON PRESS · OXFORD

OXFORD

UNIVERSITY PRESS

Great Clarendon Street, Oxford O X 2 6D P

Oxford University Press is a department of the University of Oxford.
It furthers the University's objective of excellence in research, scholarship,
and education by publishing worldwide in

Oxford New York

Athens Auckland Bangkok Bogotá Buenos Aires Calcutta
Cape Town Chennai Dar es Salaam Delhi Florence Hong Kong Istanbul
Karachi Kuala Lumpur Madrid Melbourne Mexico City Mumbai
Nairobi Paris São Paulo Singapore Taipei Tokyo Toronto Warsaw

and associated companies in Berlin Ibadan

Oxford is a registered trade mark of Oxford University Press
in the UK and certain other countries

Published in the United States
by Oxford University Press Inc., New York

British Library Cataloguing in Publication Data

Data available

Library of Congress Cataloging in Publication Data

John Dryden: tercentenary essays / edited by Pal Hammond and David
Hopkins.
p. cm.
Includes bibliographical references and index.
1. Dryden, John, 1631–1700—Criticism and interpretation. 2. Dryden, John,
1631–1700—Contemporaries. 3. English literature—Early modern, 1500–1700—History
and criticism. 4. Politics and literature—Great Britain—History—17th century.
I. Hammond, Paul, 1953–II. Hopkins, David, 1948–
PR3424.J64 2000   821′.4–dc21   00-026212
ISBN 0-19-818644-4

1 3 5 7 9 10 8 6 4 2

Typeset by Kolam Information Services Pvt Ltd, Pondicherry, India
Printed in Great Britain on acid-free paper by
Biddles Ltd,
Guildford and King's Lynn

TO THE MEMORY OF

JOHN DRYDEN

1631–1700

The Soul returns to Heav'n, from whence it came;
Earth keeps the Body, Verse preserves the Fame.

PREFACE

THIS volume is designed to celebrate and to reassess the work of John Dryden (1631–1700) in the tercentenary year of his death. It assembles specially commissioned essays by scholars from Australia, Canada, the United Kingdom, and the United States, essays which differ widely in their approach, assumptions, emphasis, and style. While no attempt has been made to address every aspect of Dryden's voluminous and wide-ranging output, special attention is paid to his political writing, his literary collaborations, his drama, and, in particular, to his translations, still an undervalued part of his *œuvre*. Much of Dryden's writing was occasional in origin, having been written in response to contemporary events and issues, to meet the demands of performance, or to assist friends. Accordingly, several of the essays in this volume offer detailed consideration of the personal and public circumstances in which these works were composed and received. But, as Dryden's own contemporaries and early admirers realized, the intellectual and imaginative world which the poet inhabited was larger than that of Restoration England; for as well as being astutely engaged with the actualities of the present, Dryden's mind was continually engaged in dialogue with his literary predecessors—classical, medieval, and Renaissance. Moreover, his work was to be read and admired in circumstances very different from those in which it initially appeared. So as well as reading Dryden's work in its contemporary contexts, the present collection also considers the poet's communings with the past and his reception after his death, thus attending to the ways in which he might be thought a writer not only for an age, but for all time.

P.F.H., D.W.H.

CONTENTS

Contents

A NOTE ON CONTRIBUTORS

JOHN BARNARD is Professor of English Literature at the University of Leeds. He is the editor of Etherege's *The Man of Mode* (1979), and co-editor of *A History of the Book in Britain*, vol. iv: *1557–1695* (forthcoming).

JENNIFER BRADY is Charles R. Glover Chair of English Studies and Professor of English at Rhodes College. She is co-editor of *Ben Jonson's 1616 Folio* (1991) and of *Literary Transmission and Authority: Dryden and other Writers* (1993).

HOWARD ERSKINE-HILL is Professor of Literary History at the University of Cambridge. He is the author of *The Augustan Idea in English Literature* (1983), *Poetry and the Realm of Politics: Shakespeare to Dryden* (1996), and *Poetry of Opposition and Revolution: Dryden to Wordsworth* (1996).

PAUL HAMMOND is Professor of Seventeenth-Century English Literature at the University of Leeds. He is the author of *Dryden and the Traces of Classical Rome* (1999), and editor of *The Poems of John Dryden*, vol. i: *1649–1681* and vol. ii: *1682–1685* (1995).

DAVID HOPKINS is Reader in English Poetry at the University of Bristol. He is the author of *John Dryden* (1986), and co-editor of *The Poems of John Dryden*, vols. iii: *1686–1693* and iv: *1693–1696* (forthcoming).

PAULINA KEWES is Lecturer in English at the University of Wales, Aberystwyth. She is the author of *Authorship and Appropriation: Writing for the Stage in England, 1660–1710* (1998).

HAROLD LOVE is Professor of English at Monash University. He is the author of *Scribal Publication in Seventeenth-Century England* (1993), and editor of *The Works of John Wilmot, Earl of Rochester* (1999).

TOM MASON is Lecturer in English at the University of Bristol. He is co-editor of *Abraham Cowley: Selected Poems* (1994).

Note on Contributors

NICHOLAS VON MALTZAHN is Professor of English at the University of Ottawa. He is the author of *Milton's 'History of Britain': Republican Historiography in the English Revolution* (1991).

CEDRIC D. REVERAND II is Professor of English at the University of Wyoming. He is the author of *Dryden's Final Poetic Mode: The 'Fables'* (1988).

ADAM ROUNCE is Part-time Tutor at the University of Bristol.

ROBIN SOWERBY is Senior Lecturer in English at the University of Stirling. He is the author of *The Classical Legacy in Renaissance Poetry* (1994).

JAMES A. WINN is Professor of English at Boston University. He is the author of *John Dryden and his World* (1987) and *'When Beauty Fires the Blood': Love and the Arts in the Age of Dryden* (1992).

STEVEN N. ZWICKER is Stanley Elkin Professor in the Humanities at Washington University, St Louis. He is the author of *Politics and Language in Dryden's Poetry: The Arts of Disguise* (1984) and *Lines of Authority: Politics and English Literary Culture, 1649–1689* (1993).

A NOTE ON TEXTS AND ABBREVIATIONS

Unless otherwise stated, Dryden's texts are quoted from the California edition of *The Works of John Dryden*, ed. H. T. Swedenberg *et al.*, 20 vols. (Berkeley, 1956–   ), abbreviated as *Works*. Poems are cited by line numbers (e.g. ll. 12–34), plays by act, scene, and line numbers (e.g. I. ii. 34–56), and prose works by volume and page number (e.g. i. 23–45).

The principal exception is material from *Fables Ancient and Modern* (1700), which has not yet appeared in the California edition; this is quoted from *The Poems of John Dryden*, ed. James Kinsley, 4 vols. (Oxford, 1958), cited as *Poems*, ed. Kinsley.

Two other editions are cited by short title:

Letters	*The Letters of John Dryden*, ed. Charles E. Ward (Durham, NC, 1942)
Poems, ed. Hammond	*The Poems of John Dryden*, vol. i: *1649–1681* and vol. ii: *1682–1685*, ed. Paul Hammond, Longman Annotated English Poets (London, 1995)

INTRODUCTION: IS DRYDEN A CLASSIC?

PAUL HAMMOND

When H. A. Mason in 1962 asked Latinists the question, 'Is Juvenal a Classic?',[1] he was challenging them to lift their eyes above the minutiae of philological and historical scholarship to address the large issues which affect human and humane living. Does Juvenal, he wondered, deserve a place amongst those writers who enlarge and refine our understanding of human nature and society? Is he a classic in the sense that Homer and Shakespeare are classics? Mr Mason's question was framed by a humanism which he learned from long study of Greek and Latin literature, of Dante, of More and Erasmus, and of Shakespeare, Dryden, and Pope; and his pursuit of 'the classic' was repeatedly inflected by invocations of Matthew Arnold and Arnold's search for the 'central, truly human point of view'. Looking back now at Mason's generation—the generation of *Scrutiny*, and in America the generation of men like Lionel Trilling and Walter Jackson Bate—I am tempted to say, as Dryden did of his predecessors, 'Theirs was the Gyant Race, before the Flood'.[2] The liberal humanism of my teachers at Cambridge—Mason himself, L. C. Knights, Theodore Redpath[3]—seems to many in the post-

---

[1] H. A. Mason, 'Is Juvenal a Classic?', in J. P. Sullivan (ed.), *Critical Essays on Roman Literature: Satire* (London, 1963), pp. 93–176. The essay first appeared in *Arion* the previous year.

[2] 'To my Dear Friend Mr. Congreve, On His Comedy, call'd *The Double-Dealer*', l. 5.

[3] Pupil of Wittgenstein, editor of Shakespeare and Donne, translator of Sophocles, exponent of Hobbes and Leibniz, barrister, intelligence officer, and wine-merchant, Theodore Redpath would have been comfortably at home in Will's Coffee House.

modern academy to be *passé* if not actually pernicious. In the 1980s and 1990s 'liberal humanist' became in some quarters a term of abuse. The supposition that there are common human questions and experiences which transcend time, race, and gender; that human behaviour is recognizable in Homer as in George Eliot; that there are great writers of individual genius whose insights sustain and disturb us—such notions were anathema. That liberal humanism at its best also entailed a profoundly historical understanding of texts and their cultural milieux, and an imaginative engagement with other ways of thinking, mattered little to those who sought in literature only their own shibboleths. To such readers the question 'Is Dryden a Classic?', asked in the year 2000, will seem not simply *une question mal posée* but one which is retrograde and even reprehensible. Is not the very idea of 'a classic' ahistorical and elitist? And on a superficial reading Dryden himself seems so obviously alien to politically correct notions that few have thought it worth exposing him. Of late he has slipped off many undergraduate syllabuses, and excites little interest among those looking for research topics. While he has, for the most part, been spared the sneering superiority with which Shakespeare and Milton have been handled, yet the comparative neglect of Dryden by our best critics and brightest students has led to him now being the least appreciated of our great poets.

Perhaps times are changing. There are, I think, signs that literature is being reclaimed by scholars and critics who are exploring a humanistic agenda with renewed confidence, particularly through close reading and the patient construction of intellectual histories, while drawing upon the best of recent critical developments. The new humanism is informed by a more imaginative historiography, excited by Foucault's big ideas and the colourful anecdotalism of New Historicism, but more attentive to the status of evidence, the distortions wrought by anachronistic agendas, and the perils of drawing large inferences from small examples. It is inspired, too, by interest in gender and sexuality, while not parading outrage at the past for daring to have values and domestic arrangements different from our own. And it deploys a deconstructive awareness of the unsteady character of those major terms and modes of argument through which we construct our humanity, while not itself becoming hermetic, and comprehensible only to initiates. Within such a reinvigorated humanism, it should be possible to ask the question 'Is Dryden a Classic?'

In response, one might point to two facets of his work. The first is the inventive way in which the literary, political, and religious issues of his day are translated into poetry, mythologized, and brought into contact with classical culture: the present is read through the past. The second is the reverse of the same coin: his translation of classical texts into an idiom which is that of the present while retaining something of the stylistic traits as well as the habits of thought of the original. This reciprocal translation of past and present shows that a common heritage does exist, but it is not unchanging or transhistorical: it has to be rediscovered and reinvented. These two axes of Dryden's work—his relations to his contemporary culture and to his predecessors—form the twin themes of this volume. Such an understanding of the nature and stature of Dryden's achievement is confirmed by the reception which he was accorded by later readers, itself a recurring motif in this collection.

᠁

Dryden's involvement with his own culture has been well expounded by modern scholars and critics, though there has been an unfortunate tendency to see this as the work of the 'journalist in verse', to quote Mark van Doren's unhappily durable phrase.[4] We have had illuminating studies (particularly from American scholars) of the political and cultural milieux out of which his major poems emerged, and in which they found their first readers.[5] *Annus Mirabilis* took its title from Nonconformist pamphlets which saw the plague and the Fire of London as divine judgements on the dissolute and ungodly ways of the Carolean court.[6] *Absalom and Achitophel* engaged in detail with the tropes and arguments of the Exclusion

[4] The title of chapter 5 of Mark van Doren, *John Dryden: A Study of his Poetry* (New York, 1920). The actual discussion is subtler than his title suggests.

[5] Steven N. Zwicker, *Dryden's Political Poetry: The Typology of King and Nation* (Providence, RI, 1972) and *Politics and Language in Dryden's Poetry: The Arts of Disguise* (Princeton, NJ, 1984); the extensive commentaries in the California edition of Dryden's *Works*; and other studies cited below. Amongst British work, notable contextual readings include Howard Erskine-Hill, *The Augustan Idea in English Literature* (London, 1983), *Poetry and the Realm of Politics: Shakespeare to Dryden* (Oxford, 1996), and *Poetry of Opposition and Revolution: Dryden to Wordsworth* (Oxford, 1996).

[6] Michael McKeon, *Poetry and Politics in Restoration England: The Case of Dryden's 'Annus Mirabilis'* (Cambridge, Mass., 1975).

3

Crisis, rhetorically offering itself both as another quasi-seditious pamphlet and as a biblically authoritative verdict on rebellion.[7] *Mac Flecknoe* used an extensive knowledge of the works of Flecknoe and Shadwell to turn those writers into ridicule, assuming that the allusions would be understood and enjoyed by the coterie readership targeted by the poem's manuscript circulation.[8] *Religio Laici* and *The Hind and the Panther* emerged from a thorough grounding in the theological and controversial literature of the period, dramatizing in dialogic form arguments from Protestant, Catholic, and Deist tracts.[9] But such a description risks implying that Dryden did no more than versify the pamphlets which he collected from the bookstalls which lined St Paul's churchyard. On the contrary, his treatment of such materials shows a poetic genius.

First, his handling of the present, its personalities, texts, and beliefs, is frequently inflected by gestures which summon into the poem the language, myth, and history of classical literature.[10] Latin vocabulary and Roman narratives lurk within his account of Restoration phenomena, suggesting modes of reading which frame the present; the present is subtly transposed into a Romano-Restoration world whose initiator is Dryden, but whose co-creator is the reader who recognizes these classical traces and gathers them for himself into a new and various texture as he reads. Far from this being the *modus operandi* of the journalist, it is a form of writing which changes the time of the present into a fictive time, one built up from different historical moments and diverse mythic materials, each of which bears traces of distinctive and not always compatible ways of apprehending the world. Dryden is too intelligent to simplify, too well-read to consider his own culture to be the culmination of human progress, too diffident and sceptical merely to assert his own beliefs without leading us to entertain other ways of thinking.

---

[7] W. K. Thomas, *The Crafting of 'Absalom and Achitophel'* (Waterloo, Ontario, 1978); Phillip Harth, *Pen for a Party: Dryden's Tory Propaganda in its Contexts* (Princeton, NJ, 1993).

[8] Richard L. Oden, *Dryden and Shadwell* (Delmar, NY, 1977); Paul Hammond, 'Flecknoe and *Mac Flecknoe*', *Essays in Criticism*, 35 (1985) 315–29. Howard Erskine-Hill's essay below reminds us that the context for the poem was political as well as literary.

[9] Phillip Harth, *Contexts of Dryden's Thought* (Chicago, 1968); Anne Barbeau Gardiner, *Ancient Faith and Modern Freedom in John Dryden's 'The Hind and the Panther'* (Washington, DC, 1998); George Myerson, *The Argumentative Imagination: Wordsworth, Dryden, Religious Dialogues* (Manchester, 1992).

[10] Paul Hammond, *Dryden and the Traces of Classical Rome* (Oxford, 1999).

Then, Dryden's handling of language is that of the skilled poet, setting words in relations which suggest unsuspected shades of meaning, playing with the culture's key abstract nouns (liberty, nature, reason, sense) while also developing clusters of associations around words which came to hold special philosophical significance for him (fortune, business, anxious care, ease), words which achieve extended definition through their varied repetition. Increasingly, Milton is the primary English source for the vocabulary through which Dryden rethinks the great issues of good and of evil, of freedom and servitude, of paradise and its loss.[11] Nor is Dryden's language primarily an abstract or abstracting neo-classical diction, for his interest in Hobbes and in the Royal Society, his reading of scurrilous satire, his boyish wonder at Ovid's tales of nature's changes and of human passion, and his long immersion in the tragic violence of Virgil and Homer—all these gave his English a subtle and disturbing force, the force of an imagination which lived fully in the physical world. The words are at once precise, and fertile with implication. The resulting texture is rarely coolly 'neo-classical', for Dryden always had an extravagant, mischievous fancy which could lead him beyond the bounds of sober decorum.[12] Critics seldom address the language of Dryden's verse with close, imaginative rigour, but it amply repays such attention.[13] His own contemporaries and successors found it a rich source.[14]

Finally, there is Dryden's polemical appropriation of the imagery of his opponents, which seeks to mythologize contemporary history in a way which implies that his is the true application of the image: 1666 is a year of wonders because it shows God's providential care for Charles and for London, not (as the Puritans had claimed) his wrath; Shadwell is the heir to Flecknoe, not (as Shadwell's rhetoric had claimed) to Jonson; the Church of Rome is not (as Protestants

[11] J. R. Mason, 'To Milton through Dryden and Pope', unpublished Ph.D. thesis, University of Cambridge, 1987. Dryden's engagement with Milton is explored below by Nicholas von Maltzahn.

[12] See Harold Love, 'Dryden's "Unideal Vacancy"', *Eighteenth-Century Studies*, 12 (1978) 74–89, and 'Dryden's Rationale of Paradox', *ELH* 51 (1984) 297–313, an argument extended in his essay below.

[13] For one such example see Eric Griffiths, 'Dryden's Past', *Proceedings of the British Academy*, 84 (1994) 113–49.

[14] This is exemplified in the essay below by Tom Mason and Adam Rounce, and in various items in the Appendix.

had claimed) the beast of Revelation and whore of Babylon, but a gentle, virginal white hind, while it is the Church of England which is a beast, a potentially noble but corrupted and dangerous panther. These corrective claims to be putting forward the true and definitive interpretation of people and causes, however, are never as complacent and totalizing as this summary might suggest. In each case the newly applied imagery is set to work within a dialogue, encountering oppositional voices which call into question the stability of the poem's case: though these opposing views are, of course, scripted by Dryden, they often have a vigour and a cogency which cannot altogether be contained within the poem's overt framework and ostensible purpose. For Dryden was, fundamentally, a dramatist, a writer who loved dialogue and impersonation, and delighted in giving voice to conflicting ideas.[15] (This does not mean that he therefore wrote consistently good plays: in those one misses the sophisticated narratorial irony which inflects his non-dramatic dialogues.) The poems both effect a translation of the historical moment into mythologized form, and at the same time make self-critical gestures of demurral which recognize the case against the 'unerring guide'[16] which the poem appears to be. Such an authority, Dryden knew, was not to be found in human texts.[17]

In addressing the contemporary literary world too, Dryden's work contrives a form of translation between past and present, his poems to Roscommon, Maidwell, Oldham, and Congreve setting their achievement within the conceptual framework of a neo-Roman culture: classicism and modernity are engaged in a movement of reciprocal definition and qualification. But it would be wrong to represent this as a triumphalist or self-congratulatory trope: the memorial poem to Oldham notoriously stresses Oldham's failures as well as his achievements, and ends on a note of pure

---

[15] Paulina Kewes's essay below explores Dryden's literal staging of oppositional tropes, while Cedric D. Reverand II examines his quasi-dramatic assumption of various personae in his late verse.

[16] *Religio Laici*, l. 277; *The Hind and the Panther*, i. 65.

[17] Is this one reason why he failed to publish any edition of his collected poems? The mode of publication of his poetry is considered in my article on 'The Circulation of Dryden's Poetry', *Papers of the Bibliographical Society of America*, 86 (1992) 379–409. David Hopkins's essay below explores the difficulties of producing an edition of Dryden's poetry which is in touch both with the original conditions of its publication, and with the needs of readers three centuries later.

classical pessimism: 'But Fate and gloomy Night encompass thee around.'[18] Moreover, that poem deploys the comparison of Dryden and Oldham with Nisus and Euryalus in such a way as to imply that it is not only Oldham who has fallen, but Dryden too: the former in death, the latter through some kind of failure as a poet.[19] And the poem to Congreve writes Dryden's own career into literary history as another form of failure, neither heroically strong like Shakespeare nor elegantly civilized like Congreve.

As Dryden develops in his essays and prefaces a new style of literary criticism, his elucidation of the distinctive characteristics of classical and modern authors takes the form of a double movement, charting both filiation and fraternity.[20] Sometimes this is overt ('*Milton* was the Poetical Son of *Spencer*, and Mr. *Waller* of *Fairfax*'[21]), sometimes implicit, as in this seminal description of Shakespeare:

> To begin then with Shakespeare; he was the man who of all Modern, and perhaps Ancient Poets, had the largest and most comprehensive soul. All the Images of Nature were still present to him, and he drew them not laboriously, but luckily: when he describes any thing, you more than see it, you feel it too. Those who accuse him to have wanted learning, give him the greater commendation: he was naturally learn'd; he needed not the spectacles of Books to read Nature; he look'd inwards, and found her there.[22]

This is Shakespeare the original genius, by implication the English Homer who is the fount of the national poetry. It is also a Shakespeare who shares characteristics with Virgil, of whom Dryden was writing simultaneously: 'when any such Image is to be set before us . . . we see the objects he represents us with in their native figures, their proper motions'.[23] But of course, Shakespeare the implicitly

---

[18] 'To the Memory of Mr. Oldham', l. 25.

[19] Dustin H. Griffin, 'Dryden's "Oldham" and the Perils of Writing', *Modern Language Quarterly*, 37 (1976) 133–50.

[20] Jennifer Brady, 'Dryden and Negotiations of Literary Succession and Precession', in Earl Miner and Jennifer Brady (eds.), *Literary Transmission and Authority: Dryden and Other Writers* (Cambridge, 1993), pp. 27–54; David Bruce Kramer, *The Imperial Dryden: The Poetics of Appropriation in Seventeenth-Century England* (Athens, Ga., 1994). Jennifer Brady develops her argument in respect of Dryden and Congreve in her essay below.

[21] 'Preface to *Fables*', l. 30.

[22] *Works*, xvii. 55.

[23] 'An account of the ensuing Poem' prefixed to *Annus Mirabilis* (*Works*, i. 54). The idea was a commonplace: cf. Poussin, writing to Chantelou on 24 November 1647: 'Virgile . . .

Homeric and Virgilian master, and intimate companion of Nature—that ostensibly ahistorical *signifié transcendantal*[24]—is also located by Dryden in a culture which was comparatively unrefined in its language and its sense of dramatic decorum. Dryden wants us to see both the contingent and the transcendent.

It was largely Dryden who established the English poetic canon: he promoted Chaucer through his translations in *Fables Ancient and Modern* (which also included an accessible reading text of Chaucer's originals), and through the Preface which placed him in the company of Ovid and Boccaccio as witty storytellers; Shakespeare is recognized as the presiding genius of the English stage, both through critical evaluations in essays and prologues, and through adaptation and imitation in *The Tempest*, *Troilus and Cressida*, and *All for Love*; while Milton is increasingly (if unobtrusively) the dominant English voice in Dryden's poetry. It was also largely Dryden who established a canon of Latin and Greek poetry in English, with the help of his publisher Jacob Tonson. Their complete translations of Juvenal, Persius, and Virgil, and their substantial selections from Homer, Horace, Lucretius, Ovid, and others, brought the classics into English with a lucidity and panache missing from most earlier versions. The compact Dryden–Tonson miscellanies, and their handsome folio volumes of Juvenal and Persius, and of Virgil, brought the classics to a non-specialist readership, fashioning in the process a new sense of national culture.[25]

There remains the problem of his religious and political consistency: his shift from being an employee and eulogist of Cromwell to being a defender and Laureate of Charles; from being an Anglican to being a Roman Catholic—or perhaps he had been a Hobbist,[26] or perhaps 'an Atheist exceeding Lucretius',[27] as one contemporary thought. Was his conversion opportunistic and mercenary, or principled and (in worldly terms) a costly error of judgement? Well-

---

accommode le propre son du vers avec tel artifice que proprement il semble qu'il mette devant les yeux avec le son des paroles les choses desquelles il traite' (Nicolas Poussin, *Lettres et propos sur l'art*, ed. Anthony Blunt (Paris, 1989), p. 137). Blunt notes that Poussin's source is Giuseppe Zarlino's *Istituzioni Harmoniche* (Venice, 1558).

[24] Jacques Derrida, *L'Écriture et la différence* (Paris, 1967, repr. 1994), p. 411.
[25] See John Barnard's essay below on the Dryden–Tonson Virgil.
[26] See Nicholas von Maltzahn's essay below, pp. 32–3.
[27] See p. 368 below.

informed and sympathetic biography[28] can clear Dryden from the charge of being unprincipled, in so far as one can see into the heart of another human being. The poems which address these issues are lively, committed, and complex, the work of a man who had thought hard about matters of religion, but was not prepared to put into print work of an intimate devotional or agonistic character. He was no Donne, no Herbert. The rare moments of spiritual autobiography suggest above all an awareness of his own capacity for error. Such is the tenor of the confessional passage in *The Hind and the Panther*, in which both the tenets and the imagery of *Religio Laici* are recalled and repudiated:

> My thoughtless youth was wing'd with vain desires,
> My manhood, long misled by wandring fires,
> Follow'd false lights; and when their glimps was gone,
> My pride struck out new sparkles of her own.
> Such was I, such by nature still I am,
> Be thine the glory, and be mine the shame.[29]

Perhaps the most directly self-revealing passages in Dryden's *œuvre* come in the dedications to his plays, notably those to *Aureng-Zebe* and *Don Sebastian*, where he admits his own changeability, and we see that among the writers who most truly reflected back the image of his own self was Montaigne: 'As I am a Man, I must be changeable; and sometimes the gravest of us all are so, even upon ridiculous accidents.'[30] It was, one supposes, in order to seek some form of stability and assurance in this world of change, to rest from the Sisyphean labours of individual reason, that Dryden embraced the Church of Rome, and accepted its claim to embody the faith through unfailing tradition and unerring words. Typically, however, that conversion in no way lessened his search for enlightenment and consolation in the poets of Greece and Rome.

§

The second area of Dryden's work, his engagement with his predecessors, has already crept into this discussion, so difficult is it to

---

[28] James Winn's *John Dryden and his World* (New Haven, 1987) is both magisterial in its research and sympathetic in its judgements.

[29] *The Hind and the Panther*, i. 72–7.

[30] Dedication to *Aureng-Zebe* (*Works*, xii. 157). See, further, Hammond, *Dryden and the Traces of Classical Rome*, pp. 59–68.

address the one without the other, to separate the contemporary in his poetry from the classical. After long neglect by critics (though not by appreciative readers, including the major Romantic poets), Dryden's translations have recently been claimed to constitute a major achievement, and perhaps the major achievement of his *œuvre*. Certainly they include some of his finest poetry, whether this is judged by linguistic skill, psychological insight, philosophical power, tonal range, or emotional depth. H. A. Mason was the pioneer in this field, both in his published work on Dryden's Homer and Horace,[31] and in his promotion of research;[32] others have followed, particularly with studies of Dryden's contributions to the miscellany *Sylvae* (1685) and his final collection, *Fables Ancient and Modern* (1700).[33] To show that Dryden's translations are themselves classics, not simply versions of classics, we need to establish that they bring into the language something distinctive and profound. The characteristic which distinguishes them from earlier English translations is, first of all, their clarity: to read Dryden after immersion in Golding's Ovid or Chapman's Homer (let alone the impenetrable doggerel of Barten Holyday's Juvenal) is to meet a proto-Enlightenment lucidity of language and syntax without any loss of a richly connotative semiotics, the work of one who thinks in verse paragraphs while maintaining a variety of rhythm and verse-

[31] H. A. Mason, *To Homer through Pope* (London, 1972), ch. 3, on Pope and Dryden's translations of *Iliad* I; 'The Dream of Happiness', *Cambridge Quarterly*, 8 (1978) 11–55 and 9 (1980) 218–71, on Dryden's translation of Horace's *Epode* II; 'Living in the Present', *Cambridge Quarterly*, 10 (1981) 91–129, on Dryden's translation of Horace's *Carmina*, iii. 29; 'The Hallowed Hearth', *Cambridge Quarterly*, 14 (1985) 205–39, on Dryden's translation of Horace's *Carmina*, i. 9.

[32] Among the contributors to the present volume are his son Tom, and three of his students, Paul Hammond, David Hopkins, and Robin Sowerby.

[33] An early student of the translations was William Frost in *Dryden and the Art of Translation* (New Haven, 1955). Subsequent books include Cedric D. Reverand II's *Dryden's Final Poetic Mode: The 'Fables'* (Philadelphia, Pa., 1988), and my own *Dryden and the Traces of Classical Rome*. Some of the best work on the translations is found in articles, including David Hopkins, 'Dryden and Ovid's "Wit out of Season"', in *Ovid Renewed*, ed. Charles Martindale (Cambridge, 1988), pp. 167–90; 'Dryden and the Tenth Satire of Juvenal', *Translation and Literature*, 4 (1995) 31–60; and 'Nature's Laws and Man's: The Story of Cinyras and Myrrha in Ovid and Dryden', *Modern Language Review*, 80 (1985) 786–801; Emrys Jones, 'Dryden's Sigismonda', in *English Renaissance Studies Presented to Dame Helen Gardner* (Oxford, 1980), pp. 279–90; Tom Mason, 'Dryden's Version of *The Wife of Bath's Tale*', *Cambridge Quarterly*, 6 (1975) 240–56; Robin Sowerby, 'The Freedom of Dryden's Homer', *Translation and Literature*, 5 (1996) 26–50. The essays below by Robin Sowerby and James Winn seek to redress the comparative lack of attention previously paid to Dryden's Homer.

music from line to line (a greater variety, indeed, than Pope). Meanwhile, as Dryden himself insisted, the principal work of the translator is to render his original in all its distinctiveness, or at least to evoke as much of it as can be replicated in another language and another epoch. Dryden gives us the witty turns of Ovid, the tragic majesty of Virgil, the unsettling directness of Homer. But there is a larger, more significant argument to be made, namely that through these translations Dryden is bringing to English readers his own vision.

Without wishing to play down their variety of subject-matter or style, or to deny the pleasure which Dryden hoped that his readers would obtain by moving between such different spirits as Horace and Ovid, Homer and Virgil, it seems clear that the characteristic element which recurs in Dryden's translations, and gives them their special stamp, is his fascination with mutability.[34] Both Lucretius and Ovid allowed him to explore the nature of the universe in terms which lay outside the conceptual frameworks of his own culture (whether Christian or scientific) but interacted with them in curious ways. Here the material world is animated, mechanistically or mythologically; human beings have no privileged place in a universe of atoms moving around by chance, or one in which jealous and capricious gods change mortals into animals, plants, or stones. Dryden selected passages from *De Rerum Natura* and the *Metamorphoses* which allowed him to explore the strange ways in which the universe seems at once anthropomorphic and resistant to any attempts to understand it. Such a vision makes the human body itself part of a labile world, sometimes hardly to be distinguished from the earth of which it is formed.

And if the precariousness of human fabrics haunted Dryden's imagination at this level, so too Virgil's poignant epic of the loss and incomplete recovery of man's dwelling-place became the central text of Dryden's *œuvre*, whether in his magisterial translation, or as the pre-text which shadows so much of his original verse. No account of Dryden's religious thinking can afford to neglect his Ovidian and Lucretian translations, because there he gave his imagination free rein to explore other philosophies, while imparting his own distinctive stamp, especially his interest in the materiality of the

---

[34] Steven N. Zwicker explores this further in his essay below.

world, and his concern for man's enslavement to passion and fortune. (He was a true Stoic and Epicurean, as well as a thoughtful
Christian.) Equally, no account of Dryden's political thinking
should neglect his *Aeneis*, not simply for the occasional topical
allusions but for the sustained contemplation of the workings of
power, whether in rulers or mobs, the motives and consequences of
war, the resilience of men in adversity; and, ultimately, the ways in
which exile may become a new kind of kingdom. Other translations
present more exploitative rulers than Aeneas: Agamemnon in 'The
First Book of Homer's *Ilias*' is rapacious and brutal, while in the
same poem Zeus is a comically beleaguered husband who nods off
in a drunken haze: 'The thund'ring God, | Ev'n he withdrew to
rest, and had his Load'.[35] Plato would not have approved. Perhaps
Dryden should be one of the first to be banished from the republic:
not for opposition in any party political sense (he grew increasingly
resigned to William's government *de facto*, though not *de jure*) but
rather because he relished the absurdity of human power as much as
he reverenced its genuine majesty: already intertwined in *Absalom
and Achitophel*, these twin perceptions of authority become more
marked in the later translations.

It was translation, too, which gave Dryden further scope to
explore psychology: to represent the human mind in disorder as it
is taken over by forbidden desire in Ovid and Boccaccio, or by fear
of death in Lucretius; by contrast, in his versions of Horace's odes he
shows how we can spurn Fortune and enjoy the present. In *Epode* II
and in Virgil's *Georgics* man makes himself a home in the world,
which is at once an agricultural and a phenomenological matter.
And in the *Fables* we see how life may be quietly sustained by
reverent love for the gods and for one's partner, exemplified in
Baucis and Philemon. For it is possible for man to be human and
humane despite the violence and the chaos: Sigismonda, faced with
the gruesome death of her lover, and her own imminent punishment, delivers a long and eloquent speech to her tyrannical father
Tancred on the nature of true nobility. Like the building of empires,
the assertion of nobility is easily sneered at now, but it is part of
Dryden's genius to have made such ideas real components in the
shelters which we build against tyranny or dissolution—in a word,

---

[35] 'The First Book of Homer's *Ilias*', ll. 812–13.

against Saturn. At the end of 'Palamon and Arcite' Theseus faces a world in which Saturn plays his malevolent games, but where a deity can still be thought to order and sustain life:

> The Cause and Spring of Motion, from above
> Hung down on Earth the Golden Chain of Love:
> Great was th' Effect, and high was his Intent,
> When Peace among the jarring Seeds he sent.
> Fire, Flood, and Earth, and Air by this were bound,
> And Love, the common Link, the new Creation crown'd.
> The Chain still holds; for though the Forms decay,
> Eternal matter never wears away:
> The same First Mover certain Bounds has plac'd,
> How long those perishable Forms shall last;
> Nor can they last beyond the Time assign'd
> By that All-seeing, and All-making Mind.[36]

This fuses Roman and Christian terminology into a vision which is a contemplative, imaginative form of natural religion, placing man safely in a benign and even loving universe.

An answer to the question 'Is Dryden a Classic?' might take two forms. The first response would be to point to those areas of his work where the poetic imagination is fully engaged in translating quotidian experience into fictive form, deploying and simultaneously holding up to scrutiny a range of mythologies, fashioning a new world for the reader's imagination. This, says Dryden, is what it means to be human, to build states and to see them destroyed, to believe and to doubt, to feel desire and its disappointment, to dream a harmonious world while schooling oneself to encounter chaos. And all this carried off with an eloquence which ranges effortlessly from the jolly to the tragic. Such achievements would, surely, speak to any literate age. Secondly, Dryden's work exemplifies Eliot's argument that tradition—specifically, the literary heritage—is not static or constrictive; rather, it is a dynamic resource which the individual must work to fashion for himself:

Tradition . . . cannot be inherited, and if you want it you must obtain it by great labour. It involves, in the first place, the historical sense . . . and the

---

[36] 'Palamon and Arcite', iii. 1024–35.

historical sense involves a perception, not only of the pastness of the past, but of its presence; the historical sense compels a man to write not merely with his own generation in his bones, but with a feeling that the whole of the literature of Europe from Homer and within it the whole of the literature of his own country has a simultaneous existence and composes a simultaneous order. This historical sense, which is a sense of the timeless as well as of the temporal and of the timeless and of the temporal together, is what makes a writer traditional. And it is at the same time what makes a writer most acutely conscious of his place in time, of his own contemporaneity.[37]

This is the work of the classic poet, but it is also the work of the humanistic reader. Dryden's work is the achievement of a man who in many respects lived in a different world from that of his historical contemporaries, one whose companions were not only Oldham, Dorset, and Congreve, but Homer, Virgil, and Shakespeare. His beliefs may have been derided, his conduct vilified, and his public causes lost, but there is a serenity—indeed, a positive joy—in Dryden's later work which is that of a man who has shaped his own world, and peopled it with his chosen companions. As the world turned on its dark side, he read and thought himself into being a classic.

---

[37] T. S. Eliot, 'Tradition and the Individual Talent', in *Selected Essays* (London, 1932, repr. 1972), p. 14.

2

MAC FLECKNOE, HEIR OF AUGUSTUS

HOWARD ERSKINE-HILL

I

The aim of this essay is to balance a largely literary-critical account
of *Mac Flecknoe*, certainly correct so far as it goes, with a historical
and political account. For a start we may briefly review some of the
salient points of the poem's reception during the last forty-seven
years. Ian Jack's *Augustan Satire* (1952) insisted on the work's mock-
heroic logic: high terms used, ironically, to ridicule a low subject.[1]
On the occasion of the poem, James Kinsley, in his edition *The
Poems of John Dryden* (1958), candidly stated that while the critical
disagreements between Dryden and Shadwell concerning the
achievement of Jonson and the nature of comedy were 'the basis
of *Mac Flecknoe*' yet 'the occasion of the satire on Shadwell is
unknown'.[2] Kinsley found no personal animosity on Dryden's
part in his critical exchanges with Shadwell, and was unable to
explain Dryden's sudden change to poetic satire without positing
'some personal quarrel' thus far undiscovered.[3] Prompted, probably,
by Kinsley, H. T. Swedenberg Jr., in Volume II of *The Works of
John Dryden* (1972), suggested that the occasion of the poem
may have been Shadwell's remarks in the Dedication of his *The
Virtuoso* (1676), on the relative economic circumstances of the two

---

[1] Ian Jack, *Augustan Satire: Intention and Idiom in English Poetry, 1660–1750* (Oxford, 1952),
pp. 43–52.
[2] *Poems*, ed. Kinsley, iv. 1914.
[3] Ibid. 1914–15.

playwrights.[4] (Shadwell had remarked that if he had had Dryden's pension as Laureate he might have been able to write better than Dryden.) This hypothesis was adopted by James Anderson Winn in his biography *John Dryden and his World* (1987), with additional detail concerning Dryden's financial difficulties in 1676.[5] We may nevertheless feel some disproportion between the occasion and motive here proposed and the resultant poem. This may have persuaded Dryden's most recent editor, Paul Hammond, in his valuable new edition, to ignore entirely the quest for a personal occasion and motive (he does not even refer to Kinsley, Swedenberg, or Winn in this connection) and to treat *Mac Flecknoe* as a poem virtually explicable in terms of Dryden's critical debates with Shadwell.[6] This radical decision is supported by a demonstration of how all the chief issues in the Dryden–Shadwell exchanges are alluded to in the satiric myth of Dryden's poem.[7] A consequence of this presentation is, arguably at least, that it leaves Dryden's transition to satire under-explained, and implies that the character of the satire is largely literary.

While an unauthorized printing came out in 1682, *Mac Flecknoe* has long been known to have been composed and alluded to some years before. The year of composition is now convincingly established as 1676. A growing interest in recent decades in scribal publication now throws a clearer light on *Mac Flecknoe*, a poem scribally circulated eight years before Dryden permitted the poem to be printed. *Mac Flecknoe* thus stands out as Dryden's only major poem to have been scribally published.

This fact raises critical questions. Dryden could, without doubt, have written a poetic discourse to settle on his side of the debate his critical disputes with Shadwell. There is no reason why such a poem should not have been printed, however, and *Mac Flecknoe* is evidently something different from a critical discourse in verse. Harold Love, in his study *Scribal Publication in Seventeenth-Century England* (1993), lays out several different kinds of scribal publication, some, for example publication through one copy, clearly inapplicable to *Mac Flecknoe*. The two forms of scribal publication which seem

---

[4] *Works*, ii. 305–6.
[5] James Anderson Winn, *John Dryden and his World* (New Haven, 1987), pp. 289–90.
[6] *Poems*, ed. Hammond, i. 306–9.
[7] Ibid. 308.

relevant to this poem are the personal lampoon and the political satire. Of the many sub-types of the former Love writes that 'all comes in the end to the parade of personal attacks and it is rare to find a formal conclusion, a couplet or two normally sufficing to terminate the slaughter'.[8] On political satire Love tellingly quotes from the Licenser, Sir Roger L'Estrange. In 1675 L'Estrange was as anxious to prosecute 'Libells in Writing' as 'Printed Libells' since 'Copyes of them may passe indifferently from one to another, by other hands.' He outlines some possible modes of prosecution of those who circulate, receive, or conceal written libels, but it seems clear that prosecution would be more difficult than in cases of printed works.[9] Later in his book Love writes of the relation of scribally published works with 'the exercise of power'. 'A good deal of this writing (in verse as well as prose) filled a function similar to that of a report or position paper . . . the writers might themselves be civil servants, either in form . . . or on a salaried basis, as in the cases of Marvell and Dryden.'[10] Scribal publication could usually impose some limits on the readership of a work (the history of the 'Sceptre Lampoon' on Charles II is a spectacular case of where through sheer carelessness Rochester overstepped the limit) and in the case of dangerous allusions scribal publication was likely to target an appreciative readership while avoiding the giving of direct offence to those ridiculed or assailed. If this sometimes turned out to be wishful thinking, we may suppose that scribal publication was *by convention* less offensive.

II

Before turning to the text of *Mac Flecknoe* I want briefly to consider three earlier satires on poets and poetry which, if they circulated before print as two of them certainly did, circulated in scribal form. These poems are Marvell's 'Flecknoe, an English Priest at Rome' and 'Tom May's Death', and Rochester's 'An Allusion to Horace', currently dated at 1675, the year before the composition of Dryden's poem.

---

[8] Harold Love, *Scribal Publication in Seventeenth-Century England* (Oxford, 1993), p. 235.
[9] Ibid. 74–5.
[10] Ibid. 174–5.

'Flecknoe, an English Priest at Rome' (1645–6, or somewhat later) is a free and ingenious adaptation of a well-known Horatian episode: *Satires*, I. ix, the poet's encounter with the impertinent or bore. In manner it has much in common with Donne's adaptation of the same text of Horace, in the first part of *Satyre* IV. Marvell's poem is thus loosely Horatian in form. The narrator, 'Oblig'd by frequent visits of this man', seeks him out in his coffin-like room only to find himself entrapped by a recitation of Flecknoe's 'hideous verse': 'sure the *Devil* brought me there' (ll. 1–22). As at the end of Horace's poem, the narrator here makes a lucky escape in the end;

> He hasted; and I, finding myself free,
> As one 'scaped strangely from captivity,
> Have made the chance be painted; and go now
> To hang it in Saint Peter's for a vow.   (ll. 167–70)[11]

Much else here requires notice. Part of the comedy is the prolific nature of Flecknoe, as Catholic priest-poetaster and lute-player, compared with his extreme thinness: 'He only fed had been | With consecrated Wafers: and the *Host* | Hath sure more flesh and blood than he can boast' (ll. 60–2). He makes himself more consubstantial by a coating of manuscripts, circumscribing himself in rhymes and 'a close Jacket of poetick Buff' (l. 70). Much farcical humour is devoted to mocking Flecknoe's religion, none more so than when the narrator and Flecknoe, wishing to descend the narrow stair, are confronted by a visitor coming up. 'There can no Body pass | Except by penetration hither', yet the space is too narrow to allow a sword to be drawn; 'nor can three Persons here | Consist but in one substance' (ll. 87–101).

'Flecknoe' is a virtuoso piece: a confident Protestant physical farce in which Marvell's detailed wit plays like a hail of silver bullets upon the dwindling body of the papist-poetaster. Sometimes this wit runs into sheer distaste. Flecknoe, the narrator can feel, is not merely ridiculous but repellent: 'Those papers which he pilled from within | Like white fleaks rising from a Leper's skin . . .' (ll. 133–4).

'Tom May's Death' has a good claim to be the first Augustan satire. 'Flecknoe' may recall Donne, *Satyre* IV, and also anticipate

---

11 Andrew Marvell, *Miscellaneous Poems* (London, 1681; facsimile edn., Menston, Yorks., 1973), pp. 54, 59.

Pope, but 'Tom May's Death' anticipates Dryden.[12] In its concern
with literary succession, true or false, it has much in common with
Mac Flecknoe—and *The Dunciad*. In its critical awareness of the
fitness or unfitness of the 'Romane cast similitude' (l. 44) it shares
a vision with the Augustan imitation. It ridicules the vanity, in-
competence, and inconstancy of a poetaster in disordered or divided
times. Not only does May make a transient visit, in the comical
Lucianic narrative of Marvell's poem, to an Elysium where Virgil
and Horace are to be found, but he is first hailed, and in a roaring
rage finally dismissed, by the shade of none other than Ben, the same
Jonson about whom Dryden and Shadwell found it so hard to agree.
What comes most strongly out of the poem—it is the crescendo of
Ben's denunciation of May—is the bond between poetic calling and
political fidelity:

> When the Sword glitters ore the Judges head,
> And fear has Coward Churchmen silenced,
> Then is the Poets time...   (ll. 63–5)

Poetry is here seen in the realm of politics. Indeed in the career of
May the two are closely entwined.[13]

Rochester's 'Allusion to Horace', the third poem here to be
compared to *Mac Flecknoe*, is a Horatian discourse, a worldly *sermo*,
rather than a Horatian narrative like 'Flecknoe' or a Lucianic
narrative like 'Tom May's Death'. In imitating Horace, *Satires*, I.
x, Rochester attempted (and in my view failed) to achieve the
flexible and judicious critical balance found in his predecessor.
The poem is, just about, a serious piece of literary criticism concerning nature and art, literary fertility and critical restraint, the
value of revision, and the respect due to the public position of a
poet. On the other hand—and this is part of Rochester's skill—'An
Allusion to Horace' ends up as only, barely, *not* a lampoon on
Dryden, so prominent is he at the start and near the end of the
poem. In part this is because, in the freedom of his imitation,
Rochester parallels Dryden with Horace's Lucilius: a poet who
was a forebear not a contemporary of Horace, now likened to a
poet who was a contemporary not a forebear of Rochester. This

---

[12] As observed by Mr B. G. T. Milnes (private communication).
[13] This important poem of Marvell is fully discussed in Howard Erskine-Hill, *The Augustan Idea in English Literature* (London, 1983), pp. 189–94.

comparison is sharpened when we recall that Dryden, in his 'Defence of an Epilogue', had played the part of Horace.[14] Rochester thus turns the tables on Dryden. Of course, the proper treatment of a predecessor (Horace striking a balance in his judgement of Lucilius) recalls the critical exchanges about Jonson between Dryden and Shadwell. Dryden is thus put down, given a taste of his own medicine, and presented as, almost, one who is now out of date, closely associated with the heroic drama of the 1660s which in the mid-1670s was beginning to seem excessive and hollow. Once literary taste moves on will Dryden be a more worthy predecessor than Jonson, Rochester implicitly asks?

In so far as Rochester achieves anything like a balance of judgement it is in his earlier interrogation of Dryden:

> Well Sir, 'tis granted I said Dryden's Rhymes
> Were stollen, unequal, nay dull many times.
> What foolish Patron is there found of his
> So blindly partial to deny me this?
> But that his Plays embroyder'd up and down
> With witt and learning, justly pleasd the Town
> In the same Paper I as freely own.
> Yet having this allow'd, the heavy masse
> That stuffs up his loose Volumns must not pass: (ll. 1–9)[15]

These are not the lines of a writer looking for a synthesis, but of one who, having made a fair concession, throws in another criticism as harsh as his first. As often when Rochester seems to engage in a debate, one side, Rochester's own, breaks through the literary structure of exchange and balance of views. When we come to the reintroduction of Dryden, later in the poem, such a conclusion seems even more to the point. Here we have a characteristically Rochesterian outburst of bawdy, quite un-Horatian:

> Dryden in vain tryd this nice way of Witt,
> For he to be a tearing Blade thought fitt.
> But when he would be sharp he still was blunt:
> To frisk his frolick fancy hee'd cry, Cunt;
> Wou'd give the Ladyes a drye bawdy bobb,
> And thus he gott the name of Poet Squobb.

---

[14] John Wilmot, Earl of Rochester, *The Complete Works*, ed. Frank H. Ellis (Harmondsworth, 1994), p. 381.

[15] John Wilmot, Earl of Rochester, *Works*, ed. Harold Love (Oxford, 1999), p. 71.

But to be just, 'twill to his prais be found,
His Excellencyes more than faults abound;
Nor dare I from his sacred Temples tear
That Lawrell which he best deservs to wear.   (ll. 71–80)

After the bawdy we might think Rochester had quite lost interest in equipoise. It is thus hard to take seriously ll. 77–80, unctuously pious as the final couplet seems. Welcome as it might have been to Dryden to know that Rochester did not propose to run an alternative Laureate against him, it is in its imbalance of sentiments and its wild swings of tone that the poem may be thought to fail. And, as it happens, Rochester's bawdy sequence revives a lampooning attack on Dryden by Shadwell in his *The Humourists* (1670), and appears to retail other Shadwellian reports about Dryden of a personal, insulting, but perhaps not inaccurate kind.[16] Soon, characteristically, Rochester goes over onto the attack again, and again raises the critical issue between Shadwell and Dryden, and with it the question of whether Dryden is a Horace or a Lucilius: 'But does not Dryden finde even Johnson dull . . .' (ll. 81–94). After the phrase 'sacred Temples' no more criticism should have been made (if there was more it should have been made earlier), but Rochester continues to worry away at his prey.

All this, however clumsily managed, is effective criticism of Dryden the early critic and pre-*Mac Flecknoe* poet. As we have seen, however, it is far from being mere critical discourse; it is patronizing, personal, intimately wounding as well. For all the merits of this historically significant poem, and all the literary values it affirms—who could argue, for example, that Dryden was as good a writer of comedy as Wycherley in 1675?—still the reader has the impression that Rochester is pursuing Dryden through the structures of the text. The poem, for its part, contains just enough general discussion, and just enough general reproof of the group of writers Rochester finally endorses (ll. 119–24), to lend an air of conviction to this censure of Dryden.

For Dryden himself, plotting in the mid-1670s a satire on the poet Shadwell, any of these poems might have been a model. We might think the two Horatian imitations would have been especially attractive, though the more lofty comedy of 'Tom May's

---

[16] Rochester, *Complete Works*, ed. Ellis, p. 100, and p. 383.

Death' proved to be more close to the poem Dryden actually wrote. A final point arises from Rochester's poem. We may be wrong to seek the occasion of *Mac Flecknoe* in the writings of Shadwell alone. The challenge to which Dryden responded was equally, perhaps, that of a party or interest group.

III

Certainly, in the mid-1670s, a social and literary configuration was taking shape larger and more dangerous than the rivalries of particular poets or the usual pursuit of political office and advantage, though we may think that interest was the heart of the matter. Dryden's difficulty arose from lack of effective assistance from king and court. No natural courtier himself, Dryden did not receive the pension he had been granted without extraordinary efforts made on his behalf, and this despite Charles II's courtesy towards him and intelligent interest in his productions. He had in 1673 sought the patronage of Rochester, who seemed intimate and influential with the king. Some short-term assistance may have been gained, but, as we have seen, Rochester could not be relied on to stay even neutral in the literary rivalries of the time. Dryden found a steadier patron in Rochester's enemy the Earl of Mulgrave, to whom *Aureng-Zebe* was dedicated in November 1675. Dryden's Dedication is notable both for its adherence to an Augustan ideal of the patronage of poetry— 'The times of *Virgil* please me . . . because he had *Augustus* for his Patron'—and for its depiction of Charles II's court: "Tis true, that the nauseousness of such Company [self-interested middle-ranking courtiers] is enough to disgust a reasonable Man; when he sees he can hardly approach Greatness, but as a Moated Castle; he must first pass through the Mud and Filth with which it is encompass'd.'[17]

---

[17] John Dryden, *Aureng-Zebe*, ed. Vinton Dearing (*Works*, xii. 150, 155). In his opening commentary on *Aureng-Zebe* Vinton Dearing, in debt to McFadden and Winn, still enters a caveat against too detailed a political interpretation of the play. Caution is wise, but the terms of his discussion are notably unrefined. For example, because many politically suggestive features of the play are found in Dryden's main source it does not mean that they can have no contemporary charge: rather they show that Dryden chose his source material with an eye to what would be politically suggestive. Again, Dearing thinks that a play cannot display a series of contemporary political allusions and also have 'enduring value as a structure of ideas' (p. 379). In neither example are we faced with mutually exclusive alternatives. In particular, the 'structure of ideas' is what gives political allusions a more than ephemeral force. I have

Evidence of Dryden's disillusionment with England's new Augustus is obvious here: he holds to the ideal, he does not of course directly challenge the monarch himself, but he is disgusted at the court practice. He even invokes the vocabulary of dunces and dullness ('Dulness has brought them to what they are', p. 149).

The significance of Mulgrave is that, while he successfully carried Dryden over the muddy moat into the royal presence, he was really a duke's man rather than a king's man. On this and other grounds George McFadden has convincingly argued that Dryden came to be a duke's man himself in the 1670s, and Winn has followed this lead.[18] To use such terms, to write even of a king's party and a duke's party, is not of course to write about organized political movements. The word faction might have been better were it not for Dryden's own use of it, in *Absalom and Achitophel* l. 568, to denote what was subversive and incipiently rebellious. We are really thinking about different clienteles: groups looking chiefly either to the king, or to his heir the Duke of York, for protection and advantage. Politically the two groups had much in common, providing (and it may sometimes have seemed a large proviso) that Charles remained as loyal to James as James was to Charles. For each prince the prospects were different, however, in regard to the all-important question of succession. Charles, having no issue from the queen, Catharine of Braganza, had either to stand by his brother, or consider an alternative, such as legitimating his eldest illegitimate son, the Duke of Monmouth. The Catholic James, with two Protestant daughters in the line of succession, had at this time married again: a Catholic princess from Modena. Any male child from this marriage, likely to be brought up a Catholic, would take precedence in the succession over the duke's Protestant daughters.

All this is familiar to the student of the forthcoming Succession Crisis and *Absalom and Achitophel*, but it also has connections with literature of the earlier period. *Aureng-Zebe* itself is Yorkist in

---

attempted to demonstrate a more inclusive mode of political analysis, in regard to Shakespeare, Dryden, and others, in *Poetry and the Realm of Politics* and *Poetry of Opposition and Revolution* (both Oxford, 1996).

[18] George McFadden, *Dryden: The Public Writer, 1660–1685* (Princeton, NJ, 1978), pp. 91, 111–202 (chs. 4 and 5); Winn, *John Dryden and his World*, pp. 243–75. McFadden's analysis of the opposing 'parties' or clienteles led by Buckingham, on the one hand, and Mulgrave, on the other, is endorsed by Harold Love in his edition of Rochester's *Works*, pp. 424 and 428.

political tendency, sympathizing with the fidelity of a long-suffering heir, critical of the self-indulgence of the Old Emperor, the monarch on the throne. The Emperor's own concluding words to Aureng-Zebe may be thought to have set up some contemporary resonances:

> Receive the Crown your Loialty preserv'd.
> Take you the Reins, while I from cares remove,
> And sleep within the Chariot which I drove.   (v. i. 673–5)

The group of writers endorsed by Rochester at the end of 'An Allusion to Horace' seem not to have been associated with such views. None was close to the duke. After Rochester himself, Buckingham was the most prominent writer-politician, he who would, according to Dryden, seek to be part of the exclusionist plot against the king and the duke, and in favour of Monmouth. Sedley, Buckhurst, and Sheppard were at this time close to Buckingham. The political tensions of the time were yet to come into full definition, and Rochester would die before the breaking of the crisis. The group resists simple political definition. But considering how important it was that the royal patron of each of the two great clienteles should perpetuate his interests through having an immediate male heir, it is no surprise to find Rochester or his circle celebrating the arrival of the duke's new wife to London with the scurrilous lampoon 'Seigneur Dildoe'. This gentleman came to England in the train of the Italian princess and the general association of the princess and the signor mockingly suggests that nobody need fear the birth of a Catholic heir to the crown.

A few points emerge from this discussion. The literary dispute between Dryden and Shadwell, unlikely on its own to have occasioned *Mac Flecknoe*, was inextricably bound up with, firstly, Shadwell's personal satire on Dryden; secondly, the way in which, the year before, critical disagreements and personal matters had all been brought together by Rochester in 'An Allusion to Horace', a poem alluding to the Laureateship and stopping just short of being a lampoon on Dryden; thirdly, Shadwell's own obtrusively competitive remarks on talent and the Laureateship in his Dedication to *The Virtuoso*. Closely connected with these provocations but if anything more important was Dryden's deep disappointment with king and court, which drew him towards the duke's party and its leader,

Rochester's adversary, Mulgrave. The occasion of *Mac Flecknoe* had thus its partisan and public dimension, as a result of which Dryden came to see the question of true and false succession in a new light.

IV

Unlike the Lucianic narrative of 'Tom May's Death', the Horatian modes of 'Flecknoe' and 'An Allusion to Horace', and some other earlier satires on poets, *Mac Flecknoe* is resoundingly Virgilian. Its mode is not really apt, like Rochester's satire, for literary discourse, but well judged if attention is to be turned from Augustan critical issues to the depiction of the central figure of Augustan civilization: the true, or false, Augustus himself. A more public satire is thus intimated, and if we put this together with the implications of scribal publication, personal offence, and public danger, we begin to see what Dryden may have in play. Further consideration reminds us that if *Aeneid* VI revealed a long posterity for Aeneas, Virgil never depicted an Augustan ruler pondering the succession. Yet the idea of succession supplies the action of Dryden's poem. Its vision of Augustus is, as it were, belated, purporting to represent the last decision of the *princeps*. Belatedness is contemporaneity here, and at the point in the text where the forthcoming coronation of the chosen heir begins to be described the name of '*Ogleby*' (l. 102) would clinch the point, were any confirmation required, that Dryden is recalling the 1661 Royal Entry devised by John Ogilby for Charles II as he passed from London to Westminster to his coronation. The name '*Ogleby*' has a crucial significance here. It does not simply betoken a low subject (the world of bad writing) which is being mock-heroically satirized by the high figure of the '*Empress Fame*' (l. 94).[19] Before *Mac Flecknoe* and *The Dunciad*

[19] In quoting from *Mac Flecknoe*, here and subsequently, I have decided on a compromise. Despite Hammond's tenacious defence of his thoughtfully modernized text (*Poems*, vol. i, pp. xvi–xxi), and David Hopkins's arguments in favour of modernization in the present volume, it seems clear that Dryden expected his printer to italicize and capitalize plentifully, even though he did not (so far as we know) issue exact instructions as to how this should be done. This is borne out by plates 2 and 8 in *Poems*, ed. Hammond, vol. i, the latter reproducing the opening of *Mac Flecknoe* in the scribal copy in Leeds, Brotherton Library, MS Lt 54; and in the first unpirated printing of *Mac Flecknoe* in *Miscellany Poems* (1684). That the *1684* printer knew what he was about (whether or not at the prompting of Dryden) is suggested by his capitalization of the words 'Mug' (l. 121) and 'Large' (l. 195): neither of these words would be an obvious candidate for capitalization, unless one had intelligently responded to Dryden's

Ogilby, like Shadwell, had not seemed a dunce, and in the 1660s his handsome illustrated folios of classical translation must have seemed impressive. He must have seemed a candidate to be Laureate, though his verse was inferior to that of Waller and Dryden. Ogilby devised the ceremonial procession of the king from London to Westminster, of which the four triumphal arches each invoked Augustus in one connection or another. His handsome and learned folio *The Entertainment of His Most Excellent Majestie Charles II* (1662), describing these triumphal arches and narrating the coronation itself, was not low or ridiculous but part of the genuine splendour of the occasion, attested by many witnesses. Ronald Knowles's learned and subtle introduction to his edition of Ogilby's *Entertainment* brings out the charismatic but transient appeal of the 'Roman-cast similitudes' upon which the 1661 ceremonial rested. *Mac Flecknoe* seizes upon this transience. Ogilby's very coronation folio, perhaps, is with his other works part of the learned lumber of the bookshops which now helps to choke the ceremonial thoroughfare. The naming of Ogilby shows us something which had been genuinely high, of heroic hope, but which has become low through the disappointments of time.

Allusions to the Royal Entry and coronation are frequent in *Mac Flecknoe*, and in view of the action of the poem—succession and coronation—we may think them as important as the allusions to different works of Flecknoe and Shadwell. At ll. 27–8 the Virgilian oak from *Georgics* II, familiarized as an emblem of power and protection, also (as Hammond notes) seems to allude to the Royal Oak on Ogilby's first arch: *Adventus Augusti*. Like the Old Emperor at the end of *Aureng-Zebe*, the monarchical oak has become supine. The mysterious episode of Shadwell and the 'royal barge' (ll. 37–59) picks up the riparian imagery from Ogilby's second arch, the Naval Arch, on which the Thames and its tributary rivers were prominently displayed.[20] 'No *Persian* Carpets' (l. 98) contrasts with the 'Blew Cloth', 'large Carpet', and 'silk Carpet' which Ogilby noted

text. I therefore think the poem should be read in seventeenth-century printing style. On the other hand, in following Kinsley's text based on *1684*, I have filled out the more important proper names which are still represented by blanks in the copy-text. Thus I have quoted '*Shadwell*', as found in the best scribal versions, rather than the '*Sh——*' of *1684*.

[20] *The Entertainment of His Most Excellent Majestie Charles II*... by John Ogilby (London, 1662), a facsimile edn., introd. Ronald Knowles (New York, 1988), pp. 43–66.

as having been laid down for the coronation[21]—this detail may also recall the new 'Persian' style of costume which Charles's court had attempted to make fashionable in 1666, as Pepys noted in his Diary on 13 October 1666 and Evelyn on 18 October of the same year. '*Herringman* was Captain of the Guard' (l. 105) is notable not only because Herringman had printed Dryden's 1660 panegyric, *Astraea Redux*, indeed all his works to date, recently much of Shadwell, and once one work of Flecknoe, but also because the Captain of the Guard with the Captain of the Pensioners brought up the rear in the Royal Entry procession.[22] Flecknoe's throne, introduced with Miltonic echo (l. 107), corresponds with Charles's '*Throne* of *Estate*' ('a Square raised five Degrees') in Ogilby's narrative,[23] while Shadwell as 'our young *Ascanius*', 'Rome's other hope' (ll. 108–9) replicates (as Hammond records in an exceptionally rich note) 'the *Duke of York*', as 'SPES ALTERA' on Ogilby's Naval Arch.[24] (If Shadwell as the Duke of York is surprising from a duke's man, one must note that Dryden's comedy plays impartially over the whole ceremony. Shadwell as Ascanius is also rapidly succeeded by Shadwell as Hannibal.) At his coronation Charles was handed two sceptres, 'one with the Cross' and 'one with the *Dove*',[25] recalled as Shadwell is given 'instead of Ball' 'a mighty Mug of potent Ale' and a copy of Flecknoe's *Love's Kingdom*, 'at once his Sceptre and his rule of Sway' (ll. 120–3). Finally, Dryden remembered from the coronation the several moments of popular acclaim: 'and all the *People* shouted';[26] compare 'He paus'd, and all the people cry'd *Amen*' (l. 144).

Jack's precise definition of mock-heroic, devised to distinguish it from travesty and burlesque, should not mean, as has sometimes been assumed, that the high terms and diction deployed are themselves impervious to satiric scrutiny as embodying the positive standards of judgement proposed. Dryden's invocation of Ogilby reveals a more complex poetic operation. The reader is here confronted by three historical levels of action. On the highest are Aeneas, Ascanius, and Augustus. On the vulnerable middle level are Charles II and James, Duke of York, hailed as England's new Augustus and new Ascanius respectively in the 1661 Royal Entry.

---

[21] Ibid. 171, 174.   [22] Ibid., opening plate section 20, and p. 172.
[23] Ibid. 173.   [24] Ibid. 93.   [25] Ibid. 181.   [26] Ibid. 183.

On the lowest level are Flecknoe and Shadwell, false Augustus and false Ascanius respectively. Ogilby, translator of Homer and Virgil, deviser of the Royal Entry, and author of the *Entertainment*, seems to link the three levels. Heroism and hope in themselves are never repudiated. But the recalled Entry and coronation are drawn down into the world of Flecknoe's and Shadwell's London: this is what the Restoration had come to.

Dryden's satiric transformation of London's Augustan ceremonies is quite inclusive. His allusion to 'little *Maximins*' (l. 78) may be read as an act of penitence for his own excessive drama *Tyrannick Love* (1670), while the part played by Herringman involved Dryden as well as many other writers of the time, as the *Term Catalogues* show. Dryden casually adds himself to what is satirically seen as a collective literary failure.

Full explanation of why Shadwell was chosen as heir to what had promised to be the English Augustan moment does not really explain why Flecknoe was made its Augustus. Here something of the ludic wickedness of Dryden's satire is apparent. He would not have needed to know Marvell's poem (possibly available to him at some time in manuscript) to appreciate the general character of Flecknoe, fertile in failed literary production, always about to retire but never retiring from his opportunistic works. The Catholicism of this priest-poet would not in the mid-1670s have the dangerous associations it would attract in the time of the Popish Plot, but for Shadwell to be dubbed 'Mac Flecknoe' must still have been an awful provocation as Dryden teasingly entangled him in papistry, Irishness, and bad writing. Further, if Dryden and others did know Marvell's poem, there was a joke to be made about bodily stature. Flecknoe, so thin as to be virtually invisible, chooses his heir according to the principle of resemblance:

> Nature pleads that He
> Should onely rule, who most resembles me
>
> .   .   .   .
>
> Besides his goodly Fabrick fills the eye,
> And seems design'd for thoughtless Majesty: (ll. 13–14, 25–6)

A nice comic adjustment of scale is involved here: Flecknoe's slight stature expresses his talent. The resemblance between Flecknoe and the 'goodly Fabrick' of Shadwell implies that the latter's largeness is illusory: a bad fat writer is, after all, like a bad thin writer.

A further opportunity for Dryden arose from the fact that both Flecknoe and Shadwell prided themselves as lute-players. Marvell had mocked Flecknoe's lute-playing while Flecknoe himself, in his *Relation of Ten Years Travells* (1656), recounted how he had entertained the musical King of Portugal, father of Catharine of Braganza, with his performances on the lute. The 'glorious day' to which Flecknoe's entertainment of the King of Portugal was prelude seems to have been a ceremonious and public episode involving a royal barge on the Thames, preceded apparently by a boat in which Shadwell, 'Commander' and 'Prince' of his 'Harmonious band', celebrated some royal personage with music and song. Dryden draws also on *Aeneid* VIII, the voyage up the Tiber, and on Waller's *Of the Danger His Majesty Escaped in the Road at St. Anderes*; the repeated echoes of the latter underline the significance of the 'Celestial charge' (l. 40) in Dryden. Shadwell's role might seem a demeaning one (musicians were no better than servants) but its celebratory character as he conducts the music (ll. 51–2) suggests a Laureate-like part. All this might be fiction were it not that the general mode of Dryden's poem, filled with verifiable allusions to the lives and works of Flecknoe and Shadwell, suggests some real event as the basis of this passage. If the excellent suggestion of Mrs E. E. Duncan-Jones (acknowledged in Hammond's edition) that the 'Celestial charge' was Queen Catharine be accepted, then Dryden would have followed a Portuguese theme from the life of Flecknoe to the life of Shadwell. It is notable that many printings of Ogilby's *Entertainment* concluded with an engraving of Catharine of Braganza.[27] Finally, by featuring the queen, Dryden would have been quietly reminding his readers that, she being barren, the English Augustus had no legitimate child as heir.

V

Having argued that some of the high terms of Dryden's mock-heroic, the Entry and coronation, Charles II as a new Augustus, are not unquestioned here but are the objects of Dryden's disappointed

---

[27] *Entertainment*, introd. Knowles, facing p. 192.

mockery,[28] in a scribal 'position paper' which constituted his first political satire, I might be thought to have offered an account in which *Mac Flecknoe* disarms itself, as it were, before its enemy. Dryden, as we have noticed, seems to connect himself with the low scene of Shadwell's coronation. But against this Dryden's kingly poetic manner, appropriate for Virgilian heroes and sacred monarchs, lends the poem a loftiness and absoluteness of expression which produces most effective satire. First, it masterfully shifts a literary-critical dispute over into a satiric myth of succession—noting Shadwell's hints that he might have been a better Laureate than Dryden. It unhesitatingly deploys in its satire the vocabulary of dullness and dunces. Then its literary idiom is so lofty and confident that it has no need to pursue its quarry, or pierce him in a hundred places as Marvell did Flecknoe. The poem thus makes supremely simple and devastating statements: '*Shadwell* never deviates into sense' (l. 20). The absolute 'never' is ironically enforced by 'deviates', recognizing a reliably faithful fool. '*Shadwell*'s genuine night admits no ray . . .' (l. 23). His quality, like Dryden's style, is absolute. Shadwell is not merely murky but pitch black.

> The hoary Prince in Majesty appear'd,
> High on a Throne of his own Labours rear'd.   (ll. 106–7)

The mock-heroic magnification of Flecknoe seems almost generous, as one might properly defer to the Old Emperor in *Aureng-Zebe*. Only as one ponders 'of his own Labours' is a muted but mocking critical note heard. More obviously festively comic is the 'enthronization'[29] of Shadwell:

> In his sinister hand, instead of Ball,
> He plac'd a mighty Mug of potent Ale;
> Love's Kingdom to his right he did convey,
> At once his Sceptre and his rule of Sway . . .   (ll. 120–3)

This is a Falstaffian tableau: the association seems begun with reference to Shadwell's 'mountain belly' (l. 193). He is a Son of Ben at least in this respect, but also a son of Falstaff, clinched by Dryden's

---

[28] The argument of this essay was first put forward, in much briefer form, in Howard Erskine-Hill, *The Augustan Idea in English Literature* (London, 1983), pp. 222–3, as part of a larger discussion of Dryden.

[29] Ogilby's word, p. 184.

Shakespearian echo: 'A Tun of Man in thy Large Bulk is writ...'
(l. 195), alluding significantly enough to the words of Prince Hal to
Falstaff after the latter has played the King in the Eastcheap tavern.
While Shakespeare and apparently Hal know Falstaff for what he
is, Dryden's association of Shadwell with Falstaff hardly betokens
virulent satire or bitter personal animosity. In his presentation of
Mac Flecknoe at this point his princely largeness of expression
follows a comic rather than satiric decorum.

The brilliant farce of the conclusion is Dryden's better answer to
the problem of how (as Love points out) so many merely personal
lampoons simply break off. Dryden retains the abruptness of such
endings but in a satirically inventive way. *Something* has to be done
to stop Flecknoe's apparently interminable oration, and Dryden
brings it off by adroit allusion to Shadwell's *The Virtuoso*. There,
as Hammond notes, Clarinda and Miranda set a trap, literally, for Sir
Formal and thus precipitate him below stage. Here Bruce and
Longvil, two spectators in the same play, have plotted the same
disrespectful conclusion, as a result of which Flecknoe's prophetic
mantle, borne aloft by a 'subterranean Wind' (l. 215; compare the
same phrase in Shadwell's *Tempest*), now mingles priesthood and
monarchy with a thoroughly low, if Rabelaisian, smell.

3

DRYDEN'S MILTON AND THE THEATRE OF IMAGINATION

NICHOLAS VON MALTZAHN

Among the many satires deploring Dryden's conversion to Rome, one of the more obscure describes him as hanging '(like Mecha's tomb) | Twixt Malmsbury and Helicon'.[1] If Dryden had been long thus suspended between Hobbesian and classicizing thought, his conversion in the mid-1680s must have brought him relief. Unlike the satirist, we may view his choice of faith more sympathetically, as Dryden's attempt to free himself from the pains this suspension had caused—pains we may see as almost existentialist, except that they were also shaded by the often punitive cast of seventeenth-century soteriology. In the mid-1680s, then, Dryden had converted less from Protestantism to Catholicism, or from scepticism to fideism, than from an almost Hobbesian determinism to a more traditional Christian voluntarism.[2] I am interested in the poetic consequences of the shift, with reference to his changing reaction to that epic of choice, *Paradise Lost*. On the 'Malmsbury' front, it had been Dryden's Hobbism that already shaped his first response to Milton's example in the 1670s, when in *The State of Innocence* he

This work has been supported by the Social Sciences and Humanities Research Council of Canada.

[1] 'An inversion of Mr. Dryden's Answer to Sr George Etheridge's Letter to my Lord Middleton by way of Essay', in National Library of Scotland, Advocates MS 19.1.12, fo. 154^r, marginal date 1686 (also *Familiar Letters of Love, Gallantry, and Several Occasions* (London, 1718), pp. 206–10).

[2] Cf. Louis Bredvold, *The Intellectual Milieu of John Dryden* (Ann Arbor, Mich., 1934), and Phillip Harth, *Contexts of Dryden's Thought* (Chicago, 1968).

supplied a mechanist reaction to Milton's naturalist poetics. As Aubrey noted of Hobbes, 'Mr. John Dreyden, Poet Laureat, is his great admirer, and oftentimes makes use of his doctrine in his plays.'[3] 'Helicon', or classicism, came rather later, whether in the Longinian justification Dryden offered after the fact in publishing *The State of Innocence*, or in the volumes of translation from the classics to which he turned after this first 'translation' of Milton's epic. Dryden's imaginative investment in the notorious Hobbes found its counterpart in these translations in his fascination with the notorious Lucretius.[4]

Translation from the classics often invited expansion of the original, especially of Latin works; Dryden's translation of Milton is marked instead by its contraction of *Paradise Lost*. This work of 'radical compression' has rightly been described by James Winn as having 'a profound effect on Dryden's poetic technique' in years to come.[5] But the aphoristic turn with which Dryden, as Winn has it, 'effectively tightens Milton's luxuriant syntax' is also a denial of the animism in Milton's materialism, that continuous extension into process that his expansive poetics seeks to represent.[6] By contrast with mechanism, Milton's emphasis on the inseparability of body and soul does not collapse the latter into the former, but rather describes them as different kinds of the same substance, the nature that proceeds from and returns to God, 'if not depraved from good'.[7] To this naturalism Dryden seems at first to have reacted

---

[3] Aubrey's source here was 'Mr. Dreyden himself'. Quoted in Bredvold, *Intellectual Milieu*, p. 66, from John Aubrey, *Brief Lives*, ed. A. Clark (Oxford, 1898), i. 372.

[4] Thus Dryden has recently been described as being, like Virgil, an 'admiring but unconvinced student of Lucretius': Paul Hammond, *Dryden and the Traces of Classical Rome* (Oxford, 1999), pp. 156–70, at p. 170.

[5] James Anderson Winn, *John Dryden and his World* (New Haven, 1987), pp. 266–8.

[6] A reaction against such naturalism may inform Dryden's gibe against the Cambridge Platonist Ralph Cudworth ('Dedication of the *Aeneis*', *Works*, v. 295); on the Cambridge background, see Paul Hammond, 'Dryden and Trinity', *Review of English Studies*, NS 36 (1985) 35–57.

[7] Milton's engagement with what has been described as the 'vitalist moment'—also styled his animist (rather than mechanist) materialism, or hylozoism—has lately found a number of treatments: see especially Stephen M. Fallon, *Milton among the Philosophers: Poetry and Materialism in Seventeenth-Century England* (Ithaca, NY, 1991); William Kolbrener, '"In a Narrow and to Him a Dark Chamber": Milton Unabridged', *Common Knowledge*, 4 (1995) 72–96, and *Milton's Warring Angels* (Cambridge, 1997); John Rogers, *Matter of Revolution: Science, Poetry, and Politics in the Age of Milton* (Ithaca, NY, 1996); John Rumrich, *Milton Unbound: Controversy and Reinterpretation* (Cambridge, 1996).

sharply, and especially to the religious demands it made.[8] But his reply, in large part that of Hobbesian mechanism, had costs of its own. In naming human motivations in reductive terms, it might fail to answer the question of what affective source could yield the consolations of faith. In *The State of Innocence*, Dryden has Satan ask, 'Lives there who would not seek to force his way | From pain, to ease?'[9] Years later, writing to John Dennis, he saw the tensions in his own life in similar terms: 'For my Principles of Religion, I will not justifie them to you . . . For the Same Reason I shall say nothing of my Principles of State . . . I am sure that I suffer for them; and Milton makes even the Devil say, That no Creature is in love with Pain.'[10] But this very confession of pain seems now to mark its having eased. By the 1690s, the course of Dryden's career had run from that of a public Laureate to that more peculiar role of a private laureate. In the latter service, Milton's example was especially instructive.[11] Earlier, in the 1670s, the consolation had been to adapt Milton for present ends in reaction against that older poet's claims for inspiration. That adaptation had been in the direction of public spectacle, rewriting Milton for dramatic performance.[12] In later years, Dryden himself would direct his poetics towards less external display, and evolve a more private literary authority, centred in reading as a private act. How private remains a question, since a clearer formation of interpretative communities followed in part from the very development of Restoration criticism to which Dryden so contributed. But the work of reading on which so much of Dryden's post-revolutionary publication depends involved less the public passion of a national drama than the private reason of a personal history. If Dryden's religion and politics forced upon him such privacy, he was now secured in it by the consolations of English Catholicism, at once bound to the authority

---

[8] Here lay the deeper challenge of the enthusiasm against which Dryden opposed himself. For Andrew Marvell's judgement of the contest, see Sharon Achinstein, 'Milton's Spectre in the Restoration: Marvell, Dryden, and Literary Enthusiasm', *Huntington Library Quarterly*, 59 (1997) 1–29.

[9] *Works*, xii. 121 (*State of Innocence*, III. iii. 82–3, and note the monosyllabic emphasis).

[10] Dryden to John Dennis (1694?), *Letters*, p. 73.

[11] The point is raised from another perspective in Howard Erskine-Hill, *Poetry and the Realm of Politics: Shakespeare to Dryden* (Oxford, 1996), pp. 171–2.

[12] Milton's likely resistance to this has been charted by Steven Zwicker, 'Milton, Dryden, and the Politics of Literary Controversy', in Gerald Maclean (ed.), *Culture and Society in the Stuart Restoration: Literature, Drama, History* (Cambridge, 1995), pp. 137–58.

of an ancient church, and validated by privation. In the 1690s, then, Dryden could confess his suffering more simply, confident in the statement of his faith. With that security came a changed relation to Milton's epic, as the increase in Dryden's allusions to it shows.[13]

In the course of his career Dryden reversed his position on the hierarchy of genres, from 1668 when he had followed Aristotle in claiming tragedy superior to epic (*An Essay of Dramatick Poesie*), to 1677 when he again cited Aristotle but also Longinus to claim epic the greater form ('Authors Apology', prefixed to *The State of Innocence*), to the 1690s when the translation of Virgil invites his proclamation that 'A heroick Poem, truly such, is undoubtedly the greatest Work which the Soul of Man is capable to perform.'[14] The latter preference he would explain more fully as he refined his reader–response theory over the years. As he changed his view of persuasion, his concern that 'the propriety of thoughts and words' is lost in 'our transient view upon the Theatre' led then to richer expectations of the 'judicious Reader' and a growing confidence in the effect of the prolonged pathos available from epic.[15]

Dryden's claim that 'Tragedy is the minature of Humane Life; an Epick Poem is the draught at length'[16] was tested especially in the laboratory of *The State of Innocence*, his operatic rewriting of *Paradise Lost*. The relationship between the two works has found frequent comment.[17] My argument turns on the less familiar ways in which

[13] Zwicker, 'Milton, Dryden, and the Politics of Literary Controversy', pp. 156–8. The claim is richly substantiated in J. R. Mason's unpublished Ph.D. thesis, 'To Milton through Dryden and Pope', University of Cambridge, 1987, which describes and evaluates the very many allusions to Milton in Dryden's poetry. My thanks to Dr Mason for permitting me to draw on his searching analysis, which uncovers many hitherto unnoted recollections of Milton's poetry in that of Dryden and Pope.

[14] *Works*, xii. 88–9, 347, v. 267.

[15] *Works*, xiv. 99, 102, v. 267–74.

[16] *Works*, v. 269.

[17] Zwicker, 'Milton, Dryden, and the Politics of Literary Controversy', p. 138: 'The story is a staple of our literary histories; it has been told often, and always to the same effect.' Recent studies include Morris Freedman, 'Dryden's "Memorable Visit" to Milton', *Huntington Library Quarterly*, 18 (1955) 99–108, and 'The "Tagging" of *Paradise Lost*', *Milton Quarterly*, 5 (1971) 18–22; Bernard Harris, ' "That Soft Seducer, Love": Dryden's *State of Innocence and Fall of Man*', in C. A. Patrides (ed.), *Approaches to Paradise Lost: The York Tercentenary Lectures* (Toronto, 1968), pp. 119–36; K. W. Gransden, 'Milton, Dryden, and the Comedy of the Fall', *Essays in Criticism*, 26 (1976) 116–33; Earl Miner, 'Dryden's Admired Acquaintance, Mr. Milton', *Milton Studies*, 11 (1978) 3–27; D. W. Jefferson, 'Dryden's Style in *The State of Innocence*', *Essays in Criticism*, 32 (1982) 361–8; Jean Gagen, 'Anomalies in Eden: Adam and

Dryden's scrutiny of Milton's work invited his consideration of literary and theatrical 'imaging', and the epistemological and moral issues arising. In part this involved the sophistication of scene descriptions, in an elaboration on the page of the instructions for the stage characteristic of Restoration libretti. These were to assist the effect of drama as read, in a theatre of the imagination, as well as to vouch for the spectacle of operatic performance. *The State of Innocence* was not staged. But on the page there is no doubt of its success. It outsold *Paradise Lost* until early in the eighteenth century. Moreover, the scribal recensions and frequent printings of *The State of Innocence* show that in seventeenth-century publication it was Dryden's most popular dramatic work, and of all his works second in republication only to *Absalom and Achitophel*.[18]

The challenge *The State of Innocence* presented in production, however, lay in the contest between literary wit and theatrical spectacle. In the shift from the scribal to print publication (1677) of the work, the additional dedication to Mary of Modena emphasizes the relation between 'Admiration' and 'extasie'.[19] Courtly hyperbole aside, the 'Apology for Heroique Poetry' that follows sets aside the wit of the play itself, and citing Longinus describes imaging as 'the very heighth and life of Poetry': 'a Discourse, which, by a kind of Enthusiasm, or extraordinary emotion of the Soul, makes it seem to us, that we behold those things which the Poet paints, so as to be pleas'd with them, and to admire them'.[20] Long ago, Lily Campbell argued that there was a clash between expectations of scenic excellence and excitement on the one hand, much associated with the growing perfections of movable scenery and impressive machines, with increasingly classicist values (not least

Eve in Dryden's *The State of Innocence*', in Albert C. Labriola and Edward Sichi Jr. (eds.), *Milton's Legacy in the Arts* (University Park, Pa., 1988), pp. 139–50; Hugh MacCallum, 'The State of Innocence: Epic to Opera', *Milton Studies*, 31 (1994) 109–31. These are in some part superseded by more grateful assessments of Dryden's work by Bruce King, 'The Significance of Dryden's *State of Innocence*', *Studies in English Literature*, 4 (1964) 371–91; Winn, *John Dryden and his World*, pp. 262–72; and by Vinton Dearing in his edition of *The State of Innocence*, vol. xii of *Works* (1994).

[18] Hugh Macdonald, *John Dryden: A Bibliography* (Oxford, 1939); *Works*, xii. 460. The frequent reprintings revealingly include a pirate of the 1695 edition, backdated to 1684.

[19] *Works*, xii. 83. For the ideal courtly drama here being attempted, cf. Eleanore Boswell, *The Restoration Court Stage (1660–1702), With a Particular Account of the Production of 'Calisto'* (Cambridge, Mass., 1932), esp. pp. 154–5, 177–8.

[20] *Works*, xii. 94.

unity of place) on the other.[21] The tension invited the Longinian solution that Dryden here presents. He himself would never restate it so wholeheartedly again, although his acolytes, especially Dennis, would make much of it in later years. But his 'heroick opera', a closet drama as it had proven, and one that had at first been doubly closeted, since circulated only in scribal publication, thus came further to be framed within a Restoration literary system in which wit and wonder might be at odds.

Dryden's response to Milton also reveals his fascination with the theatre of the imagination in a second sense. This was the way in which imagination or fancy presents a spectacle available for critical and moral evaluation. Or so faculty psychology proposed: this is the moral psychology famously expressed by Milton in Adam's prelapsarian consolation of Eve, and that John Aden, Robert Hume, and Vinton Dearing describe as increasingly important in Dryden's poetics.[22] Dryden was not unusual, then, in supposing this bifurcation of imagination and judgement, and in theorizing the arbitration of fancy by reason, although he proved influential in his adaptation of Longinian categories for this purpose. But whether by the *libertins érudits* or by Hobbes himself, 'the distinction between perceptions and volitions' came increasingly to be challenged.[23] And on this point Dryden's poetry ran ahead of his poetics. Especially in reading *Paradise Lost*, his unease about distinctions between emotions of the body and those of the soul had acute consequences for his moral theology. In *The State of Innocence*, Dryden's doubts about Milton's theodicy express themselves in the less than synthesizing debate between Adam and Raphael in Act IV, in which the questioning of liberty goes too little answered. Only much later did Dryden better master his unease on this point, in a way that led to a growing appreciation of epic. Beyond its Longinian wonders, epic offered an

---

[21] Lily B. Campbell, *Scenes and Machines on the English Stage During the Renaissance: A Classical Revival* (Cambridge, 1923), pp. 251–2.

[22] *Paradise Lost*, v. 100–19; Dryden, *Works*, xii. 334–40; Dryden, *Poems*, ed. Kinsley, iv. 1613: 'The Cock and the Fox', ll. 326–41; Robert D. Hume, 'Dryden on Creation: "Imagination" in the Later Criticism', *Review of English Studies*, 21 (1970) 295–314 (esp. pp. 302–4); cf. John Aden, 'Dryden and the Imagination: The First Phase', *PMLA* 74 (1959) 28–40. For the rhetorical solution to the problem of imagination, see William Rossky, 'Imagination in the English Renaissance: Psychology and Poetics', *Studies in the Renaissance*, 5 (1958) 49–73.

[23] Susan James, *Passion and Action: The Emotions in Seventeenth-Century Philosophy* (Oxford, 1997), pp. 124–36, at p. 125.

extended rather than incidental presentation of the operation of the will in conjunction with the imagination. Moreover, it did so in a way that finally suggested a more satisfactory theodicy than Dryden had earlier been ready to contemplate.

Dryden's dramatization of *Paradise Lost* is intimately connected with the opening of the new Theatre Royal in Drury Lane, in late March 1674, for which public performance it seems to have been designed.[24] The new premises were to compete with the Duke's Theatre in Dorset Garden, whose mastery of spectacle, and especially the present vogue for semi-opera, put the King's Company at increasing disadvantage. Dryden's 'Prologue Spoken at the Opening of the New House' concedes that the rivals' 'Magnificence' contrasts with 'our plainness'. Plays, he maintains, are at a discount 'Whilst scenes, machines, and empty operas reign', and while 'Old English authors' are forsaken for companies of French actors.[25] Against such spectacle, the virtue of wit was to be celebrated in the new theatre.[26] Dryden's 'Epilogue Spoken at the Opening of the New House' returns to the point. 'To the wits we can some merit plead', he ventures, while mocking those 'loud sirs' who are 'the true forlorn of wit', and who 'rail and roar when you are drunk'. The latter provoke Dryden's raillery: 'So may Fop corner full of noise remain, | And *drive far off the* dull attentive train . . .'.[27]

'But *drive far off the* barbarous dissonance | Of Bacchus and his revellers, the race | Of that wild rout . . .'. So had written a contemporary poet, with still more to fear from intemperate Restoration reaction to his writings.[28] Dryden had been 'tagging' Milton's verses

[24] Winn, *John Dryden and his World*, pp. 262–4; Dryden, *Works*, xii. 322–5.

[25] *Works*, i. 148–51: 'Prologue and Epilogue Spoken at the Opening of the New House', ll. 20, 34–41.

[26] At this date Rochester too deplores the vulgar approval for the sensationalism offered by the Duke's Company, and prefers the sophistication of 'Covent-Garden men', better able to 'appreciate intelligence and wit' at Drury Lane. Paul Hopkins, '"As it was *not* spoke by Mr. Haines": An Unpublished Attack on Shadwell in an Epilogue by Rochester', in R. C. Alston (ed.), *Order and Connexion: Studies in Bibliography and Book History* (Cambridge, 1997), pp. 128–30.

[27] *Works*, i. 148–51: 'Prologue and Epilogue Spoken at the Opening of the New House': 'Epilogue', ll. 7–25, at ll. 17–18 (emphasis mine).

[28] *Paradise Lost*, vii. 32–4. For this and many further Milton allusions in Dryden's poetry I draw on Mason's exhaustive 'To Milton through Dryden and Pope'.

at just this date. His inflection here of the Miltonic prayer—'still govern thou my song, | Urania, and fit audience find, though few. | But drive far off...' (*Paradise Lost*, vii. 30–2)—comments on Dryden's own condition. If not quite 'fallen on evil days... and evil tongues', the dramatist was, and not for the first time, beleaguered. The Theatre Royal was not adequately capitalized, and the spectacle and song of *The State of Innocence* were not to be produced on the Drury Lane or any other stage; nor for the present was its wit to appear on the page. That summer in Oxford Dryden could again imagine 'the cool shades of wit' as a 'sweet retreat... from envy, care and strife', where recognition of 'the value of [our dead authors'] wit' might commend Shakespeare, Fletcher, Jonson.[29] He thus proposes for himself a 'retreat' to 'this happy Seat' (another of his favourite phrases from *Paradise Lost*).[30] In 1674 Milton's influence begins tellingly to register in Dryden's works, although his audience cannot have been expected to catch these allusions. At this early date, moreover, what interest Dryden has in Milton's poetic project is insistently answered by such ironic reflections upon it, that is by his wit. But *The State of Innocence* points the way to his ongoing engagements and re-engagements with *Paradise Lost* in the years to follow.

The State of Innocence, however, is perhaps best read not in comparison with *Paradise Lost*, but instead as a precocious and outstanding contribution to English libertine literature in the 1670s, in what was to prove a golden decade for sceptical, mock-heroic, and other more licentious poetic productions.[31] The surprising number of complete scribal copies of the text has been attributed, no doubt rightly, to its initially failing of stage production or publication in 1674. But this success in such recensions is more generally the consequence of one of the engines of cultural consumption in the 1670s. The cachet of coterie and libertine materials much fostered

---

[29] *Works*, i. 151–4: 'Prologue and Epilogue to the University of Oxford, 1674': 'Prologue', ll. 5–21; Winn, *John Dryden and his World*, p. 270.

[30] *Works*, i. 151–4: 'Prologue and Epilogue to the University of Oxford, 1674': 'Epilogue', ll. 1–2. Milton had liked this placing of the phrase at the end of the line, whether in Beelzebub's dangerous proposal (*Paradise Lost*, ii. 347), or in Adam and Eve's sad and final view back on Paradise (xii. 642). See also *Paradise Lost*, iii. 362, iv. 247, vi. 226. Dryden's Satan picks up on the related usage 'this happy Place' (*State of Innocence*, IV. ii. 49); his fallen Eve will 'scorn this Earthly seat' as a 'base retreat' (*State of Innocence*, v. i. 3–4).

[31] Here Dryden's contribution bears noting, even if Rochester would soon in 'An Allusion to Horace' decry his failings in 'this nice way of wit': *The Complete Poems of John Wilmot Earl of Rochester*, ed. David Vieth (New Haven, 1968), ll. 71–6.

their scribal publication, which might then eventuate in print publication too. Dryden's 'The fall of Angells' survives in no fewer than
eight recorded texts: an astonishing total for such a full-length
dramatic text, and one rivalled only by another shorter burlesque
of the heroic drama, and that with only belated and then stifled print
publication—the 'Rochesterian' *Sodom*.[32] Moreover, despite Dryden's dissociation of himself from the proliferating manuscript
copies, and their corruptions, there is evidence that some authorial
sanction may have lain behind such transmission. The transmission
of the manuscript text is for the most part distinct from that of the
print text, with the earliest exemplar featuring authorial corrections,
perhaps in Dryden's own hand.[33] Successful though Herringman
had been in registering this 'heroick opera' with the Stationers (17
April 1674), the indebtedness to Milton's work, now republished in
a second edition that summer, might yet have occasioned difficulties
for author or publisher that scribal publication could circumvent.[34]
The lasting attraction of such manuscript presentation, and the
appeal it might lend to such a text, is suggested by a late copy, in
which the manuscript draws on the print edition of 1695.[35]

Dryden's use of Milton in this context is the more striking since
in the scribal miscellanies of the day Milton is otherwise scarcely
represented, at first or second hand. On present evidence there was

[32] Peter Beal, *Index of English Literary Manuscripts*, vol. ii: *1625–1700*, 2 parts (London, 1987–93), pt. 1, pp. 426–7 (items nos. *DrJ 287–94), pt. 2, pp. 286–7 (items nos. RoJ 636–43); cf. Harold Love, 'But Did Rochester *Really* Write *Sodom*?', *Publications of the Bibliographical Society of America*, 87 (1993) 319–36; *The Works of John Wilmot Earl of Rochester*, ed. Harold Love (Oxford, 1999), pp. 496–8, 674–5.

[33] Harvard MS Thr 9. Beal, *Index*, pt. 1, p. 426 (item no. *DrJ 287) accepts that Dryden himself corrected this text, whereas Dearing in Dryden, *Works*, xii. 462–3, disputes the attribution to his hand.

[34] The censorious Charles Leslie later cites the production as 'once Happily Prevented': *The History of Sin and Heresie Attempted* (London, 1698), A2ᵛ. The date of the second edition of *Paradise Lost* remains uncertain, but it is advertised in the Trinity Term Catalogue, licensed 6 July 1674. Comparably, Dryden's title later lent itself to an evasion of the Tonson copyright in *Paradise Lost*: a prose *The State of Innocence: and Fall of Man. Described in Milton's Paradise Lost . . .* (London, 1745) translates back into English the French prose translation of the epic by St Maur.

[35] Folger MS V.a.225, item 7, transcribed 'when at least eight other editions were in circulation' (*Works*, xii. 462). This does seem anomalous, however: that print largely super-seded manuscript transmission in this instance is suggested by the latest of the six other manuscripts collated in the California edition, being (1) a folio copy bound in a volume where the other items are predominantly from 1677, with a few more through to 1680 (Huntington MS 11640), and (2) another folio copy derived from this copy and in the hand of the same scribe (Huntington MS 134227), now with belated flyleaf and title attributions to Dryden.

next to no circulation in this medium of Milton's own poems.[36] The one such manuscript to feature any of Milton's poems is one hitherto unnoted: the 'Danvers' compilation of political poetry, which once included copies of his political sonnets to Fairfax, Cromwell, and Vane.[37] Otherwise, some very dubious Milton attributions appear only in the print collections of poems on affairs of state in the 1690s and after.[38] Even at second hand, neither Milton's influence nor his infamy seem much to have registered with the scribal communities of the day—unless his very absence be conspicuous. Again the exceptions prove the rule.[39] It is Dryden first of all, then, who after Marvell (himself a special case) has the creative span to put Milton to work in the literary satire, state poems, and libertine poetry of the day. This is familiar from Dryden's use of Milton for mock-heroic ends in *Mac Flecknoe* and in *Absalom and Achitophel*. The former, as literary satire, circulated freely in manuscript. The latter, as political satire, exhibits a strikingly libertine idiom in the vein of poems on affairs of state, and as if it were a more surreptitious work that had just made its way from manuscript into print.[40] More directly in the former than in the

---

[36] Beal, *Index*, pt. 2, pp. 86–7.

[37] BL Add. MS 34362. This witness has gone unnoted because the poems have been excised from the manuscript, but the volume includes two tables of contents, both of which list the three poems as 'On Ld Fairfax—Croml + Vane', fos. 2ʳ, 165ʳ. The leaves in question are now missing, however, from this otherwise complete volume, although the stubs show their place, as well as the catchword 'Upon' at the end of p. 26. (Also missing is the next poem in the sequence, Buckingham's epitaph for Fairfax.) See also John Aubrey to Anthony à Wood (24 May 1684), Bodl. MS Wood F. 39, fo. 372ʳ (cf. also Beal, *Index*, pt. 2, p. 86).

[38] That Milton wrote Marvell's Queen Christina epigram was dubiously suggested in the biography of John Toland (John Milton, *A Complete Collection* . . . (London, 1698), pp. xxxviii–xxxix), and thus also in that of Thomas Birch (John Milton, *A Complete Collection* . . . (London, 1738), pp. lxii–lxiii). Charles Gildon's attribution of a mock epitaph for Mazarin to Milton, in *Miscellany Poems* (London, 1692), pp. 29–33, should be seen as characteristic of that editor's boldness in seeking thus to enrich the anonymous scribal materials he was bringing into print in the 1690s.

[39] The evidence requires fuller presentation elsewhere, but will contribute to my forthcoming study 'Milton and his Readers: The Making of a National Poet'. Most notable are the recollections of *Paradise Lost* in Marvell's 'Last Instructions' (dated 4 September 1667), of which at least five manuscript copies survive (listed in Beal, *Index*, pt. 2, pp. 65–6, to which add BL Add. MS 73540, fos. 1–26ʳ). This influence seems to reflect the two poets' personal association, and the pressure the epic exerted on Marvell to produce an almost epic 'painter' poem.

[40] Harold Love, *Scribal Publication in Seventeenth-Century England* (Oxford, 1993), pp. 147, 293–5. Less capable of thus synthesizing Milton's example is Oldham, who a little later, perhaps following Dryden's lead, does, however, begin to bring Milton into the world of Rochesterian poetic discourse.

latter, Milton in both these applications proves a means of effortlessly heightening the poetic register. Dryden's response to Milton is distinctive: whereas *Mac Flecknoe* echoes Cowley's *Davideis* parodically, it echoes *Paradise Lost* with rather different effect. The difference follows in part from the degree to which Miltonic phrases in *Mac Flecknoe*—'*wage immortal war* with wit', 'Shadwell alone my *perfect image* bears', '*High on a Throne of* his own Labours rear'd'— often draw on passages in *Paradise Lost* that already put the heroic into question.[41] But these and other inflections also show Dryden incorporating the example of *Paradise Lost* at the level of diction, in a way that reflects his schooling of himself in such possibilities in 'The fall of Angells and Man in Innocence An Opera'. This was the major Miltonic work to circulate much in scribal form in the Restoration. That it did so, however, seems to have owed less to its Miltonic than to its libertine qualities, as a Hobbesian recension of its more godly original.[42]

 The State of Innocence has of course suffered in comparison with its epic source. Miltonists especially have been quick to detract from it, and the glories of *Paradise Lost* can make a critical defence of Dryden's opera seem almost perverse.[43] A more fruitful project, I propose, is to compare *The State of Innocence* with other erotic literature of the 1670s. In this context Dryden's closet opera ranks as a masterpiece. The approach is suggested by Harold Love's innovation in reading *Absalom and Achitophel* as a print product trading on its evocation of scribally circulated materials, with an aura of seditious libel, however supportive of the Crown.[44] *The State of Innocence* deserves a similar reappraisal, especially if we can read it also as that manuscript 'The fall of Angells and Man in Innocence An Opera' more privately transmitted. Indeed for

[41] *Works*, ii. 235, 314–15, 319, 322.

[42] For Hobbesian wit as a libertine signature see Warren Chernaik, *Sexual Freedom in Restoration Literature* (Cambridge, 1995), pp. 22–35; Roger Lund, 'The Bite of *Leviathan*: Hobbes and Philosophic Drollery', *ELH* 65 (1998) 825–55.

[43] Cf. the negative valuations in Murray Roston, *Biblical Drama in England* (Evanston, Ill., 1968), pp. 178–9; or Anne Ferry, *Milton and the Miltonic Dryden* (Cambridge, Mass., 1968), pp. 91–2, and more especially her almost complete indifference to this work despite the title of her book. Steven Zwicker more positively construes the 'comic diminution' as Dryden's hostile comment on *Paradise Lost*, a hostility then masked in the compliments to the epic added in the introductory materials: 'Milton, Dryden, and the Politics of Literary Controversy', pp. 138, 154, 152–8.

[44] Harold Love, *Scribal Publication*, esp. pp. 293–6.

present purposes we may prefer the original title, since its later alteration to *The State of Innocence, and Fall of Man* plainly softens its subject, reflecting the occasion of its publication in 1677 as dedicated to the Duchess of York.[45]

Whatever Dryden's successes elsewhere in political and literary satire, 'The fall of Angells' is a triumph in libertine writing, if in a different key than that which he otherwise enjoyed. Its wide scribal circulation confirms the judgement, and if we read the heroic opera in the more fugitive form its own glories may be more apparent.[46] Its subsequent success in print publication then confirms that popularity. Although not designed as a closet drama, it performed beautifully as such. The costly spectacles it required might be imagined with much satisfaction, and little expense. But the attraction of 'The fall of Angells' lay deeper: in its wit, in its poetic effects, in its transgressive thematics, and in the structure of the opera as a whole. In reworking Milton, Dryden could make the most of his own flair for aphorism, either in taking over some of Milton's most aphoristic lines, or in wittily recasting the more expansive periods in his original. That these turns of phrase might serve as free-thinking *bons mots*, or even restate the Homily against Rebellion, appears for example in Lucifer and Moloch's exchange later in the first scene:

> *Lucif.* . . . 'Tis just to win
> The highest place; t'attempt, and fail, is sin.
> *Mol.* Chang'd as we are, we're yet from Homage free;
> We have, by Hell, at least, gain'd liberty:
> That's worth our fall; thus low tho' we are driven,
> Better to Rule in Hell, than serve in Heaven. (i. i. 61–6)

Dryden also enjoys the satirical possibilities in such representations of hell, notably in his well-known slur against the Dutch where Lucifer affirms that the devils 'rise States-General of Hell', and also in his subtler association of the devils with pro-Dutch feeling at this

---

[45] The earliest manuscripts and the entry of the title to Henry Herringman in the Stationers' Register have the 'and' title; the later have 'or' instead. *A Transcript of the Registers of the Worshipful Company of Stationers; from 1640–1708 A.D.*, ed. G. E. Briscoe Eyre and Charles Rivington (London, 1913–14), ii. 479.

[46] The quarto presentation especially lends lustre to the play, where the placing of the act and scene divisions in the earliest (Harvard MS Thr 9) copy seems more advantageous than in the later folio copies (Huntington MSS 11640 and 134227). The quarto print edition also sets the divisions in the play off to good effect.

date against (French) 'Universal Monarchy'.[47] That Dryden was committed to his aphoristic 'turns' for their literary value appears from his rebuttal of criticism on this point.[48] And there are many of such turns, some 'metaphysical' in their elaboration.[49] It may also be supposed that Dryden's phrases were the more admirable to an early readership not yet so schooled in the Miltonic original. Long before T. S. Eliot admired Dryden's evocation of 'all the sad Variety of Hell', Matthew Prior had adapted the line to describe a tableau of the defeated Western Rebellion as 'a sad variety of sin'.[50] Dryden's emotional engagement with that theme shows again in Lucifer's exit line at the end of the first act, where he encourages the fallen angels to 'Seek to forget, at least divert your pains' (i. i. 201).

But Dryden's rewriting does not rest with epigrammatic effects. The success of 'The fall of Angells' drew on its combination of Dryden's distinctive thematic interests with the structure of his closet opera as a whole. The nihilism of the fallen angels, for which Dryden drew freely on the heroic posturing in his drama to date, encouraged the Almanzor-like rant of his Satan or Moloch, whom Lucifer aptly styles 'hot Braves' (i. i. 172). Indeed, it has been claimed that later in 'The fall of Angells' Dryden may be writing in reaction to his own earlier work, for 'when Raphael shows Adam the future consequences of the Fall, he makes him the first spectator of a heroic play'.[51] But the pleasures of verbal aggression lead in 'The fall of Angells' to the erotics of Adam and Eve, and more

---

[47] Dryden, *Works*, xii. 101 (i. i. 86, 90); for the politics of the allusion see Steven Pincus, 'From Butterboxes to Wooden Shoes: The Shift in English Popular Sentiment from Anti-Dutch to Anti-French in the 1670s', *Historical Journal*, 38 (1995) 333–61.

[48] Citing others' disparagement of a passage where 'Sathan' notes how 'Seraph and Cherub . . . all dissolv'd in Hallelujahs lye'—'I have heard (sayes one of them) of Anchove's dissolv'd in Sauce; but never of an Angel in Hallelujahs'—Dryden does not allege this as a diabolical breach of decorum, but instead as a commendable, indeed Virgilian, turn of phrase. Dryden, *Works*, xii. 95 (i. i. 6), 102.

[49] e.g. Lucifer's 'Before yon' Brimstone-Lake thrice ebb and flow, | (Alas, that we must measure Time by woe!) | I shall return': Dryden, *Works*, xii. 104 (i. i. 194–6).

[50] Dryden, *Works*, xii. 326; *Poems on Affairs of State*, gen. ed. George Lord (New Haven, 1963–75), iv. 47. See also Samuel Woodford, *A Paraphrase Upon the Canticles* (London, 1679), sig. c3^r, and Edward Ecclestone, *Noah's Flood, or, The Destruction of the World. An Opera* (London, 1679), sigs. A2^v–A4^v.

[51] Derek Hughes, *Dryden's Heroic Plays* (Lincoln, Nebr., 1981), pp. 12–13. The example of this work, however, registered as 'an heroick Opera', has not found adequate discussion in relation to Dryden's heroic drama—e.g. Anne T. Barbeau, *The Intellectual Design of Dryden's Heroic Plays* (New Haven, 1970), p. 145—although this direction is shown in David B. Haley, *Dryden and the Problem of Freedom* (New Haven, 1997), pp. 204–10.

especially to the spectacle of their desire and its satisfaction.[52] These have been prepared for by Milton's anthropology in *Paradise Lost*, the uses of which Dryden was quick to see. He reassigns to Lucifer the comparison of human to angelic modes of intellection, which had in the epic been Raphael's.[53] Fleshliness and discourse thus linked, Adam's negotiation for a partner leads to the erotic climax of the opera in Act II, scene iii, and Act III, scene i.

The first of these scenes (ii. iii) progresses from Adam's fantasy of Eve to Eve's own self-discovery, in which infantile erotics progress to narcissism. Thus she experiences herself as viewed from above ('The feather'd kind peep down, to look on me') and below ('Beasts, with upcast eyes . . . gaze, as if I were to be obey'd'), before she meets her own gaze in the fountain. Adam, in winning Eve from Eve, further evokes the boundlessness of desire: 'What more I shall desire, I know not yet, | First let us lock'd in close embraces be; | Thence I, perhaps, may teach my self, and thee' (ii. iii. 49–51). Eve's negligible resistance only enhances Adam's triumph, as his self-assertion—'In vain!' he exults, 'My right to thee is seal'd . . .' (ii. iii. 56)—is fulfilled by her willing credulity (ii. iii. 74). Prelapsarian sex proceeds off stage, with the energies of the spectatorial gaze dramatized instead by Lucifer, whose plans for 'Seducing Man' (iii. i. 20) are closely related to the consummation off stage. When Adam and Eve then return they speak of the ecstasies of love. Adam claims what seems at first a prelapsarian transcendence of the limits of ardour—'I, still desiring, what I still possess' (iii. i. 26)—although this may invite a darker reading of the perpetuities of lust, and recall Rochesterian complaints about unfulfilment. At first it seems that modesty requires that the pleasure in love be his, and the pride hers (iii. i. 29–30). But in keeping with the voyeur's vantage, Adam describes their union in a way that begins with the exfoliating of love, only to reduce this to others' witness of 'the triumph' (these others being 'The furr'd and feather'd kind', with even 'Fishes' leaping 'the passing Pomp to view').[54] This externalizes

---

[52] For the comparable instance of sight and touch as means of desire rather than understanding in the Dryden–Davenant *The Tempest*, see Derek Hughes, *English Drama 1660–1700* (Oxford, 1996), p. 52.

[53] Dryden, *Works*, xii. 103 (i. i. 146–53).

[54] iii. i. 37–8. Adam's satisfactions recall the oriental leisure of Dryden's Boabdil, in *The Conquest of Granada* (*Works*, xi. 23 (i. i. 1–4, etc.)), suggesting Dryden's investment in this opulent fantasy.

the event, away from his subjective passion, and restores to it some more objective value. Likewise in an erotic vein, and thus as a woman now less alert to her own spectacle, and more lost in immediate experience, Eve proceeds through 'trembling...wishes ...[and] a warmth, unknown before' to a condition in which

> What follow'd, was all extasie and trance;
> Immortal pleasures round my swimming eyes did dance,
> And speechless joys, in whose sweet tumult tost,
> I thought my Breath, and my new Being lost.

(III. i. 41–6)

This confession yields objective value another way, presenting Eve anew as the object of desire. Dryden registers the latter response again through Lucifer's envious reaction. To frame the scene Lucifer had earlier appeared rueful but decided in his course of action; that roué's determination now issues, however, in a paroxysm of aggression against Eve, whom he wishes to 'Enjoy and blast...in the act of love' (III. i. 95).

Dryden had a gift for evoking the 'pain' of 'Gazing to wish, yet hopeless to obtain' (III. iii. 116–17). In 'The fall of Angells' this pain is assuaged by the voicing of dissent against the human condition that requires such suffering. In the arresting opening of the opera, the devils' Rochesterian nihilism includes hopes of again contesting heavenly rule. But the opera conducts its own rebellion against the logic of divine decree, not least as expressed in *Paradise Lost*. The questions Dryden brought to his reading of *Paradise Lost* may be expressed in his own words:

> If Fate be not, then what can we foresee,
> Or how can we avoid it, if it be?
> If by free-will in our own paths we move,
> How are we bounded by Decrees above?
> Whether we drive, or whether we are driven,
> If ill 'tis ours, if good the act of Heaven.[55]

Thus Dryden's Prospero, in the Davenant–Dryden *Tempest*, whose final rejoinder here sounds like a complaint, rather than the consolation that might be read into these last words. The epigram is sufficiently distinct to suggest an origin separate from the writing of

[55] William Davenant and John Dryden, *The Tempest* (London, 1670), III. v. 157–62 (*Works*, x. 64).

this play;[56] it also stands alone in at least two manuscript miscellanies, the earlier of which is a source near the royal household, *c.*1674, with variants that seem to derive from oral or scribal circulation,[57] perhaps fostered now by the new and more operatic production of the Davenant–Dryden *Tempest* being staged by the Duke's Company that April. But the epigram already shows the difficulties that Dryden might encounter when confronted with Milton's theodicy. We may imagine it as an early Drydenic response to *Paradise Lost*, a pearl of wit he then incorporated when opportunity arose amid the 'delight' of working on Davenant's Shakespeare.[58] The last couplet may recall Milton's similar turn on 'drive . . . driven' in Beelzebub's proposal of Satan's dire stratagem.[59] And some contemporary of Dryden's saw fit to inscribe a copy of the 1680 edition of *Paradise Regain'd* and *Samson Agonistes* with this couplet,[60]

[56] Prospero's preceding prose now yields to verse, and the epigram works as a final flourish, if something of a departure from the scene it brings to a close.

[57] Bodleian MS Don. b. 8 (the 'Haward' manuscript), p. 499: 'Mr Drydens Verses'. The arrangement of the Haward manuscript is in large part conspicuously chronological, and the Dryden epigram is bracketed by Rochester poems ('Satire on Man', 'Chorus from Seneca's Troas') and 'A pretended libellous Speech . . .' of February 1675 (this is the satirical 'The Kings Speech' sometimes associated with Marvell). See Paul Hammond, 'The Dating of Three Poems by Rochester from the Evidence of Bodleian MS. Don. b. 8', *Bodleian Library Record*, 11 (1982–5) 58–9; Harold Love, 'Rochester's "I" th' isle of Britain": Decoding a Textual Tradition', *English Manuscript Studies 1100–1700*, 6 (1997) 200; and Love, *Scribal Publication*, pp. 211–17. Further corruption of the text (presumably owing to oral transmission) emerges in an example likely to be from the 1690s, published in Paul Hammond, 'The Robinson Manuscript Miscellany of Restoration Verse in the Brotherton Collection, Leeds', *Proceedings of the Leeds Philosophical and Literary Society: Literary and Historical Section*, 18/3 (1982) 277–8, 308–9.

[58] *Works*, x. 4 ('Preface to the *Enchanted Island*'). This *Tempest* was first performed on 7 November 1667, and thus very near the first publication of Milton's epic in the preceding weeks (N. von Maltzahn, 'The First Reception of *Paradise Lost* (1667)', *Review of English Studies*, NS 47 (1996) 487–8). Dryden's prologue for *The Tempest* as published is dated 1 December 1669.

[59] That Dryden associated the 'driv'n . . . Heav'n' rhyme with issues in *Paradise Lost* also emerges in 'The Fall of Man', where he rewrites Satan's epigrammatic 'Better to reign in Hell, then serve in Heav'n' (*Paradise Lost*, i. 263) to yield: 'That's worth our fall; thus low tho' we are driven, | Better to Rule in Hell, than serve in Heaven': *Works*, xii. 100 (i. i. 65–6). Christopher Ricks observes that the turn is now only witty, where in Milton it had been heroic: *Milton's Grand Style* (Oxford, 1963), p. 31; but it may be noted that Dryden also turns aside the anti-regnal thrust of Milton's line.

[60] Christ's College, Cambridge, EE.4.28, flyleaf (by permission of the Master and Fellows of Christ's College, Cambridge). The seventeenth-century hand does not seem to be Dryden's, however, and is heavily crossed out. The last line in this version develops its parallel construction more hypermetrically, like the corrupt version of this hexastich in the Robinson miscellany (Leeds MS Lt 54), which has: 'If bad 'tis ours: If good t'is the act of Heaven' (Hammond, 'Robinson Manuscript', pp. 308–9).

a peculiar confirmation that it supplies some judgement on Milton's theodicy. The manuscript examples show the interest an epigram on this subject could generate among Restoration readers—comparable material can be adduced from Rochester's *Valentinian*[61]—since it spoke to the central theological issue with which libertine thinking was concerned, that of determinism.

When *The State of Innocence* moves from its erotic to its philosophical climax, in the debate over free will (Act IV), and in the overreaching transgressions of the Fall (Acts IV and V), Dryden presents a libertine reaction against Milton's libertarian theodicy. Hence Charles Leslie's later complaint about Milton's epic inviting some such decline towards 'the Entertainment of Prophane Raillery'.[62] Questions about the nature of evil had already been raised in the Davenant–Dryden *Tempest*, and dramatized especially through its use of natural men. Dryden's fascination with sexual freedom notwithstanding, he was plainly interested also in the implications of Prospero's supernatural powers, and the resulting questions of causation that could be raised against theodicy. These *Paradise Lost* had also raised, and Dryden thought himself equipped to offer a response. His confidence followed from his familiarity with the terms of the debate in which such points had previously been controverted, especially between Hobbes and Bishop Bramhall. It has long been understood that Dryden gives to Adam the Hobbesian position, with Raphael and Gabriel supposed to have been given Bramhall's.[63] The difficulty is that Dryden's sympathies are sufficiently Hobbesian that these angels propose not Bramhall's defence of human freedom but a more dubious compatibilism—maintaining that 'free will does not preclude determinism and vice versa'.[64] As one of his contemporaries put it, Dryden had acquainted Adam 'with all the arguments of the Supralapsarians . . . in the Mysterious Controversie about Freewill', and so much so that 'Bayes' may

---

[61] King, 'Significance of Dryden's *State of Innocence*', p. 375.

[62] Leslie, *History of Sin*, sig. A2^v, and see also p. 51.

[63] Bredvold, *Intellectual Milieu*, pp. 66–8; King, 'Significance of Dryden's *State of Innocence*', pp. 373–88; Melissa Cowansage, 'The Libertine–Libertarian Dichotomy in Dryden's *The State of Innocence*', *English Language Notes*, 3 (Mar. 1984) 38–44. On the theological basis for Dryden's reaction to Milton's theodicy I am grateful for the advice of Phillip Donnelly.

[64] Dennis Danielson, *Milton's Good God* (Cambridge, 1982), p. 132; James, *Passion and Action*, pp. 276–9.

boast that 'I made this great Progenitor of ours, so baffle the Arch-angel in the intricate point of Free-will, that I should have been most mortally afraid that the discontented Gabriel had carried some dregs of Calvinism along with him into Heaven, and infected the rest of his fellow Angels...'.[65] Systematic discourse characterizes the debate in Act IV, whether angelic or Adamic. The theodicy Adam will question is proposed first of all by Raphael, leading to the summary claim that 'pow'r then is giv'n | Of doing good; but not compelled by Heav'n'. Of Raphael's speech it has been remarked by Vinton Dearing that it is 'A clearer exposition of a fundamental understanding in Christianity than Milton's' or the Bible's.[66] But this is exactly the problem: such systematic reasoning, even if 'clearer', is not adequate even in Dryden's opera, where the strength of Adam's counterclaims is confirmed by the dramatic emphasis of his concluding remarks, made solo (IV. i. 113–20). By contrast with the fuller affective thrust of biblical or Miltonic narration, the narrowness of such rationality, of angels making 'use of Syllogism', thus lends itself to the mock that Dryden's Adam 'Proposes Mediums, solves Objections, tells his guest that his Major was open enough to let a whole Shoul of Arminians in at the Breeches; that his Minor would not hold water... that his inferences had no more relation to the premises, than the Alcoran to the Four Evangelists.'[67]

Dryden's argument is too little enacted in the plot of the opera, and doctrine floats free of its origin in incarnated history. Moreover, he resorts to scholastic distinctions in a way informed less by Bramhall's assurance of their intelligibility than by Hobbes's scorn for them as deceptions. Without them Bramhall's position becomes untenable. Adam in debate remains a simpler Hobbesian than Dryden. But when Dryden attempts to escape Hobbesian determinism by seeking to distinguish between acting and choosing, he not unsurprisingly fails adequately to dramatize the scholastic categories required to sustain that distinction.[68] As the Cartesian cast of

---

[65] Thomas Brown, *The Reasons of Mr. Bays Changing His Religion* (London, 1688), pp. 19–20.

[66] *Works*, xii. 123 (IV. i. 23–30), 370. Cf. 'Dryden's strategy is always, it seems, to cancel Miltonic ambiguity': Joseph Wittreich, 'Milton's Transgressive Maneuvers', in Stephen Dobranski and John Rumrich (eds.), *Milton and Heresy* (Cambridge, 1998), p. 249.

[67] Brown, *Reasons*, p. 19.

[68] Much later in his career, and after his conversion, he returns to the topic at some length in 'The Cock and the Fox', considerably expanding on his Chaucerian original to speak of the

Adam's first reflections indicates, Dryden is more of a dualist than a truly monist Hobbesian. The compatibilism of Dryden's angels does not challenge the determinist position as much as try to work around it. This does not save him from making God the author of evil. If choice in this heroic opera is constrained, action is supposed to remain unconstrained. This is only possible in so far as the soul is abstracted from corporeal causation, standing outside the mechanist nexus.

The extreme interiority of such a freedom goes to the issue of the theatre of imagination. As Dryden's Raphael has it, 'though the cause suffice, | Yet often [man] his free assent denies' (IV. i. 87–8). The soul is remote from the body in this construction, and operates as a disembodied subjectivity, granting or withholding assent from embodied choice. This may be likened to Dryden's fascination with the 'detached calm' that Lucretius had commended in Book II of *De Rerum Natura*.[69] That withholding of the self from what is witnessed accorded with an Epicurean valuation of the absence of pain.[70] Milton, by contrast, had in the course of his career become dismissive of the Stoics' 'philosophic pride', and in *Paradise Regained* has the Son denounce Satan's offer of such a 'severe' but false virtue, and instead prefer a more genuine patience on 'grace depending'.[71] He was more holistic in describing the freedom granted by God through conditional decrees, with his more integrated psychology following from his monism.[72] Dryden's heroic opera, by contrast, invites a fatalist displacement away from such a description of agency and responsibility. When, after the Fall, Dryden's Eve persists with determinist complaint, Adam urges her to desist (V. iv. 126–33), but his stoicism does not much address her premiss, which he himself had earlier articulated. It has long been observed that

distinction between 'simple' and 'conditional' kinds of 'strict necessity'. He is now readier to concede uncertainty on these points, and exploits his agility in mock-heroic with better results than his handling of the point in his 'heroick Opera'. Cf. Dryden, *Poems*, ed. Kinsley, iv. 1617–19 ('The Cock and the Fox', ll. 507–51), and *The Riverside Chaucer*, ed. Larry Benson and F. N. Robinson, 3rd edn. (Boston, 1987), pp. 258–9: Nun's Priest's Tale, vii. 3234–50.

[69] Derek Hughes, *Dryden's Heroic Plays*, pp. 65–6, and *English Drama 1660–1700* (Oxford, 1996), p. 50; Hammond, *Dryden and the Traces of Classical Rome*, pp. 63–4. For Dryden's return to this Lucretian motif just after 'The fall of Angells', see his dedication of *Aureng-Zebe* (1676), *Works*, xii. 153–4 and notes.

[70] Hammond, *Dryden and the Traces of Classical Rome*, pp. 164–5.

[71] *Paradise Regained*, iv. 280, 300–21.

[72] Danielson, *Milton's Good God*, p. 140.

prelapsarian idiom in *The State of Innocence* is not very distinguishable from postlapsarian idiom, where contemporary libertine discourse especially informs Adam's misogynist commonplaces (v. iv. 62–77), and also Eve's romantic disillusionment. Dryden's Miltonic opera cannot escape the determinism it articulates with such flair. Indeed, its success follows in some part from the pessimistic satisfaction of this failure in theodicy. The success may hold even for a readership more conversant with Milton's original, and able to assess Dryden's reaction against Milton's strenuous assertion of free will. It is in capitulation to determinism, for better or worse, and in its dualist abstraction of the soul, that *The State of Innocence* masters its source.

Milton's 'mystic reason' was to be 'clear'd' by 'Sense'. The phrase is that of Dryden's acolyte Nathaniel Lee, in a commendatory poem supplied for the print publication of *The State of Innocence*. Posing Milton as a 'sullen Saturn', Lee sees in the rewriting of *Paradise Lost* the signature of a new literary and political epoch, distinctively social and polite.[73] Dryden's modest demur notwithstanding,[74] there is much to indicate that Lee's opinion here was agreeable to the Laureate himself, and to the critical confidence of a new generation persuaded of its own aesthetic standards. The next year, in a preface directed to the Earl of Danby, Dryden echoed Lee's formulation in order now to praise the Lord Treasurer. The trope of imposing order on chaos was not unusual in Restoration literature: Dryden himself was to translate Ovid's great evocation of such creation, and this in terms tellingly coloured by Milton's influence.[75] But in the Preface to *All for Love*, Dryden tellingly turns the trope towards a discussion of liberty:

'Twas indeed the policy of their old Forefather, when himself was fallen from the station of Glory, to seduce Mankind into the same Rebellion with him, by telling him he might yet be freer than he was: that is, more free than his Nature wou'd allow, or (if I may so say) than God cou'd make him. We have already all the Liberty which Free-born Subjects can enjoy; and all beyond it is but License.[76]

---

[73] John Dryden, *The State of Innocence* (London, 1677), sig. A4ʳ⁻ᵛ: *Works*, xii. 537–8.
[74] *Works*, xii. 86.
[75] Mason, 'To Milton through Dryden and Pope', pp. 40–4.
[76] *Works*, xiii. 3–4, 7.

The relation of aesthetics to politics here is apparent, since some quite consequential rhetoric against rebellion follows, implying a Hobbesian association of rebellion with intellectual and linguistic confusion. The suspicion of claims for heavenly gifts—'If their Call be extraordinary, let them convince us . . .'—transposes easily into questions of poetics, where the rhapsodic utterance of the *vates* requires some better ordering. Lee had spoken to the shaping force that characterizes Restoration civility:

> To the dead Bard, your fame a little owes,
> For Milton did the Wealthy Mine disclose,
> And rudely cast what you cou'd well dispose:
> He roughly drew, on an old fashion'd ground,
> A Chaos, for no perfect World was found,
> Till through the heap, your mighty Genius shin'd;
> His was the Golden Ore which you refin'd.[77]

Lee adds of Milton and Dryden that 'Betwixt ye both is fram'd a nobler peice, | Than ere was drawn in Italie or Greece.' This was a Propertian compliment already proposed for Milton by 'Selvaggi' in *Poems* (1645), and also by Samuel Barrow in the second edition of *Paradise Lost* (1674); Dryden was to make this his own enduring compliment to Milton in the epigram he supplied for the fourth edition of *Paradise Lost* (1688).[78] But the claims to a further refinement sound through even Dryden's commendations of *Paradise Lost* in later years, at the same time as his poetry shows him accommodating Milton's example much more comfortably.

Aubrey's report *circa* 1680 that Dryden 'very much admires' Milton is consistent with other such references: whether the commendation in 1677 that *Paradise Lost* is 'one of the greatest, most noble, and most sublime Poems, which either this Age or Nation has produc'd', or the dubiously tangled story of Dryden's response to the publication of Milton's epic—'*that Poet had cutt us all out*'—when the 'Earl of Dorset produc'd' it.[79] Dryden, however, seems to have explained to Dennis that he had not at the time of *The State of Innocence* known 'half the Extent of [Milton's]

---

[77] *Works*, xii. 537; MacCallum, 'The State of Innocence: Epic to Opera', p. 112.

[78] John Milton, *Poems* (1645), 'Poemata', sig. A2ᵛ—for 'Selvaggi' see Gordon Campbell, *A Milton Chronology* (London, 1997), p. 63; *Paradise Lost* (1674), sig. A2ʳ⁻ᵛ; *Paradise Lost* (1688), frontispiece.

[79] Winn, *John Dryden and his World*, pp. 81, 558.

Excellence'.[80] There is also evidence from Dryden's poetry that his regard for Milton only increased, especially after the mid-1680s. The need to refine Milton remained, and Dryden's reservations on this score found expression in the 1680s and 1690s, not least regarding Milton's diction, excessive biblicism, and blank verse; that he should cite such flaws recalls Nathaniel Lee's verdict on Milton's 'Ore'. Dryden also found it problematic that the 'Event' of *Paradise Lost* 'is not prosperous', which poem had been better if 'the Devil had not been his Heroe instead of Adam'.[81] *The State of Innocence* had been 'an heroick Opera', but Dryden seems on this point not quite to have understood some of his own claims about obedience, and their potential for defining an altogether different kind of heroic drama.

But in the course of the 1680s Dryden experienced some renewal of his will to believe, in a departure made famous by his conversion to Roman Catholicism in the reign of James II. The change made him correspondingly receptive to *Paradise Lost*, on which he draws with new freedom in his later poetry. The masque *Albion and Albanius* (1685) shows the attraction for Dryden of the political irony available in depicting demonic or rebellious figures in a suitably Miltonic idiom, an inflection that accords with Paul Hammond's claim that the Platonist colouring of the earlier court masque was less and less convincing to Dryden, alert as he was to Restoration *Realpolitik*.[82] In his narrative poetry, by contrast, the use of Milton seems increasingly sympathetic, and still more so in later years. As a religious poet, Dryden enriched his work by drawing on his great predecessor, and sometimes more than incidentally, most spectacularly in his bravura rewriting of the first half of *Paradise Lost*, Book III into the apology for Roman 'spiritual Royalty' in *The Hind and the Panther* (1687).[83] Miltonic notes also help elevate Dryden's tone in a number of poems from this date: *Threnodia Augustalis*, 'To the Pious Memory of . . . Mrs. Anne Killigrew', *Song for St. Cecilia's Day, 1687*, *Eleonora*, and *Britannia Rediviva*.

---

[80] John Dennis, *Original Letters* (London, 1721), p. 75.

[81] *Works*, iii. 17 (Preface to *Sylvae*, 1685); iv. 14–15 ('Discourse of Satire'); v. 276 (Dedication to the *Aeneis*); xv. 67 (Preface to *Don Sebastian*).

[82] *Works*, xv. 30–1; Paul Hammond, 'Dryden's *Albion and Albanius*: The Apotheosis of Charles II', in David Lindley (ed.), *The Court Masque* (Manchester, 1984), pp. 170, 179–80.

[83] *Works*, iii. 153–4 (*Hind and Panther*, ii. 499–525).

As a translator, Dryden made striking use of Miltonic idiom for a range of classical and later texts. In part this followed from what seems to have been a delighted recognition of Milton's responses to classical poetry, which in turn allowed Dryden better to express the potential in English of his Latin and Greek originals. But the recourse to Milton as intermediary could also assist Dryden in elevating classical poetry, or even in putting a more Christian stamp on it. The libertine thrust of his translation of Theocritus, for example, finally celebrates sexual consummation with some Miltonic phrasing, expanding on the original:

> The god of love was there, a *bidden guest*,
> And present at his own mysterious feast.
> His azure mantle underneath he spread,
> And *scattered roses* on the nuptial bed;
> While folded in each other's arms they lay,
> He blew the flames, and furnished out the play,
> And from their forehead wiped the *balmy sweat* away.[84]

And J. R. Mason has shown how Dryden exalts the Jove of Ovid's *Metamorphoses*, Book I (the Giants' War) in terms drawing on Milton, as if to make Ovid's a more monotheistic work. More generally, in Dryden's translations of Homer (especially the first book of the *Iliad*), of Horace, and of Ovid, he is notably quick to recognize Milton's earlier adaptations of those authors, and to apply them back to the original. Revealing too are his uses of Milton for his translations from Chaucer, notably in Book III of 'Palamon and Arcite', and especially in 'The Cock and the Fox'. Here Dryden enlivens his handling of the Boethian arguments in his medieval source by addressing them in sometimes Miltonic terms.[85] With Chaucer as his ally, Dryden now works with great assurance in mock-heroic response to *Paradise Lost*. Milton's, then, became part of the poetic language with which Dryden responded to the classical and also the medieval tradition. The narrative poetry in *Fables Ancient and Modern* includes many echoes of the more recent poet, as if his diction provided a means of refining the ore or

---

[84] Emphases mine; *Works*, iii. 76–7 (*Daphnis*, ll. 122–8); cf. *Lycidas*, l. 118, *Paradise Lost*, iv. 773, viii. 255.

[85] Taylor Corse, 'Dryden and Milton in "The Cock and the Fox"', *Milton Quarterly*, 27 (1993) 109–18.

transmuting the gold of the earlier poetry now presented anew. In these echoes, moreover, there are often distinct inflections where Dryden comments on his strenuous Puritan predecessor. But it is in Dryden's translations of Virgil, especially in the *Georgics* and in the *Aeneis*, that this Miltonic idiom plays the greatest part in sustaining a prolonged work of imagination, embodying the will to believe.

How might the soul best be regulated in response to the passions raised by experience, or roused by imagination or memory? Where might freedom be experienced, not subject to physical necessity? The dualist answer to the mind–body problem insisted on some inner theatre, where the will assisted by reason might judge the drama enacted before it. The place of this theatre remained uncertain, as did its material or spiritual operation. But in so far as reading might exercise judgement, it might contribute to the successful functioning of the will, especially when the individual reading was conditioned by that of an interpretative community. Passions might be shared; so, too, the response to those passions. In translation, the work of narration was not a series of choices, as with original composition. But the co-operation with tradition offered other freedoms. Not least in epic narrative, the poet could over time display at length the creative force of nature, but also realms beyond the natural. These advantages followed from the genre, which 'works leisurely; the Changes which it makes are slow; but the Cure is likely to be more perfect'.[86] Dryden's translation of the *Georgics* shows him at his most Miltonic in the Lucretian passage in the second book where Virgil celebrates the coming of spring. Here there is much of the language of 'new creation' that J. R. Mason has shown as Milton's great legacy to Dryden, where 'The womb of earth the genial seed receives.'[87] This was a spectacle that the theatre of imagination as prompted by poetry could present much better than any dramatic stage. In both the *Georgics* and the *Aeneis*, Dryden in inventing his Virgilian diction seems to have had frequent recourse to Milton's example; the *Aeneis* especially offers many such examples, many incidental and some more substantial, of the language of *Paradise Lost*, in word and phrase, sounding through

---

[86] *Works*, v. 270.

[87] Mason, 'To Milton through Dryden and Pope', pp. 56–67, comparing *Georgics*, ii. 439–73 with *Paradise Lost*, i. 21, iii. 661, 717, vii. 102, 256, 276–82, 454, and viii. 515, *inter alia*.

Dryden's evocation of Virgil's voice.[88] Often these pieces of poetic diction had featured already in earlier of Dryden's works, Virgilian or otherwise. He now takes pleasure in recovering more fully the relation between his classical original and Milton's response to that original. But it was where Dryden turned from the natural world to other worlds less available to direct experience that he drew on Milton more insistently still. For this the *locus classicus* is his translation of Book VI of the *Aeneid*. Swift to recognize Milton's recollections of Virgil's description of the underworld, Dryden incorporates them with such frequency that it can fairly be said he was reading Virgil here through Milton; that the sublimity of Milton's description of Hell is pacified by being read into the piety of Aeneas' quest. Such obedience was not unpolitical, however: in the 1690s there might be strong Jacobite implications in thus invoking filial duty, and attempting a reconciliation with the past. This was a test of virtue, grounded in the experience of loss, but conducted in the realm of the marvellous. Evil was something against which faith must endure, and in the *Aeneis* it endures at length, making the 'Event' of that epic most truly 'prosperous'.

With patience the will subordinates the passions, encounters pain and survives it. Of Dryden's great effort with Virgil it could at this date be reported that 'He is so old that it is looked upon as his leaving the woreld of poetry.'[89] Especially in the *Aeneis*, but also more widely in his later poetry, Dryden in response to Milton increasingly turns from wit to wonder: wonder at the work of Nature and, beyond the realm of the probable, at the marvels of heaven and hell. These epic could present in a way that tragedy could not. The result may seem a distinctly Augustan theodicy, but it is a theodicy all the same.

[88] In addition to those allusions noted in Dryden, *Works*, vi, there are many more noted in Mason, and in Taylor Corse, *Dryden's 'Aeneid'* (Cranbury, NJ, 1991), *passim*.

[89] John Barnard, 'Early Expectations of Dryden's Translation of Virgil (1697) on the Continent', *Review of English Studies*, NS 50 (1999) 203.

4

DRYDEN AND THE STAGING OF POPULAR POLITICS

Paulina Kewes

My theme in this chapter is Dryden's distinctive contribution to the theatrical representation of popular politics, in particular of the mechanisms by which public opinion is swayed and controlled. By 'popular politics' I mean the role played in political conflict by people outside those elites of power which centred on the king, court, and Parliament: that is, by people who would not normally have had a say in policy-making, but whose opinions had none the less to be taken into account, especially in times of political crisis.

To define 'popular politics' in this way may seem an over-simplification. First, as Tim Harris and others have shown, late seventeenth-century lower orders played a prominent part in government, even if only at the local level. For example, they participated in law enforcement in the city (and in rural parishes) in their capacity as constables and members of the militia.[1] Second, to use terms such as the 'commonalty', the 'people', the 'populace', as I shall in this essay, is no doubt to bypass significant distinctions of geography, social rank, income, and gender: distinctions between the urban and the rural population; between masters, apprentices, and journeymen; between different trades and companies; between exclusively male crowds (for example, during apprentice riots) and

I am grateful to Professors Paul Hammond, Robert D. Hume, and Blair Worden for their comments, criticism, and encouragement.

[1] See Tim Harris, *London Crowds in the Reign of Charles II: Propaganda and Politics from the Restoration until the Exclusion Crisis* (Cambridge, 1987), pp. 14 ff.

mixed-gender crowds (for example, during Pope-burning processions). Yet it seems to me justified to use the phrase 'popular politics'
in a discussion of theatrical representation, since the plays of the
period rarely distinguished among those various constituencies of
the population which modern research has delineated. When their
political survival is at stake, Restoration stage kings and queens tend
to refer to, or to be concerned about, the views of the 'people', a
term which loosely covers the lower-class population. In most cases
they have in mind the lower-class inhabitants of the capital city.[2]

Literary critics have paid virtually no attention to the theatrical
representation of popular politics and of forms of mass political
persuasion and agitation in Restoration drama.[3] Yet that representation is closely aligned to the development of participatory politics in
the London which audiences knew. The drama, I shall contend,
reflected not only the intensity of public political manipulation
but the diversity of its techniques. On the stage as in life, popular
opinion was swayed sometimes by the ruling power, sometimes by
its opponents.

After a brief spell of royalist euphoria, the 1660s and 1670s were
marked by increasing disillusion with the Stuart regime, although
initially that disillusion did not manifest itself through open popular
protest. In the years 1678–82, the time of the Popish Plot and the
Exclusion Crisis when the Restoration settlement came close to
being overturned, mass political agitation and crowd activity were
at their highest since the mid-century crisis. Those historical shifts
are mirrored in the drama. Broadly speaking, early Restoration
heroic drama is the domain of high politics. However, I shall
question the prevalent critical view that it has no popular sphere.
I shall show how the people's role in changes of government is
figured in the early Restoration heroics by the chief Stuart apologist

---

[2] Dryden's *The Spanish Fryar*, produced in the autumn of 1680, uncharacteristically
registers the different responses of the rich and the poor to political conflict: '. . . the wealthier
sort, | With Arms a-cross, and Hats upon their Eyes, | Walk to and fro before their silent
Shops: | Whole droves of Lenders crowd the Banquers doors, | To call in Money; those who
have none, mark | Where Money goes; for when they rise 'tis Plunder: | The Rabble gather
round the Man of News, | And listen with their Mouths; | Some tell, some hear, some judge
of News, some make it; | And he who lies most loud, is most believ'd' (*The Spanish Fryar or,
The Double Discovery*, in *Works*, vol. xiv (v. ii. 53–62).

[3] Susan J. Owen's account of crowd politics in the plays of the Exclusion Crisis in her
Restoration Theatre and Crisis (Oxford, 1996) is a rare exception.

and Laureate, John Dryden. The collective agitation initiated by the Whigs and later taken up by the Tories during the years of the Popish Plot scare and the Exclusion Crisis led to an activation of mass public opinion on a scale unknown since the 1640s and 1650s. That development, I shall argue, was reflected in the proliferation of crowd scenes, both in new plays and in adaptations of old ones. Having demonstrated the thematic functions and theatrical effects, in selected Whig and Tory plays of the late 1670s and early 1680s, of placing the populace on the stage, I shall focus on Dryden and Lee's *The Duke of Guise* (1682). Like other Exclusion Crisis plays, it exhibits a close preoccupation with popular politics and with the methods of swaying public opinion and sowing sedition. Yet it is unique in not merely representing propaganda but also analysing it. In it a range of techniques of public persuasion—preaching, news-writing, pamphleteering, oratory, the circulation of verses—is not only portrayed but anatomized. They become instruments both of plotting and of thematic exploration. Still more than the other plays which dramatize the workings of propaganda, *The Duke of Guise* offers points of contact and recognition between the fictional world it portrays and the current political experience of its audience.

I

I begin with the first half of Charles II's reign, the 1660s and earlier 1670s, when popular engagement in politics was less direct than it would be in the second half. One useful if rather crude indicator of public satisfaction or discontent is the incidence and nature of crowd activity. In the first decade and a half after the Restoration —an event which had been greeted with near-universal relief and jubilation—the streets of London were virtually free from popular unrest except for the bawdy house riots of Easter 1668 that were precipitated by the growing persecution of dissent.[4] Even so, as Steven Pincus has convincingly argued, the role of public opinion in that period was greater than ever before. According to Pincus the public sphere—in Habermas's sense—existed in pre-Glorious Revolution England, its most clear manifestation being the emergence of space for political discussion and dissemination of

---

[4] Harris, *London Crowds*, pp. 62 ff.

news provided by the coffee-houses which proliferated both in London and in the provinces. Access to the coffee-houses was restricted by neither gender, class, nor political sympathies.[5] Drawing on personal correspondence, diaries, manuscript newsletters, printed news-sheets, diplomatic dispatches, poems, pamphlets, parliamentary speeches, ballads, and broadsides, Pincus has also shown how widespread was the public interest in foreign affairs. The political impact of that preoccupation became evident during the Third Dutch War of 1672–4, when a shift of opinion from an anti-Dutch to an anti-French position forced the king to switch alliances.[6] The growing importance of public opinion in the first two decades of Charles II's reign found expression, I shall contend, where we would perhaps least expect it: in early Restoration heroics.

The strong ideological cast of the rhymed heroic drama which emerged and flourished in those years, and its preoccupation with kingship, have long been recognized. We know from the work of Nicholas Jose, Nancy Klein Maguire, and others how prominent the themes of regicide and restoration were in early Restoration heroic plays and tragicomedies.[7] Most scholars have, however, been content to regard the intrusion of popular politics into the drama as a development of the Exclusion Crisis. Crowd scenes were indeed largely absent from the heroics produced by Orrery, Dryden, Settle, Lee, and Otway, in the first decade and a half after the Restoration. The politics of those plays are essentially high politics. They centre on palace revolutions engineered by the rejected favourites, or treacherous relations, of the ruler. Yet that does not mean that there was no popular sphere in those plays. Even the most resolutely congratulatory theatrical celebrations of the return of the Stuart king addressed, albeit cautiously and discreetly, those dangers of civil unrest and popular revolt which had toppled his father. In this section of my essay I wish to challenge the current view of Restoration heroic drama as being *exclusively* the province of

---

[5] Steven A. Pincus, '"Coffee Politicians Does Create": Coffeehouses and Restoration Political Culture', *Journal of Modern History*, 67 (1995) 807–34.

[6] Steven A. Pincus, 'From Butterboxes to Wooden Shoes: The Shift in English Popular Sentiment from Anti-Dutch to Anti-French in the 1670s', *Historical Journal*, 38 (1995) 333–61.

[7] Nicholas Jose, *Ideas of the Restoration in English Literature, 1660–71* (London, 1984), esp. pp. 120–41; Nancy Klein Maguire, *Regicide and Restoration: English Tragicomedy, 1660–1671* (Cambridge, 1992).

high politics by focusing on the representation, in Dryden's pre-Exclusion Crisis plays, of the role of the people in bringing about and resolving political conflict.

Dryden's heroics have generally been seen as exercises in the promulgation of the Stuart principle of the divine right of kings.[8] There is much to be said for this view even if the ambivalence of his portrayals of kingship may make one wonder whether the heroic plays can be simple statements of monarchist faith. Yet pro-monarchical drama need not be solely about monarchs. Readers (and critics) of, for instance, *The Indian Queen* or *The Conquest of Granada* tend to remember, and concentrate on, the larger-than-life heroes and heroines: the huffing and ranting Montezuma, the lustful Zempoalla, the self-proclaimed *femme fatale* Lyndaraxa. Though easy to overlook in reading, the role of the populace in those plays would have been impossible to ignore in the theatre, where, even if the people were rarely seen on the stage, their voice was often distinctly heard.

In both his early pro-Stuart poems and his early heroics, even as he acknowledges the culpability of the people for rebellion and regicide, Dryden emphasizes the subjects' unanimity and joy in welcoming the returning monarch. In *Astraea Redux. A Poem on the Restoration of Charles the Second* (1660) 'the Vulgar', who had been 'gull'd into Rebellion' 'by their designing Leaders', are transformed into the 'swarmes of English' going to fetch their monarch from Holland, and the 'Crowds on *Dovers* Strand' eager 'to welcome [him] to Land' (ll. 33, 31). A year later, *To His Sacred Majesty, A Panegyrick on His Coronation* (1661) declares that now Charles's 'glory's may without our crimes be shown': the past is all but forgotten as 'Loud shouts the Nations happiness proclaim' (ll. 20, 35). *Annus Mirabilis* (1667) vindicates the people's right to make their political views known and develops a conception of policy-making—specifically in connection with the proclamation of war against the Dutch—which harmoniously blends popular voice and royal will:

> And still his Subjects call'd aloud for war:
> But peaceful Kings o'r martial people set,
> Each others poize and counter-ballance are.   (ll. 46–8)

[8] For example by Maguire in her *Regicide and Restoration*, pp. 190–214.

Charles's solicitude for the commonalty is not limited to his own subjects. In contrast to Louis XIV, who issued several hostile proclamations against foreigners, the English king offers protection to strangers, a policy whose magnanimity would make him the winner if kings were appointed by some process of international election:

> Were Subjects so but onely by their choice,
> And not from Birth did forc'd Dominion take,
> Our Prince alone would have the publique voice;
> And all his Neighbours Realms would desarts make. (ll. 173–6)

Although the poem does contain an occasional dig at the lower orders—for example, it deplores the rapaciousness of 'th'ignoble crowd' (l. 999) in the wake of the Great Fire of London—the prevailing vision is that of the unity of all classes in the face of both war effort and natural disaster.

That vision informs the dedication of *Annus Mirabilis* to 'the Metropolis of Great Britain, the Most Renowned and Late Flourishing City of London, in its Representatives the Lord Mayor and Court of Aldermen, the Sheriffs and Common Council of it'. The people and their leaders are praised for their loyalty and solidarity. Yet fifteen years later, in *The Duke of Guise*, the City is reviled for its seditious and vulgar democracy. We find a similar anti-populist rhetoric in the plays and poems Dryden wrote between 1678 and 1682: *Oedipus* (1678), *The Spanish Fryar* (1680), *Absalom and Achitophel* (1681), and *The Medall* (1682). Why did this change come about? And how was it represented on the stage?

There are several dramatic techniques that can be used to represent the popular dimension of politics in the theatre. First there can be references to public opinion and crowd activity in dialogues, soliloquies, and, less often, asides. Here dramatic decorum is preserved. No unruly mob intrudes upon the stage, but the impact on the audience is smaller than in the second case, when the mob, though unseen, can be heard. 'Noises off', whether threatening or adulatory, can be an extremely effective means of conveying to the audience the mood of the off-stage crowd, and of determining their response to the on-stage action. Third, the populace may be both visible and audible in full-blown crowd scenes. Fourth, on rare occasions the rabble can be represented by an allegorical figure, for example Democracy in Dryden's opera *Albion and Albanius*. Of course playwrights could and often did use a combination of these techniques so that in some plays, in addition to extended references to the commonalty in dialogue, the popular clamour is heard by the audience; in others 'shouts within' anticipate the appearance of the mob on the stage.[9] The spectators' sympathies will vary depending on whether concern about the public reception of a given political move is voiced by a usurping tyrant or a legitimate and just ruler, and whether the mob is shown to be loyal, seditious, or cowardly. With these possibilities in mind, let us see what happens in Dryden's plays.

The imaginative treatment of the 'restoration' in his early drama, as in his early poetry, involves a high valuation of popular, lower-class support. In the final scene of *The Indian Queen* (1664), his first heroic play, written in collaboration with Sir Robert Howard, the rightful heir Montezuma is restored to the throne of Mexico with the full backing of the populace. The crowd, fired by instinctive loyalty to the legitimate ruler, is instrumental in overthrowing the usurping queen Zempoalla and bringing about Montezuma's reinstatement. With the people still off stage, the progress of the popular rising in his favour and the mounting threat to the current regime are reported by three successive messengers:

> *1 Messen.* . . . the danger's near:
> From every quarter crowds of people meet,
> And leaving houses empty, fill the street.
>
> .   .   .   .
>
> *2 Messen.* Prepare to fight . . . the Banisht Queen,
> With old *Garrucca* in the streets are seen.
>
> .   .   .   .
>
> *3 Messen.* King *Montezuma* their loud shouts proclaim,
> The City rings with their new Sovereigns name;
> The banish'd Queen declares he is her Son,
> And to his succor all the people run.
>
> (v. i. 181–3, 188–9, 192–5)

[9] It is tempting to speculate that when noises off were called for by the script all the actors behind the scenes (and perhaps some stage-hands as well) joined in. However, contemporary prompt-books analysed by Edward A. Langhans provide little information about the staging of crowd scenes or the provisions for noises off other than the sound-effect cues warned by the prompter. See e.g. Langhans's discussion of Thomas D'Urfey's *The Injured Princess* in *Restoration Promptbooks* (Carbondale, Ill., 1981), pp. 38–9. In a manuscript of John Wilson's *Belphegor* which contains prompt notes designed for a production at the Smock Alley Theatre in Dublin *c.*1677–8 the cue 'Call Rable & Boyes' is followed by a stage direction 'Enter Boys & Rabble whooping' (v. i). This manuscript is reproduced in full in Appendix B of Langhans's book.

We then see the loyal party appear on the stage and drive away the remaining adherents of the usurper. Another play dramatizing a restoration, *Marriage A-la-Mode* (1671), likewise attests to the desirability of lower-class support, for it shows a party of Sicilian citizens assisting the legitimate heir Leonidas to regain his throne. In the event, the loyal citizens are captured—'*some like Citizens as prisoners*' (IV. iv)—and scornfully interrogated by the usurper, the final restoration being accomplished—quite improbably: a fact which the parody of it in the Duke of Buckingham's *The Rehearsal* gleefully exploits[10]—by a handful of soldiers.

In both *The Indian Queen* and *Marriage A-la-Mode* the people are tactfully exonerated from complicity in the original regicide. In the former, the rightful king had been assassinated by Traxalla, a rebel in love with the king's sister, Zempoalla, whom he placed on the throne. In the latter, the usurper Polydamas had gained the throne by a military coup. In neither case was the change of government a result of a popular insurrection.

Yet while these plays dramatize 'popular restorations', others show that people's motives and actions can and do pose a threat to legitimate government. Thus in Dryden's first solo heroic play, *The Indian Emperour* (1665), Montezuma—the same whose restoration had been portrayed in *The Indian Queen*—not only has to contend with the invasion of Mexico by the Spaniards but is also faced with a mutiny of his subjects who, famished and exhausted by the siege, are ready to surrender to the enemy: 'Their wants are now grown Mutinous and loud' (IV. ii. 1). Still more ominously in *The Conquest of Granada* (1670–1) Boabdelin the king of the Moorish Granada torn by a tribal conflict between the Abencerrages and the Zegrys and under attack by the Spanish is threatened and nearly unseated by popular unrest and disorder. In the first part he is unable to appease the warring factions, and it is only the noble stranger Almanzor who frightens them into submission in what is effectively an early instance of a crowd scene:

---

[10] While '*The two Usurpers steal out of the Throne, and go away*' and '*The two right Kings of Brentford descend in the Clouds*', Bayes, the Dryden mouthpiece, boasts about his artistic dexterity in bringing about the restoration: 'Look you now, did not I tell you that this would be as easie a turn as the other?' (George Villiers, Duke of Buckingham, *The Rehearsal*, ed. D. E. L. Crane (Durham, 1976), V. i. 38–9).

Alman. . . . Now, let me see whose look but disobeys.
Omnes. Long live King *Mahomet Boabdelin!*
Alman. No more; but hush'd as midnight silence go:
He will not have your Acclamations now,
Hence you unthinking Crowd—
> [*The common people go off on both parties.*
Empire, thou poor and despicable thing,
When such as these unmake, or make a King!   (I. i. 280–6)

In the second part a crowd of discontented subjects forces the king
to recall Almanzor, their preferred military leader, in a scene which
deploys a strategy similar to the one we have encountered in *The
Indian Queen*, the escalating demands of 'the many-headed Beast'
(I. ii. 29), as Boabdelin calls them, being communicated to him by
three messengers:

> *Enter a Messenger.*
> *Mess.* Their fury now a middle course does take:
> To yield the Town, or call *Almanzor* back.
>
> .   .   .   .
>
> *Enter a Second Messenger.*
> *Sec. Mess.* Haste all you can their fury to asswage:
> You are not safe from their rebellious rage.
> *Enter a Third Messenger.*
> *Third Mes.* This Minute if you grant not their desire
> They'll seize your Person and your Palace Fire.
>
> (I. ii. 65–6, 76–9)

Once again the menace and power of the multitude, and their
ascendancy over the weak ruler, are made painfully obvious.
Though not seen, the mob is a formidable off-stage presence: it
greets the king's fulfilment of its ultimatum with '*A shout of Acclama-
tion*', but it is easy to imagine the tumult that would ensue upon its
rejection. In fact, hostile 'noises off' reflecting the rising temper of
the mob will feature prominently in *The Duke of Guise*, with as
many as six stage directions in two consecutive scenes calling for
'*Shout within*', '*Shouts again*', '*Shouts louder*', '*Shouts within*', '*Shouts
without*', '*Shouts again*' (III. i–ii),[11] though of course in that later play
the rioting mob is not only audible but visible too.

---

[11] Dryden's deployment of off-stage shouts seems to be modelled on two earlier heroic
plays: William Davenant's *The Siege of Rhodes*, Part II, and the Earl of Orrery's *Mustapha*.
Originally produced under the Commonwealth in 1656, *The Siege of Rhodes* reappeared on

Paulina Kewes

While the fates of kings, queens, and rebels in Dryden's early heroics and tragicomedies largely depend, as we have seen, on their retaining (or winning) popular support, it is the principal characters of Dryden's last and perhaps greatest rhymed heroic play, *Aureng-Zebe* (1675), who appear most obsessively concerned about their public image and their standing with the populace. In that play references to crowds, rabble, and the will of the people abound,[12] while Dryden, in the Dedication to the Earl of Mulgrave, launches a fierce attack upon those seeking popularity, a term which in his vocabulary has a profoundly derogatory meaning.[13] 'A popular

the Restoration stage in 1661 in an extended and revised two-part version. A striking feature of the second part is its depiction of the common people's forceful intervention into decision-making and conduct of the war, which is vividly rendered through off-stage noises and repeatedly commented upon and analysed by various dramatis personae, their dialogue being punctuated by 'A great Noise . . . of the People within', '[*A great shout within*', '[*A shout within*', '[*Shout agen*', '[*A shout within*' (see *The Siege of Rhodes*, part II, in *The Siege of Rhodes: The First and Second Part . . . The First Part being lately Enlarg'd* (London, 1663), Act II, pp. 11–17). In his *Mustapha* (1665) Orrery too draws the spectators' attention to the importance of popular politics by having the characters discuss its implications against the background of mounting popular clamour (see *Mustapha*, in *The Dramatic Works of Roger Boyle, Earl of Orrery*, ed. William Smith Clark II, 2 vols. (Cambridge, Mass., 1937), vol. i, IV. ii). Solyman's displeasure at his subjects' vocal expressions of support for his son is epitomized by his near-rhetorical question: 'Can any ignorant of Treason be, | Who shout for ought but victory and me?' (IV. ii. 350–1). Interestingly, both Davenant and Orrery show the populace to be correct in its political intuitions.

[12] For example, '[t]h' impatient crowd' (I. i. 51); '[t]he Rabble' (I. i. 61); 'a Crowd' (I. i. 254); 'murmuring Crouds' (IV. i. 201), etc.

[13] As the *OED* attests, in the late seventeenth century the terms 'popular', 'popularly', and 'popularity' possessed several negative meanings which have since become obsolete. For instance, 'popularity' denoted 'the action or practice of courting, or trying to win, popular favour' (3a); the adverb 'popularly' referred to acting 'in a way that wins popular favour' (3); the meaning of 'popular' was 'of lowly birth; belonging to the commonalty or populace; plebeian' (2b); 'having characteristics attributed to the common people; low, vulgar, plebeian' (2c); 'studious of, or designed to gain, the favour of the common people' (5a). Those adverse connotations are repeatedly invoked by Dryden in both his imaginative works and his prose writings. Interestingly, it was in the same period that the word 'mob' began to be used to describe 'the disorderly and riotous part of the population, the roughs, the rabble; an assemblage of the rabble; a tumultuous crowd bent on, or liable to be incited to, acts of lawlessness and outrage' (1a). Dryden's audiences and readers were alive to both the political implications and the rhetorical virtuosity of his depictions of the populace in both his drama and poetry, ranking them alongside those by Shakespeare. In early eighteenth-century anthologies of quotations such as Edward Bysshe's much-reprinted *The Art of English Poetry*, 2 vols. (London, 1702) under the headings 'Populace' and 'Popular' there are extracts only from the work of Dryden and Shakespeare (i. 286–9). The extracts derive from Dryden's *Aureng-Zebe*, *Don Sebastian*, *The Spanish Fryar*, *The Conquest of Granada*, *Cleomenes*, *Absalom and Achitophel*, the Dryden–Lee *Duke of Guise*, and Dryden's translation of Virgil; the extracts from Shakespeare come from *Coriolanus*, *2 Henry IV*, and *Troilus and Cressida*. Under the

66

man', he writes, 'is, in truth, no better than a Prostitute to common Fame, and to the People. He lies down to every one he meets for the hire of praise; and his Humility is onely a disguis'd Ambition.' And he praises his patron's 'contempt of popular applause' and 'retir'd Virtue, which shines onely to a few'.[14]

Dryden's ambivalence towards popular power finds a curious expression in the apparently inconsistent behaviour of his heroes from Montezuma and Almanzor to Aureng-Zebe. While it is the love of the common people that ensures their success, be it in regaining the throne, obtaining a loved woman, or weathering a conflict with the father-king, and while at times they themselves enquire keenly into the current state of public sympathies—as does Aureng-Zebe following his fall from favour and the promotion of his brother Morat: 'How look the People in this turn of State?' (II. i. 520)—they repeatedly express disdain for the popular following they enjoy. 'Popularity'—in its late seventeenth-century sense—seems incompatible with nobility and honour, and yet without it political victory is impossible to achieve. To show attachment and to proffer assistance to an Almanzor or an Aureng-Zebe reflects well on the political intuitions of the commonalty; but to seek or even welcome their support would reflect badly on the beneficiary. The ideological conflict is unresolvable.

To offer a comprehensive account of Dryden's engagement with popular politics in his early work is beyond the scope of this essay. Yet even this brief overview provides ample evidence that his dramatic treatment of popular threat to royal authority predates the troubles of 1678–82, even if it is only then—in *Oedipus*, *The Spanish Fryar*, and *The Duke of Guise*—that anti-populist sentiment comes to prominence. Dryden's early plays and poems had striven to exorcise the memory of popular opposition to the government of Charles I. Now that the London mob manipulated by Whig grandees has become a serious threat to the government of his son, the

---

heading 'Train-Bands', Bysshe quotes from Dryden's 'Cymon and Iphigenia' (i. 353). For a virtually identical selection see Charles Gildon's *The Complete Art of English Poetry*, 2 vols. (London, 1718), ii. 305–8, 400.

[14] *Works*, xii. 151. Cf. Dryden's 'Translation of the Latter Part of the Third Book of Lucretius: Against the Fear of Death': 'The *Sisyphus* is he, whom noise and strife | Seduce from all the soft retreats of life, | To vex the Government, disturb the Laws; | Drunk with the Fumes of popular applause' (ll. 200–3).

representations of, and references to, crowds in Dryden's poetry and drama become increasingly negative and contemptuous. However, the ubiquity of satirical portrayals of the crowd was itself a problem. For if the mob is usually disobedient and factious, then a 'popular monarch'—such as Dryden envisioned Charles II to be in *Annus Mirabilis*—is merely the idol of a misguided people. The official rhetoric predicated on appeals to 'beloved and loyal subjects' suddenly loses its sense. The only way out of this conundrum is to show people as basically inclined to the good, if dangerously gullible and liable to be misled by demagogues.

II

The Popish Plot and the Exclusion Crisis of 1678–82 brought popular opinion to the forefront of national politics. During that time the survival of the established government was placed under threat on a scale unseen since the Puritan Revolution. In that earlier period, too, political debate had involved widespread public participation. Then, too, plays (and pamphlets in dramatic form) had represented, indeed been part of, the manipulation of public opinion, a point to which I shall return. Those plays, perforce, had not been performed. In the crisis of Charles II's reign highly partisan plays were performed. In them the popular dimension of politics is almost as prominent as it was in the public life on which they comment.

The political propaganda which emerged during the years 1678–82 assumed a variety of written, oral, and visual forms.[15] In the Civil Wars, the volume and effectiveness of printed and scribally transmitted materials—tracts, newspapers, pamphlets, broadsides, plays, poems, almanacs, prints, and woodcuts—had added a new dimension to political conflict.[16] First under Cromwell, then under Charles II, censorship had reduced, but not halted, the flow of

---

[15] See Harris, *London Crowds*, pp. 96–158.

[16] See Lois Potter, *Secret Rites and Secret Writing: Royalist Literature, 1641–1660* (Cambridge, 1989); Nigel Smith, *Literature and Revolution in England, 1640–1660* (New Haven and London, 1994); Joad Raymond, *The Invention of the Newspaper: English Newsbooks, 1641–1649* (Oxford, 1996); Louis B. Wright, 'The Reading of Plays during the Puritan Revolution', *Huntington Library Bulletin*, 6 (1934) 73–108; Dale B. J. Randall, *Winter Fruit: English Drama, 1642–1660* (Lexington, Ky., 1995); and Susan Wiseman, *Drama and Politics in the English Civil War* (Cambridge, 1998).

publication. Steven Pincus has shown that the appetite of an increasingly literate public for political discussion was high.[17] In the spring of 1679 the lapse of the Licensing Act, which removed an essential control of censorship, brought a flood of printed polemic onto the market.[18] Other forms of persuasion, however, are likely to have reached a wider audience: sermons, spectacles of Pope- and Jack Presbyter-burnings, and popular entertainments. These were collective activities, which required the presence and often participation of groups of citizens. We know from Tim Harris's *London Crowds in the Reign of Charles II* how prominently and frequently collective agitation figured in the politics of the years around 1680. For dramatists, the crowd was the chief theatrical vehicle for the representation of popular politics. The crowd scene, largely absent from new dramatic writing since the Puritan Revolution, was restored to it. In the late 1670s, in plays as well as in politics, crowds became increasingly common. Their prevalence was related, as we shall see, to the efforts of political leaders to secure public support.

Hitherto Restoration plays had contained few scenes in which the people were wooed, or seen to act in their own right.[19] When extras had been needed, it had been almost exclusively in order to represent clashing armies or cheering multitudes. Divisions within the body politic tended to be portrayed in terms either of religious polarization or else of tribal warfare. In both cases the conflicts are so entrenched as to be beyond the power of persuasion to alter them. The confrontation between the Pharisees and the priests of the

---

[17] Steven A. Pincus, *Protestantism and Patriotism: Ideologies and the Making of English Foreign Policy, 1650–1668* (Cambridge, 1996). On the steady growth of literacy see David Cressy, *Literacy and the Social Order: Reading and Writing in Tudor and Stuart England* (Cambridge, 1982).

[18] Timothy Crist, 'Government Control of the Press after the Expiration of the Printing Act in 1679', *Publishing History*, 5 (1979) 49–77. On the contest between the government and opposition press during the Exclusion Crisis see James Sutherland, *The Restoration Newspaper and its Development* (Cambridge, 1986), pp. 147–78.

[19] My focus is on political disorder as exemplified in serious drama. A different line of enquiry might pursue the representation of social unrest in Restoration comic drama. It would take into account the portrayal of, for example, the storming of a brothel by 'the many-headed-monster-Multitude' in Thomas Duffett's *The Mock-Tempest* (1674) and, in Thomas Shadwell's *The Virtuoso* (1676), the siege of the virtuoso's house by '*a great rabble of people*' made up of ribbon weavers who are enraged by a report that he has invented the engine loom. See *The Mock-Tempest: or The Enchanted Castle*, in Montague Summers (ed.), *Shakespeare Adaptations* (New York, 1922, repr. 1966), I. i. (p. 117), and *The Virtuoso*, ed. Marjorie Hope Nicolson and David Stuart Rodes (London, 1966), v. iii.

Sanhedrin in John Crowne's *The Destruction of Jerusalem by Titus Vespasian* (1677) is an example of the former. The rivalry between the Abencerrages and the Zegrys in Dryden's *The Conquest of Granada* exemplifies the latter, though even in that play, as we have seen, the tribal conflict is overlaid with popular sedition. By contrast, in the plays of the Exclusion Crisis we observe, time and again, the division and mutability of hitherto like-minded citizens.

The increasingly divided loyalties of the English, which led to the emergence of political parties and the labels Whig, Tory, and later Trimmer, were emblematically expressed on the stage in the pro-liferation of scenes of civil commotion, rioting, and mob violence. The model for such scenes, which characterize plays set both in republican regimes and in monarchies, had been established by Shakespeare in his Roman plays, notably *Julius Caesar* and *Coriolanus*, and in the English histories, especially *Henry VI*. *Julius Caesar* may have been revived during the Exclusion Crisis.[20] *Coriolanus* appeared on the stage in Nahum Tate's version called *The Ingratitude of a Commonwealth* (1681), and the *Henry VI* plays were revived in two separate adaptations by John Crowne, *The Misery of Civil-War* (1680) and *Henry the Sixth: The First Part* (1681).[21] Crowds were also introduced into new redactions of Shakespeare's plays which had previously lacked them. In Tate's version of *Richard II* (1681), Bullingbrook, the consummate mob politician, courts the rabble made up of 'A Shoemaker, Farrier, Weaver, Tanner, Mercer, Brewer, Butcher, Barber, *and infinite others*' in a scene which the adapter has added to the original.[22] Similarly, in Tate's *The History of King Lear* the newly blinded Gloster resolves to make political capital out of his pathetic condition:

---

[20] The fact that the date 1681 has been inscribed against the cast list in the copy of the 1684 edition of the play seen by W. W. Greg may indicate that there was a revival (Greg, *A Bibliography of the English Printed Drama to the Restoration*, 4 vols. (London, 1939–59), iii. 1268–9). For a claim that *Julius Caesar* was deliberately withheld from the stage during the Exclusion Crisis see Michael Dobson, '"Accents Yet Unknown": Canonisation and the Claiming of *Julius Caesar*', in Jean I. Marsden (ed.), *The Appropriation of Shakespeare: Post-Renaissance Reconstructions of the Works and the Myth* (New York, 1991), pp. 11–28, at pp. 14 and 25–6 n.

[21] For an overview of adaptations of Shakespeare during the Exclusion Crisis see Michael Dobson, *The Making of the National Poet: Shakespeare, Adaptation and Authorship, 1660–1769* (Oxford, 1992), pp. 62–90.

[22] Nahum Tate, *The History of King Richard The Second Acted at the Theatre Royal, Under the Name of the Sicilian Usurper* (London, 1681), II. iv.

> ... with these bleeding Rings
> I will present me to the pittying Crowd,
> And with the Rhetorick of these dropping Veins
> Enflame 'em to Revenge their King and me.[23]

It is against the background of factional warfare and of the canvassing of popular support in the Rome of Marius and Sulla that the star-crossed love of Romeo and Juliet, renamed Marius and Lavinia, unfolds in Thomas Otway's *The History and Fall of Caius Marius* (1680).

These Shakespearian offshoots have parallels with the other plays premièred in the wake of Titus Oates's spurious revelations about the Popish Plot. In the heroic plays of the early Restoration the ideology of absolutism and divine right—however strained—prevails. Rebels tend to be villains over whom legitimate rulers triumph in the end. But in plays of the Exclusion Crisis, even Tory ones, the prerogatives and virtues of kings are much less clear. Their reigns are caught up in national political movements which are beyond their control, and which sometimes destroy them. They are obliged to attach importance to the opinions of the ruled. Equally, the threat that their enemies will manipulate the crowd fills them with alarm. The charge of courting the masses is levelled by suspicious monarchs at virtuous individuals whose true offence is to enjoy public esteem. Theocrin, the loyal general in Nahum Tate's play of that title (1680), is falsely accused of

> ... Court[ing] ... the Popular Fame ...
> Whil'st diving low from his Triumphant Chair,
> The Rabble at each Hault he did salute,
> Then eagerly inclin'd his Lawrell'd Head,
> To catch the buzzing Praises of the Crow'd ...[24]

Those in power habitually represent the wooing of the populace as treason. In Nathaniel Lee's *Theodosius: or, The Force of Love* (1680) the emperor's sister Pulcheria assumes that a rebel will characteristically

---

[23] Nahum Tate, *The History of King Lear* (London, 1681), Act III (p. 39). Tate eliminates the invasion by the French, and shows the support for Lear's restoration to originate with English peasantry roused by Gloster.

[24] Nahum Tate, *The Loyal General* (London, 1680), Act III (p. 21).

Paulina Kewes

> . . . haste to the Army,
> Grow popular, and lead the multitude:
> Preach up [his] wrongs, and drive the giddy Beast
> To kick at *Caesar.*[25]

In John Banks's *The Unhappy Favourite* (1682) Queen Elizabeth learns of the Earl of Essex's treason. Adopting the very tactics which Shakespeare's Coriolanus had eschewed, Essex uses 'subtile means to gain [her] Subjects Hearts'. He

> . . . counted all his wounds,
> Unstrip'd his Vest, and shew'd his naked Scars,
> Telling them what great Wonders he had done,
> And wou'd do more to serve 'em and their Children;
> Begging still louder to the stinking Rabble,
> And sweated too so many eager drops, as if
> He had been pleading for *Rome*'s Consulship.[26]

Though Essex's tactics do not avail him, other rebels who appeal to the crowd are more successful. In William Whitaker's ultra-royalist play *The Conspiracy or The Change of Government* (1680), the Sultan bewails the subversive machinations which have lost him the backing of his people:

> Oh horrid Traitors to my Crown and Name!
> The City Rages in Rebellious Flame:
> The Commons are incourag'd by the Peers,
> *Vizier* and *Bectas* head the Mutiniers . . .[27]

Whitaker strives to give pictorial representation to the popular clamour. When the Sultan's plight momentarily induces some

[25] *Theodosius: or, The Force of Love*, in *The Works of Nathaniel Lee*, ed. Thomas B. Stroup and Arthur L. Cooke, 2 vols. (New Brunswick, NJ, 1954–5), vol. ii (II. i. 226–9).

[26] John Banks, *The Unhappy Favourite; or The Earl of Essex* (London, 1682), Act IV (p. 45). Cf. also the speech of Shakespeare's Henry V before the battle of Agincourt: 'He that shall see this day and live old age | Will yearly on the vigil feast his neighbours, | And say "Tomorrow is Saint Crispian." | Then will he strip his sleeve and show his scars, | And say "These wounds I had on Crispin's day"' (*King Henry V*, ed. Andrew Gurr (Cambridge, 1992), IV. iii. 44–8); see also Dryden's rendition of the speeches of *Ajax and Ulysses* from Ovid in his *Fables* (1700): 'At this he [Ulysses] bar'd his Breast, and show'd his Scars, | As of a furrow'd Field, well plough'd with Wars' (see *Poems*, ed. Kinsley, vol. iv (ll. 410–11)).

[27] William Whitaker, *The Conspiracy or The Change of Government* (London, 1680), Act III (p. 20).

citizens to relent, a stage direction specifies: '*Poor Sultan, brave Prince, and the like words of kindness murmur'd among the People*'. Other stage directions demonstrate what Londoners well knew—and what indeed the competing hissings and clappings which greeted representations of politics in the theatres themselves confirm—the capacity of public gatherings to divide: '*The People quarrel and are divided*', '*One part of the People fall off to the Sultans side, and cry* a Sultan, a Sultan*; the other part stick to the* Vizier, *and cry* Justice, Justice. *They all fight*' (Act III, p. 28 misnumbered as p. 26).

For rebels, no less than monarchs, the command of the multitude is essential. In John Crowne's *The Ambitious Statesman* (1679) the Constable of France, the arch-plotter and title character, is confident that his seditious schemes will prosper:

> For I have spread such lies against the Government,
> Have frighted all the people from their Wits.[28]

The Constable's son and opponent, the Duke of Vendosme, who is the king's 'loyal favourite', recognizes the danger inherent in his father's policy:

> An Orator will set the World a dancing
> After his pipe when Reason cannot stir it.
> Fanatick canting Priests, will o'return Kingdoms
> Only by tones, and thumping upon Pulpits.   (Act III, p. 32)

In the context of acute civil instability the dangers posed by popular opinion take on an altogether more distressing reality.

Exclusion Crisis drama, then, registers the mounting significance of the public mandate, of what was called 'popularity'. In pro-government drama scenes of mob violence serve as a warning against civil disobedience and rebellion, in opposition plays Protestant crowds are presented as essentially loyal and trustworthy, brutality and disorder being associated with the popish rabble.[29] Whether Whig or Tory, however, and whether set in courts or camps, England, Turkey, or ancient Rome, contemporary plays make apparent the power that resides in the multitude.

---

[28] John Crowne, *The Ambitious Statesman, or The Loyal Favourite* (London, 1679), Act I (p. 7).
[29] See Owen, *Restoration Theatre and Crisis*, pp. 149 ff.

III

The plays of the years 1678–82 by Tate, Otway, Banks, Lee, and Whitaker basically equate political propaganda with direct oral appeals to the populace. Some settings precluded the representation of other forms of persuasion. After all, there were no printing presses in ancient Greece or medieval Italy. Yet even where playwrights might have brought in a range of manipulative techniques, they did not do so.

To that rule, *The Duke of Guise* provides a revealing exception. Written in collaboration by Dryden and Nathaniel Lee in the late spring of 1682, it was banned before an intended performance in July of that year, but cleared for production in November. Uncompromising in its Tory partisanship, the play is an assault, thinly disguised behind the veneer of allegory, on the Whigs in general and the Duke of Monmouth in particular. The politics of *The Duke of Guise* have received much critical attention. It has been regularly cited as an example of a direct parallel play.[30] It has also been situated both in the context of Dryden's Tory propaganda, dramatic and non-dramatic,[31] and in that of the drama of the Exclusion Crisis.[32] Yet the play's intense preoccupation with, and representation of, the means of gaining and maintaining the support of the populace has passed virtually unnoticed. Dryden and Lee's play dramatizes, or at least alludes to, the whole spectrum of devices of propaganda used in the England of its time. It emphasizes the public appeal of stage-managed appearances by charismatic party leaders and dissects the mechanics of seditious preaching, verse-making, and fraudulent newsmongering. *The Duke of Guise* is a work of Tory propaganda. Yet it also explores the phenomenon to which it belongs. In a self-conscious manner, it asks how propaganda, which in the play is the exclusive province of the opposition, can be used to persuade, manipulate, and mislead.

[30] See e.g. John M. Wallace, 'Dryden and History: A Problem in Allegorical Reading', *ELH* 36 (1969) 265–90, at p. 280; Alan Roper, 'Drawing Parallels and Making Applications in Restoration Literature', in Richard Ashcraft and Alan Roper, *Politics as Reflected in Literature*, Papers Presented at a Clark Library Seminar, 24 Jan. 1987 (Los Angeles, 1989), pp. 29–65, at pp. 48–52.

[31] Phillip Harth, *Pen for a Party: Dryden's Tory Propaganda in its Contexts* (Princeton, NJ, 1993), pp. 188–205.

[32] Owen, *Restoration Theatre and Crisis*, esp. pp. 147–50, 169–71.

Most plays produced during the Exclusion Crisis engaged closely with the political controversies of the day. Several adopted a clear Whig or Tory line. Yet it was *The Duke of Guise* which proved the most controversial play not only of the Exclusion Crisis but of the whole later seventeenth century. Its uncompromising loyalism exasperated the Whigs and delighted the Tories. That was not least because Dryden, the Stuart Laureate, was joined in this composition by Nathaniel Lee, who had been hitherto perceived as a Whig sympathizer.[33] Lee's change of allegiance did not bode well for the prosperity of the Whig cause. It is therefore not surprising that Whigs repeatedly accused Dryden of having corrupted his partner's sound political views.[34]

Dryden replied to these and other charges in a lengthy pamphlet called *The Vindication of the Duke of Guise* (1683). In it he specified his and Lee's shares in the play: 'I shall not arrogate to my self the Merits of my Friend. *Two thirds* of it belong'd to *him*; and then to *me* only the *First Scene* of the Play; the whole *Fourth Act*, and the *first half*, or somewhat *more* of the *Fifth*'.[35] However approximate, this estimation allows us to explore the political slant of Dryden's and Lee's respective contributions. More than a mere piece of party writing, *The Duke of Guise* owes its impact to the wit and acuteness of its satire of the opposition, the skilful handling of the melodramatic love story, and the spectacular special effects called for by a quasi-Faustian subplot which involves a pact with the devil and the horrific destruction of its perpetrator. The consistency and pervasiveness of the play's treatment of propagandists, of their sponsors, audiences, programmes, and techniques, give the lie to those who, like its contemporary Whig critics, assume that *The Duke of Guise*,

---

[33] On Dryden's contribution to the Tory cause see Harth, *Pen for a Party*. For discussions of Lee's whiggishness see Roswell Gray Ham, *Otway and Lee: Biography from a Baroque Age* (New Haven, 1931), pp. 116–31; Robert D. Hume, 'The Satiric Design of Nat. Lee's *The Princess of Cleve*', *Journal of English and Germanic Philology*, 75 (1976) 117–38; John Loftis, *The Politics of Drama in Augustan England* (Oxford, 1963), pp. 15–17; and Susan J. Owen, '"Partial Tyrants" and "Freeborn People" in *Lucius Junius Brutus*', *Studies in English Literature*, 31 (1991) 463–82. For assessments of Lee's political views prior to the writing of *The Duke of Guise* as more moderate see Richard E. Brown, 'Nathaniel Lee's Political Dramas, 1679–1683', *Restoration*, 10 (1986) 41–52; 'The Dryden–Lee Collaboration: *Oedipus* and *The Duke of Guise*', *Restoration*, 9 (1985) 12–25; J. Douglas Canfield, 'Royalism's Last Dramatic Stand: English Political Tragedy, 1679–1689', *Studies in Philology*, 82 (1985) 234–63.

[34] For an account of the play's reception and its collaborative authorship see my *Authorship and Appropriation: Writing for the Stage in England, 1660–1710* (Oxford, 1998), pp. 162–76.

[35] *Works*, xiv. 311.

rather than being a sustained effort of collaboration by Dryden and Lee, constitutes Dryden's perversion of his partner's more neutral political views.

A historical drama set in late sixteenth-century France, *The Duke of Guise* establishes twin parallels with the politics of the Exclusion Crisis. Both the French Holy League of 1576, and the Presbyterian Solemn League and Covenant of 1643, correspond to the abortive Whig Association of 1681. 'Our Play's a Parallel', asserts the prologue, 'The Holy League | Begot our Cov'nant: *Guisards* got the Whigg' (ll. 1–2).[36] According to the Tories, the Association, whose existence was dramatically revealed during Shaftesbury's Grand Inquest in autumn 1681, confirmed that, if foiled in achieving their aims through parliamentary means, the Whigs would resort to armed rebellion. Dryden and Lee's play illustrates this claim. It shows the meteoric rise to power, and ignominious fall, of its eponymous hero, who, as was widely realized, represents Charles II's bastard son, the Duke of Monmouth, to whom the play offers a clear warning. Guise foments rebellion against his king, Henry III, his chief goal being the exclusion of the Huguenot Henry of Navarre—the alter ego for the Catholic Duke of York whose exclusion was sought by the Whigs—from succeeding to the French throne. When on the verge of success, Guise is killed by the exasperated monarch's henchmen. The Whigs alleged that the assassination of Guise was tantamount to a call for Monmouth's death. They rallied around their darling leader, proclaiming: 'Let him live safe tho' Murther'd on the Stage.'[37]

Dryden and Lee's earlier collaboration, *Oedipus* (1678), had deployed anti-populist rhetoric and featured several full-blown crowd scenes in which Creon and his cronies incite the Thebans to rebellion. Yet the representation of the people is not unequivocally negative: not only are the Thebans afflicted by the plague which elicits the audience's sympathy, they initially turn to their king for succour and later show compassion for his predicament. They may be giddy and easily manipulated, but because they have had their

---

[36] In fact, as Dryden himself acknowledged in the *Vindication*, the play had originally been called *The Parallel* and only the appearance of John Northleigh's tract *The Parallel: Or, the New Specious Association, an Old Rebellious Covenant* in March 1682 induced him and Lee to change the title to *The Duke of Guise* (*Works*, xiv. 314, 479).

[37] *Sol in opposition to Saturn. Or A a [sic] short return to a late Tragedy call'd The Duke of Guise* (London, 1683).

share of suffering, and because the calamities that have befallen them can be blamed, not unreasonably, on Oedipus, their proneness to rebellion is understandable even if not excusable. In Dryden's *The Spanish Fryar* (1680) there is no vulgar mob, the citizens rising in defence of their rightful king and against the usurper. It is debatable how justified they are in opposing the *de facto* ruler, but they are not shown as despicably treacherous or gullible. It is not until *Absalom and Achitophel* and *The Medall* in poetry and *The Duke of Guise* in drama that the anti-populist sentiment comes to the fore.

In developing the theme of partisan politics, Dryden and Lee may have drawn inspiration from the principal source of the play, Enrico Caterino Davila's *Historia delle Guerre Civili di Francia* (1630). Davila's narrative frequently touches on the part played by printed and oral propaganda in provoking religious and political unrest. He notes the role of the written word in propagating Calvin's doctrine (pp. 39–40),[38] and in publicizing the political goals of the warring factions: 'Many Writings are published on each side' (pp. 110–11); 'At the first . . . their pens were more active then their swords' (p. 123); 'The copyes of this League framed with so much art by the Guises . . . were very carefully, and with much cunning dispersed, by the hands of discreet wary men' (p. 451). The historical Duke of Guise emerges from Davila's account as a shrewd co-ordinator of a multi-pronged propaganda campaign on behalf of the Holy League. He is said to have 'made use of popular eloquent men to divulge [his reasons] from their Pulpits, and infuse them in private discourses among the people, thereby to win their affections, and procure the enlargement and spreading abroad of the League' (p. 505).

The diverse forms of propaganda recorded by Davila feature prominently in *The Duke of Guise*. Yet in Davila the manipulation of opinion is hardly a major theme. In Dryden and Lee's play it becomes one. The range and forms of propaganda techniques represented by the collaborators bring home to its audience the correspondence between the popular politics of sixteenth-century France and those of Restoration England. Parallels are explicitly

---

[38] Davila's history was translated into English by Charles Cotterell and William Aylesbury and first published as *The Historie of the Civill Warres of France, Written in Italian by H. C. Davila* (London, 1647). The second edition, *The History of the Civil Wars of France . . . The Second Impression*, appeared in 1678. Dryden used the first edition, Lee the second (Dryden, *Works*, xiv. 487). This and all subsequent citations of Davila are given in the text, and are from the first English edition.

drawn between the susceptibility of the Parisian citizenry to demagogues and the gullibility of the whiggishly inclined London
crowds. At the same time the corruption of the French churchmen,
statesmen, and nobility, who attempt to strike at their rightful king
by alienating his subjects' trust, points to the manœuvres of the
dissenting clergy, Shaftesbury, Monmouth, and their adherents.
The play cautions the spectators to be on their guard by exposing
the mechanics of misinformation and mass agitation.

Much of the savagery of the play's wit is directed at seditious
clergy. The perversion of religious doctrine by mercenary priests
who undermine royal prerogative and promote civil disobedience is
reduced *ad absurdum*. Already in the first scene, written by Dryden,
the Curate of St Eustace relates his 'godly pains, to satisfie some
Scruples rais'd amongst weak Brothers of our Party' (I. i. 11–12).
The Curate's invaluable contribution to the Leaguers' cause is
hailed by the Cardinal of Guise: 'all his Prayers are Curses on the
Government; | And all his Sermons Libels on the King' (I. i. 100–1).
The effects of the Curate's teachings are borne out in the sheriff's
description of the city bands as 'Preach'd up, and ready tin'd for a
Rebellion' (I. i. 117). The mechanics of seditious preaching are
further revealed in a lengthy exchange between Guise's adviser,
Malicorne (a satirical portrait of Shaftesbury), and Melanax, the
devil to whom Malicorne has sold his soul:

> *Mal.*—But why in this Fanatick Habit, Devil?
>   Thou look'st like one that preaches to the Crowd,
>   Gospel is in thy Face, and outward Garb,
>   And Treason on thy Tongue.
> *Mel.*   Thou hast me right,
>   Ten thousand Devils more are in this Habit,
>   Saintship and Zeal are still our best disguise:
>   We mix unknown with the hot thoughtless Crowd,
>   And quoting Scriptures, which too well we know,
>   With impious Glosses ban the holy Text,
>   And make it speak Rebellion, Schism and Murder,
>   So turn the Arms of Heaven against it self.
>
> (IV. ii. 7–17)[39]

---

[39] Shaftesbury has been identified as the satirical target of this and other scenes involving
the devil and his victim in Rachel A. Miller, 'Political Satire in the Malicorne–Melanax
Scenes of *The Duke of Guise*', *English Language Notes*, 16 (1979) 212–18.

We soon have a chance to see the infernal minister in action: '*Enter Citizens, and* Melanax *in his Fanatick Habit, at the head of 'em*' (IV. iv). What makes the situation all the more diverting is that the devil is preaching to the converted: his seditious sermonizing appears almost a model of moderation when confronted with the citizens' extremist political views. The vicious satire of the Parisian rabble (that is, the London citizenry) in this scene recalls the representation of the mob in Dryden and Lee's *Oedipus* (1678). In that earlier collaboration the equally fickle if less blameworthy Thebans are easily swayed by Creon and his confederates to abandon their rightful king Oedipus, and are only recalled to their duty by the remonstrations of the blind prophet Tiresias (I. i. 211 ff.).

The references to Melanax's 'Fanatick Habit' and the rhetorical pretence of 'Saintship' and 'Zeal' adopted by the devilish crew of priests leading the multitude to rebellion firmly associate French Catholics with English Dissenters.[40] The oppositional stance of both groups has been articulated early in the play by the Curate of St Eustace, who freely admits to having drawn his seditious arguments from a book written by a 'Calvinist Minister of *Orleans*' (I. i. 18). To disparage the Whigs, who styled themselves the king's true and loyal Protestant subjects—a claim reflected in the titles of the newspapers they sponsored, such as the *Impartial Protestant Mercury*, the *True Protestant Domestick Intelligence*, the *True Protestant Mercury*[41]—for their alleged alliance with dissent was a standard Tory move. Dryden himself had recently made this point in his 'Epistle to the Whigs' prefixed to *The Medall* and in the poem itself.[42] However, to have the Curate incriminate himself by affirming to his associates (and hence to the audience) the interchangeability of Nonconformist and popish justifications of regicide would have added punch to the accusation.

[40] Cf. Dryden's attack on Shaftesbury in *The Medall*: 'He cast himself into the Saint-like mould ...But ...There split the Saint: for Hypocritique Zeal | Allows no Sins but those it can conceal' (ll. 33, 36–9).

[41] Tories, in their turn, published a series of newspapers whose titles such as *The Loyal Protestant Intelligence* and *The True Protestant Intelligence* were designed to cast doubt on the veracity of Whig claims to represent the Protestant majority. The development and eventual demise of Whig newspapers have been treated in Harris, *London Crowds*, pp. 106–7; and Harth, *Pen for a Party*, pp. 32–3, 49, 73–4, 207–8.

[42] 'Epistle', ll. 38–43; and *The Medall*: 'Whether the plotting Jesuite lay'd the plan | Of murth'ring Kings, or the *French* Puritan, | Our Sacrilegious Sects their Guides outgo' (ll. 201–3).

Dryden charges the clergy with two other strategies of mis-information: perjury and the spreading of slanderous reports. In order to discredit the testimony of a sheriff loyal to the king, the Cardinal counsels instantaneous character assassination: 'Give out he's Arbitrary; a *Navarrist*; | A Heretick; discredit him betimes; | And make his Witness void'. The Curate readily volunteers to 'swear [the sheriff] Guilty' (I. i. 139–42).[43]

The laity are as guileful as the clergy. Like the Duke of Mon-mouth, the Duke of Guise stoops to soliciting popular support in person. Monmouth's appearances in the capital routinely attracted crowds and sparked bonfires, enthusiastic followers drinking his health and inviting (sometimes coercing) passers-by to join in.[44] The 'Protestant duke', as he was dubbed by his supporters, made several progresses in the provinces, such as his tour of the West Country in the summer of 1680 during which he was welcomed as if he were indeed heir apparent to the crown; he manifested his religious credentials—impeccable in contrast to the Catholic Duke of York's—by attending church each time he returned to London; he touched for the King's Evil or scrofula, his healing gift being trumpeted as a sure sign of both his royalty and his legitimacy;[45] and he graciously conversed with lower-class adherents of the Whig cause such as Stephen College, the Protestant Joiner, who remem-bered, with understandable pride, that when he was summoned by the duke and other Whig lords and enlisted to search for papist plotters, 'The duke of *Monmouth* called me to him and told me he had heard a good report of me, and that I was an honest man and one that may be trusted.'[46] Guise's techniques of winning mass support are equally impressive. They include extensive consulta-tions with city authorities—'the whole Sixteen | That sway the

---

[43] Cf. Grillon's condemnation of pulpit propaganda in Dryden's part of Act V: 'when the Preachers draw against the King, a Parson in a Pulpit is a devilish Forehorse' (v. i. 20–2).

[44] For accounts of widespread support for Monmouth see Harris, *London Crowds*, pp. 158–61, 186–8; Mark Knights, *Politics and Opinion in Crisis, 1678–81* (Cambridge, 1994), pp. 136–7, 171, 206, 275.

[45] See Harold Weber, *Paper Bullets: Print and Kingship under Charles II* (Lexington, Ky., 1996), pp. 77 ff.

[46] *The Speech and Carriage of Stephen College At Oxford, Before the Castle, on Wednesday August 31. 1681, 'Taken exactly from his own Mouth at the Place of Execution'* (London, 1681), p. 3, quoted in Weber, *Paper Bullets*, p. 179. For a detailed discussion of College's contribution to Whig propaganda, his trial for treason, execution, and afterlife in the Tory press see Weber, *Paper Bullets*, pp. 172–298.

Crowd of *Paris*' (I. i. 4–5)—and with the clergy—who 'cry Religion to the Crowd' (v. i. 214)—and direct appeals to the Parisian mob. He shrinks from neither flattery nor self-abasement. '[*B*]*owing, and Bare-headed*', as the stage direction tells us, the Duke addresses the rabble as 'Countrey-men', asserting fellowship and solidarity with his social inferiors: '*French* we are all, and Brothers of a Land' (IV. iv. 116, 121).

Dryden and Lee stress the readiness of opposition leaders to calculate their actions with a view to their publicity value. In a scene designed to recall Monmouth's return to London in November 1679 against Charles's express command, Guise insolently resolves to see the king despite the hazard it involves: 'Therefore I will see him, | And so report my danger to the People' (III. i. 396–7). Dryden picks up the theme (initiated by Lee) of Guise's self-fashioning by having the Duke disclose his motives for sparing the lives of Grillon and other captives to his associates: 'to kill 'em were to shew I fear'd 'em' (IV. iv. 137). His brother Mayenne endorses Guise's decision in what amounts to a mini-exercise in mob psychology:

> . . . 'Tis rightly judg'd:
> And let me add, who heads a Popular Cause,
> Must prosecute that Cause by Popular Ways:
> So whether you are merciful or no,
> You must affect to be.   (IV. iv. 141–5)

This construction of mercy (or rather of pretended mercy) as a political expedient contrasts with true mercy, a sign of true kingship, which Dryden elsewhere associates with Charles II (and his father),[47] and which Guise merely apes. More broadly, such publicity-conscious actions and sentiments of the dramatis personae would have reminded the audience of the carefully prepared appearances of Monmouth, York, and others in London's public spaces, the Duke's and the King's Theatres among them.

In the play as in the Exclusion Crisis, public appearances by party leaders are exploited in print. Like Monmouth, Guise employs a host of hack writers who target the literate in their pamphlets and manifestos and the uneducated in their ballads and songs. In the second scene of the play, written by Lee, Marmoutier, the pathetic

---

[47] For example in *Astraea Redux, To My Lord Chancellor, Annus Mirabilis, Absalom and Achitophel*, and *Threnodia Augustalis*: see *Poems*, ed. Hammond, ii. 396 n.

heroine, torn between love of Guise and abhorrence of his regicidal schemes, reproaches the Duke for the self-serving ends of his crowd politics:

> ... every hour I see you Court the Crowd,
> When with the shouts of the Rebellious Rabble,
> I see you born on shoulders to Cabals ...
>
> .   .   .   .
>
> While all the Vermin of the vile *Parisians*
> Toss up their greasie Caps where e're you pass,
> And hurl your dirty Glories in your Face.
>
> .   .   .   .
>
> ... you seek it with your Smiles and Bows,
> This Side and that Side congeing to the Crowd ...
>
> (I. ii. 116–18, 126–8, 131–2)

There is a double allusion here which indicates the self-consciousness of Lee's treatment of the crowd. First the lines recall Casca's account of the Roman populace, who, when Antony offered Caesar the crown, 'threw up their sweaty nightcaps, and uttered such a deal of stinking breath ... that it had almost choked Caesar'.[48] Secondly they point to Dryden's portrayal of Monmouth in *Absalom and Achitophel*, a work for which Lee had supplied a commendatory poem:

> Th'admiring Croud are dazled with surprize,
> And on his goodly person feed their eyes:
> His Joy conceal'd, he sets himself to show;
> On each side bowing popularly low:
> His looks, his gestures, and his words he frames,
> And with familiar ease repeats their Names.   (ll. 686–91)

Like Caesar's, and like Monmouth's, Guise's cultivation of the masses is rewarded by adulation. It is also immediately publicized. Lee echoes Dryden's opening lines, where the Leaguers hail Guise as '*Moses, Gideon, David*', and '*The Saviour of the Nation*' (I. i. 1–3). Now Lee's Marmoutier launches a vehement attack on hireling scribblers using virtually identical appellations:

> You have your Writers too, that cant your Battels,
> That stile you the New *David*, Second *Moses*,
> Prop of the Church, Deliverer of the People.

---

[48] Shakespeare, *Julius Caesar*, ed. Arthur Humphreys (Oxford, 1984), I. ii. 243–5.

Thus from the City, as from the Heart they spread
Thro all the Provinces...   (1. ii. 133–7)

The printed propaganda disseminated from the League's City head-
quarters carries a series of parallels between Guise and biblical
figures which derive from Davila's account:

all the streets, and every corner of Paris, resounded with the praises of the
Duke of Guise, celebrated in Verse and Prose by a thousand Writers, with
the title of the *new David*, the *second Moses*, the *deliverer of the Catholike
people*, the *prop and pillar of the holy Church*; and the Preachers in their
wonted manner, but with greater license, openly inveighing against the
present affairs, filled the ears of the people with wonders, or rather miracles
(so they called them) of this new *Gideon*, come into the world for the
desired safety of the Kingdom... (p. 670)

Though inspired by hints from Davila, those biblical analogies
conform to a prevalent pattern of contemporary sermons, pamphlets, and poems which concealed the chief political actors under
scriptural names.[49] In *Absalom and Achitophel*, itself indebted to this
allegorical tradition, Dryden described Absalom–Monmouth in
terms which anticipate those he and Lee used in their characteriza-
tion of Guise: he is the 'second *Moses*' (l. 234), '*Saviour*' (l. 240),
'young *Messiah*' (l. 728), and 'Young *Samson*' (l. 955). Whig writers
responded by appropriating and revising Dryden's identifications: in
Samuel Pordage's(?) *Azaria and Hushai* (1682), for example, Azaria
represents Monmouth, Hushai Shaftesbury, and Shimei Dryden
himself.[50]

In the early stages of the Exclusion Crisis, Tory propaganda had
trailed behind that of the Whigs in both its scope and effectiveness.
Taking advantage of the lapse of the Licensing Act in summer 1679,
the Whigs launched a vigorous journalistic offensive, the newspapers providing them with an ideal platform for attacking the
government's handling of the plot and disseminating their arguments in favour of exclusion. In addition to the newspapers, Whig
presses were producing a flood of pamphlets, ballads, and broadsides; the Whig-inspired bonfires and Pope-burning processions
attracted thousands of Londoners; and their Petitioning Movement
urging the king to allow Parliament to meet gained massive support

[49] For an overview see Harth, *Pen for a Party*, pp. 3–17, 36–42, 106–37.
[50] For another example see Elkanah Settle's *Absalom Senior; or, Achitophel Transpros'd* (1682).

both in the capital and in the provinces. Tory publications, by contrast, were few and far between, and their bid to counteract the Whig petitions of 1679–80 with the Abhorrence Movement proved, in the words of Phillip Harth, 'the greatest public-relations disaster the government would suffer in a year filled with political setbacks'.[51] It was only towards the end of 1680,[52] or, as other commentators have argued, in the months following the dissolution of the Oxford Parliament in March and the issuing of *His Majesties Declaration to All His Loving Subjects* in April 1681,[53] that the Tory offensive took off. By 1683 the efforts of the indefatigable Roger L'Estrange and other loyalists to '*Undeceiv*[e] . . . the *People*' had been crowned with success.[54] Ironically, the Tories, who had previously condemned their opponents' populist tactics, owed their propaganda victory to a clever exploitation of the same means of mass agitation: direct appeals to the people through street politics, the press, the pulpit, and the carefully co-ordinated Loyal Address movements. They also emulated and reversed several of their rivals' political slogans, locating arbitrary power and tyranny, not, as the Whigs did, in the abuse of royal prerogatives, but in the rule of the multitude.[55]

The Duke of Guise, itself a Tory triumph, shows the price of failure to control public opinion. Henry III's inability to act decisively and win back popular support almost leads to his downfall. In particular, Henry fails to use the judicial system to his advantage by having the mutinous Duke publicly tried and executed. The efficacy of such exemplary punishment is illustrated in Nathaniel Lee's *Lucius Junius Brutus* (produced and banned 1680; published 1681). That play closes with the pathos-ridden public death of Brutus' sons, decreed by their uncompromising father so as to 'stop the mouth of loud Sedition'.[56] Marmoutier's advocacy of Guise's exemplary public execution should he prove a traitor—'If he dares come, were I a Man, a King, | I'd sacrifice him in the City's sight' (III. i. 352–3)[57]—lends some justification to Henry's ensuing murder of

---

[51] *Pen for a Party*, p. 32.   [52] Knights, *Politics and Opinion in Crisis*, p. 168.
[53] Harris, *London Crowds*, pp. 132 ff.; Harth, *Pen for a Party*, pp. 72 ff.
[54] Roger L'Estrange, *Observator*, 13 Apr. 1681.
[55] Knights, *Politics and Opinion in Crisis*, pp. 306 ff.
[56] Nathaniel Lee, *Lucius Junius Brutus*, ed. John Loftis (Lincoln, Nebr., 1967), V. ii. 42.
[57] And later: 'His Charms prevail, no, let the Rebel dye' (III. i. 362).

his haughty antagonist, although the Duke's surreptitious assassination is a far cry from the kind of lawfully ordained capital punishment, meted out in full view of, and as a warning to, the unruly populace, that Marmoutier clearly has in mind. None the less the appearance of her troubled soliloquy in Lee's portion of the play contradicts the charge that in *The Duke of Guise* Dryden single-handedly promotes Monmouth's death.

Too weak to venture a public trial of his opponent, Henry III is also without pamphleteers, newswriters, and poets to uphold his policy and bolster his authority. Yet he comes to appreciate the benefits that his enemies reap from their expertly handled propaganda campaign. In a speech which recalls Marmoutier's denunciation of mercenary Whig hacks in Lee's part of the play, the King in Dryden's fifth act renews the attack on hostile writers and their sponsors. His venom is almost a tribute.

> ... when your Rhimes assassinate our Fame,
> You hug your nauseous, blund'ring Ballad-wits,
> And pay'em as if Nonsence were a merit,
> If it can mean but Treason.   (v. i. 231–4)

Implicit in this condemnation is a judgement of real-life party writing. The vocabulary used to describe enemy propagandists, which includes words such as 'nonsense', 'blundering', 'treason', recalls Dryden's earlier satirical portrait of Thomas Shadwell in *Mac Flecknoe* and his recent attack on Shadwell and Elkanah Settle—'*Og* and *Doeg*... Two Fools that Crutch their Feeble sense on Verse' (l. 409)—in *The Second Part of Absalom and Achitophel.*[58] Seditious verse-making and fraudulent newsmongering by the Shadwells and Settles in Whig pay may rarely deviate into sense, but they are nevertheless a menace to reckon with. *The Duke of Guise* issues a forceful warning about the threat to monarchy and stability posed by seditious propaganda.

---

[58] I am grateful to Professor Paul Hammond for drawing my attention to these allusions. In *Mac Flecknoe*, Shadwell is entrusted with absolute dominion over 'all the Realms of *Non-sense*', his claim to the throne of dullness being undisputed, for he 'never deviates into sense' (ll. 6, 20). His writing is again arraigned for dullness and lack of sense in *The Second Part of Absalom and Achitophel*, these charges being now compounded by its treasonable intent—'Treason botcht in Rhime will be thy bane' (l. 485). The ineptitude of his partner in crime, Settle-Doeg, who 'without knowing how or why, | Made still a blund'ring kind of Melody; | Spurd boldly on, and Dash'd through Thick and Thin, | Through Sense and Non-sense, never out nor in' is such that 'This Animal's below committing Treason' (ll. 412–15, 434).

IV

How typical is such a stance towards oppositional party writing? Two specific comparisons will help us see *The Duke of Guise* more clearly, both in its immediate context and in a longer perspective. Where Dryden's verse satires of the early 1680s consistently belittle the accomplishment of anti-government propagandists, the play, as we have seen, shows them in the ascendant. In this respect it aligns itself with royalist closet drama of the 1640s and 1650s rather than with current pro-Stuart stage fare. The anonymous *The Famous Tragedie of Charles I* of 1649, and its adaptation *Cromwell's Conspiracy* of 1660, provide telling parallels and contrasts with Dryden and Lee's play. So, from a different angle, does a play exactly contemporaneous with *The Duke of Guise*, John Crowne's *City Politiques*.

In its concern about the impact of opposition propaganda, the Dryden–Lee tragedy exhibits a close affinity with royalist plays written during the Puritan Revolution. The affinity reflects the return in the Exclusion Crisis of that element of mass politics which had figured so prominently during the earlier upheaval. Like *The Duke of Guise*, *The Famous Tragedie of King Charles I* dramatizes the workings of anti-royalist propaganda. Without the guise of allegory, it shows the arch-villain and regicide-to-be, Cromwell, sponsor a multifaceted propaganda campaign whose chief instrument is the Puritan divine Hugh Peters, a common figure both of fun and of vilification among enemies of godly zeal. Valued for his 'insinuating perswasive art', Peters supplies rabidly anti-monarchical sermons, ballads, and pamphlets for which, as the stage direction specifies, Cromwell *'gives him Gold'*.[59] However ridiculous Peters is made to appear—at one point Cromwell orders him to sing one of his versified contributions to the cause—it is clear that his efforts have assisted the rebels to gain their ends. Like *The Duke of Guise*, the playlet shows that the lack of an effective propaganda machine will render any government powerless and easy to topple. More particularly, Peters's boast that his 'Sermon (such as *Ignatius Loyalla* [sic] himselfe, were he to morrow to supply my place, for dangerous Doctrine, direfull Use, and dreadfull Application, would glory to name his) . . . shall confirme our Faction ten times more | Then all that they have known, or heard before' (Act I, p. 2), and his vow

---

[59] *The Famous Tragedie of King Charles I* (n.p., 1649), Act I (pp. 1, 3).

that 'it shall be my taske, both at Presse and Pulpit, to render Kingly Government obnoxious and incompatible with the Peoples Rights' (Act I, pp. 4–5), anticipate the vaunts of the Curate of St Eustace and other seditious priests in *The Duke of Guise*. Similarly, Peters's and Cromwell's humorous self-condemnations foreshadow the self-incriminations of Dryden and Lee's villains. Given that Dryden admitted to having written a draft of a play about the Duke of Guise soon after the Restoration,[60] it is unsurprising that the presentation of the various forms of manipulating public opinion in the play as we now have it should hark back to the pamphlet playlets of the 1640s and 1650s. It is equally unsurprising that, on the advice of friends, he should have withheld the play from the stage: in the triumphalist political climate of the 1660s its scaremongering would have been singularly injudicious.

When *The Famous Tragedie* came to be revised and republished in 1660, the new version, retitled *Cromwell's Conspiracy*, introduced two alterations which bear on the theme of popular politics. First Peters's campaign of lies and blandishments is counteracted by a series of loyalist sermons delivered by Dr Hewet, who is perceived by Cromwell as sufficiently threatening to be summarily executed: 'The Man . . . is our chiefest Foe; | One that upholds *Charles Stuarts* Interest | More than another single man could do, | And by sly Oratory tells the people, that | My Government is Tyrannous and unlawful'.[61] Secondly, now that the Restoration is a *fait accompli* the playlet makes a point of emphasizing the widespread public support for the return of Charles II, in the process legitimizing the people's participation in politics. In the closing scene of the play, the Mayor of London welcomes General Monck to the capital while the '*People cry a King, a Monk, a Free Parliament; a King, &c.*' Their loud acclamations are warmly appreciated by both men, the mayor pointing to 'the peoples gladsome voice' and Monck praising their commitment to monarchical government:

> 'Tis well done fellow subjects, to express
> Your zeal to true Establishment and Peace.

---

[60] *Vindication*, in *Works*, xiv. 309; Charles H. Hinnant, 'The Background of the Early Version of Dryden's *The Duke of Guise*', *English Language Notes*, 6 (1968) 102–6.

[61] *Cromwell's Conspiracy. A Tragy-Comedy, Relating to our latter Times. Beginning at the Death of King Charles the First, And ending with the happy Restauration of King Charles The Second. Written by a Person of Quality* (London, 1660), IV. ii (p. 19).

> Go home, Ring Bells, and make good lusty fires;
> A King you crave, you shall have your desires.   (v. v, p. 35)

Left unstated and unexamined is the implication that if popular support helps uphold the monarchy, popular opposition can prove fatal to it.

How powerful was propaganda? Historians such as Tim Harris and Mark Knights have stressed its critical impact upon the development and resolution of the Exclusion Crisis. As I have argued in this essay, *The Duke of Guise* was unique among partisan dramas of the time in its representation of the workings and effects of collective agitation. Dryden and Lee provide a disturbing view of enemy propaganda. In this regard John Crowne's almost exactly contemporaneous comedy, *City Politiques*,[62] makes a striking contrast. Crowne, too, emphasizes the value of maintaining the upper hand in the ongoing paper war. But in his play it is the Whigs, not the Tories, who lose the battle for the people's minds. *City Politiques* portrays a quintessential Whig scribbler, Craffy, who with characteristic zeal, and equally characteristic lack of wit, sets out to counter Dryden's brilliant satires. 'I'm now writing an answer to *Absalom and Achitophel*', he announces early in the play. Two acts later Craffy is 'answering the *Meddal*... Who must answer these things then? There's ne're a man o' wit of our party but my self, and my things are discommended.'[63] Crowne is as self-conscious and directly topical in his preoccupation with hostile party writing as are Dryden and Lee. Consider, for instance, the self-condemning declaration made by the Bricklayer, a satiric alter ego of the Protestant Joiner Stephen College:

---

[62] *City Politiques* was suppressed at the same time as *The Duke of Guise*, and eventually produced in January 1683. See Robert D. Hume, *The Development of English Drama in the Late Seventeenth Century* (Oxford, 1976), p. 366.

[63] *City Politiques*, in *The Comedies of John Crowne: A Critical Edition*, ed. B. J. McMullin (New York, 1984), II. i. 202, IV. i. 234. Craffy is a caricature of either Elkanah Settle or Samuel Pordage, both of whom have been credited with anti-Tory satires *Azaria and Hushai* and *The Medal Revers'd* (introduction to the play, p. 168). For a Whig view of Tory propaganda see the 'Epistle to the Tories' (modelled upon Dryden's 'Epistle to the Whigs'), prefixed to *The Medal Revers'd. A Satyre against Persecution. By the Author of Azaria and Hushai* (London, 1682): 'It is your common practise to slander or villifie others, your gross Libels swarm in the Streets, and fly in the Face of Magistracy it self, at such an impudent rate as is not to be parallel'd, in the most licentious Common-wealths, and yet you have a Confidence to cry out of the *Whiggs* for their Clubs, whilst your damme Bullies hector and roar in every Coffey-house' (p. 4, first pagination).

For the justification of our proceedings, we will print a *Narrative of the Pilgrim under the Gown*. As paper, in Holland, passes for money, pamphlets with us pass for religion and policy; a bit of paper in Holland, from a man of credit, takes up goods here, pays debts there. A pamphliteer is the best fool-maker in the nation. (IV. i. 229)

Although they share a preoccupation with party writing, *City Politiques* and *The Duke of Guise* approach the subject differently. First Crowne unequivocally identifies anti-government agitators through personal satire, an instrument which Dryden and Lee eschew. Secondly, he breaks the fictitious frame of his play by citing real-life titles of Tory verse, a device which designates the propaganda camp to which he himself belongs. By avoiding such direct-ness, Dryden and Lee are able to maintain at least a semblance of impartiality and detachment, a strategy which renders their partiality all the more effective. The manipulation of public opinion, they indicate, may be an unpleasant business, but governments need to engage in it. Neglect of that strategy threatened to destroy Henry III in the play and Charles II in real life.

V

We have seen that the drama of the Exclusion Crisis illustrates a transition from politics as a predominantly court-centred activity to the involvement of a wider public. As the Restoration settlement came under strain, and as both opposition and government re-doubled their efforts to control public opinion, dramatic representa-tions of the making of politics changed in significant ways. More and more plays on both sides of the political divide included scenes representing the swaying of public opinion. The most striking instance of this process is Dryden and Lee's *The Duke of Guise*. In it we find Dryden carrying to an extreme his long-standing pre-occupation with popular politics, showing us the terrifying consequences of the mob turning against legitimate authority. In effect, the play was an outrageously offensive—and an outrageously effective—piece of propaganda. It was a triumphant exercise in that very art of public persuasion which it so incisively delineates and to which it gives so sinister a cast.

If the Exclusion Crisis revived the crowd scene, the crushing of the Whigs after the Rye House Plot in 1683 banished it once more.

Crowd activity, whether oppositional or loyalist, virtually ceased. As in the years after the Restoration, the politics of the drama were predominantly high politics. It was not until 1686 that rioting in London resumed, as a response to James II's pro-Catholic policies, and not until the Revolution of 1688–9 that political divisions were once again acknowledged in plays. The theatrical response to that event was, however, slack. Perhaps that was because of the sudden-ness and rapidity of the political upheaval, perhaps because of the financial straits of the one surviving theatre, the United Company, perhaps because of a lull in dramatic creativity. Crowds do now reappear, but not in full-length dramatic scripts.[64] Instead they figure in pamphlet plays—*The Bloody Duke, The Abdicated Prince, The Royal Voyage, The Royal Flight, The Late Revolution: or, the Happy Change*—which gloatingly recount the liberation of the realm.[65] Here, of course, the populace is in the right, rebelling against tyranny and Catholicism (though, as several of these playlets attest, even the Protestant architects of the 'Glorious' Revolution, how-ever eager they may have been to capitalize on the nation's sup-posed unanimity in welcoming William and Mary, sought to dissociate themselves from their plebeian adherents' tumultuous expressions of joy).

Dryden was among the opponents of the Revolution. In his late plays and translations we find an anti-populism reminiscent of his Exclusion Crisis writings. For instance, the African mob in *Don Sebastian* (1689) is shown as characteristically volatile and disloyal, and thus an easy prey to manipulation by an opportunistic priest, a treasonous favourite, and a self-styled 'Captain of the Rabble'. Dryden's revisions of Virgilian diction in his translation of the *Aeneid*, too, testify to his distrust of the multitude, and his abhor-rence of rabble-rousers.[66] Yet that anti-populism now mingles with

---

[64] A striking example of a post-Revolution play featuring scenes of mob violence and rebellion is Thomas D'Urfey's two-part *The Famous History of the Rise and Fall of Massaniello* (1699), itself a redaction of R.B.'s mid-century closet drama *The Rebellion of Naples, or The Tragedy of Massenello* (London, 1649).

[65] For a discussion of pamphlet plays written at the time of the 'Glorious' Revolution see Lois Potter, 'Politics and Popular Culture: The Theatrical Response to the Revolution', in Lois G. Schwoerer (ed.), *The Revolution of 1688–1689: Changing Perspectives* (Cambridge, 1992), pp. 184–97.

[66] See Paul Hammond, *Dryden and the Traces of Classical Rome* (Oxford, 1999), pp. 240–9. By contrast, in 'Cymon and Iphigenia' from Boccaccio which he included in *Fables* Dryden's

a very different sentiment. Dryden's Jacobite leanings produce a crowd scene in which the audience is invited to side with those who attempt to stir the people to rise. In *Cleomenes* (1692), the titular Spartan hero and his few virtuous followers try to mobilize the Egyptian populace to fight for 'Liberty' (v. iv). Sadly, the cowardice of the citizens prevents them from hearkening to the call and from rising for their own good. Far removed from both the inherently loyal subjects of Dryden's early heroics, and the seditious and gullible mobs represented in his Exclusion Crisis plays, the Egyptians are exposed as being too lazy and too servile to resist the legitimate if tyrannical government and take the side of the just and honourable rebels. With William and Mary on the throne and James in exile in France, Dryden's treatment of popular rebellion becomes both more complex and more equivocal than it had been when the Stuart brothers were in power.

'[T]o gratifie the barbarous Party of my Audience', Dryden writes in the Preface to *Cleomenes*, 'I gave them a short Rabble-Scene, because the Mobb (as they call them) are represented by *Plutarch* and *Polybius*, with the same Character of Baseness and Cowardice, which are here describ'd in the last Attempt of *Cleomenes*.' 'They may thank me, if they please, for this Indulgence,' he continues, 'for no *French* Poet would have allow'd them any more than a bare Relation of that Scene, which debases a Tragedy to show upon the Stage.'[67] However disingenuous in political terms (there is in fact no mention of the rabble in Polybius), this statement carries a telling aesthetic judgement. The logical inference from it is that not only *Cleomenes*, but also his earlier heroics and tragedies—*The Indian Queen*, *The Conquest of Granada*, *Oedipus*, *The Duke of Guise*, and *Don Sebastian*—are all 'debased'. Towards the end of his playwriting career Dryden thus seems to imply that by his representation of popular politics, which we have seen to be so extensive and so innovative, he had compromised his artistry.

depiction of mob violence is headily insouciant rather than aggressively satirical (see 'Cymon and Iphigenia' in *Poems*, ed. Kinsley, vol. iv (ll. 399–412 and 605 ff.)).

[67] *Works*, xvi. 77–8.

5

CONSTRUCTING CLASSICISM: DRYDEN AND PURCELL

HAROLD LOVE

> Waller was smooth; but Dryden taught to join
> The varying verse, the full resounding line,
> The long majestic march, and energy divine.

So Pope in the 'The first Epistle of the Second Book of Horace Imitated' (ll. 267–9), placing Dryden at a crucial point in the evolutionary narrative of English poetry—a point at which force marries with elegance of form in a way that constitutes the 'classical'. Dryden had been complicit in the construction of an earlier version of this narrative, which saw the reign of Charles II identified as the Augustan age of English poetry—exhibiting the same refinement of cruder precedents as had been achieved by Virgil, Horace, and Ovid, while not yet overtaken by the restless striving for effect that afflicted their successors, Persius, Seneca, and Lucan.[1] Later adjustments to this model were concerned with the exact chronological placing of the apex—whether, for instance, the truly Augustan reign might have been Anne's rather than Charles's. But there was a clear understanding that the writers of the Restoration stood closer to the summit than their Jacobean and Caroline predecessors and that this distinction resulted from a more faithful conformity to the practice of the best ancients.

---

[1] For one articulation of this model, see John Fowler, 'Dryden and Literary Good-Breeding', in Harold Love (ed.), *Restoration Literature: Critical Approaches* (London, 1972), pp. 226–7 and 240–5. Dryden's best-known statement of the idea is in a passage from the 'Discourse Concerning Satire' in which he distorts chronology in order to place Persius in the period proper to his supposedly decadent stylistic features (*Works*, iv. 51).

But Dryden was also influential in the development of a rival narrative that was to shift the era of greatest achievement back to the generation of Shakespeare. He may not quite have intended this— in the famous passages of homage he is still judging from the viewpoint of a greater literary knowingness and with regret for crudities that resulted from Shakespeare's having lived at a too early stage of the ideal paradigm.[2] Yet, as early as the Preface to *All for Love* (1678), he had acknowledged 'the Divine *Shakespeare*' as his master, and, by implication, the source to which all subsequent writers in English should return for inspiration. This rival narrative was to triumph with the Romantics and remains dominant in our own time. Under it the classical age in one of the senses of the word (the period of greatest achievement and influence; the apex in the graph of cultural ascent and decline) is not classical in the other sense (imitation of Greek and Roman precedents; bringing form and energy into lucid equilibrium; achieving the perfection of structure that Aristotle admired in Homer and Sophocles). Under the Shakespeare-apex model, the reign of Charles II dwindles to an episode that saw a departure, under French influence, from the true native strain, giving us a Dryden who was a classicist merely in the stylistic sense.

What both narratives ignore is that Dryden's adherence to 'classical' values, however defined, is more a matter of profession than of actual practice. Despite his veneration for the Roman Augustan poets, his creative allegiances were at least as strongly to the silver age as to the golden. Moreover, his strongest artistic debt as a young writer was to native and Continental Mannerism. The 'classical' Dryden is the Dryden of the later verse and the translations, and even these pose problems.[3] The Dryden of the heroic plays is England's Corneille, not her Racine. It is this that makes the satire of *The Rehearsal* so bitter. To the critics of the Buckingham circle— self-conscious disciples of Ben Jonson—Mr Bayes was an irresponsible literary avant-gardist prepared to sacrifice all classical decorums in order to provoke momentary spasms of astonishment. This was

---

[2] See in particular the 'Defence of the Epilogue', *Works*, xi. 203–18.

[3] Dryden's unclassical classicism is on display in the translations as a compulsion to make their language more metaphorical than that of the originals. See my 'The Art of Adaptation: Some Restoration Versions of Ovid', in Antony Coleman and Antony Hammond (eds.), *Poetry and Drama 1570–1700: Essays in Honour of Harold F. Brooks* (London, 1981), pp. 136–55.

also the criticism made a century later in a trenchant passage of Johnson: 'Next to argument, his delight was in wild and daring sallies of sentiment, in the irregular and excentrick violence of wit. He delighted to tread upon the brink of meaning, where light and darkness begin to mingle; to approach the precipice of absurdity, and hover over the abyss of unideal vacancy.'[4] This Dryden, who is also that of Macaulay's early nineteenth-century critique, fits into neither of the narratives just mentioned.[5] Nor is he really accommodated by a third narrative which would trace a 'line of wit' from Donne and the Metaphysicals to Eliotan modernism: Dryden's place in that now superannuated story, in so far as he was allowed a place at all, was the Arnoldian one of a restorer of prose virtues in poetry. We have still to devise a story that will restore visibility to Buckingham's, Johnson's, and Macaulay's Dryden.

The master narrative of English music afforded a similar prominence to Purcell as the 'Orpheus Britannicus' from whom subsequent English composers were encouraged to draw inspiration. The earliest stage of this process is documented in the classicizing memorial verses reprinted by Zimmerman.[6] A German composer, Jakob Greber, giving advice *circa* 1704 to a compatriot on how to succeed in London, included among his Machiavellian instructions 'Praise the deceased Purcell to the skies and say there has never been the like of him.'[7] In Purcell's case the clash between the bestowal of classical status and Mannerist stylistic practice was even more glaring, since, while Dryden still had his imitators as late as the nineteenth century, Purcell as a compositional model was almost immediately replaced by Corelli. Even so admiring a contemporary as Roger North, writing in 1728, lamented that Purcell 'unhappily began to shew his great skill before the reforme of musick *al' Italliana*, and while he was warm in the persuit of it,

---

[4] *The Lives of the English Poets*, ed. George Birkbeck Hill, 3 vols. (Oxford, 1905), i. 460. Johnson accompanies this with examples of Dryden's enormities.

[5] In the *Edinburgh Review* of January 1828, p. 1, Macaulay wrote: 'By trampling on laws, he acquired the authority of a legislator. By signalizing himself as the most daring and irreverent of rebels, he raised himself to the dignity of a recognized prince. He commenced his career by the most frantic outrages.'

[6] Franklin B. Zimmerman, *Henry Purcell 1659–1695: His Life and Times* (London, 1967), pp. 329–59.

[7] Harold E. Samuel, 'A German Musician Comes to London in 1704', *Musical Times* (Sept. 1981) 591. Could this advice have percolated through to Handel? See R. J. S. Stevens's anecdote cited at Zimmerman, *Henry Purcell*, p. 359.

dy'd'.[8] Charles Burney's judgement that Purcell 'is as much the pride of an Englishman in Music, as Shakespeare in productions for the stage, Milton in epic poetry, Lock in metaphysics, or Sir Isaac Newton in philosophy and mathematics' was qualified by sharp criticisms of his part-writing and harmonic practice.[9] In the service in B♭ 'the same crudities of the sharp 3d with the flat 6th, and flat 3d, 4th, and 5th, as have been elsewhere censured, occur; which, I hope, in spite of my reverence for Purcell, the organists of our cathedrals scruple not to change for better harmony'.[10] In the twentieth century Purcell fared better, with composers as eminent as Britten and Tippett designating him (rather than, say, Dunstaple, Tallis, Byrd, Lawes, or Jenkins) as the point of departure for the modern national tradition, arranging his music, and at times imitating features of his style. However, they did not do so because of any imagined classical qualities (in the stylistic sense) but for the very asperities and contrapuntal intricacy that annoyed the Corellians— in other words as a forerunner of modernism, much as Donne and Marvell were enrolled as forerunners of modernist poetics.

Here I must digress briefly to explain that, while literary historians and musicologists both understand more or less the same thing by modernism, they have different terminologies for distinguishing varieties of 'classicism'. Classicism in English literature is timeless and recurrent, but the period of its recognized aesthetic dominance is essentially that from the mid-seventeenth century to the early nineteenth: roughly Waller and Denham to Crabbe and Landor. Yet, as is well known, the earliest manifestations of the classical tendency belong to the heyday of the Metaphysicals, while its later phase overlaps with Romanticism. 'Classical' music, when the adjective is not used in its demotic sense to refer to all art music in the Western tradition, refers more narrowly to the music of the closing decades of the eighteenth century and the opening decade of the nineteenth (Mozart, Haydn, and early Beethoven). The period of the formation of the classical style (roughly corresponding to the 1750s and 1760s) has no single agreed name and is usually discussed

---

[8] *Roger North on Music*, ed. John Wilson (London, 1959), p. 307. For the impact of Corelli on musical style in England, see ibid. 358–9.

[9] Charles Burney, *A General History of Music, from the Earliest Ages to the Present Period (1789)*, ed. Frank Mercer (1935, repr. New York, 1957), ii. 380.

[10] Ibid. 385.

in terms of a variety of fashions and regional styles ('style galant', Mannheim school, Italian overture style, *Sturm und Drang*, French rococo, etc.). But there is general agreement that Bach (d. 1750) and Handel (d. 1759) represent the culmination of a distinct earlier movement known both popularly and to musicologists as the Baroque, which had its origins in early seventeenth-century Italy and against which classicism was in conscious reaction. Purcell's agreed place in this narrative is as an English foreshadower of the achievements of Bach and Handel in whom a native heritage from predecessors such as Lawes and Locke of densely contrapuntal and frequently dissonant part-writing is chastened by a progressive acceptance of the new Italian harmonic disciplines. Even so subtle and sympathetic an account of Purcell's musical style as that of Martin Adams is still in thrall to a narrative of this kind, in that, despite the author's praise for Purcell's musical conservatism, it is the more 'modern' works (those anticipating 'high Baroque') that are seen as most significant. Thus, having praised 'the ruggedly independent inner parts' of the dances in *Dioclesian*, Adams criticizes the work as a whole because it lacks the 'direct communication that makes *Dido and Aeneas* such a success', ignoring that *Dioclesian* was much more popular in Purcell's own time.[11]

In insisting on judging Dryden and Purcell by reference to their anticipations of an exemplary future, or, in Dryden's case, as an artist caught between an exemplary future and even more exemplary past, we condemn them, unfairly, to a transitional status that brands much of their actual practice as an artistic mistake that, with greater understanding, they would have felt obliged to rectify. It also requires us—this time correctly—to dismiss the exemplarity claimed for them by their contemporaries as another kind of mistake, one that in correctly estimating the magnitude of their achievement mistook the nature of that achievement. In this second case we are at least able to explain how the mistake came to be made. The first reason was the need to establish first the Restoration and then the Revolution of 1688 as new births of arts and sciences as well as of reformed constitutions.[12] This is a perfectly fair claim in that the Restoration did see a rebirth of court culture and the

---

[11] *Henry Purcell: The Origins and Development of his Musical Style* (Cambridge, 1995), p. 63.
[12] On the first of these see Nicholas Jose, *Ideas of the Restoration in English Literature 1660–71* (London, 1984).

Revolution accompanied a maturation of town culture, marked in Purcell's professional sphere by the invention of the public concert and the stage musical, and in Dryden's by the new literary camaraderie of the coffee-houses. The promotion of the two as cultural icons was also encouraged by developments in book publishing in England, which led for the first time to the notion of a canon of British 'classics' (musical as well as literary) to be kept permanently in print in carefully prepared editions. Dryden's role, as a writer of prefaces, in this process of canon formation, and the enormous influence of Tonson's folio publication of the *Juvenal and Persius*, the *Virgil*, and *Fables*, during the 1690s, followed by a host of octavo and duodecimo reprints, are too well known to need discussion;[13] but it is not always appreciated that Purcell's alliance with the Playfords was just as influential in his own field as Dryden's with Tonson. The posthumous *Orpheus Britannicus* and its companion volume *Amphion Anglicus* (devoted to the work of Purcell's teacher, John Blow) exploited the same new desire to monumentalize the work of contemporary creators. Henry Hall, in his commendatory poem to *Orpheus Britannicus*, was in no doubt that without Henry Playford there would have been much less public awareness of Purcell:

> Yet he, ev'n he, had scarce preserv'd a name,
> Did not your press perpetuate his fame,
> And shew'd the coming age as in a glass,
> What our all-pleasing Britain's Orpheus was.[14]

It is significant that both Dryden and Purcell worked as editors for the publishers who sustained their standing. Dryden, besides the verse miscellanies, co-ordinated group translations of Ovid, Juvenal with Persius, and Plutarch for Tonson, while Purcell revised the section on composition for the twelfth edition of John Playford's *An Introduction to the Skill of Musick* (1694) and edited Henry Playford's *Harmonia Sacra: or Divine Hymns and Dialogues* (1687).

That the institutional corpus of canonical English literature and music arose from a base in the published work of these two artists

---

[13] Aspects of this process are discussed in Keith Walker, 'Jacob Tonson, Bookseller', *The American Scholar*, 61 (1992) 424–30, and in my 'Refining Rochester', *Harvard Library Bulletin*, NS 7 (1996) 40–9.

[14] Zimmerman, *Henry Purcell*, p. 349.

was in itself an important reason for the status that was afforded them. It was Dryden's and Purcell's good fortune to be present at the right time to be cast in the leading roles of a particular cultural story: it was less fortunate that, in order for them to be fitted into it, the actual nature of their achievement had in certain respects to be misrepresented and has, apart from the exceptions cited earlier, remained so. In the remainder of this essay I will look at aspects of their aesthetic assumptions and artistic practice which constitute a 'moment' which is distinctly their own, not merely part of a historical transition.

THE LONG MAJESTIC MARCH

Apart from their professional collaborations, both Dryden and Purcell were protégés at different times of Dr Busby at Westminster School. Dryden, a King's Scholar, had the major part of his education there, while Purcell, as well as receiving a bequest in the music-loving Busby's will, was on the books as a 'Bishop's Boy' between 1678 and 1680. In this respect they shared both an intellectual and an institutional heritage. While Dryden seems to have known relatively little about music, Purcell displayed an exceptional sensitivity to verse: otherwise he would not have set it so brilliantly. Addison conceded as much when he wrote that 'the *Italian* Artists cannot agree with our *English* Musicians in admiring *Purcell's* Compositions, and thinking his Tunes so wonderfully adapted to his Words, because both Nations do not always express the same Passions by the same Sounds'.[15] Dryden took special care to supply Purcell with well-written, singable lyrics. So an initial connection can be established through their common concern with the expressive use of English words.

A second connection is their preference for episodic forms. Both were brilliant originators of structures which incorporate autonomous substructures, possessing an epigram-like completeness, into a looser discursive whole which commands attention through its energetic forward movement rather than through any predictable overall plan. *Absalom and Achitophel* will serve as an example of

---

[15] *The Spectator*, ed. Donald F. Bond (Oxford, 1965), i. 121. See also Zimmerman, *Henry Purcell*, p. 334.

Dryden's success in this mode: it is essentially a bundle of 'characters', speeches, narratives, descriptions, exhortations, apophthegms, and passages of argumentation placed sequentially in such a way that each drives the reader irresistibly on to the next—one manifestation of Pope's 'long majestic march'. The same building of compositions from sequentially articulated musical 'epigrams' can be observed in any of Purcell's odes or anthems, or in an extended theatre song such as 'No, no, resistance is but vain', from the music to Southerne's *The Maid's Last Prayer*.[16] In Purcell's larger-scale compositions, there are of course formal 'movements', but these themselves will often be composed of a series of sectional ideas with only minimal recapitulation. He came only slowly to the *da capo* aria. The two practices—musical and poetic—assimilate to each other in the Restoration 'Pindaric' ode, which was written in stanzas which then served as separate movements in a cantata-like musical setting or might be even further divided. Dryden wrote several odes of this kind, one of them lamenting the death of Purcell. In these works, at least, the structural methods of Dryden closely resemble those of Purcell.

The process by which the poet and the composer maintain forward momentum through works so liberally sprinkled with arresting local and episodic detail requires closer inspection. In Dryden, as is so often noted, it frequently takes the form of logical or mock-logical argument. Dryden's choice of the heroic couplet as his verse medium imposes a basic structure of statement followed by contradiction or qualification, as in the following from IV. i of *The Indian Emperour*, where Cortez is explaining to Almeria that he is forced to reject her offer of love because he is already enamoured of her sister:

> *Cortez.* Things meant in Jest, no serious Answer neede.
> *Almeria.* But, put the Case that it were so indeed.

---

[16] Carefully analysed in terms of its component sections in Adams, *Henry Purcell*, pp. 321–3. Adams's conclusion that 'No multi-sectional song before this one so securely and cogently uses harmonic process as a primary means of providing continuity across wide stylistic variety' is unexceptionable; but it locates the primary aesthetic interest of the piece in the continuity rather than the variety, which is surely to miss the point a little. Similarly, his disparagement of the anthem 'Let God Arise' (a very popular work in Purcell's time) for being, in effect, *too* episodic (p. 20) signals an excessive deference to twentieth-century ideals of musical coherence.

Cortez. If it were so (which but to thinke were pride)
  My constant Love would dangerously be try'd:
  For since you could a Brother's death forgive,
  Hee whom you save, for you alone should live:
  But I the most unhappy of mankind,
  Ere I knew your's, have all my Love resign'd:
  Tis my own Losse I greive, who have no more;
  You goe a begging to a Bankrupt's doore.
  Yet could I change (as sure I never can)
  How could you Love so infamous a man?
  For Love once giv'n from her, and plac'd in you,
  Would leave no ground I ever could be true.   (ll. 83–96)

Each of these couplets demands admiration for the unexpected new impetus it gives to what is essentially a sequence of interlocking syllogisms, which both resolve and demand a further resolution. They also show an obvious indebtedness to the processes of dialectical question and response institutionalized in the academic disputation.[17]

This ratiocinative movement in Dryden's writing has a homology in Purcell's fondness for developing ideas through imitation or a tight interweaving of motivic fragments. Adams analyses numerous examples of both practices. In music, imitation is most straightforwardly interpretable as argument when the answering phrase is at another pitch (usually that of the dominant), since the harmony will also change and the melodic outline of the answer will require adjustment to give what writers on fugue call a 'tonal' rather than a 'real' answer. When the subject is inverted, as happens occasionally in Purcell, it becomes a contradiction rather than just a qualification of the original. But even when an imitation is at the same pitch, there is always a secondary logical opposition between that and the countersubject. While the etymological meaning of 'fuga' is flight or pursuit, a sense can as easily be created of the two upper lines of a vocal duet or trio sonata as being in competition with one another or as throwing ideas backwards and forwards, which is exactly what happens in space if we envisage them in live perfor-

---

[17] Undergraduates were expected to dispute regularly in Latin with their tutors. Dryden would have experienced the practice at Trinity College, Cambridge. To earn their degrees they were required to dispute publicly. The wider cultural significance of academic disputing is examined in Walter J. Ong, *Fighting for Life* (Ithaca, NY, 1981).

mance. (The delightful 'The Maids and the Men' from *The Fairy Queen* takes this to the point of parody.) Very often the competing parts will occupy the same pitch range, crossing frequently. This mimicry of verbal argument is particularly marked in music, such as Purcell's, that asks us to listen horizontally as well as vertically.

An analysis of the experiences of reading and listening would also have to attend to the ways that the end of each 'epigram' creates an expectation for the next. Often both in Dryden (poems and plays alike) and Purcell the conception is a theatrical one: the larger structure (scene or composition) represents a series of 'passions' arising from a situation of tension which then progress towards a moment of action. In this, both arts enact Hobbes's notion of the will as 'the last Appetite, or Aversion, immediately adhæring to the action, or to the omission thereof'.[18] 'Will', Hobbes stresses, is not a 'faculty' of the soul but simply the cessation of deliberation, itself imagined as nothing more than a progressive supplanting of one appetite by another. While both poet and composer base their art on the portrayal of the passions, the passions they present are generally part of such a process of deliberation. The interaction between Almeria and Cortez in the scene quoted earlier is an intensely dynamic one: in the first phase (not quoted) she is brought by stages to the action of an imprudent declaration of love. The counter-action that follows leads to Cortez's action of rejection, which while left unspoken in the scene concerned is to have dire effects in what follows. In Purcell's 'No, no, resistance is but vain' the only difference is that the conclusion is a reprise of the original dilemma. However, now, with the options having been worked through, it is clearly the time for resistance to cease and action to begin. In Handel's operas, by contrast, attention seems to be requested more for the depiction of the state than its projection of a consequence, which is reserved for the recitatives.

The motivic means of creating musical momentum in Purcell are easy enough to perceive: the most prominent are ostinati, ground basses, 'walking' or 'running' quaver basses in common or duple time, leaping crotchet basses in three-four time, and chromaticism in either the bass or the melody. Less easy to account for in formal

---

[18] Thomas Hobbes, *Leviathan* (1651), pt. 1, ch. 6; ed. C. B. Macpherson (Harmondsworth, 1968), p. 127.

terms is an underlying impatience to be moving onwards that is also present in Lawes, though in his case less obedient to the directing power of tonality.[19] The force of these effects is particularly evident in the two sets of trio sonatas (1683 and 1697), especially when set beside the near-contemporary sets of Bassani, Buxtehude, and Corelli. Purcell, in these works, shows neither Buxtehude's genius for extended musical conversations and storytelling nor Corelli's balanced phrasing and chordal conceptualization of dissonance. Instead the sonatas, and particularly their canzonas and allemandes, display a condensed, agitated quality which is unsettling in its refusal to allow the listener moments of repose (an effect often achieved by 'adroitly postponing cadences with suspensions and sequential devices'[20]). Despite Purcell's obeisance to Italian models, the phrasing is not as a rule symmetrical. Often such practices seem to signal to the ear that the musical lines are so keen to progress that they tangle together, producing a momentary sense of confusion. This is especially prone to happen in the frequently crossing upper parts. Once such a tangle is recognized it has, cognitively, to be untangled, an effect that by checking the apprehension of movement demands that the listener then 'catch up' with the unfolding of the wider structure. In addition, as indicated earlier, the harmonic movement is often wayward by post-1700 standards. Bukofzer instances as examples of Purcell's asperities 'the simultaneous use of suspensions and retardations . . . the resolution of a suspension in a new harmony', and 'insistence on cross-relations, especially in cadences'.[21] It is sometimes suggested that these progressions might not have sounded as unusual to Purcell or his first listeners as they do to us; and yet he must have been aware how very different his practice was from that of his Continental contemporaries, not to mention English predecessors such as John Jenkins (1592–1678), whose sense of tonal direction is consistently modern.[22] For all these reasons it is

---

[19] Pinto refers to Lawes's 'blunderbuss tactics' in his transitions between keys (introduction to Charles Colman, *The Four-Part Airs* (London, 1998), p. vii).

[20] Manfred Bukofzer, *Music in the Baroque Era from Monteverdi to Bach* (New York, 1947), p. 214.

[21] Ibid. 215.

[22] Andrew Ashbee, *The Harmonious Music of John Jenkins* (London, 1992), p. 309 praises the composer's 'masterly handling of tonality', illustrating this in many passages of his analysis of Jenkins's viol fantasias. His far-ranging but seamless modulation is further studied from a notational perspective in Christopher Field, 'Jenkins and the Cosmography of Harmony', in

often hard at the end of a movement to reconstruct the aural journey along which the listener has been taken.

These are all 'early' or 'middle' Baroque features as described by Bukofzer in his still useful classification of 1947.[23] They also have something in common with Dryden's style of restless argumentation, with no conclusion allowed to stand without challenge. A second analogy might be with the verbal pyrotechnics of Restoration comedy, dazzling the listener with a stream of similes, paradoxes, and apt allusions which always require to be capped or answered. The music overwhelms by the density and profusion of short events, leaving any awareness of their coherence to retrospection, but, far from losing impetus because of this, must strain for it continually for exactly this reason.

MUSICAL AND POETIC WIT

It is possible to speak of the more intense of these local effects as a form of 'wit' in the sense in which the word is used in the study of seventeenth-century poetry. Both poetic and musical 'wit' resist the forward march by offering moments of intensified stimulation. In Dryden's case the art is one that gives sparkle and distinction to the individual balanced couplet or polished verse paragraph. It should be stated for the benefit of any musicologists charitable enough to read these musings that poetic wit has nothing to do with jokes. The issue before us is therefore quite different from that addressed by Gretchen Wheelock in her delightful study of Haydn's musical humour.[24] In the generation before Dryden the term was applied to those rhetorical figures that helped generate a 'strong line', chiefly paradox, antithesis, and catachresis. Dr Johnson in his life of Cowley famously censures catachrestic wit as 'heterogenous ideas . . . yoked by violence together'.[25] By the generation following Dryden the opposed ideal had come to prevail of wit as a satisfying

Andrew Ashbee and Peter Holman (eds.), *John Jenkins and his Time: Studies in English Consort Music* (Oxford, 1996), p. 174. The North brothers, Francis and Roger, with whom Purcell is known to have played his trio sonatas, were friends, patrons, and pupils of Jenkins, and would have heard Purcell's part-writing through ears schooled by their admired master.

[23] *Music in the Baroque Era*, pp. 16–19.
[24] *Haydn's Ingenious Jesting with Art: Contexts of Musical Wit and Humour* (New York, 1992).
[25] *Lives*, i. 20.

propriety of words and sense (Pope's 'What oft was thought but ne'er so well expressed'), with Dryden's own conceptions falling a little uneasily between. In 'An account of the ensuing Poem' prefaced to *Annus Mirabilis* (1667) he writes:

Wit written, is that which is well defin'd, the happy result of thought, or product of that imagination. But to proceed from wit in the general notion of it, to the proper wit of an Heroick or Historical poem, I judge it chiefly to consist in the delightful imaging of persons, actions, passions or things. 'Tis not the jerk or sting of an Epigram, nor the seeming contradiction of a poor Antithesis, (the delight of an ill judging Audience in a Play of Rhyme) nor the gingle of a more poor *Paranomasia*: neither is it so much the morality of a grave sentence, affected by *Lucan*, but more sparingly used by *Virgil*; but it is some lively and apt description, dress'd in such colours of speech, that it sets before your eyes the absent object, as perfectly and more delightfully then nature.[26]

There are actually three separate definitions here. The first ('that which is well defin'd') points to the Popean one. Johnson was to remonstrate that Pope 'reduces it from strength of thought to happiness of language'.[27] The second (wit as a 'delightful' propriety in representation) does not here refer to verbal wit at all but is an attempt to define the normative delight produced by heroic writing, or, rather, the ground to which verbal wit is an interruption or embellishment. But seeing that Dryden's business at the time was writing 'plays of rhyme', it is there among the jerks, stings, and seeming contradictions that we should look for his actual working aesthetic, and perhaps Purcell's as well.

This third kind of wit—the kind for which Mr Bayes was taxed in *The Rehearsal*—falls under Johnson's dictionary definition of 'sentiments produced by quickness of fancy'. Fancy in this sense is the opposite of judgement. If pressed Dryden might even have agreed with Locke that wit was a genius at 'putting those [ideas] together with quickness and variety, wherein can be found any resemblance or congruity', while judgement got on with the more philosophical task of 'separating carefully *Ideas* one from another' which might otherwise have become confused.[28] His own image of fancy was as a 'nimble Spaniel' whose task was to search memory for 'the species

---

[26] *Works*, i. 53.   [27] *Lives*, i. 19.
[28] See *An Essay Concerning Humane Understanding* (London, 1690), II. xi. 2 (p. 68).

or Idea's of those things which it designs to represent' and which sometimes required to 'have Cloggs tied to it, least it out-run the Judgement'.[29] But he does not offer a formal definition of wit that might be applied to other arts besides his own. To obtain this we have to turn from his theory to his practice.

If one asks what it is above all that allows us to distinguish the witty parts of a discourse, whether verbal or musical, from those that produce a normative kind of delight, the first characteristic must be that wit is interruptive—something that breaks the regular flow of musical or poetic discourse with a different, contrasting kind of perception. It follows from this that it should surprise. All art forms that move in time employ a basic rhythm of expectations aroused and fulfilled, though never, if interest is to be maintained, perfectly fulfilled. In music this often takes the form of a melody built through harmonic transformations of a single module or two contrasted modules (the pattern that was to lead to sonata form). In the Baroque this was often done within a two-section structure in which the first section progressed from the tonic to the dominant and the second section, more circuitously, from the dominant back to the tonic. Wit complicates our awareness of this modular process through what theorists of the time would have recognized as a form of the passion of wonder or astonishment.

Most Augustan discussions of the role of the passions in music and poetry invoke the psycho-physiology of Descartes, according to which wonder is credited with the physiological effect of drawing the 'animal spirits' ('animal' as belonging to the anima, or soul) together to the place in the brain occupied by the image of the wonder-provoking event, and thereby leaving the other functions unprovided.[30] This displacement produced a momentary paralysis during which even respiration might be suspended, after which the spirits would course back violently to their former place, producing a sudden revivification. The most striking portrayals of this passion

---

[29] *Works*, i. 53, viii. 101.

[30] This mechanistic account of the passions was enunciated by Descartes in *Traité des passions de l'âme* (1649) as an outcome of his theories of the functioning of the body as a hydraulic engine operated by fluids that were themselves assemblages of particles. This had enormous influence on the description of affect in art, music, and theatre. A useful sub-Cartesian account of the two passions mentioned will be found in Aaron Hill, 'An Essay on the Art of Acting', in *The Works of the Late Aaron Hill, Esq*, 2nd edn. (London, 1754), iv. 368–373 [= 371].

were seen in tragedy—as in Hamlet's semi-paralysis (famously recorded in a portrait of Garrick in the role) when he first sees the ghost—or in fiction—as in Defoe's account of Crusoe's reaction to his discovery of the footprint. But interruptive wit employs an evanescent version of the same physiological mechanism: its philosopher should be Longinus, not Aristotle. The Cartesian account of wonder is still helpful today in understanding the effects of this mode of wit. Of course, one instance of wit may lead directly into another or a chain of others, offered as responses or supersessions. In that case the forward momentum of the discourse is maintained in a new way. But more often, by initially drawing attention to itself, it checks or retards the current of attention in a way that, as we have seen, requires the listener to engage in a process of mental catching up. This check, it should be added, is cognitive, not experienced as an aspect of the performance: far from slowing down in real time to emphasize its witty moments, a play or piece of music is likely to toss them off lightly.

A second mark of wit is a sudden increase in the frequency of semantic events: a conceptual busyness. In poetry the witty remark is simply more complex and more difficult to paraphrase. However, the presence of wit is not detectable through the mere look of the page: a witty statement will not use more, or fewer, words than an unwitty one. In music an increase in the frequency of semantic events will often be detectable graphically through characteristics of notation. This is certainly true of the use of ornaments, such as, to use Purcell's own terminology, the forefall, the backfall, the shake, the shake turned, and the beat, and simple 'divisions', though it is only the more arresting examples that actually become 'witty'.[31] Beyond this a vocal line may be embellished through taking isolated individual words as the basis for striking passages of figuration in short note-values. Such local events encountered in the course of characteristic Purcellian long melodies allow us to identify the presence of one common kind of musical wit.

[31] For an example of a standard ornament transformed into a sublime piece of musical wit see the rising dotted figure leading into the final chord of the principal theme of the slow movement of Mozart's piano concerto in Bb, K595. Then compare this with how a very similar triplet figure, which first appears at bar 14 in the slow movement of Beethoven's Fifth Symphony, remains just that—an ornament.

The qualification needs to be entered here that the kind of musical wit most likely to be detectable through its graphical appearance would correspond to what rhetoricians used to call 'auricular' figures (alliteration, rhyme, chiasmus, etc.) rather than 'figures of sense' (metaphor, metonymy, antithesis). These auricular figures are ways of patterning language by placing words into a more striking or symmetrical order that does not, however, significantly modify either their meaning or that of the passage. So, to take an instance from *Hamlet*, the syntax of 'The courtier's, soldier's, scholar's, eye, tongue, sword' could be normalized without any effect on the paraphrasable sense of what was communicated. Because a musical 'sentence' is built to a far greater extent than a poetic one on repetition or near-repetition of its constituent phrase-modules, auricular patternings of this kind are not interruptive, but belong rather to the normative effects of melody-building. So a kind of patterning that would be witty done with words in a poem might not be so in a piece of music. This is less of a problem with Purcell than with Corelli or Handel because his melodies are, on the whole, less obviously modular in their construction than theirs; but this absence of symmetry creates the opposite problem that it becomes more difficult to classify a particular event as anomalous and therefore an example of melodic wit.

Purcell's melodic or 'auricular' wit can be illustrated in its elementary form in 'I attempt from love's sickness to fly in vain', set to Dryden's words from *The Indian Queen* as a triple-time rondo with two episodes (ABACA). In the first line, 'love's' carries a conventional ornament that prepares us for an example of musical wit in the two bars of descending quavers on 'fly' which then invite a falling long appoggiatura on 'in vain' as a kind of musical soft landing. The second line of the couplet, 'Since I am myself my own fever and pain', is built round a figure of three rising crotchets which contains nothing interruptive or surprising until we reach the cadence on the tonic which is decorated by four falling quavers. This plainness in the second part of the A section is appropriate since the wit is at this point supplied by Dryden in the form of an outrageous catachresis ('I am myself my own fever'); however, we might note that a Victorian arranger could not resist adding some 'feverish' quavers to the bass.[32] The melisma on 'fly in vain' comprises an example of auricular wit, with the remainder of the strain, in its predictable patterning, representing the modular norm. In this case the auricular wit also involves an element of pictorialism of a kind very frequent in Purcell.[33] A further example of pictorial wit in the song comes in the C episode when the phrase 'make us seek ruin' is set to a falling quaver figure which on its repetition takes the singer to the lowest note of the whole piece.

The other possible sign of musical and poetic wit is an element of semantic tension or contradiction, which corresponds in a broad sense to the rhetorician's 'figures of sense'. In Dryden's case this is most commonly performed by antithesis, or 'seeming' antithesis ('Cool was his kitchen but his brains were hot') or paradox ('I am myself my own fever'), and what he refers to generally as his 'jerks and stings'. While the paradoxical figures are only one species of wit among several deployed by Dryden (his use of the Ovidian 'turn' is of another nature), they have a particular interest for the present study. In two earlier papers I tried to ask in what ways the cognitive effect of Dryden's paradoxical figures differed from that of the metaphysical poets, who were his principal early masters.[34] The answer offered was that, while offering the *form* of paradox or radical antithesis, they did not offer the content. What the seeming paradoxes of the heroic plays provide is a musculature of argument that exists primarily to be flexed and displayed like the poses of a body builder: a spectacle of technique detached from function. Paradox had been a natural mode of expression for Donne and the poets of his school because it was a valid means of understanding mysteries such as the Trinity and the Incarnation which were themselves paradoxical. But neither paradox nor radical metaphor (formerly justified as a means of knowing a universe composed of occult correspondences) had a place in the new stylistic ideals promoted

---

[32] *The Songs of England . . . in Three Volumes*, ed J. L. Hatton and Eaton Faning (London, n.d.), p. 1.

[33] Musical word-painting corresponds to physical mimicry, universally agreed to be the lowest form of social and verbal wit, but rather more respected in Virgil, where it goes under the name of onomatopoeia. For further examples from Purcell, see Robert King, *Henry Purcell* (London, 1994), pp. 95–6, 101, 104, 152–3, 197, 225, and *passim*.

[34] See Harold Love, 'Dryden's Unideal Vacancy', *Eighteenth-Century Studies*, 12 (1978) 74–89, and 'Dryden's Rationale of Paradox', *ELH* 51 (1984) 297–313. These may be consulted for further examples of the phenomena described.

from the 1660s by the Royal Society. In an age of material explanations and Latitudinarian rationalization of the mysteries, there was no longer either scientific or metaphysical work for paradox to perform. Consequently, the philosophical assumptions of Donne's two 'Anniversaries' were clearly incomprehensible to Dryden when he imitated some superficial features of the poems' style in *Eleonora*.

Instead, paradox often became a means of performing playful transgressions of the new epistemological boundaries erected *within* the no longer unified realm of knowledge by dualistic thinkers such as Descartes and Hobbes in order to quarantine mental and vitalistic explanations of phenomena from material and mechanical ones. Wit of this kind, which is especially frequent in the dramas, shocks not through revealing unexpected connections but in confounding the very categories of cognition. A good example of the co-presence of incompatible systems of explanation is given by the opening lines of Dryden and Lee's *Oedipus* (for which Purcell composed the famous 'Music for a while'):

> *Alcander*. Methinks we stand on Ruines: Nature shakes
>   About us; and the Universal Frame
>   So loose, that it but wants another push
>   To leap from off its Hindges.
> *Diocles*. No Sun to chear us; but a Bloody Globe
>   That rowls above; a bald and Beamless Fire;
>   His Face o're-grown with Scurf: the Sun's sick too;
>   Shortly he'll be an Earth.[35]

The logical tension of this catachrestic presentation of the sun as a face disfigured with plague sores arises from its also representing Descartes's mechanistic model of planet formation. According to this model, the earth itself had once been fiery like the sun, but had been gradually covered over by *maculae* of the 'third element', identical in their nature to sun-spots.[36] What we experience is a collision between vitalistic and mechanistic explanations of the same event, the first offering a moral reason for the sun's darkening, in the sin of Oedipus, and the second a purely scientific one. Whether we

[35] *The Works of Nathaniel Lee*, ed. Thomas B. Stroup and Arthur L. Cooke (New Brunswick, NJ, 1954), i. 379. Also Dryden, *Works*, xiii. 121.
[36] Further explained in Harold and Rosaleen Love, 'A Cartesian Allusion in Dryden and Lee's *Oedipus*', *Notes and Queries*, NS 25 (1978) 35–7.

describe this collision as superimposition or simultaneity depends largely on whether we regard the contradictory explanations as being mutually exclusive or complementary; but there can be no doubt about their transgressive nature.

That something similar was recognized in Purcell is indicated by Robert Gould's lines quoted by Zimmerman:[37]

> How in that mystic order cou'd he join
> So different notes! make contraries combine
> And out of discord, cull such sounds divine.

The simplest form of a superimpository musical wit would be the long cadential appoggiatura in which a note from a previous chord is held as a dissonance for an appreciable part of the duration of the chord of resolution: in effect a co-presence of two competing harmonies. A more intricate kind of harmonic wit arises from clashes and false relations created by allowing the logic of the individual line to override that of the anticipated progression, an effect very frequent in Purcell. Westrup in his classic study describes one common form of this:

A frequent, and in general a successful, application of the principle [of independent movement] in simple harmonization is one that might be described as 'overlapping'. Two alternative solutions of a cadence present themselves, and the opportunity afforded by several parts, whether vocal or instrumental, induces the composer to use both simultaneously.[38]

This is suggestive of the simultaneous employment of incompatible systems of explanation that we have already noted in Dryden and which are further illustrated in the two articles cited. Purcell's equivalent to Dryden's contradictory appeals to vitalistic and mechanistic explanations is that in which false relations are produced through the simultaneous use of modal (equatable with vitalistic) and tonal (equatable with mechanistic) melodic movement in different voices. A number of examples of this are discussed by Westrup on pages 248–52. Such musical 'figures of sense' may not be evident graphically (apart from the presence of conflicting

---

[37] *Henry Purcell*, p. 345.
[38] J. A. Westrup, *Purcell*, rev. edn. (London, 1960), p. 248. Westrup's most striking example of this, taken from the chorus 'Full fathom five' from *The Tempest*, is now believed to be by Purcell's pupil John Weldon.

accidentals) to the extent suggested for melodic wit, but are still marked by surprise and a sudden increase in semantic density. These are exactly the passages where players may well pause to check the score in case there is an error or the editor has recorded a variant. They have been known to give rise to heated arguments in rehearsal between those who would resolve the anomaly in one direction or another. But the truth of the matter will often lie in listening through the apparent contradiction to a deeper simultaneity of alternatives, both of which possess their own rightness.[39]

These moments, melodic and harmonic, of elaboration or overlapping within a characteristic Purcellian long phrase may be compared with the working of verbal wit in Dryden's couplets: the longer-range syntactic and deliberative structures that sustain the forward movement are regularly checked by wit whose function is to arouse wonder and admiration, and having done so will encourage the mind to linger briefly in pleasurable contemplation. In Dryden, especially in the heroic plays, this desire to startle will sometimes stifle the onward movement, producing a series of jewels held up one by one for our delighted inspection but at the expense of any consideration of the larger structures of argument, character, or scene. Similarly, Purcell will sometimes pile on decoration so extravagantly that it is the individual detail rather than the advance of the structure that dominates our attention, as in a song such as 'Sweeter than roses'. But generally the two elements, the eager forward movement and the retarding force of the individual conceit or figure, are kept in a balance which is the essence of the appeal of both the writings and the music. Or, if we do not experience them as a balance, we can at least argue that each has the effect of intensifying the vigour of the other.

At the beginning of this essay I looked at the means by which a 'classical' status was constructed for both Dryden and Purcell. I have also now considered a number of ways in which their common artistic assumptions are significantly unclassical by the terms of that construction. The narrative of classicism falls down in their case

---

[39] There is something similar to this in the notion of 'musical metaphor' as it is developed in chapter 5 of Joseph Swain's *Musical Languages* (New York, 1997), pp. 95–118. 'Metaphor' in Swain's specialized sense 'stretches the syntactic coherence of a composition' (p. 111). It is perceived as an incongruity in a syntax whose task is that it 'mediates the relation of tension and resolution in musical languages' (p. 28).

because it fails to predict the nature of the practices we actually encounter when we look at their work without preconceptions. At best it can afford them an uneasy transitional status towards a summit of achievement represented by Pope and Johnson in literature and Bach and Handel in music: a status which makes their most vital and characteristic work a kind of mistake which, had they lived a little later, they would never have made. This is a view we need to correct. In the case of Purcell it involves recognizing that if he was an Orpheus he was equally a Timotheus, impatient of predictable sequence and regular transitions. (And surely Dryden's Timotheus in *Alexander's Feast* is his tribute to Purcell, although Purcell was never to set this greatest of odes for music.) In Dryden's case it involves reorienting ourselves to the way in which he was seen by Buckingham, Johnson, and Macaulay in the passages cited, as a wild artist rather than a tame one, but without their negativity, which was itself the product of an inappropriate application of 'classical' values.

6

DRYDEN AND CONGREVE'S COLLABORATION IN *THE DOUBLE DEALER*

JENNIFER BRADY

Congreve shall preserve thy fame alive,
And *Dryden's* Muse shall in his Friend survive.

(Joseph Addison, 'An Account of the Greatest
English Poets', 1694)

But whither, whither wouldst Thou fly
My feeble Muse? The Quarry's much too high.
To some great Genius leave his praise,
    Which may survive to After-days:
Let *Congreve* then in Deathless Song,
        His Father's Loss deplore;
Congreve must his Fame prolong,
In such soft rural Strains, as once he Sung before.

(John Freud, 'Upon the Death of *John Dryden*, Esq;
A Pindarique', 1700)

A writer turns to a partner not from a practical assessment of
advantages, but from a superstitious hope, a longing for replen-
ishment and union ...

(Wayne Koestenbaum, *Double Talk*, 1989)

I want to thank my colleagues at Rhodes, Gail Murray, Sandra McEntire, and Brian
Shaffer, for their steadfast support and intellectual help during the writing of this essay, and
the editors of this volume for their painstaking reading of it at a later stage. I want also to thank
my dear friends Earl Miner, for giving me my first break in Dryden studies, and Andy Silber,
who sparked my interest in Dryden some thirty years ago.

On 12 March 1700, less than two months before his death, John Dryden wrote to Mrs Elizabeth Steward with the happy news of the long-awaited publication of his *Fables*, 'my new Poems...which are not come till this day into my hands'.[1] He shared with his correspondent his delighted sense that *Fables* was poised to become a popular and critical success. 'The Town encourages them with more Applause than any thing of mine deserves',[2] Dryden reported in March, and by 11 April the glowing early reviews were in. 'The Ladies of the Town have infected you at a distance', he joked in a second letter. 'They are all of your Opinion; & like my last Book of Poems, better than any thing they have formerly seen of mine.'[3] In retailing the warm reception of his *Fables* to his relation, Dryden celebrated what must have seemed to him a vindication long over-due: the deposed Poet Laureate, 68 years old and in poor health, had produced a last major work.

There was yet another notable literary debut in the spring of 1700. William Congreve's comedy *The Way of the World* opened at the Lincoln's Inn Fields Theatre, apparently the same week that *Fables* was published. In his 12 March letter Dryden protested at the reception accorded Congreve's play: 'Congreves New Play has had but moderate success; though it deserves much better.'[4] This pro-tective response on his part to Congreve's setback was revealing. On the day when he held his 'new Poems' in his hands for the first time, Dryden's triumph was shadowed by his concern for the lukewarm reception of his protégé's play. Dryden's extraordinary investment in Congreve, publicly proclaimed in his 1693 verse address, 'To my Dear Friend Mr. Congreve, on His Comedy, call'd *The Double-Dealer*', was reaffirmed in the quiet tones of this private letter. When Dryden died on 1 May 1700, their friendship had spanned most of the previous decade, during the years when Congreve wrote the five plays on which his reputation as a playwright securely rests. Paradoxically, the two debuts in March of the same year were also both authors' swan-songs: the playwright in Congreve did not survive his influential sponsor, who had choreographed his career in its formative years. After *The Way of the World*, Congreve retired from writing stage plays.

---

[1] *Letters*, p. 134. [2] Ibid. [3] *Letters*, p. 135. [4] *Letters*, pp. 134–5.

Dryden's and Congreve's close co-operation throughout the 1690s amounted to a partnership that benefited both writers. They assumed a variety of supportive roles in relation to each other's work: mutual editing of manuscripts, the exchange of commendatory verses, and co-translating, among other kinds of assistance. Each man supplied the other with prefatory poems that endorsed specific projects. Dryden's 1692 translation of Persius, for example, was published with Congreve's 'To Mr. Dryden, on his Translation of Persius'[5] as its only accompanying preface. Dryden's famous epistle to Congreve in the same year served a complementary function in *The Double Dealer*. Dryden commissioned Congreve, then in his early twenties, to work on his translation of Juvenal; the title-page hailed it as a collaborative work 'BY Mr. DRYDEN, AND Several other Eminent Hands'.[6] Dryden's Dedication to *Examen Poeticum*, which included 'two fragments of *Homer*', one translated 'by Mr. Congreve . . . and the other by my self', proposed Congreve to its dedicatee, Lord Radcliffe, as 'more capable than any Man I know' of embarking on a translation of Homer's epic.[7] Dryden not only employed Congreve as a co-translator on his classical projects, but he envisaged other large undertakings for him, using his accumulated prestige to advance his colleague's career. At the same time, Dryden relied on Congreve's tact, equanimity, and legal training in negotiating the details of his contracts with their mutual publisher, Jacob Tonson. The two writers edited and revised each other's works in progress, with Dryden volunteering his help in preparing Congreve's *The Old Batchelour* for the stage and Congreve in turn correcting Dryden's translations of classical authors. In 1717 Congreve wrote the foreword to an important posthumous edition of Dryden's dramatic works being published by Tonson.

Congreve's and Dryden's professional collaboration has received little sustained recent attention from Restoration scholars, despite the long-standing availability of their letters and other crucial documents in John C. Hodges's and Charles E. Ward's ably edited collections.[8] In part, Congreve's phenomenal impact on Dryden

---

[5] *Works*, iv. 809.   [6] *Works*, iv. 2.   [7] *Works*, iv. 372–4.

[8] Ward's edition of Dryden's letters is a valuable resource. See also *William Congreve: Letters and Documents*, ed. John C. Hodges (New York, 1964), in which Hodges makes a compelling case for the mutual benefits realized by Dryden and Congreve in their productive collegial relations. Cited below as *Letters*, ed. Hodges.

has been discounted by scholars who focus on the disparity of some forty years in their ages and who, like James Winn, sceptically assume Dryden to be inflating his estimation of Congreve's precocity in his epistle.[9] Dryden's importance for Congreve is more readily acknowledged by theatre historians and theorists exploring the revival of satiric comedy in the 1690s, yet most readings of *The Double Dealer* give at best only perfunctory attention to its pre-text.[10] While the full title of Dryden's verse address, 'To my Dear Friend Mr. Congreve, on his Comedy, call'd *The Double-Dealer*', insists on the crucial ligament connecting his poem to Congreve's second play, in practice critics abbreviate Dryden's cumbersome title, thus masking or suppressing the attachment of his poem to the occasion of its first publication. Interpretations of 'To my Dear Friend Mr. Congreve' typically centre on its place in Dryden's development as a writer of patrilineal succession poems, an emphasis that has illuminated his understanding of literary history while obscuring his ardent sponsorship of Congreve. Finally, in the ethos that favours the single author as the object of study, the claims of one writer are typically lodged at the expense of another, and collaborations are devalued, regarded as 'a mere subset or aberrant kind of individual authorship', in Jeffrey Masten's words, rather than as a different—and often constructive—model of inter-authorial relations.[11]

Jack Stillinger has challenged both our traditional and our postmodern conceptions of authorship in provocative ways in his *Multiple Authorship and the Myth of Solitary Genius*. He investigates in Romantic and modernist writers

the joint, or composite, or collaborative production of literary works that we usually think of as written by a single author. This kind of multiple authorship . . . is also an extremely common phenomenon; a work may be

---

[9] James Anderson Winn, *John Dryden and his World* (New Haven, 1987), pp. 465–6.

[10] For exemplary readings of Dryden's influence on Congreve's drama, see Robert D. Hume, *The Development of English Drama in the Late Seventeenth Century* (Oxford, 1976), esp. pp. 381–90, where Hume argues convincingly that during the half-decade of 1689–94 the satiric comedies written by Dryden, Southerne, and Congreve represented 'a deliberate attempt under Dryden's sponsorship to revive and advance the Carolean mode. Southerne and Congreve were his [Dryden's] instruments' in this endeavour (p. 382). See also Robert Markley, *Two Edg'd Weapons: Style and Ideology in the Comedies of Etherege, Wycherley and Congreve* (Oxford, 1988), in which Markley offers cogent readings of both Southerne's and Dryden's influential pre-texts; and Harold Love, *Congreve* (Totowa, NJ, 1974).

[11] Jeffrey A. Masten, 'Beaumont and/or Fletcher: Collaboration and the Interpretation of Renaissance Drama', *ELH* 59 (1992) 341.

the collaborative product of the nominal author and a friend, a spouse, a ghost[writer], an agent, an editor, a translator, a publisher, a censor, a transcriber, a printer, or—what is more often the case—several of these acting together or in succession.[12]

In the cases Stillinger studies, the individual author's apparent autonomy dissolves into a more complicated allocation of part-shares in the work when he examines in detail the successive manu-script versions of a Keats sonnet, transcribed but also edited by the Romantic poet's several helpers, or the traces of collaboration with colleagues, friends, or partners inscribed in acknowledgements pages. The paradigm Stillinger develops offers several advantages: it reasserts, post Barthes and Foucault, the importance of establish-ing historical authorship; it embeds 'literary works [in] . . . the social, cultural, and material conditions in which they were produced';[13] and it represents the collaborative process as utterly common for writers, while acknowledging the multiplicity of roles collaborators can assume in the social production of literature.

In exploring Dryden's and Congreve's participation in each other's professional lives, I begin by documenting their attachment as it is revealed in letters and other published sources from the 1690s. Dryden's letters and prefaces shed light on his complex investment in Congreve, including his efforts to create opportunities for him

---

[12] Jack Stillinger, *Multiple Authorship and the Myth of Solitary Genius* (New York and Oxford, 1991), p. v. See further, on the subject of literary collaboration, Gordon McMullan, *The Politics of Unease in the Plays of John Fletcher* (Amherst, Mass., 1994), pp. 132–55, where he concludes that 'The logic of collaboration puts paid to the myth of the author as sole controller of the text. . . . Infection, contamination, compromise, and all the other words used of the collaborative process describe not an atypical situation but the inevitable condition of writing' (p. 155). A more romantic view of male literary collaboration is offered in Wayne Koestenbaum's provocative *Double Talk: The Erotics of Male Literary Collaboration* (New York and London, 1989), in which Koestenbaum interprets collaboration as entailing a sublimation of homoerotic desire for Victorian and modernist writers. He is most convincing in his focus on the collaborator's 'wish for a partner' (p. 2) to complete him, a psychological emphasis that accords with my own sense of Dryden and Congreve's dynamics, although I do not follow Koestenbaum's explicit homoerotic bias in my reading of these early modern writers. Paulina Kewes construes collaboration far more narrowly than do Masten, McMullan, Koestenbaum, and Stillinger in her recent study, *Authorship and Appropriation: Writing for the Stage in England, 1660–1710* (Oxford, 1998), where collaboration becomes synonymous with professed 'dual authorship' of works. Even though she concludes that fewer playwrights collaborated on plays, she instances Dryden as a major exception to her findings in an interesting discussion of Dryden and Lee's collaborations on two plays, *Oedipus* (1678) and *The Duke of Guise* (1682) (pp. 154–76).

[13] Stillinger, *Multiple Authorship*, p. 183.

with publishers and prospective patrons. Throughout their friendship, Dryden repeatedly made Congreve the beneficiary of his own astute professionalism. Dryden's diminished confidence in his stature as a writer after the Revolution of 1688 is also caught in these public and private professions. His epistle formally nominating Congreve as his successor and confronting in print his own painful loss of the post of Laureate is, I shall argue, a crucially formative text in articulating Dryden's wish for an heir who would serve in turn as his defender and apologist. 'To my Dear Friend Mr. Congreve' also responds to the playwright Thomas Southerne's commendatory poem 'To Mr. *Congreve*', published several months earlier in 1693. Both of these influential poems rework Dryden's satire *Mac Flecknoe* into a patrilineal fable starring Dryden and Congreve in place of Flecknoe and Mac Flecknoe, the mocked king and prince of dullness. Dryden diverges from Southerne's awed portrait of him as the presiding monarch of contemporary literature, however, in his epistle, which offers a poignant view of his situation and appeals to Congreve to 'be kind to my Remains'.[14] In turning to *The Double Dealer*, my focus will be on Congreve's treatment of a literary collaboration in a subplot of his second play. *The Double Dealer* exposes to ridicule a self-infatuated novice writer, Lady Froth, whose heroic poem attracts the attention of Brisk, who volunteers to vet her manuscript so that it will pass muster with the critical reading public. Congreve thus represents collaboration on stage in his comedy at the same time as he is working closely with Dryden on a publication highlighting works by both authors and designed to enhance Congreve's reputation. Finally, I will consider Congreve's dedication to Thomas Pelham-Holles, first Duke of Newcastle, of Dryden's dramatic works in 1717, a testimonial in which Congreve expresses his continuing sense of obligation—intermixed with gratitude—to his friend, colleague, and former sponsor.

I

'His Friendship, where he profess'd it, went much beyond his Professions',[15] William Congreve wrote about John Dryden, in a

---

[14] This request was recalled by Congreve in the preface to Dryden's *Dramatick Works* (1717). *Letters*, ed. Hodges, p. 126.

[15] Ibid. 127.

compliment that applied with equal justice to his own gift for sustaining close friendships, both personal and professional, over his lifetime. Dryden's fervent attachment to Congreve was expressed in his letters to Tonson, Walsh, and Steward, and, with barely more reserve, in his critical prefaces where Dryden's growing sense of isolation after the Revolution of 1688 and his advocacy of Congreve's talents were cherished topics for the ex-Laureate. Whether he was writing to his publisher, Jacob Tonson, or his cousin's daughter, Mrs Steward, dedicating his *Examen Poeticum* to Lord Radcliffe, or even supplying a preface to his son's 1696 comedy, Dryden introduced—or obtruded—discussion of Congreve into his text. There was a steadfastness in Dryden's high regard for the brilliant young writer; in semi-public, private, and public forums Dryden consistently proclaimed Congreve's importance for him.

Significantly, their attachment arose in the immediate aftermath of Dryden's loss of the Laureateship, which was a key source of both his intellectual self-esteem and his livelihood. His letters and prefaces reveal his increasing vulnerability in the 1690s when, given his impolitic loyalty to James II and his Catholicism, Dryden was forced to resign the salaried posts of Laureate and Historiographer Royal. As he complained in 1692 to the Earl of Dorset in his 'Discourse Concerning Satire', 'since this Revolution...I have patiently suffer'd the Ruin of my small Fortune, and the loss of that poor Subsistance which I had from two Kings, whom I had served more Faithfully than Profitably to my self...And now Age has overtaken me; and Want, a more insufferable Evil, through the Change of the Times, has wholly disenabl'd me'.[16] Dryden's representation here of his losses had a measured pathos that moved many of his contemporaries to identify with his grievances. In *Luctus Britannici*, the volume of elegies published by Henry Playford and Abel Roper in 1700 to commemorate Dryden's career, the booksellers pointedly hail Dryden on the title-page as the 'LATE | Poet Laureat to Their Majesties, K. *Charles* and K. *James* the Second' and many of the elegists protest at the laurels 'torn' from Dryden on William's accession to the throne.[17]

---

[16] *Works*, iv. 23.
[17] *Luctus Britannici: or the Tears of the British Muses . . . for the Death of John Dryden, Esq.*, in

On 30 August 1693 Dryden sent a worried letter to his publisher Tonson, detailing his frustration at yet another financial setback and anticipating an attack from Thomas Rymer, his successor in the post of Historiographer Royal, in retaliation for Dryden's anti-government stand in the Dedication to *Examen Poeticum*. At the close of his letter, he turns abruptly to an appeal (routed through Tonson) to Congreve: 'I am Mr Congreve's true Lover & desire you to tell him, how kindly I take his often Remembrances of me: I wish him all prosperity; & hope I shall never loose his Affection.'[18] The thought of Congreve's partisan support consoled Dryden in the midst of his other anxieties, most immediately Rymer's impending attack on his plays. In the context of the pressures detailed in the rest of the letter to Tonson, his wish that Congreve and their friendship prosper gained in urgency.

Congreve also played a role in mediating Dryden's sometimes fractious dealings with Jacob Tonson, who published both writers' works. As J. M. Treadwell's research into tax returns for St Dunstan parish in London has shown, Congreve was a lodger at his publisher's Fleet Street address by the mid-1690s.[19] He witnessed Dryden's contracts for his translation of Virgil and later the *Fables*, and Dryden seems to have entrusted to Congreve, who had considerable legal training, the oversight of both contracts. When Dryden was to meet with Tonson in June 1695, to settle the arrangements for the second subscription of his *Works of Virgil*, he asked his publisher in an edgy letter to 'be ready with the price of paper, & of the Books', adding that 'Mr Congreve may be with us, as a Common friend; for as you know him for yours, I make not the least doubt, but he is much more mine'.[20] Within months Dryden pressured Tonson again to keep him informed on the progress of the second subscriptions:

Drydeniana XIV (New York and London, 1975). See especially the elegies written by Ch. Vi. (pp. 1–4), Henry Hall (pp. 16–20), and S.F. (pp. 25–30), which echo Dryden's sense of injured merit. Hall, for example, sides with Dryden's scornful dismissal in 'To my Dear Friend Mr. Congreve' of his new rival, Thomas Rymer, who replaced Thomas Shadwell in 1692 in the office of Historiographer Royal from which Dryden had been ousted: 'The Sacred Wreath, that long so well was worn, | Shall now no more be from His Temples torn; | No more of slighted Merit we complain, | Now Tom the Second, may securely reign' (ll. 5–8), Hall writes, quoting the ex-Laureate.

[18] *Letters*, p. 59.
[19] J. M. Treadwell, 'Congreve, Tonson, and Rowe's "Reconcilement"', *Notes and Queries*, 22 (1975) 265–69. [20] *Letters*, p. 76.

'When you have leysure, I shou'd be glad to see how Mr Congreve & you have worded my propositions for Virgil.'[21] Dryden had evidently delegated to Congreve the oversight in London of his complicated business transactions with Tonson, including among Congreve's responsibilities aspects of Dryden's public relations as well as his contractual obligations, all of which bore directly on the former Laureate's livelihood after 1694. As these data suggest, Dryden placed a rather extraordinary trust in Congreve, valuing his judgement, his business acumen, and his tact, and, just as important, his personal loyalty.

In return, Congreve was the beneficiary throughout the 1690s of Dryden's exertions on his behalf, exertions that included hiring the younger writer to work on Dryden's heavily subscribed translations, or, in another shrewd showcasing of his protégé's talents, soliciting commendatory verses from Congreve for what seemed likely to be prestige publications. In a letter written to William Walsh in May 1693, for instance, Dryden responded as a seasoned professional writer to the anticipated publication early that autumn of Wycherley's poems: 'I ... believe it [the volume] will be extraordinary. ... Congreve & Southern & I, shall not faile to appeare before it. & if you come in, he [Wycherley] will have reason to acknowledge it for a favour.'[22] Wycherley did not publish his *Poems* until 1704, but, as Dryden recognized, the cachet associated with supplying pre-texts for Wycherley's poems would have made this an important opportunity for Congreve in 1693, when he was a young writer about to publish his second comedy. Dryden arranged the pre-texts to Wycherley's *Poems* with two aims in mind: to certify Congreve and Southerne as putative heirs to the Restoration tradition of satiric comedy that Wycherley represented, and to position them, implicitly under his and Wycherley's joint sponsorship, as the most important writers of the new generation. Dryden had, of course, more control over the release of his own texts and, when he brought out his *Satires*, he advertised his favouring of Congreve over the 'Several other Eminent Hands'[23] who had, like Congreve, translated individual satires of Juvenal for the volume by asking him to supply its only commendatory poem, 'To Mr. Dryden, on his Translation of Persius'.

---

[21] *Letters*, p. 79.   [22] *Letters*, p. 54.   [23] *Works*, iv. 2.

Perhaps the most revealing of Dryden's interventions on Congreve's behalf involved his appeal to Lord Radcliffe, the dedicatee of *Examen Poeticum*, to sponsor Congreve in translating Homer's *Iliad*. Dryden told Jacob Tonson that he had never expected Radcliffe to pay him for his Dedication, and implied as much in his address to Radcliffe: 'my Lord, you have it in your Nature, to be a Patron and Encourager of Good Poets, but your Fortune has not yet put into your Hands the opportunity of expressing it. What you will be hereafter, may be more than guess'd, by what you are at present.'[24] Projected into the future, this vision of Radcliffe's *vera nobilitas* bypasses Dryden's own career when he nominates Congreve in his stead as the most deserving recipient of the aristocrat's patronage.[25] Later in his Dedication, Dryden identifies his co-translator as Homer's most gifted contemporary interpreter: 'I wish Mr. *Congreve* had the leisure to Translate him, and the World the good Nature and Justice, to encourage him in that Noble Design.'[26] At this stage of Dryden's appeal, the 'world' becomes synonymous with the potential largesse of Lord Radcliffe, who is deftly complimented through an evocation of the patron he may be 'hereafter' and pointed unmistakably in the direction his patronage of the arts should take. It may well be unprecedented for a writer versed in the patronage system to use his dedication as a springboard to solicit long-term financial support from his patron for a fellow writer, but that is precisely what John Dryden attempts to engineer here for his friend Congreve.

There is another prong to Dryden's energetic promotion of Congreve as 'more capable than any Man I know'[27] to undertake the translation of Homer. Dryden, famously, chose to translate Virgil's epic while advocating in print that his friend emulate his choice by taking on the *Iliad*, 'the best and most absolute Heroique Poem'[28] in classical literature—or perhaps, the *other* best epic, given Dryden's balanced admiration of both Homer and Virgil. He was particularly drawn to the idea of Congreve translating Homer

---

[24] *Works*, iv. 369.
[25] On the subject of *vera nobilitas*, see Michael McCanles, *Jonsonian Discriminations: The Humanist Poet and the Praise of True Nobility* (Toronto, 1992), pp. 46–65.
[26] *Works*, iv. 374.
[27] Ibid.
[28] *Works*, iv. 27.

because he himself would embark within the year on a parallel course in his verse translation of Virgil. Had Congreve in the mid-1690s followed his mentor's script, he and Dryden would have been paired as the premier translators into English verse of the two foundational Western classical epics. In a fitting postscript to this unfulfilled dream of John Dryden's, Alexander Pope chose to follow Dryden's suggestion in undertaking a verse translation of *The Iliad of Homer*, published in instalments from 1715 to 1720. Pope's grasp of literary history could be uncanny: in a tribute designed as much for Dryden, the originator of the project, as for his first choice to translate Homer's epic, Pope dedicated his elegant work to his friend William Congreve.[29]

As this survey of Dryden's and Congreve's professional relations suggests, Dryden championed Congreve to the extent of trying to choreograph his career, and simultaneously relied on him for various kinds of support that mitigated Dryden's marked sense of isolation after his forced abdication of the Laureateship. Over and over in his correspondence of the 1690s Dryden promoted Congreve. His Dedication of *Examen Poeticum* warmly honoured his co-translator, 'Mr. *Congreve* (whom I cannot mention without the Honour which is due to his Excellent Parts, and that entire Affection which I bear him)'.[30] Even his Preface to his son John's 1696 comedy, *The Husband His own Cuckold*, reserved its praise for Congreve's prologue and Dryden's matching epilogue: 'my son and I are extreamly oblig'd to my dear Friend Mr. *Congreve*, whose excellent Prologue was one of the greatest Ornaments of the Play. Neither is my Epilogue the worst which I have written.'[31] By incorporating the title of his famous poem 'To my Dear Friend Mr. Congreve'

[29] Pope's phrasing in his dedication is revealing not only of his own attachment to Congreve but of the kind of link to his friend Dryden had wanted to forge when he first proposed that Congreve undertake a verse translation of Homer. Pope writes: 'let me leave behind me a memorial of my friendship, with one of the most valuable men as well as the finest writers, of my age and country: One who has try'd, and knows by his own experience, how hard an undertaking it is to do justice to *Homer*...to him [Congreve] therefore... I desire to dedicate it [*The Iliad of Homer*]; and to have the honour and satisfaction of placing together, in this manner, the names of Mr. CONGREVE, and of | A. POPE' (*Letters*, ed. Hodges, p. 233). Dryden had repeatedly joined his name with Congreve's in his prefaces and correspondence of the 1690s, but it was Pope who finally coupled his name with Congreve's in his dedication.
[30] *Works*, iv. 372.
[31] *Works*, iv. 472.

into this comparatively obscure preface written three years later, Dryden ratified his choice of Congreve as his defender and heir over all other candidates, including his own son. Their partnership, as Dryden conceived it, would continue beyond his death.

II

When Dryden supplied Congreve with a commendatory poem for *The Double Dealer*, he was engaging in a customary practice institutionalized by print culture, in which writers endorsed each other's work in poems that were produced as a favour to the author (or as a repayment of favours in kind). As G. E. Bentley has shown, Renaissance playwrights often collected such verses from their colleagues to defend plays of theirs that had failed on stage, as Ben Jonson did in the sheaf of pre-texts he marshalled when he published the lavish quarto *Sejanus* in 1605.[32] Jonson also wrote some thirty-five commendatory poems for his contemporaries' works, and his example is matched by Dryden's recruiting of contributors to write pre-texts for Wycherley's collected poems, or his close supervision of Congreve's *The Old Batchelour*, whose first edition included commendatory poems by Southerne, Marsh, and Higgons.[33] Some years ago Annabel Patterson drew scholars' attention to the political significance of the front matter of early modern texts, decrying the editorial practice in some modern editions of dropping the pre-texts or relegating them to appendices.[34] This material is also crucial in another respect, as evidence of writers' close professional ties to each other. The poems published as front matter are invited and in that sense co-operative undertakings and, as G. E. Bentley has said of all collaborations, their writing requires 'one author to accommodate his writing to that of another'.[35] The

---

[32] G. E. Bentley, *The Profession of Dramatist in Shakespeare's Time, 1590–1642* (Princeton, NJ, 1971).

[33] On the practice of peer endorsement in early modern writers, especially Jonson, see Arthur F. Marotti, *Manuscript, Print, and the English Renaissance Lyric* (Ithaca, NY, and London, 1995), p. 322. I have taken the number of commendatory poems Ben Jonson wrote from Marotti's important book.

[34] Annabel Patterson, *Censorship and Interpretation: The Conditions of Writing and Reading in Early Modern England* (Madison, Wis., 1984), p. 48.

[35] Bentley, *The Profession of Dramatist*, p. 197.

commendatory poem is, in other words, an important site for investigating not only the invention and ideology of authorship in the early modern period but paradoxically the fact of multiple authorship that calls into question the fetish we make of the individual author.

There are two crucial pre-texts to Dryden's 1693 verse address to Congreve, Thomas Southerne's 'To Mr. *Congreve*', which heads the three congratulatory poems printed in *The Old Batchelour*, and Dryden's own satire of literary succession, *Mac Flecknoe*, written in 1676. Earl Miner has remarked that *Mac Flecknoe* and 'To my Dear Friend Mr. Congreve' are 'uncannily alike', so much so that 'Dryden could only have been aware that he was seriously parodying his own earlier poem'.[36] The more immediate catalyst for Dryden's self-collaboration is the playwright Southerne's important poem. His 'To Mr. *Congreve*' previews in detail the patrilineal fable developed in Dryden's poem to Congreve, not surprisingly since Southerne too is mining *Mac Flecknoe* for his encomium on the two writers.

Southerne's poem is addressed formally to Congreve, but Dryden, referred to in the third person, is assumed to be its other most engaged contemporary reader:

> DRYDEN has long extended his Command,
> By Right-divine, quite through the Muses Land,
> Absolute Lord; and holding now from none,
> But great *Apollo*, his undoubted Crown:
> (That Empire settled, and grown old in Pow'r)
> Can wish for nothing, but a Successor:
> Not to enlarge his Limits, but maintain
> Those Provinces, which he alone could gain.
> . . . .
> CONGREVE appears,
> The Darling, and last Comfort of his Years:
> May'st thou live long in thy great Masters smiles
> And growing under him, adorn these Isles:
> But when—when part of him (be that but late)
> His body yielding must submit to Fate,

---

[36] Earl Miner, 'Introduction: Borrowed Plumage, Varied Umbrage', in Earl Miner and Jennifer Brady (eds.), *Literary Transmission and Authority: Dryden and Other Writers* (Cambridge, 1993), p. 17.

Leaving his deathless Works, and thee behind,
(The natural Successor of his Mind)
Then may'st thou finish what he has begun:
Heir to his Merit, be in Fame his Son.
What thou hast done, shews all is in thy Power;
And to Write better, only must Write more.[37]

Southerne glosses over Dryden's loss of the Laureateship in this poem, which casts Dryden, like Flecknoe, as 'Absolute Lord' of his empire, a monarch 'grown old in [a] Pow'r' that is uncontested, who wishes above all for a worthy male heir. I have quoted extensively from Southerne's poem because he so closely hews to the plot and diction of *Mac Flecknoe* in his characterization of Dryden as the ageing monarch of contemporary literature. In *Mac Flecknoe*, Flecknoe too 'had govern'd long' and 'was own'd, without dispute | Through all the Realms of *Non-sense*, absolute' (ll. 4–6). There are numerous parallels between the commendatory poem and Dryden's *Mac Flecknoe*, including the imperialist strain in Southerne's and Dryden's allusions to literary empires, the son's projected role in defending the father's realm, and his ideal fitness to inherit the throne. Congreve is to 'maintain | Those provinces' (ll. 24–5) of literature pacified by Dryden, while Mac Flecknoe is advised by his cautious father to 'chuse for thy command | Some peacefull Province in Acrostick Land' (ll. 205–6). In Dryden's satire, Flecknoe wonders which of his progeny should inherit his throne until he recognizes that '*Sh*—— alone my perfect image bears, | Mature in dullness from his tender years' (ll. 15–16). Southerne reviews the various candidates for inheriting Dryden's crown—Wycherley, Etherege, Lee, and Otway (whose names appear in the text in discreet italics)—before 'CONGREVE appears', in capitals, as the precocious son in whom 'DRYDEN' is well pleased: 'Heir to his Merit, be in Fame his Son' (ll. 30, 39). The type style used in the first quarto of *The Old Batchelour* underscores the inevitability of Congreve's succession, linking the two writers and enlarging their names over those of other contemporary contenders for literary greatness.

Southerne must negotiate the delicate matter of Dryden's mortality in his commendatory poem to Congreve. The nervous halt

---

[37] Thomas Southerne, 'To Mr. *Congreve*', in *The Complete Plays of William Congreve*, ed. Herbert Davis (Chicago, 1967), p. 31, ll. 18–25, 30–41. Citations of Congreve will be from this edition.

in the line that first anticipates Dryden's death reveals Southerne's nearly overwhelming awareness that 'To Mr. *Congreve*' has two readers, one of whom must die for the other to inherit his estate. Southerne confronts this reality hesitantly: 'But when—when part of him (be that but late) | His body yielding must submit to Fate, | Leaving his deathless Works, and thee behind' (ll. 34–6). This passage is remarkable in several respects, not the least of which is Southerne's discomfort at the thought that Dryden will shortly be reading his poem. His pious wish, '(be that but late)', resists the thought of Dryden's death, as though Southerne is resigned to its inevitability yet wants to postpone it indefinitely. The circumlocutions that evade ever quite naming death have a similar function in the poem. Southerne's equivocal language seeks to protect his two primary readers from recognizing the enormity of their impending separation. There is one major consolation offered John Dryden in this tense passage anticipating his dying and the transfer of his power to his much younger colleague. In Southerne's poem, Congreve is for the first time identified as the custodian of Dryden's 'deathless Works'.

Congreve's role as Dryden's protégé is carefully scripted in Southerne's 1693 poem, which anticipates in several ways Dryden's epistle to Congreve written later that same year. Whether or not Dryden explicitly authorized Southerne's 'To Mr. *Congreve*' cannot be established from surviving documents, but Southerne's account of Dryden's intervention in the revisions of *The Old Batchelour* suggests that he might also have had a consultative role in preparing the play and its front matter for its first printing.[38] As Robert Markley has argued, Southerne's 'lines are weighty with images of authority, kingship, and orderly succession from a dying father to a dutiful heir'.[39] Congreve is made the conservator of Dryden's literary empire, not an innovator who might foray into new terrain. He is expected to continue to 'grow...under' (l. 33) Dryden in his remaining years, earning his sponsor's approval through adopting an attitude of filial submission. Finally, 'To Mr. *Congreve*' imgines Dryden 'leaving his deathless Works, and thee behind' to 'finish what he has begun' (ll. 36, 38), thus severely constraining Congreve's choices.

---

[38] *Letters*, ed. Hodges, p. 151.   [39] Markley, *Two Edg'd Weapons*, p. 197.

Dryden revisits Southerne's poem in the appeal Dryden makes to his friend in his closing lines, but with a quite different emphasis. He writes: 'Be kind to my Remains; and oh defend, | Against Your Judgment Your departed Friend! | Let not the Insulting Foe my Fame pursue' (ll. 72–4). Evidently Dryden expects assaults on his reputation to continue after his death and seeks to enlist Congreve as his defender. According to Dryden, both his works and his reputation are vulnerable to his enemies' slander, and it is only Congreve's intervention that secures a hearing for the embattled ex-Laureate. In Southerne's account of the succession, by contrast, Congreve is conscripted into a caretaking role: he protects and maintains the father's estate. Dryden too wants his protégé to mount a partisan defence of his works after his death, but his pitch to Congreve is based on their kinship as writers ('Be *kind* to my Remains'), rather than on the contractual model of their relations proposed by Southerne. To recast this point, where Southerne would oblige, Dryden trusts more in the power of the personal appeal in his approach to Congreve.

Nor does Dryden skirt the painful issue of his forfeited government posts in his epistle, where he confronts the loss not only of the Laureateship but of the post of Historiographer Royal, offices occupied by Thomas Shadwell and Thomas Rymer. As I have argued elsewhere, Dryden's willingness to bestow his crown on Congreve is complicated by the fact that Dryden has been ousted from his throne, where '*Tom* the Second [now] reigns like *Tom* the first' (l. 48). His sarcasm betrays Dryden's continuing bitterness over the transfer of his prestigious titles to his rivals in the theatre. 'Well had I been Depos'd, if You had reign'd!', he laments, 'For only You are lineal to the Throne' (ll. 42, 44). Dryden's ousting is also Congreve's loss, he reasons, since Shadwell and Rymer occupy his son's rightful places, offices Dryden had been holding for his successor. By advancing this narrative of his exclusion, Dryden argues that his removal from office was politically motivated and unjust and, a subtler point, that Congreve's legitimate claim to the Laureateship in England has been subverted by Dryden's political opponents. Congreve is thus coached or pressured to identify with Dryden's anger and adopt his mentor's grievances.

Elsewhere in the poem Dryden compares his exclusion from the Laureateship to a forced abdication. Resorting to historical analogy, he writes: 'Thus when the State one *Edward* did depose; | A Greater *Edward* in his room arose' (ll. 45–6). On one level Dryden rewrites history as a kind of *felix culpa* in which the deposing of Edward II is more than compensated for by the glorious achievements of Edward III. Dryden cannot risk comparing his experience of being deposed as Laureate to the most recent instance of this pattern in English history, the Revolution of 1688 in which James II was dethroned in favour of William, not only because of Dryden's own political and religious allegiances but because he would then have to liken his protégé Congreve to the victor William, whose policies Dryden steadily opposed. Even so, his overly bland account of a king's abdication—'Thus when the State one *Edward* did depose'—should make us wonder at his choice of historical analogy. Two readings seem possible here. The first is that references to the deposing of Edward II would necessarily, in 1693, trigger memories in English readers of the recent removal of James II from the throne. Dryden's identification with the figure of the deposed king establishes his loyalties clearly, while the *felix culpa* construction he places on the analogy insulates him from (more) government-sponsored repercussion. The second gloss I would place on this passage relates to the terrible brutality of Edward II's murder. In likening his political misfortunes to those of Edward II, Dryden implies that he experienced the seizure of his offices by 'the State' in 1688 as a violation of his public identity. When Dryden cites Edward's abdication as a historical parallel to his own case, it is difficult to overlook the king's quasi-sodomitical murder by Mortimer's agents or to pass blithely over Dryden's allusion to the deposed king to focus on the success story of Edward III that Congreve's career seems poised to repeat.[40] The *culpa* seems to outweigh the *felix* in Dryden's controversial choice of historical precedents, despite his assurance that 'a greater' Congreve will arise in his vacated place.

Throughout his epistle Dryden promotes the view that Congreve's career will be more fortunate than his own. That contrast is explicitly argued in the comparison the ex-Laureate makes between his present miseries and Congreve's bright prospects:

---

[40] On the murder of Edward II, see John Boswell, *Christianity, Social Tolerance, and Homosexuality* (Chicago, 1980), pp. 298–300.

> Already I am worn with Cares and Age;
> And just abandoning th'Ungrateful Stage:
> Unprofitably kept at Heav'ns expence,
> I live a Rent-charge on his Providence:
> But You, whom ev'ry Muse and Grace adorn,
> Whom I foresee to better Fortune born... (ll. 66–71)

Paul Hammond has pointed us to the twin movements of mourning and celebration in Dryden's late works, and they are particularly pronounced in his verse address to Congreve where Dryden mourns his own misfortunes yet still finds the generosity to celebrate Congreve's meteoric rise.[41]

Dryden rewrites his own *Mac Flecknoe* in his epistle to Congreve, casting himself in the role of the prophet foretelling his illustrious son's ascent to the throne of wit. He relegates his self-absorbed thoughts to asides that interrupt—but only briefly—Congreve's elevation.

> Yet this I Prophecy; Thou shalt be seen,
> (Tho' with some short Parenthesis between:)
> High on the Throne of Wit; and seated there,
> Not mine (that's little) but thy Lawrel wear. (ll. 51–4)

With this public declaration endorsing William Congreve as his successor, Dryden fulfils the expectation created several months earlier in 1693 by Southerne's poem. Most of the contributors to *Luctus Britannici* accepted Dryden's nomination at face value, with only one disgruntled elegist consigning Congreve to Mac Flecknoe's bad eminence as the reigning prince of dullness.[42]

In 'To my Dear Friend Mr. Congreve' Dryden both answers the challenge extended to him in Southerne's poem and complicates the stakes, chiefly by refusing to gloss over the humiliating loss of the Laureateship and his other titles. Instead of 'deathless Works',

---

[41] Paul Hammond, *John Dryden: A Literary Life* (Basingstoke, 1991), p. 158. In *Dryden and the Traces of Classical Rome* (Oxford, 1999), pp. 9–16, Hammond offers a moving reading of the Congreve epistle that focuses on Dryden's tendency to displace himself altogether from his poem: 'it is an intensely personal poem', he concludes, 'but one which almost makes Dryden disappear from the cultural scene and from his own text, as his [literary] "Remains" are handed over' to Congreve (p. 16).

[42] In 'Upon the Death of Mr. DRYDEN', Digby Cotes parodies *Mac Flecknoe* to demean Congreve's talents, in what amounts to a sophomoric play on Dryden's satire. See *Luctus Britannici*, pp. 31–2.

the 'Remains' Dryden leaves to Congreve will, he predicts, need defending. Dryden's laurels cannot compare with Congreve's, as his sad parenthesis disparaging his own literary achievement makes clear. Dryden contests the portrait of him that Southerne draws in his poem: the patriarch confidently surveying his empire, bequeathing it to his dutiful son. The self-portrait Dryden presents us with in his verse address to Congreve is of a far more vulnerable man with a more uneasy relation to his literary corpus, a writer who petitions his friend to 'be kind to [his] ... Remains' (l. 72).

III

In his brilliant study of satiric narratives, Michael Seidel adapts Freud to comment suggestively on the tactics satirists use to disguise their unavoidable but also largely unacknowledged implication in their subject-matter. In Seidel's view,

Satirists generate their own insecurities and then elaborate a fable in which they attempt to displace themselves from what they have generated. . . . [It] has always been a persistent part of the satiric fiction for the satirist to try to protect (or insulate) himself from his material. He hopes, almost prays, that whatever out there threatens him does not by a stretch of his own imagination absorb him. . . . [He] works to distance himself from the debasing, deforming, encroaching and contaminating nature of his subjects by placing surrogate figures in his fiction. He literally invents expendable versions of himself (with whom he is only partially identified) to do his dirty work.[43]

Seidel's argument clarifies Congreve's investment in his subplot in *The Double Dealer* that satirizes literary collaboration through the figures of Lady Froth and Brisk, who together are editing her impossibly bad heroic poem in order to defend it from the anticipated criticism of a reading public they disparage as 'the vulgar'. On one level, Congreve conspicuously distances himself and by extension his professional relations with Dryden from the self-indulgent literary couple in his satiric comedy who glibly rationalize bad writing and whose composite work is a vanity production in every sense of the word. On another, Congreve is engaged in his subplot in an anxious distancing of his own activities in producing

[43] Michael Seidel, *Satiric Inheritance, Rabelais to Sterne* (Princeton, NJ, 1979), pp. 11–12, 14.

his plays with Dryden's help from the collaboration of Lady Froth and Brisk, his surrogates in the play. Congreve has so resolutely separated himself from his targets that they seem to inhabit different universes: his dilettante writers in *The Double Dealer* operate as inverted mirror-images of the playwright's earnest self-presentation in his dedication of the play.

'I heartily wish this Play were as perfect as I intended it', Congreve writes to Lord Charles Montagu in his fussy preface, which offers an elaborate vindication of his comedy, including his boast that he has 'resolved to preserve the Three Unities of the Drama, which I have visibly done to the utmost severity'.[44] By contrast, the writers in *The Double Dealer*—Saygrace, Brisk, Lady Froth, and, proleptic-ally, her infant daughter Sapho—represent a culture of licence. Saygrace, an impudent social-climbing chaplain who is interrupted by Maskwell in the course of writing an acrostic poem, jokes that he will 'but pen the last Line of an Acrostick, and be with you in the twinckling of an Ejaculation' (v. i. 273–4). His trifling taste is confirmed by Saygrace's choice of acrostics, the genre Dryden had particularly condemned in *Mac Flecknoe*, whose dull protagonist is urged to 'Leave writing Plays, and chuse for thy command | Some peacefull Province in Acrostick Land' (ll. 205–6). Congreve writes plays, his character Saygrace acrostics, their genres prescribed by the competing realms of wit and dullness represented in Dryden's satire. But the contrast extends further in the undeclared contest between Congreve's poetasters and himself: his comic art is severe, classical in design, and disciplined in execution, while Saygrace's occasional poems are the product of his excessive idleness.

Congreve's unremitting perfectionism, heralded in his dedication of *The Double Dealer*, is juxtaposed within the comedy to Lady Froth's experiments in automatic writing. During her courtship, as she recalls for the reserved heroine Cynthia, Lady Froth 'gave ... vent' to 'Whymsies and Vapours': 'O I Writ, Writ abundantly', her overwrought sensibilities and arrogance prompting her to tackle indiscriminately 'Songs, Elegies, Satyrs, Encomiums, Panegyricks, Lampoons, Plays, or Heroick Poems' (ii. i. 11–17). Her habits of

---

[44] *Complete Plays*, ed. Davis, pp. 118–19. On the subject of Congreve's defence in his Dedication of his even-handed disparagement of his male and female characters in *The Double Dealer*, see Pat Gill, *Interpreting Ladies: Women, Wit, and Morality in the Restoration Comedy of Manners* (Athens, Ga., 1994), p. 98.

revision are equally slapdash and unconsidered. When Brisk objects to a simile in her heroic poem, Lady Froth half-concedes his point, then detours into an ingeniously stupid defence of her faulty comparison, finally cobbling together a quatrain that salvages much of her original line while answering Brisk's criticism:

Lady Froth. For as the Sun shines every day,
                      So of our Coach-man I may say.
Brisk. I'm afraid that simile wont do in wet Weather—because you say the Sun shines every day.
Lady Froth. No, for the Sun it wont, but it will do for the Coachman, for you know there's most occasion for a Coach in wet Weather.
Brisk. Right, right, that saves all.
Lady Froth. Then I don't say the Sun shines all the day, but, that he peeps now and then, yet he does shine all the day too, you know, tho' we don't see him.
Brisk. Right, but the vulgar will never comprehend that.
Lady Froth. Well you shall hear—let me see.   *Reads.*
                      For as the Sun shines every day,
                      So, of our Coach-man I may say,
                      He shows his drunken fiery Face,
                      Just as the Sun does, more or less.
Brisk. That's right, all's well, all's well.

(III. i. 515–33)

Their careless and hasty amending of the simile sets these writers apart from the perfectionism Congreve exhibits in his own work. He judges his plays by absolute standards; a Congreve comedy is either 'as perfect as I intended it' or, failing that, 'very imperfect'.[45] His dilettantes in *The Double Dealer* settle for another standard altogether: they content themselves with a facile compromise, 'more or less'. In fact, Lady Froth has another, unacknowledged collaborator in this quatrain from *Sillabub* that she reads aloud, as amended on the spot, to Brisk. She has already lifted a phrase verbatim from Abraham Cowley's verse translations of Anacreon, the second of which celebrates the natural world's affinity for drink: 'The busie *Sun* (and one would guess | By's *drunken fiery face* no less) | Drinks up the *Sea*.'[46] Cowley's influence is absorbed by her in the

---

[45] *Complete Plays*, ed. Davis, p. 118.
[46] 'Drinking', in *Poems of Abraham Cowley*, ed. A. R. Waller (Cambridge, 1905), p. 51, ll. 9–11, my emphasis. I owe this point to David Hopkins. In *Authorship and Appropriation*,

same undigested way as is Brisk's; she recycles his words, without improving on her source or imitating Cowley to any real purpose.

Congreve designs his subplot to provide his audience with an instructively bad instance of a literary collaboration. Brisk is so ingratiating in praising the improvements Lady Froth is making to the poem and in offering to supply 'Notes to the whole poem' (III. i. 554–5) that the infatuated co-authors soon progress from bungling quatrains in the drawing room to 'making couplets' (v. i. 513) on the lawn of the Touchwood estate. Lady Froth remains resilient in her blithe flouting of decorum: she transposes the dairy in her poem from the country to the city and her heroic poem absurdly conflates epic or biblical names with familiar and stock names.[47] Whenever Brisk questions her literary judgement, she takes refuge in the personal. Neither party tempers or corrects or even seriously challenges the other's errors. Brisk will, it seems, annotate every line of *Sillabub* rather than hold Lady Froth accountable to any principle of coherence. The aristocratic collaborators in *The Double Dealer* share an impenetrable vanity, shored up by a snobbery directed at 'vulgar' readers whose criticism they both fear and discount.

Lady Froth's literary progeny include her daughter Sapho. The infant 'has a World of Wit, and can sing a Tune already' (III. i. 619–20) according to her doting stage mother, who insists on exhibiting her daughter's precocity almost hourly before the assembly. By naming her child after the poet Sappho, Lady Froth projects her own literary ambitions onto her daughter. As Lawrence Lipking has shown in his study of the Greek poet's reception through the ages, Sappho was at once enshrined as the tenth muse who became 'the prototype of all supremely gifted women' and caricatured as the embodiment 'of wanton female sexuality'.[48] It is, of course, Sappho's triangulated relationships that Lady Froth emulates in her

---

Paulina Kewes discusses Gerard Langbaine's strictures against writers who copy from English sources in his 1688 pamphlet, *Momus Triumphans: or, The Plagiaries of the English Stage*, where he writes: 'I cannot but esteem them as the worst of Plagiaries, who steal from the Writings of those of our own Nation. Because he that borrows from the worst *Forreign* Author, may possibly import . . . *somewhat* of value: whereas the former makes us pay extortion for *that* which was our own before' (p. 113).

[47] See further, on this point, Derek Hughes, *English Drama, 1660–1700* (Oxford, 1996), p. 356. Eric S. Rump has also treated the satire of literary dilettantism in his perceptive introduction to *The Comedies of William Congreve* (Harmondsworth, 1985), pp. 9–27.

[48] Lawrence I. Lipking, *Abandoned Women and Poetic Tradition* (Chicago, 1988), pp. 61–2.

adultery, not her talent, so that the legacy she passes on to her child is unwittingly tarnished by her own behaviour. Her heroic poem *Sillabub* bears no resemblance to Sappho's art: the doggerel verse travesties the Greek poet's perfect lyrics.

Congreve separates his own comic art from the dilettantes he ridicules in his subplot, just as he explodes Lady Froth's pretensions to being the modern Sappho. His *Double Dealer* insists on the differences between himself and his targets, setting up hierarchical dualisms based on class and literary talent. As Derek Hughes has argued, the satire of the aristocracy in the English comedies of the mid-1690s reflects 'the growing confidence of the intelligent professional in his own worth and standing',[49] a confidence made possible in many ways by Dryden's career, which modelled professionalism for younger generations of writers like Congreve and Southerne.

Yet despite these distancing tactics, Congreve leaves traces of himself in the satire, smudged prints that suggest a partial if obscured identification with his targets. Lady Froth's naming of her daughter is one such instance of Congreve's implication in his material. The name Sapho, absurdly foisted on the child by a mother who wishes to dictate her daughter's destiny, would seem an uncomplicated joke at the expense of Lady Froth's literary vanity, but for one curious fact. In his letters to Joseph Keally, Congreve repeatedly expresses his devotion to his dog, Sapho, who is doted over in ways that mirror Lady Froth's apparent over-investment in her daughter: 'I was about writing to you when I received yours; but Sapho being in labour, I was forced to hold my hand till her deliverance. Among other beauties which she has brought into the world, she has reserved one most like herself for you', and, later, 'We are at present in great grief for the death of Sapho. She has left some few orphans; one of which, if it can live, is designed for you.'[50] Congreve even dates the 'great revolutions' he refers to in another letter as having happened 'since the Death of Sapho'.[51] The conjunction of the two Saphos—Lady Froth's off-stage daughter, Congreve's dog—complicates our reception of the satire in *The Double Dealer*. Lady Froth names the infant child after the Greek poet, dedicating her to Sappho as though to ensure the Pythagorean transmission of genius

---

[49] Hughes, *English Drama*, p. 333.   [50] *Letters*, ed. Hodges, pp. 16, 24.
[51] Ibid. 25.

from Sappho through her to her daughter. Congreve, also obsessed with the magic properties of names and with the transfer of literary legacies, names his beloved dog Sapho. Her name and his attachment to her confess Congreve's desire to realize Sapphic perfection in his art, at the same time as it betrays his uneasy, for the most part repressed, identification with Lady Froth, the dilettante writer whose self-indulgence draws his ridicule.

There are other signs of Congreve's implication in *The Double Dealer*'s subplot. His dedication of the play mirrors Lady Froth's preoccupation with the reception of her manuscript by 'vulgar' readers in two respects. In his preface, Congreve includes this particularly huffy passage, directed at his critics: 'I would not have any Body imagine, that I think this Play without its Faults, for I am Conscious of several, (and ready to own 'em; but it shall be to those who are able to find 'em out.)'[52] He disparages those critics who have found fault with the play's morality or its protagonists, sharply impugning their views. Lady Froth's performance whenever Brisk challenges her logic or phrasing is similar in obfuscating the objections made to her work: 'Then I don't say the Sun shines all the day, but, that he peeps now and then, yet he does shine all the day too, you know, tho' we dont see him' (III. i. 524–6). She responds defensively to criticism, a reaction that is also showcased in Congreve's preface. These points of conjunction between Congreve and Lady Froth do not collapse the factors making them representatives of opposing literary traditions and values, but the partial resemblances do suggest an unacknowledged intensity in Congreve's investment in this subplot, one that might account for the extraordinary 'stage time devoted to satirizing the corruption of wit'[53] in *The Double Dealer*.

When Lady Froth and her fawning editor Brisk correct her manuscript, their labours parody the demanding process of revision. Brisk suggests new wording, and she obligingly crams it into her text ('And when at night his labour's done, | Then too like Heav'ns Charioteer, the Sun', III. i. 535–6), or he volunteers to provide exhaustive notes to forestall criticism of her poem by the reading public. Lady Froth's response to his involvement in her work veers between being too receptive—as in her impulsive, off-the-cuff

[52] *Complete Plays*, ed. Davis, p. 118.   [53] Markley, *Two Edg'd Weapons*, p. 212.

rewriting of individual lines—and intractable stubbornness, as when she covers up her faults with tendentious explanations, instead of conceding the illogic of her metaphors.

By contrast, when Congreve wrote in 1717 about his highly productive working relations with Dryden over the 1690s, he recalled Dryden as having been 'extream ready and gentle in his Correction of the Errors of any Writer, who thought fit to consult him; and full as ready and patient to admit . . . His own Oversight or Mistakes'.[54] The collaboration Congreve represents on stage in his comedy is thus at a far remove from the helpful mutual editing he describes in his testimonial to Dryden, whose example of patient mentoring Congreve followed in his kind, painstaking, and candid response to Catherine Trotter, a young playwright whose tragedy he read and responded to in considerable detail in 1703.[55]

Yet Congreve airs some discomfort with literary collaboration in *The Double Dealer*. Seidel argues in *Satiric Inheritance* that in the genre of satire, as in dreams, 'a hostile anxiety is recessed into the deeper structure of a "plot" produced to express' the satirist's anxiety,[56] but in a disguised or altered form. Congreve probably found his mentor's choreographing of his career flattering and overwhelming, and his perfectionism was ultimately at odds with Dryden's ingrained professionalism. By 1693 Congreve was already deeply indebted to Dryden and the gift of his generous poem establishing Congreve as his sole heir only added to that debt. *The Double Dealer's* subplot satirizing collaboration suggests Congreve's recessed anxiety about the extent of his reliance on Dryden.

v

After the première of *The Way of the World* and John Dryden's death in the spring of 1700, Congreve wrote no more plays. In 1704 he became the co-manager with John Vanbrugh of the new Haymarket Theatre, but when that venture failed Congreve worked for the next thirty-five years as a civil servant.[57] Restoration scholars have

---

[54] *Letters*, ed. Hodges, p. 127.
[55] Ibid. 212–13.
[56] Seidel, *Satiric Inheritance*, p. 10.
[57] In his privately published Clark Lectures for 1997, *The Integrity of William Congreve* (Oxford, 1997), D. F. McKenzie sheds light on Vanbrugh and Congreve's conception of the

attributed his retreat from authorship after his incandescent early career as a playwright to a variety of cultural and personal pressures. Robert D. Hume has pointed to the economic instability of London's volatile theatre companies at the turn of the century, as well as audiences' new taste for sentimental drama and the cumulative impact of Collier's attacks on the so-called obscenity of satiric drama.[58] Alternatively, Voltaire's impression—that Congreve fancied himself a gentleman, not a writer—implies an unresolved tension between his social and professional identities that is also mirrored in the dedications to his plays.[59] Another version, repeated by Samuel Johnson in his 'Life of Congreve', holds that William Congreve retired in disgust to a long life of 'sociable indolence'[60] after *The Way of the World* was only a middling success on stage. Congreve's writing career has been represented as a casualty of performance anxiety, or fastidiousness, or the changing marketplace. In all likelihood his choice to give up writing plays was overdetermined, a compound of factors working in conjunction. To these various explanations, I would add another: the end of William Congreve's productive partnership with John Dryden.

Dryden bolstered Congreve in the 1690s, promoted his talents, and repeatedly sought out opportunities for his protégé to distinguish himself in the profession Dryden had done so much to establish. Their attachment was reciprocal, entailing more than Dryden's able mentoring of Congreve. He was, Congreve wrote in 1717, especially touched by Dryden's personal appeal to him in the close of his epistle. Just as Dryden had once quoted the title of his verse address to Congreve in a new context that reaffirmed his warm endorsement of his 'dear Friend, Mr. *Congreve*', so Congreve, some twenty-four years after the poem's first printing, repeated the words that had particular resonance for him in explaining to Thomas Pelham-Holles, Duke of Newcastle, why he had agreed to write the foreword to a new edition of Dryden's plays:

---

new Haymarket Theatre as a 'home . . . for a truly English opera' (p. 36) that would rival the popular Italian operas and even, they hoped, revive a court-sponsored patronage of the musical arts, as well as Congreve's partnership with John Eccles on *Semele*, an opera for which Congreve wrote the libretto and Eccles composed the music.

[58] Hume, *Development of English Drama*, pp. 380–431.
[59] *Letters*, ed. Hodges, pp. 242–3.
[60] Love, *Congreve*, p. 1.

In some very Elegant, tho' very partial Verses which he did me the Honour to write to me, he recommended it to me to *be kind to his Remains*. I was then, and have been ever since most sensibly touched with that Expression: and the more so, because I could not find in my self the Means of satisfying the Passion which I felt in me, to do something answerable to an Injunction laid upon me in so Pathetick and so Amicable a Manner.

You, my Lord, have furnish'd me with ample Means of acquitting myself, both of my Duty and Obligation to my *departed Friend*. What kinder Office lyes in me, to do to these, his most valuable and unperishable Remains, than to commit them to the Protection, and lodge them under the Roof of a Patron, whose Hospitality has extended it self even to his Dust?[61]

After 1700 Congreve undertook two literary projects of significance to this study, the publication in 1710 of *The Works of Mr. William Congreve*, collected in three volumes, and, in 1717, *The Dramatick Works of John Dryden, Esq; in Six Volumes*, edited by their publisher Tonson and showcasing Congreve's Epistle Dedicatory. The bond between Dryden and Congreve produced a final collaboration, a labour of love on Congreve's part that answered his 'departed Friend' 's wish that he honour his life's work. There was, however, an undeniable cost involved in Congreve's relinquishing of his own literary ambitions. The playwright and early-blooming genius who once built a career with Dryden's help had been superseded in later life by the friend who was now the custodian of their collective works.

---

[61] *Letters*, ed. Hodges, p. 126.

7

ALEXANDER'S FEAST; OR THE POWER OF MUSIQUE: THE POEM AND ITS READERS

Tom Mason and Adam Rounce

ALEXANDER'S FEAST, not long after its appearance, being the theme of every Critick, young Marley, among others, took an opportunity of paying his court to the author; and happening to sit next him, congratulated him on having produced the finest and noblest Ode that had ever been written in any language. 'You are right, young gentleman, (replied Dryden,) a nobler Ode never was produced, nor ever will.'[1]

It appears to have happened to Dryden (as does not always happen to poets) that the poem he valued most was most enjoyed both by its immediate audience and by succeeding generations.[2] There is a great deal of evidence to suggest that *Alexander's Feast* was seen by most of Dryden's readers (and by Dryden himself) as a masterpiece—a poem in which the poet both epitomized and excelled himself, a poem which outdid all its rivals of its kind, and which was not bettered by later writers. To take an example almost at random,

---

In this chapter underlining in quotations represents our editorial emphasis. For reasons of economy, the many works which borrow from *Alexander's Feast* are cited only by title and, where possible, date of publication. The originals, together with bibliographical information, may be located via the Chadwyck–Healey *English Poetry* and *English Drama* full-text databases, which, however, sometimes provide a text from later collected editions.

[1] *The Critical and Miscellaneous Prose Works of John Dryden*, ed. Edmond Malone, 4 vols. (London, 1800), i. 476.

[2] 'I am glad to hear from all hands', he wrote to Tonson in December 1697, 'that my Ode is esteemed the best of all my poetry by all the town. I thought so myself when I writ it; but being old, I mistrusted my own judgement' (*Letters*, p. 98).

the entry under 'Music' in *A Poetical Dictionary; or, The Beauties of the English Poets, Alphabetically Displayed, Containing the Most Celebrated Passages* (1761) consists in its entirety of a passage from Alexander Pope and a poem by John Dryden. Pope's passage (extracted from *An Essay on Criticism*) tells how, in Dryden's *Alexander's Feast*, the master musician, Timotheus, 'bid alternate passions fall and rise' and how 'the world's victor', Alexander, was 'subdu'd by sound'. This is followed by Dryden's poem itself, printed in full under the title '*DRYDEN'S fine ODE*'.

Pope's description of Dryden's poem is the culmination of a discussion of versification, the deciding and defining illustration of the maxim that 'The *Sound* must seem an *Echo* to the *Sense*'. Pope's passage, it has been frequently observed, is a reformulation of notions he shared with many of the leading writers of the previous century,[3] and a working into verse of some thoughts he had originally expressed in a letter:

It is not enough that nothing offends the Ear, but a good Poet will adapt the very Sounds, as well as Words, to the things he treats of. So that there is (if one may express it so) a Style of Sound. As in describing a gliding Stream, the Numbers shou'd run easy and flowing; in describing a rough Torrent or Deluge, sonorous and swelling, and so of the rest.

Accordingly, Pope demonstrated in the *Essay* how poetry might seem an echo to the sense when that sense concerns a gliding stream and a rough torrent, the effort of Ajax throwing a rock's vast weight, or the speed of Camilla riding through the corn.

At this point in his argument, in both the poem and the letter, Pope turns to Dryden's poem: 'This, I think, is what very few observe in practice, and is undoubtedly of wonderful force in imprinting the Image on the reader: We have one excellent Example of it in our Language, Mr. *Dryden*'s Ode on St. *Cæcilia*'s Day, entitled, *Alexander's Feast*.'[4] The mention of *Alexander's Feast*

---

[3] Roscommon in his *Essay on Translated Verse* (1684) had maintained that 'The sound is still a Comment on the Sense'. In his Preface to *Sylvae*, Dryden had observed of Virgil that his 'verse is everywhere sounding the very thing in your ears, whose sense it bears' (*Works*, iii. 6). Again, in the Preface to *Albion and Albanius*, he had argued that the 'chief secret' of writing well is 'the choice of words', in which he includes not only 'elegancy of expression', but 'propriety of sound, to be varied according to the nature of the subject' (*Works*, xv. 9).

[4] Pope to Walsh, 22 October 1706 (*The Correspondence of Alexander Pope*, ed. George Sherburn, 5 vols. (Oxford, 1956), i. 22–3).

marks a surprising shift in emphasis in both verse and prose—almost a change of subject. It is easy to see how Pope's own examples imprint the 'image' of a gliding stream or a roaring torrent on the mind of the reader. It is less easy to see what might be meant by an 'image' in relation to Dryden's poem—which, as Pope describes it, is principally concerned with the passions:[5]

> Hear how *Timotheus'* vary'd Lays surprize,
> And bid Alternate Passions fall and rise!
> While, at each Change, the Son of *Lybian Jove*
> Now *burns* with Glory, and then *melts* with Love:
> Now his *fierce Eyes* with *sparkling Fury* glow;
> Now *Sighs* steal out, and *Tears begin to flow*:
> *Persians* and *Greeks* like *Turns of Nature* found,
> And the *World's Victor* stood subdu'd by *Sound*!
> The Pow'r of Musick all our Hearts allow;
> And what *Timotheus* was, is *Dryden* now.   (ll. 374–83)

Pope's conclusion, by which Timotheus and Dryden become one, is itself presented as something which might 'surprize'. In his *Dictionary* Johnson glossed the verb 'surprize' as 'to take unawares; to fall upon unexpectedly', giving, among other examples, one from Thomson's *Autumn*: 'Who can speak | The mingled passions that *surpriz'd* his heart!' (ll. 255–6). Pope's surprise, however, is worked towards by uneven steps. The attention until the last moment has been directed towards the action of the poem—towards Alexander and Timotheus rather than Dryden. It is Timotheus' 'vary'd Lays' that 'surprize' Alexander, that 'bid' his 'Alternate Passions' rise and fall. Pope then turns from Alexander to Timotheus' audience at large—'*Persians* and *Greeks* like *Turns of Nature* found'—before emerging with his general proposition:

> The Pow'r of Musick all our Hearts allow;
> And what *Timotheus* was, is *Dryden* now.

In this passage Pope appears to be suggesting a close association between 'nature', 'various verse', and 'passion'—between the

---

[5] Samuel Cobb in *Poetæ Britannici* (1700) expressed a similar paradox. Arguing that Dryden had 'exalted' the 'proper Phrase' of our 'tongue' and that 'Perfection from his Numbers sprung', Cobb went on to assert that 'His *Images* so strong and lively be, | I hear not Words alone but Substance see. | Adapted Speech, and just Expressions move | Our various Passions, Pity, Rage and Love.'

subject-matter, the art, and burning and melting, fury and tears.[6] Pope's closing couplet seems to assume that every heart recognizes both the power of music in general and the particular power of Dryden's verse in this poem—and that the two propositions are intimately connected.

Pope shared his impression of Dryden's poem with the civil servant and amateur poet Jabez Hughes, who in a poem *Upon Reading Mr. Dryden's Fables* (1721) praised the 'energy' displayed in *Alexander's Feast* to a similar degree and by similar means.[7] Pope and Hughes express a kindred response to this poem, a response that is markedly different in its emphases from those expressed in much twentieth-century commentary. Many recent commentators see the essential and governing point of *Alexander's Feast*, or find its centre of concern, residing in the attitude towards the action. For Pope the argument of the poem is simply described: 'the *World's Victor* stood subdu'd by *Sound'*. For modern readers the poem is interesting because Alexander is (or both Alexander and Timotheus are) made to seem, in various ways and to various degrees, absurd. Attention is drawn to the ignobility of the passions that Timotheus arouses, from maudlin sentimentality to murderous revenge, and to their outcome—the wanton destruction of Persepolis. Noticing that in 'The Cock and the Fox' (in *Fables*, 1700) Dryden had coined a phrasal verb 'Alexandered up' to describe 'Princes rais'd by Poets to the Gods' in 'lying Odes' (l. 660), and that in this ode Alexander is fully persuaded of his own divinity by Timotheus, some have tended to assume that Dryden was mocking William III in the guise of Alexander the Great, or was profoundly sceptical about the power of music, or the power of verse.[8]

---

[6] Pope's emphasis on passion is a stronger version of what became the standard praise of variety of numbers in Dryden's poem throughout the eighteenth century, e.g. in Edward Young's essay 'On Lyric Poetry' (1728) (*The Poems of Edward Young*, ed. John Mitford (1896), ii. 151).

[7] Repr. in *Dryden: The Critical Heritage*, ed. James and Helen Kinsley (London, 1971), pp. 248–53.

[8] See Bessie Profitt, 'Political Satire in Dryden's *Alexander's Feast*', *Texas Studies in Literature and Language*, 11 (1970) 1307–16; John Dawson Carl Buck, 'The Ascetic's Banquet: The Morality of *Alexander's Feast*', *Texas Studies in Literature and Language*, 17 (1975) 573–89; Ruth Smith, 'The Argument and Contexts of Dryden's *Alexander's Feast*', *Studies in English Literature*, 18 (1978) 465–90; Paul H. Fry, '"Alexander's Feast" and the Tyranny of Music', in *The Poet's Calling in the English Ode* (New Haven, 1980), pp. 49–62; W. B. Carnochan, 'Dryden's Alexander', in Robert Folkenflik (ed.), *The English Hero, 1660–1800* (Newark, NJ,

For both Pope and Hughes, in marked contradistinction, it appears to have been the sequence, the alternation of passions, that most impressed. It was clear that Alexander was 'subdu'd', but that was only part of the story. As Hughes retells the narrative, 'the flatter'd Monarch' is first lifted high with 'boasted Lineage, to his kindred Sky', and is then persuaded to 'the Pleasures of the flowing Bowl' to such an extent that he 'unbends his easy Soul' in 'mellow Mirth'. But Timotheus next evokes pity, and 'humbles' and 'saddens all the Feast, | With Sense of Human Miseries express'd', so that 'Relenting Pity in each Face appears, | And heavy Sorrow ripens into Tears'. At this point in the poem, as Hughes read it, the whole company becomes amorous:

> see in ev'ry Eye
> The Gaiety of Love, and wanton Joy,
> Soft Smiles and Airs, which tenderly inspire
> Delightful Hope, and languishing Desire.

And, finally, it is the whole audience that is inspired by a frenzy of revenge:

> But lo! the pealing Verse provokes around
> The Frown of Rage, and kindles with the Sound;
> Behold the low'ring Storm at once arise,
> And ardent Vengeance sparkling in their Eyes;
> Fury boils high, and Zeal of fell Debate,
> Demanding Ruin, and denouncing Fate.

Hughes, like Pope, appears to be more interested in the audience than in the particular case of Alexander. The fictional audience responds as one mind. Pope and Hughes appear to assume that readers feel what Alexander and his peers were made to feel under the powerful control of Timotheus' song (and therefore, perhaps, are in no position to deem themselves superior to the godlike hero). Timotheus is great because he has great power over a great mind—and over the minds of readers.[9] Hughes described

1982), pp. 46–60; Robert P. Maccubbin, 'The Ironies of Dryden's *Alexander's Feast; or The Power of Musique*: Texts and Contexts', *Mosaic*, 18/4 (1985) 33–47; Howard Erskine-Hill, *Poetry of Opposition and Revolution: Dryden to Wordsworth* (Oxford, 1996), pp. 40–3; Joshua Scodel, 'Lyric Forms', in Steven N. Zwicker (ed.), *The Cambridge Companion to English Literature 1650–1740* (Cambridge, 1997), p. 125.

[9] Similarly, an anonymous contributor to *The Occasional Paper*, 3/10 (1719) 10, writing on the subject 'Of Genius' in music, quotes the poem to illustrate the power of 'Genius' to

Alexander's Feast as a 'wond'rous Song' in which a 'flow of Rage comes hurrying on amain' with 'utmost Energy of Numbers strong':

> And now the refluent Tide ebbs out again;
> A quiet Pause succeeds; when unconfin'd
> It rushes back, and swells upon the Mind.

'The Mind' in this instance would appear to include the minds of the assembled Macedonians, the mind of Alexander, and every mind that reads the poem.

There are many reasons for thinking that Pope and Hughes shared their particular response to *Alexander's Feast* with the majority of readers of poetry for well over a century. The enthusiasm of the first generation to read the ode appears to have been transmitted to the second and third. So famous and widely known was the poem that its very fame could be used to make a point. There are, for example, several references to Dryden's poem in the novels of Samuel Richardson. At one point in *Clarissa* Lovelace mocks Belford's account of the growing influence of Scripture upon him by telling a story which he had from his tutor, warning him against exposing himself by 'ignorant wonder':

> The first time Dryden's *Alexander's Feast* fell into his hands, he told me, he was prodigiously charmed with it: And, having never heard anybody speak of it before, thought, as thou dost of the Bible, that he had made a new discovery.
>
> He hastened to an appointment which he had with several wits (for he was then in town) one of whom was a noted Critic, who, according to him, had more merit than good fortune; for all the little nibblers in wit, whose writings would not stand the test of criticism, made it, he said, a common cause to run him down, as men would a mad dog.

perform 'whatever the Artist intends' with 'equal Propriety and Elegance'. The earliest response to Dryden's poem appears to occur in the third act of *The Revengeful Queen* (1698) by William Phillips, where, following a song comparing the pleasures of love and drink and contrasting both with the pursuit of honour, Aistolfus proclaims his distaste for 'low effeminating Sounds', preferring to 'hear none but the lofty Phrygian Airs'. He would be happy if 'Timotheus alone shou'd play' to him: 'Who might Inspire me, like Alexander | With so much transporting Warmth and Courage | Cou'd force me, think, | Tho' o'er my Cups, I were at th'Army's Head, | And from the Table leap, to shake my Spear.' Aistolfus sees Alexander as both deluded and inspired. His friend Alboino, however, maintains that: ' 'Twas Wine inspir'd the Hero' and not Timotheus' 'Notes'.

The young gentleman (for young he then was) set forth magnificently in the praises of that inimitable performance; and gave himself airs of second-hand merit, for finding out its beauties.

The old Bard heard him out with a smile, which the collegian took for approbation, till he spoke; and then it was in these mortifying words: "Sdeath, Sir, where have you lived till now, or with what sort of company have you conversed, young as you are, that you have never before heard of the finest piece in the English Language!"[10]

Richardson's admiration for Dryden's poem and assumption of its universal popularity is equally clear in *Sir Charles Grandison*. After tea at Sir Charles's house in London, Harriet Byron entertains the company on the harpsichord, and is encouraged to play some Handel (whose setting of *Alexander's Feast* no doubt contributed to its popularity):

Come hither, come hither, my sweet Harriet—Here's his Alexander's Feast: My Brother admires that, I know; and says it is the noblest composition that ever was produced by man; and is as finely set, as written.

She made me sit down to the instrument.

As you know, said I, that great part of the beauty of this performance arises from the proper transitions from one different strain to another, any one song must lose greatly, by being taken out of its place; and I fear—

Fear nothing, Miss Byron, said Sir Charles: Your obligingness, as well as your observation, intitle you to all allowances.

I then turned to that fine piece of accompanied recitative:

> *Softly sweet, in Lydian measures,*
> *Soon he sooth'd his soul to pleasures.*[11]

Handel's setting is seen as reflecting, not replacing, Dryden's words. The praise of Dryden's poem is at the same pitch as that of the literary critic mentioned by Lovelace—the poem is 'the noblest composition that ever was produced by man', and is as finely written as set. The poem also serves as a suitably refined accompaniment to this early stage in the endless courtship of Harriet and Sir Charles. Much later in the novel, a similar scene leads to an impromptu concert, in which Sir Charles sings (predictably perhaps) with a 'mellow manly voice, and great command':

---

[10] Samuel Richardson, *Clarissa, or the History of a Young Lady* (1748), ed. Angus Ross (Harmondsworth, 1985), pp. 1146–7.

[11] *Sir Charles Grandison* (1753–4), ed. Jocelyn Harris (Oxford, 1986), p. 239.

Alexander's Feast

The song was from Alexander's Feast: The words,

> *Happy, happy, happy pair!*
> *None but the good deserves the fair,*

Sir Charles, tho' himself equally *brave* and *good*, preferring the latter word to the former. (p. 345)

On this occasion, Dryden's poem—now suitably emended—reflects the fidelity and virtue of Sir Charles. Richardson's citations show the degree and the extent of influence that Dryden's poem could be said to hold at the mid-century—it is freshly in the mind of both a notorious rake and a model of a 'perfect man', and can be made to serve as a reference point for the character of either.

If Richardson gave evidence of *Alexander's Feast* being familiar to the wide audience of prose fiction, perhaps the most striking reference to the poem in mid-eighteenth-century poetry was made by Thomas Gray in 'The Progress of Poesy' (written between September 1751 and December 1754). Gray centred his rhapsodic praise of Dryden on *Alexander's Feast*. Two coursers of ethereal race, 'With necks in thunder clothed, and long-resounding pace' (l. 106), bear Dryden's chariot 'wide o'er the fields of glory'. Gray, like Pope, identified the poet with the musician Timotheus:

> Hark, his hand the lyre explore!
> Bright-eyed Fancy hovering o'er
> Scatters from her pictur'd urn
> Thoughts that breathe, and words that burn.   (ll. 107–10)

Gray maintained (in a note that he added to the poem in 1768) that Dryden's poem was the only English example of a 'sublime' ode, Dryden having excelled Cowley, and not having been outdone by Pope: 'We have in our language no other odes of the sublime kind, than that of Dryden on St. Cecilia's day: for Cowley (who had his merit) yet wanted judgement, style, and harmony, for such a task. That of Pope is not worthy of so great a man.' The importance of Dryden's ode to Gray's composition was stressed by an anonymous reviewer in a highly imaginative account of this stanza of Gray's poem: 'The circumstance of Dryden's having written but one ode of the sublime and truly lyric kind, and suddenly withdrawing his masterly hand from those chords he knew full well to strike, is here

147

exquisitely expressed by an image of a musician unexpectedly pausing in the midst of his strain.'[12]

Something of what Gray might have had in mind in remarking that Pope's music ode was 'not worthy of so great a man' can be gathered from Joseph Warton's *Essay on the Writings and Genius of Pope*, where it is said of the poet that

He used to declare, that if Dryden had finished a translation of the Iliad, he would not have attempted one after so great a master; he might have said with more propriety, I will not write a music-ode after Alexander's Feast, which the variety and harmony of its numbers, and the beauty and force of its images, have conspired to place at the head of modern lyric compositions.[13]

As an illustration of these propositions, Warton mentions the moment in Pope's ode when the Argonauts react to the 'animating song' of Orpheus:[14]

> Each Chief his sevenfold Shield display'd
> And half unsheath'd the shining Blade.   (ll. 45–6)

These 'effects of the song', as Warton sees them, are 'lively', but 'do not equal the force and spirit of what Dryden ascribes to the song of his Grecian artist':

When Timotheus cries out REVENGE, raises the furies, and calls up to Alexander's view a troop of Grecian ghosts that were slain and left

---

[12] Review of *A Cursory Examination of Dr Johnson's Strictures on the Lyric Performances of Gray*, in *The Gentleman's Magazine*, 52 (1782) 33. Gray's emphatic praise of *Alexander's Feast* may have convinced many eighteenth-century readers that Dryden's ode remained the finest in the language, in that the only serious rivals were Gray's own odes, particularly 'The Bard'. For instance Goldsmith, in his anonymous 1758 review of Gray's *Odes*, averred that 'The Bard' 'will give as much pleasure to those who relish this species of composition, as any thing that has hitherto appeared in our language, the Odes of Dryden himself notwithstanding' (*Monthly Review*, 17 (1757) 241); cf. 'Philo Lyristes' in *The Gentleman's Magazine*, 52 (1782) 22. In his edition of Pope's *Works*, Joseph Warton placed *Alexander's Feast* 'at the head of modern Lyric compositions', but added the comment 'always excepting *The Bard* of Gray' (*The Works of Pope*, 9 vols. (London, 1797, repr. 1822), i. 197).

[13] *An Essay on the Writings and Genius of Pope* (London, 1762), i. 50. Pope expressed a similar sentiment to Joseph Spence in 1735: 'Many people would like my ode on music better, if Dryden had never written on that subject' (*Observations, Anecdotes, and Characters of Books and Men*, ed. James M. Osborn, 2 vols. (Oxford, 1966), i. 28).

[14] This was also Johnson's favourite stanza, in which 'there are numbers, images, harmony, and vigour, not unworthy the antagonist of Dryden. Had all been like this—but every part cannot be the best' ('Life of Pope', in *The Lives of the English Poets*, ed. George Birkbeck Hill, 3 vols. (Oxford, 1905), iii. 228).

unburied, inglorious and forgotten, each of them waving a torch in his hand, and pointing to the hostile temples of the Persians, and demanding vengeance of their prince, he instantly started from his throne,

> Seiz'd a flambeau with zeal to destroy

while Thais and the attendant princes rushed out with him, to set fire to the city. (i. 53)

The liveliness of Dryden's narrative convinced Warton that 'the whole train of imagery in this stanza is alive, sublime, and animated to an unparalleled degree; the poet has so strongly possessed himself of the action described, that he places it fully before the eyes of the reader' (i. 53). It may have been this conviction that prompted Warton in his edition of Pope's *Works* to give credence to the anecdote in which Dryden was discovered one morning 'in an unusual agitation of spirits, even to a trembling', and on being asked the cause, replied: 'I have been up all night...my musical friends made me promise to write them an ode for their Feast of St. Cecilia: I have been so struck with the subject which occurred to me, that I could not leave it till I had completed it; here it is finished at one sitting' (i. 201). As Warton experienced the poem, 'The rapidity, and yet the perspicuity of the thoughts, and the glow and the expressiveness of the images, those certain marks of the first sketch of a master, conspire to corroborate the fact' (i. 82–3). The poet, as it were, saw the action himself, and 'places it fully before the eyes of the reader', who sees it too.

As was the case for Richardson, Warton's pleasure in *Alexander's Feast* was deepened but not limited by Handel's setting.[15] His appreciation rests, like that of Pope, Hughes, and Gray, partly on the comprehensiveness of the poem, in which he found Dryden to have 'introduced and expressed all the greater passions', and partly on the 'transitions from one to the other' which are 'sudden and impetuous'—particularly when the 'pathetic description of the fall of Darius immediately succeeds the joyous praises of Bacchus'. In the concert-hall as when reading in private, these transitions are such that 'we feel the effects': 'The symphony, and air particularly, that accompanies the four words, "fallen, fallen, fallen, fallen," is

---

[15] But Horace Walpole 'thought Dryden's *Ode* more harmonious before he set it than after' (*The Correspondence of Horace Walpole*, ed. W. S. Lewis *et al.*, 48 vols. (1937–83), xxviii. 354 (12 Feb. 1778)).

strangely moving, and consists of a few simple and touching notes' (i. 83). Similar thoughts seem to underlie Samuel Johnson's discussions of *Alexander's Feast*. In his 'Life of Dryden', Johnson presents himself as endorsing the common view: 'The ode for *St. Cecilia's Day*, perhaps the last effort of his poetry, has been always considered as exhibiting the highest flight of fancy and the exactest nicety of art. This is allowed to stand without a rival.'[16] Johnson presumably included the versification of the poem in the phrase 'the exactest nicety of art'. In the opening pages of *Rambler* 88, when writing about the versification of *Paradise Lost*, he maintained that 'from the proper disposition of single sounds results that harmony that adds force to reason, and gives grace to sublimity; that shackles attention and governs passion'. In *Rambler* 86 he had argued that it was the 'peculiar superiority' of poets that to the other powers 'by which the understanding is enlightened, or the imagination enchanted', the poet adds 'the faculty of joining music with reason, and of acting at once upon the senses and the passions'.[17] 'Passions' here is perhaps not quite the expected term, not quite the expected parallel with 'reason'—for which 'mind' might seem more appropriate. One effect, it would seem, of verse harmony upon the mind is passion—but passion that is governed.

Johnson's comments on *Alexander's Feast* in the 'Life of Dryden' are immediately followed by his broad estimate of Dryden's poetic abilities: 'In a general survey of Dryden's labours he appears to have had a mind very comprehensive by nature, and much enriched with acquired knowledge. His compositions are the effects of a vigorous genius operating upon large materials.'[18] Here too, Johnson appears to be reflecting common opinion, that *Alexander's Feast* embodied Dryden's essential claims to poetical excellence, to the highest flights of fancy and the exactest nicety of art. The ode was evidence of the comprehensiveness of his mind and the endurance of his poetical 'spirit', his poetical 'fire' into extreme old age. Jabez Hughes, for example, described the usual debilitating concomitants of old age which 'dishonouring our Kind, | Robs all the Treasures

---

[16] *Lives*, i. 456.

[17] *The Yale Edition of the Works of Samuel Johnson*, ed. W. Jackson Bate *et al.*, 12 vols. (New Haven, 1958–), iv. 99, 89. For Johnson on Dryden's odes, see Greg Clingham, 'Johnson's Criticism of Dryden's Odes in Praise of St Cecilia', *Modern Language Studies*, 18 (1988) 165–80. [18] *Lives*, i. 457.

of the wasted Mind', only to maintain that Dryden had defied (indeed, improved with) Time:

> But the rich Fervour of his rising Rage
> Prevail'd o'er all th' Infirmities of Age;
> And, unimpair'd by Injuries of Time,
> Enjoy'd the Bloom of a perpetual Prime:
> His Fire not less, he more correctly writ,
> With ripen'd Judgment and digested Wit.

As Hughes continues to elaborate his case, 'succeeding Years' had first 'tam'd' the 'luxuriant Ardour of his Youth' to produce 'better Growth'. Then Dryden's spirit seemed to break through the 'Body's Crust' to give 'th' expanded Mind more Room to play', a mind that shone with a light like the sun's:

> Which, in its Evening, open'd on the Sight
> Surprizing Beams of full Meridian Light,
> As thrifty of its Splendor it had been,
> And all its Lustre had reserv'd 'till then.

It appears that William Congreve was entirely representative in maintaining that Dryden's 'Parts did not decline with his Years' and that he was an 'improving Writer to his last, even to near seventy Years of Age; improving even in Fire and Imagination, as well as in Judgement: Witness his Ode on St. *Cecilia*'s Day, and his Fables, his latest Performances'.[19] There is a great deal of evidence to suggest that the esteem for Dryden's ode implied by these testimonies was almost universal until well into the nineteenth century, and that admiration for the ode played a large part in Dryden's general standing.

The claim that *Alexander's Feast* was an example of unsurpassed excellence is made explicit when Johnson returns to the poem in the course of a discussion in the *Lives* of Pope's *Ode for St. Cecilia's Day*. Again, Johnson records common opinion: Pope, in this ode, 'is generally confessed to have miscarried' (*Lives*, iii.226). Johnson then adds a comment, probably reflecting Pope's own remarks, to the effect that his ode would have been better appreciated had Dryden not written first. As Johnson saw it, Pope had 'miscarried only as

---

[19] William Congreve, Epistle Dedicatory to *The Dramatick Works of John Dryden, Esq: In Six Volumes* (1717), repr. in *Dryden: The Critical Heritage*, p. 265.

compared with Dryden for he has far outgone all others' (p. 226). The comparison with Pope prompts Johnson to use a different set of critical terms to describe *Alexander's Feast*. He now describes Dryden's poem as exciting passions—passions that are 'the pains and pleasures of real life': 'Dryden's plan is better chosen; history will always take stronger hold of the attention than fable: the passions excited by Dryden are the pleasures and pains of real life, the scene of Pope is laid in imaginary existence.'[20] Johnson's distinction between Dryden's ode and Pope's is pertinent to the present argument in that some readers, ancient and modern, seem to have found it difficult to ground their own esteem for the poem on satisfactory critical principles, or to account for its enduring popularity. Few denied the claims of *Alexander's Feast* (as of Dryden's poetry generally) to mastery and innovation of versification. But it was not always easy to go beyond that. There appeared to have been conceptual gaps, as it were, between observation of the sophistication of the 'numbers', readers' experience of being hurried out of themselves, and the critical proposition that the poem was sublime or noble—'the noblest composition that ever was produced by man'.

Walter Scott (following Johnson) argued in his 'Life of John Dryden' (1808) that though a poet 'may be possessed of the primary quality of poetical conception to the highest possible extent' he is 'but like a lute without its strings' unless he also possesses the 'power of expressing what he feels and conceives in appropriate language': 'With this power Dryden's poetry was gifted in a degree, surpassing in modulated harmony that of all who had preceded him, and inferior to none that has since written English verse. He first shewed that the English language was capable of uniting smoothness and strength.'[21] For Scott, this power was supremely demonstrated in lyrical poetry in which 'Dryden must be allowed to have no equal'. Again it is *Alexander's Feast* that was made to prove the point. That ode is alone 'sufficient to show' Dryden's 'supremacy in that brilliant department': 'In this exquisite production, he flung from him all the trappings with which his contemporaries had embarrassed the

---

[20] *Lives*, iii. 227. Warton expressed similar sentiments: 'The subject of Dryden's ode is superior to . . . Pope's, because the former is historical, and the latter merely mythological. Dryden's is also more perfect in the unity of action; for Pope's is not the recital of one great action, but a description of many of the adventures of Orpheus' (*Works of Pope*, i. 197).

[21] *The Works of John Dryden*, ed. Walter Scott, 18 vols. (London, 1808), i. 485.

ode. The language, lofty and striking as the ideas are, is equally simple and harmonious; without far-fetched allusions, or epithets, or metaphors, the story is told as intelligibly as if it had been in the most humble prose' (i. 489). Scott's experience of the poem appears to have resembled that of every other reader: 'The change of tone in the harp of Timotheus, regulates the measure and the melody, and the language of every stanza. The hearer, while he is led on by the successive changes, experiences almost the feelings of the Macedonian and his peers' (i. 490). Henry Hallam, however, reviewing Scott's edition in 1808, found the affective power of this poem more difficult to explain:

In what does this superiority consist? Not in the sublimity of its conceptions; or the richness of its language, the passage about Jupiter and Olympia alone excepted. Some lines are little better than a common drinking song, and few of them have singly any great merit. It must be the rapid transitions, the mastery of language, the springiness of the whole manner, which hurries us away and leaves so little room for minute criticism, that no one has ever qualified his admiration for this noble poem.[22]

Johnson, in contrast, in preferring Dryden's ode to Pope's, appears to be demanding a very close association of three aspects: the story, the verse, and the affective power. It is the unreality of the story in Pope's ode that leaves the sound hanging on the ear and prevents it from taking a firm hold on the mind. Dryden's poem, however, takes hold on the attention because sound is at the service of, or is an expression or embodiment of, sense and passion. Johnson complains that in Pope's ode the second stanza 'consists of hyperbolical commonplaces', the fourth and fifth 'detain us in the dark and dismal regions of mythology where neither hope nor fear, neither joy nor sorrow can be found'. Johnson seems to be making a comparison between the (relatively) empty sound of Pope's poem and the solid matter and human passions of Dryden's. In parts of Pope's poem, we have 'all that can be performed by elegance of diction or sweetness of versification'. Johnson's final judgement, however, is encapsulated in the rhetorical question: 'what can form avail without better matter?' (*Lives*, iii. 227–8). Johnson's ultimate criterion is the power of Dryden's poem on 'the mind': 'Pope is read with calm acquiescence, Dryden with turbulent delight; Pope hangs

---

[22] Henry Hallam, *Edinburgh Review* (Oct. 1808) 132.

upon the ear, and Dryden finds the passes of the mind' (iii. 227). While it was not clear if the passions of 'real life' were excited in Alexander, in the fictional audience, or in the reader, it is clearly the reader whose attention is held, the reader who feels turbulent delight, and the reader the 'passes' of whose mind are found.

In his *Dictionary* Johnson glosses 'PASS. n.s.' as a 'narrow entrance; an avenue', citing 'The straight pass was damm'd | With dead men' from *Cymbeline* (where the sense is literal), and a metaphorical use from one of Robert South's sermons: 'Truth is a strong hold, fortified by God and nature, and diligence is properly the understanding's laying siege to it; so that it must be perpetually observing all the avenues and *passes* to it, and accordingly making its approaches.' Interestingly, the 'passes of the mind' were, in verse, usually evidence of the undesirable vulnerability of the mind. Tom Brown, for example, in his 'Satire against Woman' (*ante* 1704) uses the phrase to describe the dangers presented to men by the female mind, 'that various and that changeful Thing':

> Now sprightly Motion arms her wanton Eye,
> Then in soft Languishments she'll seem to die,
> Thus all the unguarded <u>Passes of his Mind</u> she'll try;
> 'Till vanquish'd by her strong bewitching Charms,
> He falls a willing Pris'ner to her Arms,
> There meets a Veng'ance of ne'er ending Harms.

Similarly, John Williams, in a poem 'From the High Topmast of this Nether World' (1800), advised his readers to 'Avoid potations deep of Barley juice' which 'whirl the Senses in a maddening round' till 'Reason quits the <u>passes of the mind</u>', and Edward Young, in the second book of *The Force Of Religion* (1714), describes a 'subtle priest' who 'with insidious art' instils 'his poison' into the heart of his victim and finds the 'most unguarded <u>passes of her mind</u>'.

Johnson's thought is presumably that Pope's ode which 'hangs upon the ear' has no power to penetrate further, while Dryden's by subtle means finds secret passages into the recesses of the mind, where it causes 'turbulent delight'. Johnson was presumably recalling and recounting his own experience,[23] but there is a good deal of

---

[23] Johnson appears to have found any possible excuse to quote from Dryden's ode in his *Dictionary*, for example citing it under 'Allow', 'Alternate', 'Divide', 'Hiss', 'Joyless', and 'Melt'. In a letter of 21 June 1775 Johnson quotes Timotheus when telling Mrs Thrale that 'If

partially, in the mind. They imply general thought or observation upon human life that may extend beyond the immediate context. They hint at harmony in that they mark themselves as metrical units, distinguished from the irregularities of speech or prose by the clear (although slight) presence of the rhythmical patterns of sound. Commentary on *Alexander's Feast*, in the form of imitation, emulation, encomium, and parody, is so rich and various that the interaction of the poem with many minds can be minutely particularized. Johnson described the 'force' of Dryden's 'genius' as one which 'collects, combines, amplifies and animates', and it is possible to determine precisely from where Dryden collected his words and phrases, how he combined them, and by what means they were amplified, so that one may ascertain precisely what it was in the poem that Dryden added to the phrasing of his predecessors and transmitted to his successors. Those phrases that operated in the memories of later poets are often those where Dryden's contribution appears to have been minute—a tiny addition to a pre-existing formulation, a recombination of almost traditional elements. And yet some of the phrases with which the feast is described, and some of the phrases with which Timotheus controlled the passions of Alexander, seem to have constituted for many poets in the eighteenth century, and some in the nineteenth, an almost inevitable vocabulary when certain occasions or subject-matters presented themselves.

To judge from the frequency with which the phrases were borrowed, it seemed particularly important to later poets that Alexander was called '*Philip*'s Warlike son'; that Alexander and Thais sat 'Aloft in awful State'; that Alexander sat 'On his Imperial Throne'; that his valiant peers were crowned 'with Roses and with Myrtles'; that Timotheus touched his lyre with 'flying Fingers' to produce 'trembling Notes'; that Jove 'left his blissful Seats above' and rode 'on Radiant Spires'; that Timotheus was a 'sweet Musician'; that Alexander, believing himself a god, 'Heav'n and Earth defy'd'; that Darius was 'fallen, | Fallen from his high Estate'—and so on throughout every stanza (but not every line) of the poem. On a large variety of disparate occasions, Dryden's words appear to have suggested themselves to later poets, not only for incidental details, but also occasionally as more profoundly shaping elements. A selection of such phrases will illustrate the suggestive power of the poem.

FLYING FINGERS

When Thomas Gray in *The Progress of Poesy* depicted Dryden as a figure like Timotheus, he was responding to an image which seems to have provided a model for several other poets:

> *Timotheus* plac'd on high
>   Amid the tuneful Quire,
>   With <u>flying Fingers touch'd the Lyre</u>
> The trembling Notes ascend the Sky,
>   And heavenly joys <u>inspire</u>.   (ll. 20–4)

A closer examination of the origins of the phrase that Gray takes from Dryden's poem reveals an interesting and recurrent pattern: Dryden is not the originator of the phrase, but a modifier and combiner of words that had been loosely associated before. Timotheus' 'flying fingers' appear to have been acquired from Cowley's play *The Guardian* (1650), where Truman describes the woman he loves:[25]

> Did she but touch her Lute (the pleasing'st harmony
> Then upon earth, when she her self was silent)
> The subtil motion of her <u>flying fingers</u>
> Taught Musick a new art, To take the sight
> As well as th'ear.   (v. ii)

If Cowley is not Dryden's source, the most likely precedent is the description of a frieze in William Davenant's *Gondibert* (1651), from which Dryden may have derived his verbs 'touched' and 'inspire':

> Toss'd Cymballs (which the sullen Jewes admir'd)
>   Were figur'd here, with all of ancient choice
> That joy did ere invent, or breath <u>inspir'd</u>,
>   Or <u>flying Fingers touch'd</u> into a voice.   (II. vi. 191–4)

The phrase was first used by Dryden in his translation of *The Aeneid* describing the '<u>flying Fingers</u>, and harmonious Quill' of Orpheus in Elysium (VI. 879). In this case, as in many moments in *Alexander's Feast*, Dryden was epitomizing his own earlier work (particularly his Virgil). The distinct contribution made to the phrase by its setting in

---

[25] The lines appear little changed in Cowley's revised version of the play in 1663, *Cutter of Coleman Street*, the performance of which Dryden may have attended. See James Winn, *John Dryden and his World* (New Haven, 1987), p. 123.

Dryden's ode is clear from its reflection in Nicholas Rowe's tragedy *The Royal Convert* (1708), where an analogy is drawn between musicianship and successful advocacy in love:

> The String that jars,
> When rudely touch'd ungrateful to the Sense,
> With pleasure feels the Master's flying Fingers,
> Swells into Harmony, and charms the Hearers.   (III. i)

'Flying fingers' are here the sign of a master musician, such as Timotheus was. (Dryden had called him 'the Master' (l. 69) and the 'Mighty Master' (l. 93).) The attribution of 'flying fingers' to a master musician who was able thereby to 'inspire' appropriate passions appears to have constituted a template on which later poets were able to ground their imaginings. So James Thomson, in a well-known passage from *The Castle of Indolence* (1748), uses Dryden's phrase to describe the movement of the wind over an Aeolian harp:

> From which, with airy flying fingers light,
> Beyond each mortal touch the most refined,
> The god of winds drew sounds of deep delight:
> Whence, with just cause, the Harp of Aeolus it hight.
> Ah me! what hand can touch the string so fine?
>
> (I. xl–xli. 357–61)

In effect, the depersonalized fingers of the airy wind cause a succession of emotional equivalents in the music, similar to the pattern of emotions raised up by Timotheus.

In Thomson's poem, the wind-inspired music is 'above the reach of Art', like the 'nameless graces' which 'a master hand alone can reach' described by Pope in *An Essay on Criticism* (ll. 141 ff.). The more common response to Dryden's ode appears to have seen Timotheus as combining the full force of nature with the highest reaches of art. In William Collins's 'The Passions: An Ode for Music' (1746), for example, Timotheus' musical powers over the human passions become almost an emblem of the ideal poet. This is made most clear when into the procession of Collins's personified passions comes Joy:

> To some unwearied minstrel dancing,
> While as his flying fingers kissed the strings,
> Love framed with Mirth a gay fantastic round.   (ll. 88–90)

The relationship between the touch of Timotheus' fingers and the human emotions they inspire is made closer in Collins than in Dryden. Timotheus 'touched' the strings and inspired love. In Collins's poem, human love is implicit in the very action of the musician's hands, which 'kissed' the strings. By contrast, in another passage

> Next Anger rushed, his eyes on fire,
>   In lightnings owned his secret stings,
> In one rude clash he struck the lyre
>   And swept with hurried hand the strings.   (ll. 21–4)

Collins appears to have conflated the beginning and the end of Dryden's action, turning the virtuosity of Timotheus' fingers into the sharp, abrupt collision of anger with the instrument. Where Timotheus had 'touched' the lyre, Collins has the lyre 'struck' (as towards the end of Dryden's poem, Alexander is roused from his slumbers by a sudden crescendo: 'Now strike the Golden Lyre again', l. 123). A general thought about the relation between human actions and the human soul appears to have found the passes of his mind in indissoluble association with an alliterative phrase and the hint of a picture.[26]

BLOOMING EASTERN BRIDES

Byron, in a very free paraphrase from the *Prometheus Vinctus* of Aeschylus (written as a school exercise), has the Chorus addressing the chained Prometheus on the subject of his former grandeur:

> How different now thy joyless fate,
>   Since first Hesione thy bride,
> When plac'd aloft in godlike state,
>   The blushing beauty by thy side,
> Thou sat'st.[27]

---

[26] 'Flying fingers' also appear in John Dart's translation of Tibullus' fourth elegy (1720); in William Thompson's *Nativity: a College Exercise* (1736); a notebook poem of Thomas Parnell, 'To —— on the various Styles of Poetry'; Francis Fawkes's 'A Mechanical Solution of the Propagation of Yawning' (1761); William Dodd's 'Cupid Detected: To Miss W——N'; William Cowper's translation of Milton's Latin elegy 'To Charles Diodati' (1792); and Thomas Love Peacock's *The Genius of the Thames* (1810).

[27] Dated 1 December 1804. Byron, in delaying the verb, appears to be combining memories of Dryden and Milton (*Paradise Lost*, ii. 1–5).

In writing this Byron seems to have recalled Dryden's scene as a whole. For him, it appears, Alexander resembled other 'godlike' figures in that his moment of (temporarily) assured glory combined being 'plac'd aloft' with the presence 'by his side' of 'beauty':

> His valiant Peers were <u>plac'd</u> around,
> > Their Brows with Roses and with Myrtles bound.
> (So shou'd Desert in Arms be Crown'd:)
> The <u>Lovely *Thais*</u> by his side,
> Sate like <u>a blooming *Eastern* Bride</u>
> In Flow'r of <u>Youth and Beauty's Pride</u>. (ll. 6–11)

It was this image of the godlike hero seated next to his concubine that, perhaps more than any other in the poem, impressed later poets. Lovely Thais, sitting by the side of Alexander '<u>like a blooming *Eastern* Bride</u>', appears to have been peculiarly beloved.[28]

Surprisingly enough, Dryden's Thais appears to have been the first female figure to have been described as an 'eastern bride' in English poetry. It may have come into Dryden's mind that in *Gondibert* (1651) one of the Heroines is described as '<u>like</u> an <u>Eastern</u> Monarch's <u>Bride</u>' (III. i. 47). The borrowing (if it is one) would be purely verbal. Davenant's bride is bashful and hides a 'rising Heart, behind a falling Look'—entirely unlike Dryden's, who burns the whole place down. What seems more certain is that the last three feet of the line '<u>In</u> Flow'r of <u>Youth and Beauty's Pride</u>' are derived from Cowley, who wrote in 'The Chronicle' of a 'gracious Princess' who 'dy'd | <u>In</u> her <u>Youth and Beauties pride</u>' (ll. 34–5). Cowley seems to have used the word 'pride' to mean 'most excellent or flourishing state or condition' (*OED* 9). Although 'blooming youths' were common, Dryden's Thais seems to have been the first 'blooming bride' in English verse, and is therefore one of Dryden's contributions to the phrasal inheritance of the English language. Again, a very slight adjustment of inherited materials had

---

[28] In a letter to Tonson, written either just before or just after the first performance of *Alexander's Feast*, Dryden asked his publisher to 'Remember in the Copy of Verses for St. Cecilia, to alter the name of Lais, wch is twice there, for Thais; those two Ladyes were Contemporaryes, wch caused that small mistake' (*Letters*, p. 96). It looks as if Dryden, having confused two famous Greek courtesans, had given the name of Alexander's companion as 'Lais' in the copy of the poem he had sent to the printer. Interestingly, Edward Thompson (1738–86) in his *Meretriciad*, restored Dryden's adjective to the Corinthian courtesan: '<u>lovely</u> <u>Lais</u> of Trinacria's Isle, | Who all the youth of Corinth did defile'.

long consequences.[29] But the afterlife of this fragment of Dryden's phraseology appears to have been one largely independent of the intellectual colouring of its original context. Despite the resemblance of wording, in very few cases does the later poem in any way recall the earlier in terms of theme or attitude, and if Dryden's words were in the memories of later poets, they existed there almost as free-floating fragments.[30] On the other hand, that some of these blooming brides were the daughters of Dryden's Thais, and that the later use reflects a direct engagement with Dryden's imagining, is suggested by the fact that in some cases the chosen vocabulary echoes Dryden's poem in apparently insignificant detail. Dryden's parentage seems clear, for example, in Thomas Campbell's *The Turkish Lady* (1804) where 'at Rhodes the British lover | Clasped his <u>blooming Eastern bride</u>' (ll. 40–1). Similarly, *Suppressed Evidence* (1813) by George Daniel contains a description of a wedding that has distinct eastern touches, and provides an account, perhaps, of what the author saw when he read this moment in *Alexander's Feast*: 'And next him sat his youthful <u>Bride</u>, | A <u>blooming</u> nymph, <u>in beauty's pride</u>'. In many cases, it is the relative placing of bride and groom that recalls that of Alexander and his concubine. John Wolcot's *Ode to Hymen* (1816) tells the story of a man who 'dove-tail'd to a devil of a wife', who is described as 'all young and beauteous, <u>by his side,</u> | His soft, fresh-<u>blooming</u>, incense-breathing <u>bride</u>'. Tellingly, in both these cases the rhymes are Dryden's.

On these occasions, Dryden's 'blooming eastern bride' represents or contains within itself the fragment of a significant miniature narrative. In several cases, Dryden's poem appears to have contributed to the available vocabulary not of words alone, but the stock of expressive imagery—conveyed, at least in part, by metrical pattern. The adaptability of Dryden's phrases might be explained by

[29] So Thomas Blacklock in *Graham* (1774) has 'his <u>blooming bride</u>', as does Henry Boyd in *The Royal Marriage* (1793). The Chadwyck–Healey database reveals many in nineteenth-century poetry, but it is perhaps only in Christina Rossetti's 'Light Love' that there is much attempt to reinvigorate the metaphor: ' "Now never teaze me, tender-eyed, | Sigh-voiced," he said in scorn: | "For nigh at hand there blooms a bride, | My bride before the morn; | Ripe-blooming she, as thou forlorn. | Ripe-blooming she, my rose, my peach".'

[30] An example of Dryden's phrases being applied in an utterly different context is the adaptation of the line where Timotheus '<u>Chang'd</u> his <u>hand</u>, and <u>check'd</u> his Pride' in Charles Lamb's poem 'On an Infant Dying as Soon as Born': 'Shall we say, that Nature blind | <u>Check'd</u> her <u>hand</u>, and <u>changed</u> her mind'.

pointing to the absence of an inbuilt moral intention, and the presence of what was in the eighteenth century commonly called a 'thought'.[31] In this case, the thought might be associated with ideas of human happiness—Thais like a flower in bloom representing to readers of Dryden's poem the sum of earthly bliss, perhaps. What seems not to have been carried over from Dryden's poem was any suggestion that Thais was an improper object of Alexander's affections, was harbouring malicious thoughts of her own, or even that her 'prime' hinted, say, at 'the common fate of all things rare' that are 'so wondrous sweet and fair', as Waller put it.

HONOUR BUT AN EMPTY BUBBLE

The one place, however, where a 'thought', or a particular combination of image and 'thought', does seem to have carried with it some of its original import occurs in the stanza where Timotheus begins to soothe Alexander's soul by singing of the pointlessness of war and the pleasures of love:

> War, he sung, is <u>Toil and Trouble</u>;
> <u>Honour but an empty Bubble</u>.
>   Never ending, still beginning,
> Fighting still, and still destroying;   (ll. 99–102)

In the fourth edition of his *Dictionary* Johnson offers two definitions of the word 'Bubble'. The first is 'a small bladder of water; a film of water filled with wind', a definition which is illustrated by a quotation from Bacon's *Sylva Sylvarum* (1627): '*Bubbles* are in the form of a hemisphere; air within, and a little skin of water without.' The second definition is 'any thing which wants solidity and firmness; any thing that is more specious than real'. This is illustrated by two passages. One is Jaques's speech from *As You Like It*:

> Then a soldier,
> Seeking the *bubble* reputation,
> Even in the cannon's mouth.

The other is from Dryden's ode:

---

[31] As Pope in *An Essay on Criticism* complains of bad poems, where only the last couplet is 'fraught | With some *unmeaning* Thing they call a *Thought*' (ll. 356–7).

> War, he sung, is toil and trouble,
> Honour but an empty *bubble*,
> Fighting still, and still destroying.

Johnson's entry represents what appear to be the essential elements of the history of the word 'bubble' as a metaphorical poetic term—but in outline only.

The word 'bubble' (with implications close to Johnson's second definition) was, for example, a favourite of Spenser's.[32] He uses it in *The Ruines of Time* as part of a comparison of man and a glass vessel full of wind:

> Why then dooth flesh, a <u>bubble</u> glas of breath,
> Hunt after <u>honour</u> and aduauncement vaine,   (ll. 50–1)

The similarity between Spenser's vocabulary and sentiment and that expressed by Jaques becomes clear when Johnson's quotation from *As You Like It* is given in full, so that 'honour' and the 'bubble reputation' follow each other closely:

> Then, a soldier,
> Full of strange oaths, and bearded like the pard,
> Jealous in <u>honour</u>, sudden, and quick in quarrel,
> Seeking the <u>bubble</u> reputation
> Even in the cannon's mouth.   (ii. vii. 149–53)

It appears to have been Samuel Butler who brought honour and the bubble into immediate conjunction. Butler seems to have read Jaques's sentiment with Falstaff as commentary: 'What is honour? A word. What is in that word honour? What is that honour? Air' (*1 Henry IV*, v. i. 134–5). Butler's contribution to the phrasing and the idea appears to have been the rhyme between 'trouble' and 'bubble':

> <u>Honour</u> is like that glassy <u>Bubble</u>
> That finds Philosophers such <u>trouble</u>,
> .   .   .   .   .   .
> Quoth Ralpho, <u>Honor's</u> but a Word,
>   (*Hudibras*, Part 2, ii. 391–3, 395)

---

[32] 'Bubble' suggesting an existence lacking solidity and firmness, more specious than real, is also to be found in sonnet LVIII of Spenser's *Amoretti*. In 'Februarie' from *The Shepheardes Calender* 'Youngth is a <u>bubble</u> blown vp with breath' (l. 87).

It may have been a recognition of Shakespearian presence in Butler's lines that recalled to Dryden's mind the words of the witches
from *Macbeth*: 'Double, double <u>toil and trouble</u>' (IV. i. 10). Dryden's
original contribution appears, once again, to have been minute. It
consisted in no more than the addition of the word 'empty' to
'bubble' when the phrase is applied to the pursuit of honour or
(generally military) renown:

> War, he sung, is <u>Toil and Trouble</u>;
> <u>Honour</u> but <u>an empty Bubble.</u>   (ll. 99–100)

However minute, Dryden's phrase 'empty bubble' was lastingly
consequential, perhaps because it proved adaptable. It appears to
have been the 'image', rather than an attitude to war, that attracted
later poets. A string of related abstract nouns could be described as
'empty bubbles', whether of honour, or renown, or glory—or, in
one case, love.[33]

In the first scene of the third act of Nicholas Rowe's *The Tragedy
of Lady Jane Gray* (1715), for example, we find 'glory' described by
the heroine as 'a Toy I wou'd not purchase, | <u>An</u> idle, <u>empty</u>
<u>Bubble</u>'. Dryden's adjective seems to have become so firmly attached
to the bubble that it remained even when the abstract noun was
Shakespeare's. So in James Hurdis's *The Relapse* (1810) the 'empty
bubble' is conflated with Shakespeare's 'bubble of renown' to
produce 'the <u>empty bubble</u> of renoun'. Samuel Egerton Brydges's
Human Fate (written in 1831) retraces the history of the phrase:

> We lead a life of lost and anxious care
> <u>Honours</u> to win, which some pronounce a breath,
> <u>An empty bubble</u>! And which, after all,
> As Falstaff says, Detraction clouds and covers!

Shakespeare and Dryden were associated in ever odder ways and
stranger places. In his amalgamation of Shakespeare's *Measure for
Measure* and Purcell's *Dido and Aeneas*, entitled *Measure for Measure,
Or Beauty the Best Advocate* (1699), Charles Gildon placed a masque
that contains one of the earliest sustained reminiscences of Dryden's
poem:

---

[33] In Act III of Congreve's *Semele* (1710), Juno's song uses vocabulary from *Alexander's
Feast*: 'Above measure | Is the Pleasure | Which my Revenge supplies. | Love's a Bubble |
Gain'd with Trouble, | And in possessing dies.'

Fame's a <u>Bubble</u>,
<u>Honour but a</u> Glorious <u>Trouble</u>,
A vain Pride of <u>Destroying</u>,
Alarming and Arming,
And <u>Toiling</u> and Moiling,
And never <u>Enjoying</u>.
—'Twas that gave Hector

.   .   .   .

Renoun and Fame.
An <u>empty</u> Name,
And Lamentable Fate.   (II. ii)

In Gildon's masque, it is fame that is the bubble, and honour the trouble. The senselessness of war is suggested, as in Dryden, by the contrast between destroying and enjoying. Even the word 'empty' is not forgotten but transferred to Hector's 'name'.

NEVER ENDING, STILL BEGINNING

It seems to be the case that many of Dryden's phrases lodged in a poet's mind partly or largely on account of their metrical pattern, however fragmentary: Gildon uses 'hónour bút a' presumably because of the memorability of the trochaic rhythms and the internal consonances of Dryden's phrasing. In one instance it might be said that the 'thought' is carried principally by the metrical pattern—Timotheus' description of war as 'Never ending, still beginning'.

James Burnett, Lord Monboddo (1714–99), the eccentric primitivist, in a manuscript analysis of the versification of Dryden's poem, commented that

To Pity naturally succeeds Love, which he describes in the next Stanza, beginning with four Iambics . . . Then he changes to the Trochaic in which he goes on for four verses—

> 'Softly sweet in Lydian measures,
> 'Soon he soothed his soul to pleasures,
> 'War, he sung, was toil & trouble,
> 'Honour but an empty bubble

Then he goes on in the same Measure, but varying the Rhyme to alternate, instead of the common Rhyme,

'Never ending, still beginning,
'Fighting still, and still destroying,
'If the World be worth thy winning
'Think, O think it worth enjoying

At this point Monboddo added a comment as an afterthought in the margin:

where the reader may observe that the composition is agreeably varied by turning to Alexander and addressing the two last lines to him: a like figure of Speech is to be found in Virgil, and also in Milton and it may be also observed that the double Rhymes, or Rhymes of two Syllables appear to be very well adapted to the Subject and to suit that mode of music which by the Antients was called the Lydian.[34]

Again Dryden's contribution appears to have been the precise metrical arrangement, for many of these phrases appear not to have been his actual invention. In his edition of *Venus and Adonis* in *The Plays and Poems of William Shakespeare*, Malone's comment on the lines 'she kiss'd his brow, his cheek, his chin, | And where she ends, she doth anew begin' (ll. 59–60) implies that Shakespeare's poem is Dryden's source: 'So Dryden, in his Alexander's Feast: "Never ending, still beginning."' William Browne's *Britannia's Pastorals* (1613) include in the third song of the first book a love-knot wherein love is described as 'Still beginning neuer ending'. The phrase appears in a very different context in *Cynthia*, an anonymous novel of 1687, which contains the histrionic and Miltonic dying speech of Almerin, a pirate who has gained his power (appropriately) by serving as the devil's agent:

Oh no! Alas, alas, none that go to that appointed Place, ever return back again. Oh horrible! Oh fearful! Oh terrible! still beginning, and never ending Eternity; now I desire to live, because I fear to die; yet I wou'd die, because I wou'd be freed from the Fear of worse to come. (p. 165)

Dryden, however, seems to have given the rhythm of the phrase a particular implication by means of repetition, and by applying it to war: 'Never ending, still beginning | Fighting still, and still destroying'. The phrase was picked up by Samuel Rogers in *Reflections*, for example, and extended in application to the whole of life:

[34] National Library of Scotland, Edinburgh, MS 24508, fos. 117^v–118^r. Reproduced by permission.

The turmoil in this world of ours,
The turmoil <u>never ending</u>, <u>still beginning</u>,
The wailing and the tears.

Christina Rossetti, by contrast, gave the same words a more joyful application in a poem first published in 1893, which begins:

Hark the Alleluias of the great salvation
<u>Still beginning</u>, <u>never ending</u>, still begin
The thunder of an endless adoration.

AND TEARS BEGAN TO FLOW

For many readers, the stanza in *Alexander's Feast* that most obviously moved the emotions was that in which Timotheus sings of the death of Darius, deserted by those 'his former Bounty fed', and sings so well that Alexander, revolving the various turns of chance in his altered soul, begins to weep.[35] Again it appears to have been common opinion that the subject described and the verse used in the description were, in this stanza, in unusually close harmony. Monboddo observed that Dryden 'most happily changes the Verse as the Musician Changes his Music':

He then returns to the Iambic measure, which I think more proper than the Trochaic to express Grief.

'He chose a mournful Muse,
'Soft Pity to infuse

This Last Line the Reader may observe is shorter than the other consisting only of two feet and a half; and in the Second place has an Anapaestic in place of an Iambic which make the Line shorter in the pronunciation than the preceeding tho' it consists of the same Number of Syllables.

As Monboddo presents the poem, uncommon metrical effects are to be understood in terms of their function:

[35] Elizabeth Barrett Browning, whose general estimate of Dryden included reservations about his dramatic powers, 'verbosity', and 'defect of sensibility', nevertheless remembered this stanza in a letter to Mary Russell Mitford: 'I have been "<u>revolving in</u> my <u>altered soul</u>" all your gracious & good advice about a subject.' She also argued, in one of a series of papers on English poetry, that '[Dryden] reasoned powerfully in verse—and threw into verse besides, the whole force of his strong powerful being; and so he wrote what has been called from generation to generation, down to the threshold of our days, "the best ode in the English language."' See letters of 4 February 1842 and [13] October 1841 in *The Brownings' Correspondence*, ed. P. Kelley and R. Hudson, 14 vols. (1984–98), v. 232, and *The Athenaeum*, 771 (6 Aug. 1842) 707.

Then he gives an Iambic of four feet

      'He sung Darius, great and good,

then an Iambic of three feet,

      'By too severe a fate

Then follows a wonderfull Change into a measure very uncommon in English, but which suits the Subject exceedingly well. It is a Line of two Spondees and four Repetitions of the same word,

      'Fallen, fallen, fallen, fallen,

Then a Line of two Dactyles, describing as it were the precipitate motion of his fall,—

      'Fallen from his high Estate

Then he goes on in three Iambic Verses,

      'And weltering in his Blood,

      'Deserted at his utmost need

      'By those his former bounty fed.

Surprisingly perhaps, Monboddo assumes that in every case 'fall'n' constitutes one syllable, so that 'fallen from his' and 'high estate' are metrically equivalent. At this point Monboddo's metrical terminology proves inadequate. Before turning to Dryden's ode, he had assumed that all English verse could be described with three terms— iambic, trochaic, and anapaestic. Analysis of *Alexander's Feast* had taught him otherwise. In his manuscript he observes that 'Mr Dryden has shown' him that 'there are in our language likewise Spondees Dactyles and [   ] and [   ] and in short all the variety of feet in Greek and Latin' (fo. 122^r). Presumably the lacunae represented by square brackets were to be supplied when he had discovered or invented an appropriate term.

Monboddo was, however, equally impressed by the unusual and hitherto undescribed, as by the 'very fine iambic verses':

Then he varies the measure by making the first foot an anapaestic and the Second an unaccented Syllable interposed between two accented, which may be called a [   ] and the last an Iambic—

      'On the bare Earth exposed he lyes,

Then he returns again to the Iambic—

      'With not a friend to close his Eyes,

Then he lengthens his verse preserving still the same measure by adding one Iambic foot more,

'With downcast look the joyfull victor sat,

Where the Reader may observe that the last word *sat*, rhymes to *Estate* at the distance of five lines, which I am persuaded is a Rhyme without example in English. Then follow four very fine Iambic Verses, with alternate Rhymes

'Revolving in his altered Soul
'The various turns of fate [*sic*, for Chance] below,
'And now and then a Sigh he stole,
'And tears began to flow—

Where he has made an agreeable variety, by making the last verse shorter by a foot.

Pope, too, seems to have been impressed by this stanza from an early age, particularly by the death of Darius as related by Timotheus: 'Deserted at his utmost Need, | By those <u>his former Bounty fed</u>'. In a favourite extract from the *Odyssey* that he translated early in his life, Pope transferred the phrasing and the thought to Ulysses newly arrived in Ithaca: 'In his own Palace forc'd to ask his bread, | Scorn'd by those slaves <u>his former bounty fed</u>'.[36] Although this phrasing was not repeated in his complete version of the *Odyssey*, Dryden's stanza seems to have returned to Pope's mind when particular situations presented themselves in his translations of Homer. On these occasions, the phrase that is recalled came from the moment in *Alexander's Feast* when the warlike hero begins to feel the full pity of things: 'And, <u>now</u> and then, a <u>Sigh</u> he stole; | <u>And Tears began to flow</u>' (ll. 87–8). In *An Essay on Criticism* Pope's most obvious quotation from Dryden is the six syllables 'and Tears begin to flow':

<u>Now</u> his fierce Eyes with sparkling Fury glow;
<u>Now Sighs</u> steal out, <u>and Tears begin to flow</u>.   (ll. 378–9)

It would seem difficult to attribute such a simple, such an obvious, such a 'natural' set of words to the creative workings of any particular mind. Nevertheless, it does appear to be the case that Dryden was again the first to arrange precisely these words in precisely this order.[37]

[36] Pope's translation was originally included with a letter dated 19 October 1709 (*Correspondence*, i. 74). It was later reprinted, as 'The Arrival of Ulysses in Ithaca', in Steele's *Poetical Miscellanies: Consisting of Poems and Translations* (1714).

[37] There seems to be no exact precedent for Dryden's six syllables in verse before 1697. Interestingly, the nearest precedent in prose occurs once again in the anonymous *Cynthia*

Dryden in this instance was his own self-borrower, seeming to regard the phrase as suitable for the effects of a particular passion—the pity caused in the heart of the magnanimous by contemplating the untimely fall of great ones. In 'Palamon and Arcite' (1700) the phrase is applied to Theseus as he reacts to the ladies of Thebes lamenting the deaths of their unburied husbands: 'The Prince was touch'd, his <u>Tears began to flow</u>' (i. 93). The similar situations may have caused Pope to associate Dryden's phrasing with the reaction of the truly heroic mind to the thought of an unburied corpse.[38] So, in the eleventh book of Pope's *Odyssey*, Ulysses responds to the memory of the unburied body of Elpenor, just as Alexander had responded to the image of Darius:

> Sad at the sight I stand, deep fix'd in woe,
> And ere I spoke the <u>tears began to flow</u>.   (xi. 69–70)

The appropriateness of the phrase may have been its lack of ornamentation. Pope seems to have thought it peculiarly appropriate for moments in his Homer when the heroes are facing an event about which nothing can be said. This is clearest in the speech of Menelaus to Antilochus on the death of Patroclus in the seventeenth book of the *Iliad*. Pope accompanied the passage with a note taken from Eustathius, who observed that 'Homer ever represents an Excess of Grief by a deep Horrour, Silence, Weeping, and not enquiring into

(1687), when Fidelio is describing the mournful response of the doomed heroine Desdemona to the news of her lover's impending marriage: 'When on a sudden, all the former Signs of Joy vanish'd, and were dispers'd; her Visage was over-cast with a fatal Disturbance, her Breast began to pant, and a Shower of Tears began to fall from her fair Eyes, which hung on her Cheeks like Pearly Dew on a sweet-smelling Rose' (p. 78). The version in *Cynthia* can be found once in verse before Dryden. John Phillips's *Maronides: or Virgil Travestied* (1678) has: 'And <u>tears began to</u> fall like hail'. Dryden's version '<u>And Tears began to flow</u>' makes a complete line in ballad metre, and seems to have been frequently used as such in poems which in one way or another imitated the ballad. Chatterton used Dryden's line verbatim in the *Bristowe Tragedy*: 'Wyth herte brymm-fulle of gnawynge grief, | Hee to Syr Charles dydd goe, | And satt hymm downe uponne a stoole, | <u>And teares began to flowe</u>'. Goldsmith in *Edwin and Angelina*, the ballad included in chapter 8 of *The Vicar of Wakefield* (1766), has 'But nothing could a charm impart | To soothe the stranger's woe; | For grief was heavy at his heart, | <u>And tears began to flow</u>'. Macpherson may have been attempting a similar folk coloration in *Temora* (1763): ' "My bards wait him with songs. My feast is spread in the hall of kings." I heard Cormac in silence. My <u>tears began to flow</u>.'

[38] Those commentators who argue that Alexander is consistently made into a figure of ridicule in Dryden's poem would seem to differ from both Dryden and Pope, for it appears that both poets saw Alexander at this moment as experiencing a pity which exhibits an entirely becoming magnanimity.

the manner of the Friend's Death: Nor could Antilochus have express'd his Sorrow in any manner so moving as Silence':

> Patroclus on the Shore,
> Now pale and dead, shall succour *Greece* no more.
> . . . .
> The youthful Warrior heard with silent Woe,
> From his fair Eyes the <u>Tears began to flow</u>;
> Big with the mighty Grief, he strove to say
> What Sorrow dictates, but no Word found way.

(xvii. 775–6, 781–4)

From Pope the phrase passed to Fenton, who in the twenty-first book of the *Odyssey* applied it to Penelope when she goes to the treasure room to collect the bow of Ulysses.[39] It may be that in both her case and Alexander's the poet expects the moment to be read with full consciousness of the predestined end—the early death of the godlike hero, the slaughter of the suitors:

> She moves majestic thro' the wealthy room,
> Where treasur'd garments cast a rich perfume;
> There from the column where aloft it hung,
> Reach'd, in its splendid case, the bow unstrung:
> Across her knees she lay'd the well-known bow,
> And pensive sate, <u>and tears began to flow</u>.   (xxi. 53–8)

If it is more than mere chance that connects Pope's Homer and Dryden's *Alexander's Feast*, the nature of the connection might be suggested by some similarities between Joseph Warton's praise of the English and Pope's praise of the Greek poem. Warton's experience of reading Dryden's ode was that the 'train of imagery' was 'alive, sublime, and animated to an unparalleled degree'. The superiority of Dryden's ode over Pope's was that Dryden places his action 'fully before the eyes of the reader'.[40] In the Preface to his *Iliad* Pope wrote of 'that unequal'd fire and rapture, which is so forcible in *Homer*, that no man of a true poetical spirit is master of himself while he reads him'. In both cases the reader is overmastered by the power of the poet's imagination. As Pope saw it, everything that Homer

---

[39] The phrase occurs again in *Odyssey*, xiii. 240 (also ascribed to Fenton) when Ulysses, having arrived in Ithaca unawares, breaks into lamentations, 'And as he spoke, <u>the tears began to flow</u>'.
[40] *An Essay on the Writings and Genius of Pope*, i. 53.

wrote 'is of the most animated nature imaginable; every thing moves, every thing lives, and is put in action'. So it is that 'the reader is hurry'd out of himself by the force of the poet's imagination, and turns in one place to a hearer, in another to a spectator'. In both cases the power of the 'imaging' is assisted or expressed by the verse. The 'course' of Homer's verses, as Pope experienced them, 'resembles that of the army he describes . . . *They pour along like a fire that sweeps the whole earth before it.*'[41] The experience of readers of *Alexander's Feast* before the twentieth century seems to have been of this kind. What Pope called the 'stile of sound' appears to have been 'undoubtedly of wonderful force in imprinting the Image on the reader'. As Alexander, his concubine, and his peers were overmastered by Timotheus, so readers were hurried out of themselves by the force of Dryden's imagination.

Congreve's remarks on Dryden's 'fire' and 'imagination' in old age were mentioned earlier in this essay. The fact that certain phrases from *Alexander's Feast* proved so enduring may in part endorse and in part modify Congreve's praise of Dryden's style:

In his Poems, his Diction is, wherever his Subject requires it, so Sublimely, and so truly Poetical, that its Essence, like that of pure Gold, cannot be destroy'd. Take his Verses, and divest them of their Rhimes, disjoint them in their Numbers, transpose their Expressions, make what Arrangements and Disposition you please of his Words, yet shall there Eternally be Poetry, and something which will be found incapable of being resolv'd into absolute Prose.[42]

The endorsement would come from the survival of Dryden's phrases in prose, and in verse of different metres and in various metrical contexts. The modifications might be of two kinds. The first would be a reminder that Dryden's diction was not, strictly speaking, his own. The lasting phrases appeared to have the quality of a discovery rather than an invention. Dryden's phrases stayed in the memory because he had himself memorized the words of a great many predecessors—Spenser, Shakespeare, Cowley, Milton, and perhaps a host of less notable writers. The second modification would be to suggest that where Congreve uses the word 'diction'

---

[41] *The Iliad of Homer*, trans. Alexander Pope, ed. Stephen Shankman (Harmondsworth, 1996), p. 4.
[42] William Congreve in *Dryden: The Critical Heritage*, p. 266.

the term should be understood as Dryden himself defined it: 'the diction; that is . . . the choice of words, and the harmony of numbers'.[43] For Dryden there were not two stages to the process by which words were selected, one for decorum, and quite another for sound: the suitability of a word included its metrical value. As it was for the poet, so it seems to have been for his readers. The shard of an image, the hint of a thought, or the trace of a passion appears, in almost every case, to have been recalled by the force of a musical pattern, however fragmentary. The after-traces of *Alexander's Feast* appear to justify the subtitle of the poem.

When Johnson ended his 'Life of Dryden' with the immense claim that 'we owe the improvement, perhaps the completion of our metre, the refinement of our language, and much of the correctness of our sentiments' to Dryden, and that 'by him we were taught "sapere & fari", to think naturally and express forcibly',[44] the last two verbs were, perhaps, in very close conjunction. Thinking naturally, for example, would appear in this case to have been a different matter from thinking morally, and expressing forcibly to imply something more than the usual expressiveness of eloquent verse. Dryden appears to have impressed his readers as having found the 'natural' expression for the various 'natural' passions concomitant upon human life.

---

[43] Preface to *Fables Ancient and Modern*, in *Poems*, ed. Kinsley, p. 1448.
[44] *Lives*, i. 469.

8

DRYDEN, TONSON, AND THE PATRONS OF *THE WORKS OF VIRGIL* (1697)

John Barnard

The Works of Virgil published by Jacob Tonson in 1697 is a fascinating example of cultural production in the early modern period. It has attracted a good deal of recent interest among scholars. My starting-point is an article on authorship in the age of Milton and Dryden published in 1990 by Dustin Griffin, where he writes:

> In order to understand better what authorship meant in their era, how writers negotiated a balance among the claims of occasion, audience, patron, bookseller [i.e. publisher], immediate financial need, and long-term career—we need a better—a thicker—literary history. We need to acknowledge that in this period there was no simple and steady progress from a court-based to a marketplace-based literature.[1]

This is surely right, and a proper corrective to my own unwise statement, made in 1963, that the *Virgil* was 'through and through a commercial venture'.[2] However, in the book which grew out of his article Griffin discusses Dryden and Tonson's venture almost exclusively in terms of literary patronage, while Brean Hammond,

---

I would like to thank Hermione Lee, Paul Hammond, and the late D. F. McKenzie for their help and advice in the course of writing this chapter. I am very grateful to Ian Doolittle for his advice on City merchants. John Childs kindly provided details from his files on army officers.

[1] 'The Beginnings of Modern Authorship: Milton and Dryden', *Milton Quarterly*, 24 (1990) 1–7, at p. 6.

[2] 'Dryden, Tonson and Subscriptions for the 1697 *Virgil*', *Papers of the Bibliographical Society of America*, 57 (1963) 129–51, at p. 140.

writing on 'professional imaginative writing' in this period, sees the project quite differently as one in which 'business considerations interacted with aesthetic desiderata to produce beautiful books and considerable profits'.[3]

Published in 1996 and 1997, the two books risk presenting the *Virgil* as an example either of literary patronage or of commercial shrewdness. It is in fact a mixture of both, as Griffin had earlier argued. Nor is the venture a typical case. It is the first example of a major literary work by a *living* writer to be published by subscription.

I want to take up the challenge to write a 'thicker' kind of literary history. Griffin successfully demonstrates that literary patronage was a 'systematic economic arrangement, a complex exchange of benefit to both patron and client', an arrangement which gave power to the author as well as the patron.[4] However, if the *Virgil* is regarded as an unusual example of 'high' cultural production in the England of the 1690s, the symbiotic relationship between author, publisher, patrons, readers, commercial considerations, and differing contemporary political, economic, and social formations, its publication becomes an altogether more complex event. One effect is to underline the importance of Tonson's role as publisher; another is to demonstrate Dryden's adroitness in using the system for his own ends—aesthetic, financial, personal, and political.

The success of Dryden's translation depended on the way in which Dryden and Tonson, both powerful cultural brokers in their own overlapping spheres of influence in the 1690s, stood to gain both financial and cultural standing through the publication. For Dryden and Tonson, the translation was at once a joint business venture and a cultural project, one which excited interest on the Continent even before its completion.[5]

Tonson's role in enabling Dryden's translation was central to its ultimate success. His financial imperatives as publisher were at one with his need for enhanced cultural standing (a precondition for further commercial success as a literary publisher), and fitted neatly

---

[3] Brean Hammond, *Professional Imaginative Writing in England, 1670–1740: 'Hackney for Bread'* (Oxford, 1997), p. 71. Hammond rightly places more stress on theatrical income than does Griffin, but he does not grasp the workings of Dryden's second subscriptions.

[4] *Literary Patronage in England, 1650–1800* (Cambridge, 1996), p. 13. For his account of Dryden see pp. 70–98 and *passim*.

[5] John Barnard, 'Early Expectations of Dryden's Translation of Virgil (1697) in England and on the Continent', *Review of English Studies*, NS 50 (1999) 196–203.

with his long-standing relationship with Dryden. In a decade when literary patronage was shifting from court-based patronage, from which Dryden had benefited under Charles II, to one based on that of 'well-connected Court Whigs' like Lord Somers, the Earl of Dorset, and Charles Montagu, with Tonson playing a key role as publisher,[6] both writer and bookseller were interestingly placed. Dryden in his sixties was a Tory, a Catholic, out of office, in need therefore of income, and adamantly opposed to the Williamite settlement, but was undeniably England's major poet; Tonson, twenty-five years his junior, a Whig supporter of the new order, and a tradesman with good political connections, had long worked with Dryden to their mutual benefit.

The larger patterns are those described by Griffin. It was to the mutual benefit of Dryden (income) and the new Whig grandees (cultural capital) that the translation should succeed. The emergent party political Williamite grouping could ally Dryden's literary achievements and neo-classical aesthetic with its new cultural dom-ination, and Tonson was the immediate facilitator of that process. The *Virgil* grew out of a specific cultural matrix in which individuals made choices within the contradictory tensions of English society between 1694, when the poet signed the contract with Tonson, and his translation's publication in 1697.[7] Those tensions were political, social, aesthetic, cultural, and economic, with individual agents variously placed within the differing categories but all belonging, or believing they belonged, to the cultural elite.[8] Dryden's, and to a

---

[6] Griffin, *Literary Patronage*, p. 47 and *passim*.

[7] For accounts of Pope's subscribers see Matthew Hodgart, 'The Subscription List for Pope's *Iliad*, 1715', in Robert B. White, Jr. (ed.), *The Dress of Words: Essays on Restoration and Eighteenth Century Literature in Honor of Richmond P. Bond* (Lawrence, Kan., 1978), pp. 25–34, and Pat Rogers, 'Pope and his Subscribers', *Publishing History*, 3 (1978) 7–36. No attempt is made here at a comparative study, but Pope was clearly able to attract a larger proportion of aristocratic patrons. The really interesting comparative study would be with the 1688 sub-scription edition of Milton's *Paradise Lost*, with which Tonson was intimately concerned and to which Dryden subscribed, a study I hope to complete in due course.

[8] See Pierre Bourdieu, *The Field of Cultural Production*, ed. and introd. Randal Johnson (Cambridge, 1993), pp. 189–90. Bourdieu's analysis of the recurrent opposition between the avant-garde (cultural capital funded by excess wealth) and a middlebrow establishment (commercially viable), in which the former in due course takes over the latter, does not fit the later seventeenth century with any exactness. But the success of Dryden's *Virgil* is quite clearly an example of aesthetic capital being metamorphosed into cash (Dryden and Tonson) and cultural capital (the subscribers). The great strength of Bourdieu's analysis is the space it allows for individual choice by participating agents.

lesser extent Tonson's, motivation will be given particular attention. Because individual subscribers belong to more than one social and/ or political formation there will be some repetition of names, and because larger patterns are only discernible through detail there will be overlaps with Griffin's discussion of Dryden's dedications and John Brewer's account of the Kit-Cat Club. Only from within the context of that detail is it possible to appreciate how Dryden remained true to his own poetic and political beliefs while operating successfully within the new exigencies of culture and power in the 1690s.

An essential key to the *Virgil*'s success was Tonson's imaginative (and extremely shrewd) contract for the subscription edition. Dryden's subscribers were in part purchasers of the book published by Tonson in 1697, but they were also patrons in that they paid well above the market value. They were solicited by Dryden, Tonson, Congreve, Atterbury, and others. In addition, Dryden wrote three dedications, for which he received gifts, and drafted parts of his translation while enjoying the hospitality of Sir William Bowyer's Denham Court and the Earl of Exeter's Burghley House. He was also given £200 copyright money by Tonson as publisher. The bookseller was able to ensure that Dryden received a handsome prepayment from his subscribers (as well as the staged advance of copy money) during the translation, along with a final payment on publication: in all Dryden received between £910 and £1,075 from Tonson and the subscribers, and probably £400 or £500 for his dedications,[9] equivalent to three years' income to support an Esquire and his dependants.[10] For his part Tonson made around £95 from the first edition alone, and, from the second edition the following year, another £100 to £200 by 1709.[11] Both Dryden and Tonson were undoubtedly eager for income, but the relationship between author, publisher, patrons, subscribers, and other buyers is

---

[9] A hitherto unrecorded report that Dryden gained £1,000 for the *Virgil* and £500 in gifts for his three dedications occurs in a letter from Thomas Burnett to Leibniz, 20 January 1698 (Niedersächsische Landesbibliothek, Hanover, L. br. 132, fos. 69–70). Richard Graham reported Dryden's total earnings as £1,400 (see Barnard, 'Dryden, Tonson and Subscriptions for the 1697 *Virgil*', pp. 130–2).

[10] See Appendix II below.

[11] 'Large- and Small-Paper Copies of Dryden's *The Works of Virgil* (1697): Jacob Tonson's Investment and Profits and the Example of *Paradise Lost* (1688)', *Papers of the Bibliographical Society of America*, 92 (1998) 259–71.

altogether more complex than their strictly financial dealings. The cultural standing of the venture was of considerable importance for the 42-year-old bookseller's reputation: a lesser publisher might have been happy to ensure his author's immediate benefit, while carrying a loss-leader, in a fairly certain expectation of future profit. Tonson's contract made absolutely sure that Dryden, as well as himself, came out financially to the good as soon as the first edition was published.

Even more striking perhaps is Tonson's confidence, indeed courage, in going forward with the project at all in the summer of 1694, when the book trade was marked by a series of bankruptcies and the finances of the Stationers' Company were in a disastrous state.[12]

Subscription publishing had evolved as a method of publishing large expensive books either by individual scholars like Dugdale or Plot, or by entrepreneurs like Ogilby (a self-publisher) or Richard Blome, and was closely related to joint-stock subscriptions—by 1657 the East India Company was a completely joint-stock company.[13] The Dryden–Tonson venture was the first to use it to finance a new poetic work in English by a major living writer (Tonson had in 1688, in partnership with Bentley, published the posthumous subscription edition of Milton's *Paradise Lost*) and to use two subscription lists. The financial arrangements of the *Virgil* place it somewhere between a publisher's initiative and an appeal to the public for support. As such it relates to the swift and novel development of public credit in the decade following 1688.

Tonson paid copy money for the right to subsequent editions: subscribers, who in part prepaid for their copies, were at once patrons and prospective owners and readers. There were two lists of subscribers. The first, limited to 101, paid five guineas in all (three guineas initially, and a further two on receipt of the book), the second paid two guineas (both groups paying well above the cost price, which Tonson reckoned at £1). Those paying the higher price had their names and arms engraved on one of the illustrative

---

[12] Michael Treadwell, '1695–1995: Some Tercentenary Thoughts on Freedoms of the Press', *Harvard Library Bulletin*, NS 7 (1996) 3–19, at pp. 13–14.

[13] See S. L. C. Clapp, 'The Beginnings of Subscription Publication in the Seventeenth Century', *Modern Philology*, 29 (1931–2) 199–224, 'Subscription Publishers Prior to Jacob Tonson', *Library*, 13 (1932) 158–83, and 'The Subscription Enterprises of John Ogilby and Richard Blome', *Modern Philology*, 30 (1932–3) 365–79.

plates, taken from John Ogilby's earlier subscription publication of Virgil in 1654.[14] After four years' gestation, Dryden's translation was announced as ready to be delivered 'in Quires' to its subscribers in the week following 28 June 1697.[15]

In addition to Griffin and Hammond, other scholars have written about Dryden's *Virgil*. James Winn gives a survey of the political, religious, and social range of the subscribers.[16] William Frost and Steven Zwicker independently realized that Dryden used the dedications and Postscript to make coded expressions of his Jacobite political and religious allegiances, and on occasions even used the plates assigned to the first subscribers for the same purpose.[17] Of the three dedicatees, one was a Catholic, Hugh, Lord Clifford, and the others, the Earl of Chesterfield and Marquess of Normanby, had refused to take the loyalty oaths to King William.[18] Dryden's refusal to dedicate the volume to William III, despite Tonson's wishes, was a principled one. On 3 September 1697 Dryden told his two sons in Rome that Tonson had 'prepared the Book' for its eventual dedication to the king, 'for in every figure of Eneas, he has caused him to be drawn like K. William, with a hooked Nose'. With evident pleasure Dryden reports that 'he [Tonson] has missed of his design'[19] as a result of the poet's obduracy.

Winn's account of the subscribers shows that the two lists are inclusive, drawing from all political and religious sections of society. A systematic exploration of the subscribers reveals that Dryden and Tonson did indeed bring together support from all sides, so much so that they were clearly following a deliberate policy. The following account tries to do four things: to give a more detailed analysis of who subscribed to the Dryden–Tonson translation than has so far been attempted; to ask how subscribers, particularly first subscribers, regarded their copies; to explore the way in which some of the identifiable sub-groups among the subscribers for whom there is

---

[14] The plates had been used again in Ogilby's Latin edition of Virgil's works published by Thomas Roycroft (1658).

[15] *London Gazette*, 24–8 June. See Hugh Macdonald, *John Dryden: A Bibliography of Early Editions and of Drydeniana* (Oxford, 1939), p. 58.

[16] *John Dryden and his World* (New Haven, 1987), pp. 474–5.

[17] *Works*, vi. 870–6; Steven N. Zwicker, *Politics and Language in Dryden's Poetry* (Princeton, NJ, 1984), pp. 177–205.

[18] Winn, *John Dryden and his World*, pp. 484–5.

[19] *Letters*, p. 93.

evidence utilized their patronage networks; and to show how Dryden made use of the prose texts of his dedications, Postscript, and Notes to position himself and his translation within the literary and cultural world of England in 1697.

I

Dr Johnson, who knew about the book trade through his father, reported that 'the nation considered its honour as interested' in the publication of Dryden's translation.[20] Griffin glosses 'nation' as meaning 'those relatively few powerful men who constituted the *political nation* . . .'.[21] This is true enough up to a point, but Dryden's 349 subscribers[22] reach well beyond those 'few powerful men', even though all the contributors belonged to, or believed they belonged to, the dominant cultural elite. Johnson's point, that the 'polite' reading public wanted the major living English poet to succeed in his translation of Virgil, is borne out by the list of subscribers and by other evidence.

Little is known about which first subscribers were approached by Dryden and which by Tonson. The list of first subscribers was filled so quickly that Dryden found himself demanding on 29 October 1695 that Tonson find a place for Lord Chesterfield, to whom the *Georgics* were eventually dedicated.[23] Indeed, Dryden complained that Tonson's over-zealous soliciting meant that by early 1696 he was refusing would-be first subscribers.[24] The eagerness of the subscribers is proof of the public's early support of the translation. Chesterfield got his place, but another name put forward by Dryden did not. In the same letter to Tonson asking for a place for his old patron, Dryden wrote: 'And I must have a place for the Duke of Devonshyre. Some of your friends will be glad to take back their three guinneys.'[25] Although room was found for at least four

---

[20] *The Lives of the English Poets*, ed. George Birkbeck Hill, 3 vols. (Oxford, 1905), i. 448.
[21] Griffin, *Literary Patronage*, p. 41.
[22] Tonson printed 351 subscribers' copies of the first edition: two patrons, Hugh, Lord Clifford, and Robert Harley were both first and second subscribers. For a tentative estimate of the translation's success in reaching its potential audience see Appendix II.
[23] *Letters*, p. 78.
[24] *Letters*, pp. 80–1.
[25] *Letters*, p. 78.

other subscribers,[26] the Duke of Devonshire remained without a place.

The Duke of Devonshire had been one of the seven signatories to the invitation to William of Orange and one of the first to take up arms on his behalf. Dryden's eagerness to have him as a subscriber to one of the plates in his translation shows that the Jacobite poet fully appreciated the importance of bipartisan support. (The fact that his son, the Marquess of Hartington, was a first subscriber and his wife a second subscriber suggests that the duke felt it beneath his dignity to appear as anything but a first subscriber—indeed, it may be that his wife subscribed precisely because no place was found for the duke himself.) There is, then, good reason to believe that Dryden and Tonson, whose own politics were radically at odds, saw eye to eye in their search for patrons.

The following analysis of the overlapping and competing groups and networks of the first and second subscribers to the *Virgil* extends Winn's account (and, implicitly, Johnson's) of their social, political, and religious spread.[27] It also gives a better context for understanding Dryden's encoded Jacobite sentiments.

Considering that the first subscription list was full as early as 1695, the patrons honoured by plates in the summer of 1697 map onto the holders of major state office with considerable precision. The first three plates are dedicated, in the order of their precedence in processing in Parliament, to Lord High Chancellor Somers (Pl. 1),[28] the Lord Privy Seal, Earl of Pembroke (Pl. 2), and the Lord Chamberlain, Earl of Dorset (Pl. 3). This was exactly up to date.

Somers had been appointed Lord Chancellor and was made a baron in 1697, while Dorset ended his term of office that year (which is why the next Lord Chamberlain, the Earl of Sunderland,

---

[26] In addition to Lord Chesterfield, room was found for Viscount Fitzharding, Sir Walter Kirkham Blount, and the Williamite Duke of Shrewsbury (see 'Tonson's Final Accounting with Dryden', *Works*, vi. 1187). A place was also found for the Earl of Derby, another supporter of William III (*Letters*, p. 78). No place was found for Lord Petre or the Countess of Macclesfield (*Letters*, p. 78). The exclusion of the latter is not surprising: after she had two illegitimate children by Lord Rivers, her husband started divorce proceedings in the summer of 1697.

[27] What follows is based on Appendix I.

[28] The numbering of the plates is that given in the list of first subscribers: *Works* and the first edition both supply page references.

is so described on the plate dedicated to him (Pl. 80)). This represents half of the six highest-ranking officers in the land.

These first three names are a reminder that, particularly among the first subscribers, individuals were likely to be representative of more than one kind of interest. Dorset, for instance, was, like Lord Somers, a generous patron of literature, and also a member of the Kit-Cat Club, a member of the House of Lords, and a Williamite state officer, as well as being a long-standing patron of Dryden.

The number of other state officials among the first subscribers is striking. Both Secretaries of State are represented. The Duke of Shrewsbury had been appointed to the Southern Department in 1689 (Pl. 91) and Sir William Trumbull, appointed in 1695, resigned his office on 2 December 1697 (Pl. 27). The Exchequer, of critical importance during a period of currency instability and reform, is particularly well represented. Charles Montagu, Chancellor of the Exchequer and another notable patron of literature, has a plate (Pl. 10) as does its Auditor, Sir Robert Howard, Dryden's brother-in-law (Pl. 87). Although it is not mentioned on his plate, Viscount Fitzharding (Pl. 86) held one of the four lucrative posts as Teller of the Exchequer (Guy Palmes, a second subscriber, was also one of the Tellers, and William Lowndes, Secretary to the Exchequer, was another second subscriber). The Attorney General, Sir Thomas Trevor (Pl. 11), and the Solicitor General, Sir John Hawles (Pl. 12), have successive plates in order of rank. Sir Fleetwood Sheppard, Usher of the Black Rod (Pl. 66), also belongs here.

The second subscribers include the names of further state officials and administrators, sometimes named as such in the printed list. William Blathwayt was Secretary of War, Lord Clanbrassis the Paymaster General, and Richard Franklin describes himself as 'Postmaster'. Charles Ferguson was a Commissioner of the Navy, and Samuel Pepys and Will Hewer were former naval officials. William Bridgeman was Secretary to the Admiralty and clerk of the Privy Council under both James II and William III. Nathaniel Hornby was Commissioner of Excise, while William Bromley and James Vernon were future Secretaries of State.

The self-descriptions chosen by the first subscribers for their plates show a clear bias towards William III's household. Charles Beauclerk, Duke of St Albans (and illegitimate son of Charles II), was 'Master Falconer to his Ma^{ty} and Captaine of ye Honble Band of

Gent. Pensioners' (Pl. 55). James Bertie, Earl of Abingdon, who had asked Dryden to write *Eleonora* (1692) to commemorate his wife's death, describes himself as 'Cheife Justice, and Justice in Eyre of all his Maj^ts Parcks, Forests and Chaces on the South side of Trent, and Ld Lieutenant and Custos Rotulorum of the County of Oxon' (Pl. 5). The Earl of Romney was Master General of the Ordnance, Warden of the Cinque Ports, and a Gentleman of the Bedchamber (Pl. 70). Colonel George Cholmondley was a Groom of the Bedchamber (Pl. 82), while George Stepney styles himself as his Majesty's 'Envoy Extra:^ry to Severall Princes in Germany' (Pl. 72). Colonel Christopher Codrington's plate records that he is 'One of the Captains in his Ma.^ies first Regiment of foot Guards' (Pl. 84). Sir Godfrey Kneller appears as 'Principall Painter to his Majesty' (Pl. 79), and George London as 'of his Ma:^ties Royall Garden in St James Park Gent.' (Pl. 18).

This contrasts markedly with the number of those from Princess Anne's court, which had recently been established at Whitehall after her sister's death in 1694.[29] Apart from herself (Pl. 32), her husband (Pl. 31) (ordered by gender), and their 8-year-old son, William (Pl. 60), only Viscount Fitzharding, 'Master of ye Horse to Her Royall Highness the Princess Anne of Denmark' (Pl. 86) announces his place in her court (the Earl of Denbigh (Pl. 62), Master of Horse to Prince George, omits this role from his plate). Michael Dahl, the painter, who enjoyed Princess Anne's and Prince George's patronage, was a second subscriber, as was Prince George's physician, Dr Samuel Garth.

Dryden's choice of Princess Anne's family as his royal patrons makes all the more pointed his refusal to follow Tonson's wishes to dedicate *Virgil* to William III. It is true that she and her family are placed tactfully well away from the beginning of the volume, but in choosing her Dryden allies the translation with her strong Protestant beliefs, the opposite to his own, while still being able to dedicate these plates to a Stuart family rather than to their successors.

To balance this, there are a significant number of subscribers who were active in establishing William as king, including three of the seven signatories to the letter of invitation to William dated 11 December 1688—the Earl of Abingdon (who also gave £30,000

---

[29] Her court took over St James's Palace only in 1696.

towards the expedition), the Earl of Romney, and the Duke of Shrewsbury. If Dryden had succeeded in finding a place for the Duke of Devonshire, more than half of the signatories would have had their arms and names on plates in the volume. The by then disgraced Admiral, the Earl of Torrington, had delivered the invitation to William, and the Earl of Pembroke carried it. Two of the second subscribers, the Earl of Weymouth and Peregrine Bertie, were sent as messengers to Prince William. Sir Justinian Isham, a first subscriber, had raised a troop at Nottingham to guard Princess Anne so that she could desert James II. Another, Henry Herbert, Baron Cherbury, had joined William in Holland in 1688. The Earl of Sunderland was one of William's advisers, and the Earl of Derby was active on William's side after the Revolution. One of the second subscribers, Sir Bevil Granville, brought over the garrison at Jersey. Six of the first subscribers fought for William (the Dukes of St Albans, Richmond, Ormonde, and Somerset, and Colonels Cholmondley and Codrington). At least eleven of the second subscribers saw active service in Ireland or Flanders or both. Of course, it could be argued that any list like this, created in a divided nation, would naturally include names like these, but this group of people emphasizes the way in which everyone in the country was directly affected in one way or another by the decision to replace James with William.

An index of that division is provided by the Act of Attainder brought against Sir John Fenwick in the House of Commons during the 1695–6 session. Sir John was charged with being involved in a plot to assassinate William III, and the issue was hotly debated. Despite doubts about the legality of this process, Fenwick was beheaded on Tower Hill on 28 January 1697. (As his wife, Lady Mary, was a second subscriber, the *Virgil* carries a clear reminder of these events.) The 1695–6 session of the Commons was, some historians believe, critical in the development of party politics, in which the 'polarisation in the Commons had changed from Court and Country to Whig and Tory'.[30] A breakdown of the MPs sitting in this session who chose to, or were persuaded to, subscribe to the

---

[30] I. F. Burton, P. W. J. Riley, and E. Rowlands, *Political Parties in the Reigns of William III and Anne: The Evidence of Division Lists*, *Bulletin of the Institute of Historical Research*, Special Supplement No. 7 (London, 1968) 3.

Virgil shows that Dryden's and Tonson's venture succeeded in attracting patrons from both Whigs and Tories. Among first subscribers the division was almost equal: there are twelve Whigs, ten Tories, and two uncertain (Sir William Trumbull and John Lewknor).[31] Of the fifty-one second subscribers who were MPs in 1696, 63 per cent were Whigs and 37 per cent Tories. Taking first and second subscribing MPs together shows a clear and significant bias towards the Whigs (forty-two Whigs and thirty Tories, or 59 per cent and 39 per cent respectively). In all 15 per cent of those MPs who voted in 1696 subscribed to the *Virgil*, with more than twice as many second as first subscribers. These MPs make up a striking one-fifth of all subscribers, and the proportion would be even higher if those who were MPs at some point in their careers were to be included.

Given the bias towards the Whigs, it is important to note that Robert Harley, the leader of the Country Whigs, who became one element of the new Tory party, was both a first subscriber (Pl. 69) and a second subscriber. He chaired the Commission for Taking and Stating the Public Account of the Kingdom, the 'spearhead of the Country Party Opposition'[32] to William III's need to increase taxation to finance his Continental wars which led inevitably to an expansion of government bureaucracy. Three of the other five members of this Commission were also subscribers—John Granville (Pl. 30), Sir Thomas Dyke (Pl. 63), and William Bromley, a second subscriber. The Commission's last effective meeting took place on 3 December 1696, and its last entry was made on 24 April 1697, two months before the publication of the *Virgil*. The decision of John Granville, unlike Sir Thomas Dyke, to have the full title of the defunct Commission engraved at the foot of his plate may well be an affirmation of his political beliefs.

The voting record of subscribers in the Commons in 1696 is the single most compelling piece of evidence to support Dr Johnson's belief that the nation's 'honour', irrespective of party, was interested in the success of Dryden's translation. It also underlines

---

[31] These and the following figures are based on the findings of I. F. Burton, P. W. J. Riley, and E. Rowlands. For details, see Appendix I.

[32] William A. Shaw, *Calendar of Treasury Books . . . Introduction to Vols. XI–XVII Covering the Years 1695–1702* (London, 1934), p. clv. The details of the Commission's membership are given on p. clix.

the importance Dryden and Tonson gave to drawing support from across the whole political spectrum.

The financing of the *Virgil* is interestingly related to larger developments. At the heart of the political debate in these years was the question of public credit. Taxation would only go so far in supporting the European wars. After 1688 the country underwent a financial revolution, the most obvious sign of which was the founding of the Bank of England in 1694. Like the Tontine Act of 1693 and the Million Lottery of 1694, it sought to raise substantial long-term credit, borrowed directly from the public, for government use. All three of these Whig initiatives sought private subscribers and were the beginning of the National Debt which funded England's military domination of Europe and economic expansion for the rest of the century.[33] Charles Montagu, as Chancellor of the Exchequer, fought for the creation of the Bank of England and this new system of credit in Parliament, and together with William Lowndes, his highly effective Secretary, successfully established both. In addition, Montagu himself was a subscriber to the Bank's flotation in 1694, as were other of Dryden's patrons. Among those honoured by plates in the *Virgil*, Sir Robert Howard and Gilbert Dolben also subscribed to the Bank, for which Sir William Cowper, a second subscriber, put up £2,000.[34] Another of Dryden's subscribers, Peter (or Pedro) Henriques Junior, invested substantially in the Bank and the Tontine, and also took out short-dated securities like the Land Tax Loan of 1693 (£13,300).[35] Henriques was a Sephardic Jewish jobber, with an income of over £600 per year, who lived in the parish of St Gabriel Fenchurch. He, his wife, and their two children (together with a manservant and four maids) shared this house with his father, mother, brother, and two sisters, a considerable establishment.[36] There were a further eighteen patrons of the *Virgil* living within the City walls in 1695, only one of whom was a five-guinea subscriber. He was Dr Stephen Waller, the judge, who lived in Doctors' Commons with his family. The others mostly had annual

[33] P. G. M. Dickson, *The Financial Revolution in England: A Study in the Development of Public Credit 1688–1756* (London and New York, 1967), pp. 3–75 *passim*.

[34] Ibid. 258.

[35] Ibid. 259, 429.

[36] *London Inhabitants within the City Walls 1695*, introd. D. V. Glass, London Record Society, 2 (1966).

incomes of over £600 and were probably mostly merchants. They included Whitfield Hayter, a bachelor goldsmith living in Lombard Street, Paris Slaughter and Leonard Wessell, who had connections with Dryden, and Edward Haistwell (or Hastwell).[37] The latter was the largest London trader in tobacco in the 1690s: he was also a Quaker, appearing from 1699 to 1702 in defence of the Maryland Quakers.[38] In addition, he was elected to the Royal Society in 1698 (as his fellow Quaker, William Penn, had been in 1681). Another eminent merchant subscriber, not recorded as living in the City, was the Huguenot Paul Docmenique 'Esquire', aged 54 in 1697. He had been naturalized in 1662, and in 1704 bought the seat of Gatton, which he represented as MP for thirty years. Two City aldermen, Sir John Parsons and Charles Chamberlayn, were subscribers, and the latter became a director of the Bank of England in 1697–8.[39] Another second subscriber to the *Virgil*, John Smith, the Whig politician, who subscribed to the Land Tax Loan of 1693 (£7,500), was a Treasury Lord who was to become Chancellor of the Exchequer from 1699 to 1701 and again in 1708–10.[40] This strong connection among Dryden's subscribers between the moneyed interest in the City and the Whig innovations in public credit, shows that all of these were investing their money in national enterprises at the very same time that they were translating financial into cultural capital by subscribing to an ostentatiously large paper copy of *Virgil* in English, whose value was in some cases perhaps as much talismanic as literary.[41]

Other subscribers to the *Virgil* were involved in very different metropolitan cultural projects. The most long-standing of these was the Royal Society, to which Dryden himself had been elected one

---

[37] Ibid.

[38] Gary Stuart de Krey, *A Fractured Society: The Politics of London in the First Ages of Party* (Oxford, 1985), p. 105. Haistwell died *c.*7 January 1709 according to Narcissus Luttrell, *A Brief Relation of State Affairs 1678–1714* (Oxford, 1857), vi. 392.

[39] Alfred B. Beaven, *The Aldermen of the City of London Temp. Henry III–1912* (London, 1913), i. 113, 115–16.

[40] Dickson, *Financial Revolution*, p. 429.

[41] Another financial connection among the subscribers is provided by Hoare's Bank. Dryden opened an account there in 1695. At least twenty of his subscribers opened accounts before or in 1697, and another twenty or so had opened accounts by 1705. See H. P. R. Hoare, *Hoare's Bank: A Record 1672–1955: The Story of a Private Bank*, 2nd edn. (London, 1955), appendix IV. The archives of Hoare's Bank show that further subscribers, among them Paul Docmenique and Edward Haistwell, had accounts there (see Ledger 2).

of the original Fellows in 1663. Twelve of the subscribers were elected FRS by 1697 or earlier, and a further eight were elected by 1707,[42] making twenty in all. There is a very telling overlap between those elected as Fellows from 1695 onwards and those who belonged to the Kit-Cat Club.

The Club brought together patriotism, Whig politics, and an idealistic belief in literature and the arts, but the date of its foundation is uncertain. One account locates its origins in private evening meetings between John Somers, made Lord Chancellor in 1697, Jacob Tonson, and another lawyer 'before the Revolution'.[43] Kathleen Lynch describes the club as follows:

The Kit-Cat Club was composed of many but not all, of the leaders of the Whig political party in the reigns of William and Mary, and Anne. These men were indeed patriots who worked unceasingly, whether in or out of power . . . for the clear-cut objectives of the Whig party: a limited monarchy, with a strong Parliament; resistance to French aggression; the union of England and Scotland; and the succession of the House of Hanover.[44]

The Club may have been founded as early as 1696, but no survey of its membership exists before 1702.[45] Ten of the first subscribers (10

[42] For the membership of the Royal Society, see *The Record of the Royal Society*, 4th edn. (London, 1940), pp. 375–90. The following list gives the subscribers to *Virgil* who were also an FRS in chronological order. Figures in brackets indicate year of election, and whether members were first or second subscribers; PRS stands for President of the Royal Society, and political allegiance is also indicated. Thomas Thynne, Earl of Weymouth (1664) (2); Samuel Pepys (1664) (2, PRS 1684); Sir Justinian Isham (1673) (1, Tory); William Bridgeman (1679) (2); Thomas, Earl of Pembroke (1685) (1, PRS 1686–9); Sir William Trumbull (1692) (1); Charles, Earl of Radnor (1693) (2, Whig); Charles Montagu (1695) (1, PRS 1695–8, Whig); Orlando Bridgeman (1696) (2); Thomas Foley (1696) (1, Whig); George Stepney (1697) (1, Whig); Robert Molesworth (1697) (2, Whig). Between 1697 and 1707 the following subscribers were elected Fellows: Edward Haistwell (1698) (2); John, Lord Somers (1698) (1, PRS 1698–1703, Whig); Charles, Earl of Dorset (1698) (1, Whig); Anthony Hammond (1700) (1, Tory); Sir John Percival (1701) (1); George, Prince of Denmark (1704) (1); Dr Samuel Garth (1706) (2, Whig); Sir Thomas Trevor (1707) (1, Whig).

[43] John Oldmixon, *The History of England during the Reigns of King William and Mary, Queen Anne, King George I* (1735), p. 479. Cited in Kathleen M. Lynch, *Jacob Tonson: Kit-Cat Publisher* (Knoxville, Tenn., 1971), p. 38.

[44] Lynch, *Jacob Tonson*, p. 37.

[45] Ibid. 42–6. Three contemporary lists of membership which differ in details exist: Abel Boyer, *The History of the Life of Queen Anne* (1722), p. 254 n.; John Oldmixon, *The History of England during the Reign of King William* (1733), p. 479; John Faber, *The Kit-Cat Club done from the Original Paintings of Sir Godfrey Kneller* (1735). Catherine Howells, 'The Kit-Cat Club: A Study of Patronage and Influence in Britain, 1696–1720', unpublished Ph.D. thesis, University of California at Los Angeles, 1982, does not actually establish 1696 as the starting date

per cent) belonged to the Club by then and six of the second subscribers were members in that year. These are headed by Dorset, Somers, and Charles Montagu (all three literary patrons and two of them members of the Whig Junto) as first subscribers. Colonel John Tidcombe and Dr Samuel Garth were second subscribers. Those who were in their thirties in 1702 include Charles Seymour, Duke of Somerset (Pl. 37), George Stepney (Pl. 72), William Walsh, the writer, critic, and MP (Pl. 20), Arthur Mainwaring, writer and politician (Pl. 96), John Dormer of Rousham and Deputy Lieutenant of Oxfordshire in 1701 (Pl. 24), and William Congreve, a second subscriber. In their twenties at the same time were Charles Lennox, first Duke of Richmond (Pl. 21), William Cavendish, the Marquess of Hartington (Pl. 9), and the following second subscribers—Algernon Capel, Earl of Essex, Richard Boyle, and Charles Cornwallis. To their names should be added those of Sir Godfrey Kneller, who was to paint their portraits, and the Club's secretary, Jacob Tonson.[46]

The overlapping of aesthetic and political patronage within this formation is evidenced by Somers's defeat of the Tory candidate, Sir John Parsons (ironically a second subscriber), and his son in the 1698 election in Reigate. Reigate was one of forty-three burgage boroughs, in which parliamentary votes were attached to 'ancient tenements' or 'burgages', freehold properties let for two or three pounds a year or less, which, because they carried a vote, changed hands at prices quite out of line with their value. On buying the lordship of the manor, Somers's secretary George Adney immediately bought up a large number of burgages, conveying them into dependable hands. Somers used his influence in legal circles to ensure the safety of many of them, but among those who voted for him in 1698 were William Congreve and Jacob Tonson, fellow Kit-Cats and fellow supporters of Dryden's *Virgil*.[47] (Sir Godfrey

(cited in John Brewer, *The Pleasures of the Imagination: English Culture in the Eighteenth Century* (London, 1997), pp. 40, 672). However, *Luctus Britannici: or the Tears of the British Muses . . . for the Death of John Dryden . . .* (1700) refers to the lack of any '*Kit*-Cat' to grace the volume (p. 52), and the subscription list to the *Virgil* and Somers's political use of club members (discussed below) show that the pressure group was in place in 1697 and 1698. In the discussion, I follow Lynch's findings and order. On the Kit-Cat Club see also Brewer, *Pleasures*, pp. 40–3.

[46] J. Douglas Stewart, *Sir Godfrey Kneller and the English Baroque Portrait* (Oxford, 1983), pp. 67–8, believes that Dryden was a member, but his evidence comes from 1714.

[47] See 'Reigate Surveys, Abstracts of Title and Extracts from Records', Reigate Election 22 July 1698, Surrey Record Office, Ref. 445/1, and L. Sachse, *Lord Somers: A Political Portrait*

Kneller, Addison, and Tickell were later burgage holders.[48]) It is particularly striking that Tonson, after all only a tradesman, should have been sufficiently in Somers's confidence to act in this way.

This group of Kit-Cat members had an average age of 35.4 years, which is lower than that for the other subscribers (39.1 years).[49] Their relative youth and Whig allegiance went along with a belief that they represented England's future. For these men, politics did not stand in the way of their recognition and support of an English poet whose political beliefs differed from their own. The same was true of Dryden himself, who saw Congreve as his dramatic successor, while Congreve gave Dryden advice during the disagreements with Tonson over the division of the second subscriptions and wrote the Dedication for Dryden's *Dramatick Works* in 1717.

However, the five subscribers who were both FRS and members of the Kit-Cat Club suggest a further pattern. These, with the dates of their election, are Charles Montagu (1695), George Stepney (1697), Lord Somers (1698), Dorset (1698), and Samuel Garth (1706). The three most important figures are Montagu, Somers, and Dorset. When it is realized that Montagu was President of the Royal Society from the year of his election as Fellow until 1698, immediately followed by Somers from 1698 to 1703, also made President the same year he became a Fellow, and that a substantial number of Dryden's subscribers, mainly Whigs, were elected Fellows in this period, one in which the Royal Society's membership was recovering after a loss of interest, it becomes clear that for Somers and Montagu in particular a high-profile involvement in national cultural enterprises and in public patronage of the arts played an essential role in their rapid rise to political prominence. The Whig leaders and their supporters were seeking a position of cultural dominance. The Kit-Cats' appropriation of Dryden culminated in his lavish funeral, which was arranged by Dorset and Charles Montagu, the latter defraying the considerable expenses. His embalmed body lay in state in the College of Physicians, Dr Garth delivered a Latin oration, and his hearse was pulled by six

(Manchester, 1975), p. 138. Griffin discusses Somers's role as patron and cites Sachse on Congreve's and Tonson's votes (*Literary Patronage*, pp. 47–51).

[48] Wilfrid Hooper, *Reigate: Its Story through the Ages* (Guildford: Surrey Archaeological Society, 1945), pp. 120–1.

[49] The oldest subscriber was 74, the youngest 6.

white horses to Westminster Abbey, where he was buried in Chaucer's grave.[50]

The grouping of Fellows of the Royal Society and members of the Kit-Cat Club can be further linked to Tonson's 1688 subscription edition of Milton's *Paradise Lost,* for which Dryden had been a subscriber. Nicholas von Maltzahn has argued that both Somers and Dryden were involved in helping Tonson organize this edition, and that its Oxford connections were of particular importance through the young Francis Atterbury and Dean Aldrich at Christ Church. The subscription list for *Paradise Lost* shows a number of overlapping groups pointing to a cultural rapprochement 'in which the literary interests of divergent parties might lead to some non partisan destination'. In addition to a core of Westminster and Christ Church men, subscribers to the Milton venture include many of the writers associated with Dryden's and Tonson's other literary projects in the 1680s (and indeed the 1690s). 'The gathering may be seen as looking back to the formation and development of the Royal Society, and forward to that of the Kit-Cat Club.'[51] The alliance of Whig and Anglican Tory evident here had shaped the Revolution in 1688.

One other politically neutral venture, the Music Society's yearly celebrations of St Cecilia's Day (22 November), shows Dryden's and some of his subscribers' involvement in a public competition, begun in 1683, to advance English music. Peter Motteux, writing in the *Gentleman's Journal* in 1691–2, said that these occasions attracted 'most of the lovers of music, whereof many persons are of the first rank, [and] meet at Stationers' Hall in London, not thro' a principle of superstition, but to propagate the advancement of that divine science'.[52] The yearly celebrations were normally organized by four

---

[50] For the details of Dryden's funeral, see *The Critical and Miscellaneous Prose Works of John Dryden,* ed. Edmond Malone, 4 vols. (London, 1800), i. 364–78, 562–3. See also Winn, *John Dryden and his World,* pp. 512–13, 627, and Griffin, 'Beginnings of Modern Authorship', p. 1.

[51] Nicholas von Maltzahn, 'Wood, Allam, and the Oxford Milton', *Milton Studies,* 31 (1994) 155–77, at p. 169 and *passim.* Maltzahn's account does not note that Cambridge Fellows and graduates substantially outnumber those from Oxford. Trinity College was particularly significant in providing subscribers. Dryden, or Dryden's contacts, played an important role.

[52] Cited in William H. Husk, *An Account of the Musical Celebrations of St. Cecilia's Day in the Sixteenth and Seventeenth Centuries. To which is appended a Collection of Odes on St. Cecilia's Day* (London, 1857), p. 27. The details given below of the celebrations are largely drawn from this source.

Stewards, two of whom were musicians. The two lay Stewards for the first celebration in 1683, in which three odes with music by Purcell were performed, were William Bridgeman, a second subscriber, and Gilbert Dolben, a long-standing friend of Dryden's and a first subscriber. Dryden himself wrote the ode for the 1687 celebrations. Sir John Woodhouse, a second subscriber, was one of the Stewards in 1693. In 1697 Dryden was again prevailed upon to supply the ode (*Alexander's Feast*) for that year's occasion. He grumbled to his sons that the work was 'troublesome, & no way beneficiall', and said that he had only undertaken the work because the 'Stewards of the feast... came in a body to me, to desire that kindness; one of them being Mr Bridgman, whose parents are your Mothers friends.'[53] James Winn notes that in making his decision Dryden 'probably also considered' the fact that Orlando Bridgeman was a second subscriber.[54] So too were the other three Stewards, Hugh Colville, Leonard Wessel, and Paris Slaughter (the last two lived within the City walls). Another (first) subscriber, Henry St John, later Lord Bolingbroke, reputedly saw Dryden after the poet had been up all night writing the ode.[55] This hints both at the two-way relationship between Dryden and his patrons and at the extent to which Dryden was a highly visible writer in the final decade of the century. It also explains why Dryden felt under pressure to complete his translation of Virgil. In the 'Dedication to the *Aeneis*', written between early December 1696 and early February 1697, Dryden noted that he had had to translate the *Aeneid* in three years, a work which took Virgil eleven years to write, and that he needed more time to perfect the translation, but 'some of my Subscribers grew so clamorous, that I cou'd no longer deferr the Publication'.[56] If his patrons were supportive, their expectations could also be coercive. Alexander Pope, when he began translating Homer's *Iliad*, felt overcome by the weight of his task: 'What terrible moments does one feel after one has engaged for a large work!... In the beginning of my translating the *Iliad* [1713] I wished anybody would hang me, a hundred times. It sat so heavily on my mind at first that I often used to dream of it, and so do

---

[53] *Letters*, p. 93.   [54] Winn, *John Dryden and his World*, p. 493.
[55] Husk, *Account*, p. 41 (from Scott).
[56] *Works*, v. 320.

sometimes still [1739].'[57] There are a number of other constituencies of patrons which call for attention—those connected with the Church and universities, lawyers and doctors, the military, artists and writers, Catholics, and women, all of whom figure in both subscription lists.

The Church and universities are less well represented than any other professional group. Among the first subscribers, the Duke of Ormonde was Chancellor of both Oxford and Dublin universities (Pl. 101), and the Duke of Somerset was Chancellor of Cambridge (though not so named in his plate (Pl. 37)). The Church of England is represented by the bishops of Durham and Ossory (Pls. 44, 45), grouped together with Dr John Montagu, Master of Trinity (Pl. 46), Dryden's own college. Among the second subscribers are Samuel Fuller, Dean of Lincoln, two prebends of Durham, John Bowes and Theophilus Pickering, the latter, as Winn points out, Dryden's cousin,[58] William Delawn, who became President of St John's College, Oxford, in 1698, and a further eight clerics, including Francis Atterbury.

Dr Knipe, who had succeeded as headmaster of Westminster School on Busby's death in 1695, was a two-guinea subscriber, so the current heads of both Dryden's school and college wished to be associated with his translation. If Dryden's achievement reflected on the places of his education, a sense of pride in their own education probably influenced some subscribers. Ten (10 per cent) of the first subscribers were educated at Westminster (or, in the case of Dorset's 9-year-old son, Lord Buckhurst, was being educated). They include the Marquess of Hartington, Charles Montagu, Colonel George Cholmondley, the Master of Trinity College, Gilbert Dolben, a generous friend of Dryden's, and George Stepney. A further six of the second subscribers went to school at Westminster, making sixteen in all (4.6 per cent of the whole). Graduates of Trinity College, Cambridge, number sixteen, and include Sir William Bowyer, who was there at the same time as Dryden, and extended the hospitality of Denham Court to the poet in the course of the translation. They also include (again) Charles Montagu and George

[57] Joseph Spence, *Observations, Anecdotes, and Characters of Books and Men*, ed. James M. Osborn (Oxford, 1966), i. 84.

[58] Winn, *John Dryden and his World*, p. 475.

Stepney, like Sir William, both first subscribers. However, the college which provided most subscribers for the *Virgil* was Christ Church, Oxford (thirty-two out of a total of one hundred and twenty-two from Oxford and Cambridge colleges). This reflects the distinctive humanism of Christ Church teaching under John Fell and Henry Aldrich, assisted by Francis Atterbury before his recent departure to London, with its 'emphasis on [not only] the classics but also history and modern languages',[59] and was particularly true of those trained in Busby's Westminster School. This sub-group of Westminster- and Oxbridge-educated men clearly illustrates the overlapping allegiances, intellectual, social, political, and professional, which defined Dryden's audience and patrons.

A similar pattern is observable among lawyers (twenty-one subscribers) and soldiers (twenty-eight subscribers). Both groupings are marginally older than the average age for all known subscribers, and there is an even or near-even split between Whig and Tory among MPs who voted in 1696 (nine lawyers, ten soldiers), though the list of soldiers as a whole is Williamite rather than Tory. Not surprisingly, fewer soldiers attended university or the Inns of Court, though ten went to one or the other, and of these three attended both. More significantly perhaps two members of each profession were educated at Westminster and five of each at Christ Church, while Oxford degrees dominate both lists. The army names include more subscribers from the aristocracy: eight had titles whereas among the lawyers the recently ennobled Somers is accompanied by three knights. However, over half the lawyers were first rather than second subscribers (13 : 8) whereas only a third of the military were (10 : 20).

It is perhaps significant that Tonson headed the two lists simply as 'THE NAMES OF THE SUBSCRIBERS...'. Contemporary subscription lists are frequently headed, as in the 1688 *Paradise Lost*, 'THE NAMES OF THE Nobility and Gentry...'. The nobility and gentry were undoubtedly of critical importance for the success of Dryden and Tonson's venture, but what is striking about the two-guinea subscribers is the number of professional men who subscribed. In addition to lawyers and soldiers there were

[59] Maltzahn, 'Wood, Allam, and the Oxford Milton', p. 165.

government officials, doctors, and prosperous merchants. (Significantly, no booksellers subscribed to the *Virgil*, and there are few clerics or college Fellows—differing on both counts from the make-up of subscribers to the 1688 *Paradise Lost*.) Another way of describing this feature of the second subscribers' list (since many of those described as 'Mr.' or 'Esq.' are unidentified) is to note that if knights, baronets, and nobility (including Honourables) are excluded, approximately three-quarters of the names are left.

Congreve was, it is known, active in recruiting second subscribers. Not only do the actors Betterton, Anne Bracegirdle, Elizabeth Barry, and the playwright Thomas Southerne appear among those on the second subscribers' list (though their subscriptions may have had as much to do with their prior connections with Dryden as their current connections with Congreve), but so too do Congreve's lifelong friends Walter Moyle (again known to Dryden) and Charles Mein. In collecting second subscriptions, Congreve seems to have been particularly successful in recruiting from the Middle Temple, which he had entered in 1691. Walter Moyle had entered the same year, as did another friend, Joseph Keally.[60] Other Middle Templars who appear among the second subscribers are Robert Palmer (1691), Martyn Williams (1690), and Henry Maxwell (1693).

Other names connected with the arts include the authors Richard Graham and Lady Mary Chudleigh, while the painters Sir Godfrey Kneller and John Closterman, along with the Royal Gardener at St James's Park, George London, were all five-guinea subscribers (Pls. 79, 85, 18). They are joined, in the second list, by the painter Michael Dahl, the architect Nicholas Hawksmoor, and the wood carver Grinling Gibbons.

The list shows that family feeling overrode political affiliations. It includes both Sir Robert Howard and Dryden's notorious Catholic and Jacobite cousins Bernard and Craven Howard. Three children of the fervent Cromwellian Gilbert Pickering also paid two guineas for the work of their Catholic cousin—Sir John Pickering, the current baronet at Titchmarsh, his brother Theophilus, a prebendary of Durham cathedral, and their sister, Elizabeth Creed.[61]

---

[60] For Mein and Keally, see Kathleen M. Lynch, *A Congreve Gallery* (Cambridge, Mass., 1951), pp. 17–18, 23–36.

[61] Winn, *John Dryden and his World*, p. 475.

There are a number of surprising subscribers. The Catholic Henry Tasburgh (Pl. 53) appears in the first subscribers' list (as Zwicker notes),[62] as does Sir Bartholomew Shower, a Jacobite (Pl. 28). In the list of second subscribers, Chidley Brook was a collector and receiver of excise in New York.[63]

Perhaps most surprising is the dedicatory plate to James Cecil, Earl of Salisbury.[64] This can hardly be the fifth earl (1691–1728) who was only 3 or 4 when the subscription was made between June 1694 and June 1695. His father, the fourth earl, sent three guineas for 'Mr Dryden's book' before he died on 22 October 1693.[65] As William Frost points out, this could have seemed 'deliberately pointed'. The plate (Pl. 38) illustrating *Aeneis*, ii. 290, which shows Laocoön struggling with the two mysterious serpents which have already killed his two sons, symbolizes a 'hopeless minority resistance to treacherous foreign incursion'.[66] Salisbury, who had converted to Catholicism in 1687 while in Rome on a diplomatic mission for James II, was impeached on a charge of high treason for being a Catholic in 1689, was the victim in 1692 of a false accusation of plotting the death of William III, was twice imprisoned in the Tower, and was viciously lampooned by his political enemies as a Catholic and Jacobite.[67] Like Laocoön, the Trojans' high priest, who immediately saw the real purpose behind the Greeks' gift of the wooden horse and foresaw their sacking of Troy, Salisbury is cast as a prophet in his own land, warning helplessly of an impending fate, one which has now overtaken his country and himself. The plate then is a memorial of his resolute adherence to the Stuart cause and to Catholicism.[68]

---

[62] Zwicker, *Politics and Language*, p. 235.

[63] *Calendar of Treasury Books...*, ed. William A. Shaw (London, 1933), xii. 170, 173.

[64] Zwicker, *Politics and Language*, p. 192. Frost makes the same point: *Works*, vi. 872.

[65] Cited from the Hatfield House Archives in Paul Hammond, 'A Song Attributed to Dryden', *Library*, 6th ser., 21 (1999) 59–66, at p. 61. Hammond believes the payment was for *Love Triumphant*, published *c*. March 1694. However, Dryden's contract for the *Virgil* had been signed four months earlier on 10 June, and three guineas is an odd figure for a gift.

[66] *Works*, vi. 872. Zwicker, *Politics and Language*, p. 192, sees the plate as a 'memorial' to Salisbury. I am grateful to Paul Hammond for drawing my attention to the full significance of the relation between the plate and the first part of the *Aeneis*, Book II.

[67] See Frost, *Works*, vi. 872, and *Poems on Affairs of State: Augustan Satirical Verse 1660–1714*, vol. iv: *1685–1688*, ed. Galbraith M. Crump (New Haven, 1968), pp. 155–6 and nn., 325 n., 328 and n.

[68] The dedication to 'Roger Earl of Orrery...' (Pl. 40) could be a retrospective dedication, but the second earl died in 1682, and even though his widow lived until 1710 it seems more likely that this is a slip for Lionel, the third earl.

One final important group of patrons which, like serving MPs, constitutes a tenth of the first subscribers is made up of women. In addition to Princess Anne (Pl. 32), three women subscribed as the wife of a high-ranking first subscriber—the Duchess of Ormonde (Pl. 33), Anne, Countess of Exeter (Pl. 34), and the Marchioness of Normanby (Pl. 36). Subscription evidently went by families. Lady Mary Sackville (Pl. 74) was the daughter of the Earl of Dorset. The Countess Dowagers of Winchilsea (Pl. 35) and Northampton (Pl. 42) are present in their own right, as are Lady Dorothy Brownlowe (Pl. 54), Lady Giffard (Pl. 50), and Mrs Ann Baynard (Pl. 64). The last, who died on 12 June 1697 aged 25, and so never received her copy of the *Virgil*, was noted for her learning, her knowledge of languages, and her piety.[69] There are another fifteen women among the two-guinea subscribers, giving an overall total of twenty-five, which at 7.2 per cent represents a significant minority. Among them two are the wives of first subscribers, Anne, Duchess of Richmond, and Lady Jane Leveson-Gower (who had died in 1696). The Duchess of Devonshire's appearance in the second list looks across at her son's place among the first subscribers, and is a reminder of her husband's failure to find a place alongside her son. Lady Mary Chudleigh, a writer and poet, whose verses on the *Virgil* Dryden thought should have been printed in the second edition of his work,[70] was another second subscriber. As noted earlier, two of the leading actresses of the time, Elizabeth Barry and Anne Brace-girdle, gave their two guineas, and their names, in support of Dryden's venture. Elizabeth Creed, Dryden's cousin, who was at his bedside when he died and who, in her old age, erected a monument to Dryden and his family in Titchmarsh church, gave familial support in the second list. Lady Mary Fenwick's appearance in the same list has the effect, intentional or not, of memorializing her executed anti-Williamite husband. The remaining seven women are unidentified.

[69] See George Ballard, *Memoirs of Several Ladies of Great Britain, who have been celebrated for their Writings or Skill in the Learned Languages Arts and Sciences* (Oxford, 1752), pp. 349–60. This gives substantial quotations from John Prude's *A Sermon at the Funeral of Mrs. Ann Baynard . . . June the 16th 1697* (1697). This may be another memorial subscription. Her father, Edward, had subscribed to *Paradise Lost* (1688).

[70] *Letters*, p. 98. By accident or design, this never happened. For her poem, discussed below, see *Works*, vi. 1188–90.

The presence of so many women reflects their increasing influence on the arts in the 1690s. In the late 1680s and 1690s, prologues and epilogues written for the public stage identify a 'ladies' faction', which they believed was affecting the reception of comedy in particular. Although David Roberts has questioned the causal connection made by critics like J. H. Smith and Robert Hume between their presence in the audience and the movement towards sentimental comedy, demonstrating that the idea of a single 'faction' is untenable, he nevertheless admits to a heightened awareness of women's position in society in general.[71] (And women had been significant subscribers to the 1693 Tontine and the Bank of England—making up 11.9 per cent in number and 5.9 per cent in value.[72]) Certainly, Dryden takes care to address the 'Ladies' in his 'Dedication of the *Aeneis*' when discussing the possible faults of Virgil's epic: '[Aeneas] is Arraign'd with more shew of Reason by the Ladies; who will make a numerous Party against him, for being false to Love, in forsaking *Dido*. And I cannot much blame them; for to say the truth, 'tis an ill precedent for their Gallants to follow.'[73] Despite a condescending final sentence to this paragraph (Dryden says Dido's example teaches young ladies not to shelter from the rain in a cave in the company of their lover), he gives over the next five pages to dealing with this charge, and in 1691 he had written the preface to William Walsh's *A Dialogue concerning Women, being a Defence of the Sex*. A surprising number of women mentioned or wrote about Dryden in the last decade of the seventeenth century. Lady Mary Chudleigh has already been mentioned. The year the *Virgil* was published, the 18-year-old Catherine Trotter wrote a verse epistle to Congreve, whom she describes as Dryden's successor (Congreve was to correspond with her, and give technical advice on her tragedy, *The Revolution in Sweden* (1703)).[74] Elizabeth Rowe mentions Dryden favourably in her *Poems on Several*

---

[71] David Roberts, *The Ladies: Female Patronage of Restoration Drama 1660–1700* (Oxford, 1989). For the opposite view see e.g. J. H. Smith, 'Shadwell, the Ladies, and the Change in Comedy', *Modern Philology*, 46 (1948) 22–33, and Robert Hume, 'The Change in Comedy: Cynical versus Exemplary Comedy on the London Stage, 1678–1693', *Theatre*, 1 (1983) 101–18.

[72] Dickson, *Financial Revolution*, p. 256.

[73] *Works*, v. 294.

[74] *William Congreve: Letters and Documents*, ed. John C. Hodges (New York, 1964), pp. 198–200, 212–13.

Occasions (1696),[75] and on Dryden's death a group of women published a joint elegiac volume, *The Nine Muses. Or, Poems written by Nine Several Ladies upon the Death of the late Famous John Dryden Esq.* (1700).[76] Among the contributors are Catherine Trotter, Mary Pix, and Mary Manley, all three dramatists. This elegiac volume, whose title offers it as a female equivalent of *Luctus Britannici: or the Tears of the British Muses; for the Death of John Dryden* (also published in 1700), throughout presents Dryden as an enabling poetic father-figure.

The main reason for this, although his original work is praised, was Dryden's role as a translator, which made the classics available to women readers. Lady Mary Chudleigh's poems and prose, with their astonishingly wide range of references to classical literature, history, and philosophy, are proof of the effectiveness of learning based on English translations,[77] and she explicitly praised Dryden's *Virgil* for making the poet available to women:

> This Work, great Poet, was reserv'd for thee,
> None else cou'd us from our Confinement free . . .[78]

One of the recurrent themes in her own writing is the importance for women of reading widely in serious contemporary and translated literature if they are to escape their confines and to live rationally.[79] She was not alone. Aphra Behn had thanked Creech in 1683 for his translation of Lucretius which advanced women from 'the state of Ignorance | And Equallst Us to Men!'[80] Elizabeth Thomas was grateful to Dryden for translating Juvenal, Persius, and Virgil,[81] and on 10 May 1696 Elizabeth Rowe wrote that all women

---

[75] Sig. 2A4[v] (p. 8).

[76] I owe this reference to Paul Hammond. On the two elegiac volumes, see Ruth Salvaggio, 'Verses on the Death of Mr. Dryden', *Journal of Popular Culture*, 21 (1987) 75–91.

[77] The point is made by Margaret J. M. Ezell in her introduction to *The Poems and Prose of Mary, Lady Chudleigh* (New York and Oxford, 1993), p. xxvii. Ezell points out that the usual claim that Lady Mary was unhappily married is not based on any evidence.

[78] *Works*, vi. 1189.

[79] See especially 'The Resolution', in *The Poems and Prose of Mary, Lady Chudleigh*, pp. 88–111. See also 'Of Knowledge to the Ladies' (pp. 255–61) and 'Of Grief' (pp. 295–6).

[80] *T. Lucretius Carus. The Epicurean Philosopher . . . The Second Edition* (Oxford, 1683), sig. d4[r].

[81] *Luctus Britannici*, p. 13, where the poem appears anonymously. Elizabeth Thomas is identified as the author in her *Miscellany Poems on Several Subjects* (1722), which has five poems on Dryden.

could now read Plutarch, presumably referring to the Dryden–Tonson version.[82]

In 1696, in *An Essay in Defence of the Female Sex*, Judith Drake noted that women could make considerable progress in learning since translations meant that 'scarce any thing either Ancient or modern that might be of general use either for Pleasure, or Instruction is left untouch'd'.[83] As early as 1680 Dryden had recognized how the translation of *Ovid's Epistles* enfranchised women readers, while assuring them that Ovid's 'amorous expressions go no further than virtue may allow'.[84]

Indeed, in the last two years of his life, Dryden enjoyed a correspondence with two young women writers. His letters to his 26-year-old kinswoman Mrs Elizabeth Steward, whom he describes as 'a Poetess', and to Elizabeth Thomas, who had sent him verses, show the ageing poet taking considerable care in writing to them.[85] (Nor should his attitude be read as merely one of condescension. He had reason to be grateful for the critical acuity of Lady Jane Hyde, daughter-in-law of Laurence, Earl of Rochester, and daughter of Sir William Leveson Gower, who successfully fought to have the queen's stage ban on *Cleomenes* (1692) relaxed.[86]) These examples suggest that the reading, and even the writing of poetry by women, and their reading of men's translations from the classics, created a 'polite' space into which they could be admitted on more equal (if still male-governed) terms.

This analysis of Dryden's and Tonson's subscribers entirely bears out Johnson's belief that the English nation was interested in the success of Dryden's translation. More importantly, it demonstrates the complexity of the way in which Dryden's folio translation of Virgil sited itself within the fractured society that was the England of 1697. As is by now more than evident, the *Virgil* spoke to and for a wide variety of constituencies in terms of age, politics, social and professional standing, religion, and gender. A recurrent theme in Dryden's three dedications and Postscript is the belief that his

---

[82] 'To the Reader', Elizabeth Rowe, *Poems on Several Occasions* (1696), sig. a3ᵛ.
[83] pp. 41–2 (cited by Ezell in *The Poems and Prose of Mary, Lady Chudleigh*, p. xxvii).
[84] Preface to *Ovid's Epistles* (1680), *Works*, i. 114.
[85] Dryden referred to Mrs Steward as a writer on 4 March 1699 (*Letters*, p. 113), and gave Elizabeth Thomas advice on her verses and on her reading (*Letters*, pp. 125–8, 132).
[86] See Roberts, *The Ladies*, pp. 116–19.

translation is a patriotic endeavour, one undertaken on his country's behalf, one which united it in the face of the divisive political and religious tensions evident in the 1690s—and only too evident in the lived experience of those who chose to subscribe to the *Virgil* between 1694 and 1697. Dryden, Tonson, and their subscribers all believed that the translation united the nation in an aesthetic realm which transcended the fractious and unstable actualities of 1697.

II

There are at least two issues raised by this account of Dryden's 349 subscribers' social, educational, and political backgrounds. First, how exactly do the coded Jacobite messages in the dedications, Postscript, and plates square with Dryden's and Tonson's evident desire not only to attract patrons of all persuasions, but to create a sense of common national purpose through support for the translation? Second, how did the first subscribers in particular regard the single large folio volume they eventually received? The second is easier to answer than the first, but may help to explain how the apparent conflict between Tonson's Whig beliefs and Dryden's veiled Jacobitism was acceptable to the first subscribers.

For the first subscribers, who had to pay three guineas down in 1695, and for Tonson, who had to pay Dryden £200 copy money in stages between 1694 and 1697, supporting the translation was an act of faith, based on their belief in Dryden's outstanding abilities as a classicist and poet, and the cultural significance of the project itself. Dryden's receipt of the copy money and the first three guineas of the 101 subscribers (together with the one guinea from second subscribers) gave him the time to undertake the translation (done alongside other prior commitments[87]).

What the first subscribers received on paying their final two guineas in the summer of 1697 was a large-paper folio in quires which was personally customized in that one of the 101 plates had their coat of arms at the foot of the engraving with their own self-description reading across it. The individual copy could be further personalized by the choice of binding, which could have

---

[87] These are carefully detailed in the contract signed on 15 June 1694: *Works*, vi. 1179–83.

substantially increased the overall cost.[88] William Frost's notes to the California edition of the *Virgil* demonstrate that some first subscribers cared very much indeed about their individual copies. There were two particularly touchy cases. One involved a change of rank. Dorothy Brownlowe (Pl. 54) chose to describe herself fulsomely: 'Daughter & Coheiress of S.ʳ Richard Mason K.ᵗ Clerk Comtroler of yᵉ Greencloth to K. Charles yᵉ 2.ᵈ K James yᵉ 2.ᵈ Wife to William Brownlowe 2.ᵈ son to S.ʳ Richard Brownlowe Bar.ᵗ of Humby in yᵉ County of Lincolne'.[89] As is evident from the abbreviations, the engraver found this wealth of detail difficult to compress into the limited space available. Dorothy Brownlowe's insistence on her own position as 'Coheiress' suggests at least a degree of self-assertion (her husband did not subscribe), while the particularity of the description of her father's function in the courts of Charles II and James II may be a gesture of solidarity with the Stuarts now that the country was under William of Orange's rule. In the list of subscribers in both the first and second editions of the *Virgil* she is mistakenly described as '*Mrs.* Ann Brownlow' instead of 'Dorothy', an error she seems not to have noticed. But when her husband became a baronet following the death of his brother on 16 July 1697 she asked for the plate to be changed to read 'Lady' instead of 'Mrs. Dorothy' (Chicago, Folger copies). Most copies do not have this alteration to the plate. Since the *Virgil* was announced as ready for publication on 24–8 July, the engraver had no more than seven days' warning that this change was required. Each of Ogilby's 101 plates had to be machined as many as 351 times on a separate rolling press, so that a late alteration obviously presented practical problems. It must have been too late to change all 351 impressions. A few pulls from the altered plates were run off, and Tonson ensured that Lady Brownlowe or her binder were sent a corrected state, thus allowing her to have a personalized copy for herself and her family. For Lady Brownlowe her large-paper copy was, as no doubt for other subscribers, both a private *and* a public space.

A similar technical problem, though for quite different reasons, was created by Plate 17 (for *Georgics*, ii. 145), which depicts a rather

---

[88] Hugh Amory reports that what may have been John Lewknor's large-paper copy (Houghton, Typ 605.97.868F) is inscribed 'J Lewkener Pre. 6ˡⁱ: 2ˢ.' This may represent a first subscription plus the cost of binding: if so, Lewknor paid 17s. for his binding.

[89] See *Works*, v. 482, for the plate, and vi. 1014 for the changes made.

pudgy Bacchus astride a large wine barrel, holding a glass of wine in his right hand and a bunch of grapes in his left, and with a vineyard to his left. Two of the subscribers did not wish their names to be associated with such an image. Gilbert Dolben, a generous friend of Dryden and also the son of an archbishop, clearly objected to being assigned this plate. In some copies of the first edition, this plate is exchanged with that originally given to Sir Thomas Dyke (Pl. 63). This clearly grated. Sir Thomas was sufficiently concerned to ensure that, while unable to do anything about the first edition, in at least some copies his name was taken off and replaced by that of John Pulteney (originally Pl. 67) when the second edition was published in 1698. It is hard to believe that Sir Thomas's unlocated copy of the first edition did not have the same change made.[90]

All three examples show how much the first dedicatees were concerned by the statement being made about their own status in the *Virgil*. Lady Brownlowe, Gilbert Dolben, Sir Thomas Dyke, and, one would have thought, John Pulteney, cared a great deal how their names appeared in their own copy in their own house. Whether they knew that printing and binding processes beyond their control meant that other owners and readers were seeing plates inscribed with their names either inaccurately or inappositely is uncertain. John Pulteney may never have known that most of the plates in the second edition of 1698 assigned the image of Bacchus to him.

Further proof of the subscriber's strong proprietorial attitude is provided by the copy, probably that of the Marquess of Hartington, now in the library of Chatsworth. It is bound in Russia, with tooled spine, gilt edges, and the Devonshire arms are impressed and gilded on the front board. The engraved ducal bookplate is pasted onto the verso of the title-page.[91] In this copy the list of first subscribers is deliberately excised, but that of the second subscribers is kept.[92] One

---

[90] Frost, *Works*, vi. 920–1.

[91] The volume's hinges have been repaired, but it is otherwise in very good condition. There are no signs of use. It is a large-paper copy (case 27, shelf a). The bookplate is possibly that of the first duke, in which case this is the copy to which his wife was a second subscriber. More likely it is that of his son, who added the bookplate some time after he succeeded. A second, small-paper, copy (case 23, shelf c) has the signature 'George Granville' (probably that of the first Earl Granville (1773–1846), brother-in-law of the sixth duke) on the title-page. I am grateful to Mr P. Day, Keeper of Collections, for his generous help.

[92] The leaf containing 'THE NAMES OF THE SUBSCRIBERS | TO THE Cuts of Virgil. | Each Subscription being Five Guineas' is conjugate with that containing the errata

reason for this may be that the first subscribers are described more fully (and sometimes more accurately) on the plates themselves; another, and probably more important, factor is that the list of subscribers to the plates, that is, the first subscribers, says that each had paid 'Five Guineas'. The vulgarity of mentioning the price paid by first subscribers is the most likely cause for the list's omission from the Chatsworth copy. The patron's increase in cultural capital through his patronage of *The Works of Virgil* was not to be seen as a direct consequence of a financial payment by an aristocrat to an author. Even some of those who bought the second edition, to which they were neither first nor second subscribers, felt proprietorial about their copies. The Brotherton copy of the second edition has a very precise bookplate pasted onto the verso of the title-page. Engraved beneath his coat of arms is the following description: 'The Right Hon:^ble James Lord Viscount Seafield Lord Ogilbie of Cullen. Sole secretary of state for the kingdom of scotland 1698.' For the first subscribers in particular their copy of the *Virgil* was at once an object of pride and a means of self-aggrandizement.

It is likely that Tonson realized more clearly than Dryden that the first 101 copies of the *Virgil* would be regarded by the first subscribers as luxury objects and status symbols. A Williamite's focus on his or her own copy may have led them to overlook the contradictory signals from some of the plates, from Dryden's surrounding prose, and from some of the names of the second subscribers. Or, if such readers did notice, there were more than enough first and second subscribers sharing their views to make them feel representatives of one powerful section of the nation which had chosen to support the Dryden–Tonson venture.

III

The outline of the differing constituencies which make up Dryden's subscribers given so far is, necessarily, a fairly static account of what was in actuality a continuing and many-layered process of exchange between patrons and clients. Behind the public acknowledgements

---

and the 'Directions to the Binder', which is itself part of the late printed section (sigs. †–2†²) containing the complimentary poems on Dryden's translation. The binder had to cut out 2†2, but bound in the disjunct leaf (χ1), printed at the last minute, containing the names of the second subscribers.

of patronage in printed dedications or subscription lists lie complex negotiations which are usually hidden from view. One way of revealing these interconnections is to note that, while first subscribers are dominated by the Williamite court and state structure, a fifth of them had previous direct connections with Dryden, either by themselves or through family. The most important group here is those members of the aristocracy who were Dryden's former patrons or their descendants. Three of these eight families subscribed for more than one plate, giving him twelve first subscriptions.[93] While husbands and wives may have wanted two copies for their own use, this is more likely to be a form of patronal generosity. It is also noticeable that although most of these families were to a greater or lesser extent opposed to the Williamite settlement, William's Lord Chamberlain, Dorset, and his household subscribed for five copies,[94] a very public endorsement of the translation. The Earl of Exeter and his wife, whose hospitality had supported Dryden during his translation, subscribed, as did Sir William Bowyer for the same reason. Two old friends, Gilbert Dolben and John Lewknor, are numbered among the first subscribers, as are Lord Somers and George Stepney, both Williamite officials, who had contributed to works edited by Dryden. Sir Robert Howard, the poet's brother-in-law, paid his five guineas, as did the two physicians who attended Dryden while he was working on the translation, Dr William Gibbons and Dr Thomas Hobbs. All these groups of subscribers chose to do so from different motives, and if Princess Anne and her family made three subscriptions in support of a Stuart author, a quarter of all the first subscriptions are accounted for.

A glimpse into the way in which one sub-section of the *Virgil*'s patrons were mutually supportive is given in a letter written to Tonson by the diplomat George Stepney from Lippstadt on 14–24 February 1695. It is not directly concerned with Dryden's translation but with Stepney's *A Poem Dedicated to the Gracious Memory of Her Late Gracious Majesty Queen Mary* (1695), a draft of which was

[93] These are the Earl of Dorset, his son, Lord Buckhurst, and daughter, Lady Mary Sackville; Hugh, Lord Clifford, Catholic son of Dryden's patron (he was also a second subscriber); the Duke of Ormonde (grandson of Dryden's earlier supporter) and his wife; John Sheffield, Marquess of Normanby and his wife; the Earl of Abingdon; the son of the Earl of Orrery; the Earl of Sunderland; and the son of Dryden's patron, the Earl of Salisbury.

[94] Brice Harris, *Charles Sackville: Patron and Poet of the Restoration* (Urbana, Ill., 1940), p. 198.

enclosed along with Stepney's own sharp criticism of individual words and lines. Kathleen Lynch notes that Stepney not only asked his bookseller to show his draft to Dryden, Charles Montagu, and Congreve for their comments and improvements, but also trusted some of the verbal alterations to Tonson himself, and that the printed text does indeed include many alterations.[95]

In addition, the letter gives valuable information, ignored by Lynch as not to her purpose, about the nexus of clientage and patronage which produced the elegy. Stepney, who had taken up the task unwillingly, says he only wrote the poem 'at Sr W. Trumbulls com'and (to wch I always pay great deference)' (not surprisingly, as Trumbull was one of the Secretaries of State and Stepney was an official envoy), and, more unexpectedly, 'at y^r [Tonson's] desire'.[96] Stepney, who expected no payment, but hoped Tonson would not make a loss, asks him, once the poem is printed, to 'give in my name' copies to Charles Montagu (who is to decide whether it should be published anonymously or not), Sir William Trumbull, William Blathwayt (Secretary of War), the Duke of Shrewsbury, and a 'Mr Vernon', through whom Stepney had sent his letter. This must be James Vernon, Whig MP, who succeeded Sir William as Secretary of State in late 1697. Apart from Dryden and Tonson, all these men were first or second subscribers. With the exception of Dryden and Trumbull, all were strong Whigs and three were members of the Kit-Cat Club, while Dryden, Stepney, and Montagu had been educated at both Westminster and Trinity College.

This letter gives a satisfyingly complete example of how patronage worked.[97] Stepney's elegy was written at the 'com'and' of one of the Secretaries of State for obvious political reasons, and at the request of a bookseller for both political and commercial reasons. Stepney asks for advice from the leading poet of the day, Dryden, and puts his request for help very carefully: 'Perhaps the subject is not ye most agreeable to Mr Dryden; yet I am persuaded he is so much my friend as to deal impartially with me, and I hope will alter severall places in the many that want to be corrected.' Stepney also

---

[95] Lynch, *Jacob Tonson*, pp. 106–7.

[96] *The Gentlemen's Magazine*, NS 8 (Oct. 1837) 362–4. The following quotations are from this source.

[97] For the relations between Dryden and Stepney, see David Hopkins, 'Charles Montague, George Stepney and Dryden's *Metamorphoses*', *Review of English Studies*, NS 51 (2000) 83–9.

sought out the advice of another poet, Congreve, consulted Prior, and approached Montagu as politician, patron, and poet (all three Whigs). Finally, once the poem was printed, he sent copies to five influential politicians, one of whom had been asked to advise. No copies went to Dryden, Congreve, or Prior (though he did ask Tonson to send a dozen copies to his sisters). Propaganda for the king, the need to satisfy his superiors, and personal advancement are Stepney's motives. While commonplace at the time, this example is fully detailed from beginning to end. Particularly interesting is Dryden's role as an impartial father-figure, and the proactive and executive action on the part of Tonson, to whom Stepney writes with familiarity but also with a recognition of his important powers as a literary broker in 1695.

The linkage of Dryden and Tonson here is a reminder of their association since 1679, when Tonson was 24 and Dryden 48. In the early years, certainly, it was Dryden who acted as an adviser and editor for Tonson's edition of Ovid's *Epistles* (1680) and Plutarch's *Lives* (1683–6), making full use of his Cambridge connections.[98] Although there is little overlap between the translators Dryden attracted to these ventures and the subscription list for *Virgil*, there is enough overlap between those who both contributed to the four Dryden–Tonson *Miscellanies* published before 1697 and who subscribed to the translation to suggest a connection, one underlined by Dryden's frequent references to the translations from different parts of *Virgil* published in their pages. In the Postscript Dryden names three translations which he found particularly difficult to equal, the anonymous translation of *Georgics*, iii. 209–85, Roscommon's translation of *Eclogue* VI, and Addison's translation of *Georgics*, iv. 1–314. The first two appeared in *Miscellany Poems* (1684) while Addison's translation was published in the *Annual Miscellany* (1694). Dryden assumes that his reader will have ready access to this run of *Miscellanies*, for instead of giving any notes for *Eclogue* VI he writes, 'My Lord *Roscommon*'s Notes on this Pastoral, are equal to his excellent Translation of it; and thither I refer the Reader.'[99] Dryden's 'Notes

---

[98] See Arthur Sherbo, 'Dryden as a Cambridge Editor', *Studies in Bibliography*, 38 (1985) 251–61, and 'The Dryden–Cambridge Translation of Plutarch's *Lives*', *Études anglaises*, 32 (1979) 177–84. See also Paul Hammond, 'The Circulation of Dryden's Poetry', *Papers of the Bibliographical Society of America*, 86 (1992) 355–409, at pp. 401–4.

[99] *Works*, vi. 813.

and Observations' make further references to translations in *Miscellany Poems* (1684). He notes that *Pastorals* VIII and X 'are already Translated to all manner of advantage, by my excellent friend, Mr. *Stafford*' in the 1684 volume, as well as the Camilla episode in the *Aeneid* (corresponding to Dryden's xi. 962–1210) which was published in *Sylvae* (1685).[100] He also claims that Knightly Chetwood's translation of the 'Praises of Italy' in *Georgics*, Book II is 'the greatest Ornament' of *Miscellany Poems* (1684).[101] A glance at the contents pages of the four Tonson–Dryden *Miscellanies* before 1697 reveals interesting overlaps with the *Virgil*. *Miscellany Poems* (1684) is dominated by Dryden's own translations, but also includes translations by George Stepney (a future first subscriber, and another product of Westminster and Trinity) and, as already mentioned, Knightly Chetwood. The 1693 *Miscellany* includes a poem by Mulgrave, a poem and translations of Homer and Horace by William Congreve, the former highly praised in Dryden's Dedication, and Addison's 'To Mr. Dryden by Mr. Jo. Addison'. *The Annual Miscellany* (1694) again contains poems and translations by both Addison and Congreve, as well as, interestingly, Lauderdale's translation of the *Georgics*, Book I. Addison's fawning 'An Account of the Greatest English Poets' places 'Great Dryden' as the apogee of English poetry, whose Muse will survive in his friend Congreve (exactly echoing Dryden's own view of the matter), before going on to find subsequent space to praise Charles Montagu, finally directing his own Muse to Dorset. George Granville, later Lord Lansdowne, also contributed to both the 1693 and 1694 miscellanies, and contributed one of the commendatory poems to the *Virgil* (though he chose not to subscribe). Granville, who was 30 in 1697, lived in literary retirement during the reign of William III, only entering public life on the accession of Queen Anne, when he became an early patron of the young Alexander Pope.

This overlap between gentlemen writers, and those of Dryden's subscribers who also helped in one way or another with the translation of the *Virgil*, shows how the *Miscellanies* were active in several directions at once. Between 1684 and 1694 they encouraged gentle-

---

[100] *Works*, vi. 813. Frost identifies him as probably the Honourable John Stafford, a Catholic, by this time 'a prominent Jacobite at James II's court in exile' (*Works*, vi. 1116).

[101] *Works*, vi. 814. Chetwood translated *Georgics*, ii. 136–76 (corresponds to Dryden's ll. 187–246).

man translators and more serious writers to translate passages from the classics, as well as allowing Dryden to demonstrate his abilities as a translator of, among others, Virgil. Tonson, who financed the sequence of volumes, was responding to what he sensed was a literary trend, but was also creating an audience, one which would in due course support (though he could not have known that in 1684) the *Virgil*. The series of *Miscellanies*, and other translations, with Tonson as publisher and Dryden as adviser, gave them powers of cultural patronage over their contributors, whether aristocratic amateurs or ambitious young men. Contributors could make use of their association with the *Miscellanies* (and with Dryden) to further their own careers.

This is neatly demonstrated in the case of Addison, and accounts for Addison's (and Knightly Chetwood's) willingness to contribute, apparently out of generosity at the last moment, substantial anonymous prose pieces to the *Virgil*. Addison's 'An Essay on the Georgicks' is about 3,000 words long. In 1697 Addison was 25. He had arrived at Queen's College, Oxford, in 1687, his classical abilities were quickly noticed, and he was awarded a demyship at Magdalen in 1689, taking his MA in 1693. At this time he seems to have expected to take orders. He published Latin verses on the crowning of William III in an Oxford collection of 1689, followed by another Latin poem on the king in a similar collection the following year. That the appearance in *Examen Poeticum* in 1693 of a single short poem in praise of Dryden was followed in *The Annual Miscellany* of 1694 by a translation of the largest part of *Georgics*, Book IV, one admired by Dryden, along with his 'A Song for St. *Cecilia's* Day, at Oxford' and 'An Account of the Greatest English Poets', suggests that the 22-year-old quickly learnt how to use his classical abilities to put himself in the way of potential patronage. His poem to the king, published in 1695, was dedicated to the influential Whig patron of literature John Somers. At this time, too, Tonson asked him to contribute to and help edit Herodotus, and to translate the second book of Ovid (nothing came of the first, and Tonson did not publish Addison's Ovid translation until his 1704 *Miscellany*).[102] According to Steele, Congreve introduced Addison to his own patron, Montagu. Addison was probably

---

[102] *The Letters of Joseph Addison*, ed. Walter Graham (Oxford, 1941), pp. 1–2.

appointed a probationary fellow at Magdalen in 1697, the year Dryden's *Virgil* was published containing his essay on the *Georgics*. In the same year, Addison also dedicated to Montagu a Latin poem on the Peace of Ryswick. Montagu not only obtained a £300 pension for him through Somers, but also wrote to the head of Magdalen in support of Addison, who became a full Fellow the following year in 1698, a position he did not resign until 1711. By 1697, then, Addison had managed to place himself in a position to pursue a career in the Church and as a writer, at the same time that Montagu seems to have been encouraging him to think of a diplomatic career. The subsequent twists and turns in Addison's career do not affect how he perceived his position when agreeing to write and then publish his essay anonymously in Dryden's translation. Although the general public could not identify its author, Dryden's and Tonson's immediate circles would have known, and so too would Montagu. By writing the essay, Addison contributed a part of the supporting framework to the English *Virgil*, and appeared as a doubly generous friend to the older poet, first for helping him out of a difficult position, and secondly for modestly withholding his name, so that no glory would be taken from Dryden's achievement.

The recurrence of Tonson's name in these instances places him as a facilitator, go-between, entrepreneur, and cultural broker who by the 1690s had made himself a crucial figure in England's literary culture. As Keith Walker points out, the Kneller portrait of Tonson, a mere bookseller, in the National Gallery is 'a "document" of the first importance'.[103] It memorializes his role as secretary of the Kit-Cat Club, and his acquaintance with peers and Whig authors, and makes a clear statement about his own cultural importance—in his right hand he firmly holds a bound copy of Milton's *Paradise Lost*. Tonson was not simply the beneficiary of Whig patronage, but from early in his career had placed a high value on his own influence. Many years later he admitted that he had successfully forged two complimentary poems for the second edition of Thomas Creech's translation of Lucretius (Oxford, 1683) which were attributed at the time to Dryden and to Waller. Tonson's reason for risking his relationship with Dryden, then at an early stage, was to impress Creech. When Creech came up to London following the

---

[103] 'Jacob Tonson, Bookseller', *American Scholar*, 61 (1992) 424–30, at p. 424.

publication of the first edition of his translation, and was much praised, Tonson introduced him to Dryden and to Waller. When he got back to Oxford, Creech asked Tonson to persuade the two older poets to write on his behalf: as Tonson found that Dryden would not agree and he knew that nothing could be expected from Waller, Tonson made good the lack himself because he was obliged to Creech for contributing to the Dryden–Tonson *Plutarch*, and because he wanted to get the rights to publish Creech's forthcoming translation of Horace.[104] Tonson successfully fooled Creech and kept his 'secret' to himself. This curious episode is testimony to the high value Tonson placed on his own reputation as an influence in the London literary world. By the 1690s he could not only promise work to an up-and-coming young man like Addison but was himself patronizing painters. He commissioned James Maubert in about 1695 to paint Dryden's portrait (now in the National Portrait Gallery). It depicts Dryden in a gown and slippers, with his left elbow next to an open volume of Shakespeare resting against a pile of books by Homer, Virgil, Horace, and Montaigne. It is a flattering portrait showing Tonson's good taste, his aspirations to gentility, and his admiration for Dryden, who, along with *Paradise Lost*, made his fortune. It also indicates that Dryden and Tonson, despite their disputes, respected each other.

All four examples demonstrate the workings of a mutually beneficial cultural reciprocity between individual agents whose politics, class, and age could all be widely at odds.

IV

Dryden and Tonson believed rightly that *The Works of Virgil* brought a divided nation together in its common support for an important English cultural achievement, proving that the growing sense of England's expansionist commercial and imperial power was matched by English poetry, a poetry which had established itself as the equal (or more) of contemporary Continental poetry. Dryden's 'Postscript to the Reader' begins with its well-known self-portrait of the ageing poet 'strugling with Wants, oppress'd with Sickness,

---

[104] Tonson to his nephew on 22 April 1728: see G. Thorn-Drury, 'Some Notes on Dryden', *Review of English Studies*, I (1925) 196–7. See also Lynch, *Jacob Tonson*, pp. 101–2.

curb'd in my Genius, lyable to be misconstrued in all I write', lied
about by his enemies, yet nevertheless a man 'steady to my Principles'. Despite all these problems, 'I have, by the Blessing of God on
my Endeavours, overcome all difficulties; and, in some measure,
acquitted my self of the Debt which I ow'd the Publick, when
I undertook this Work.' Dryden's 'indebtedness' is no figure of
speech: the public had given him the time to translate Virgil
through their subscriptions. Not only has Dryden repaid the debt,
but has done so, he modestly implies, with interest. Imperfect as his
translation is 'for want of Health and leisure to Correct it, will be
judg'd in after Ages, and possibly in the present, to be no dishonour
to my Native Country'. Dryden goes on to claim that he has added
to English language and poetry 'in the choice of Words, and
Harmony of Numbers which were wanting, especially the last, in
all our Poets'. Even those of his predecessors endowed with genius
'have not Cultivated their Mother-Tongue with sufficient Care; or
relying on the Beauty of their Thoughts, have judg'd the Ornament
of Words, and sweetness of Sound unnecessary'. Dryden claims
nothing less than a permanent improvement for the future resources
of English poetry. Posterity will recognize his achievement (and the
wisdom of his patrons' generosity).

Dryden goes on to discuss briefly the question of reviving 'antiquated Words', a form of 'Redemption', continuing the financial
metaphor, which he believes in only when 'Sound or Significancy is
wanting in the present Language'. This allows him to mock the
ignorance of contemporary pretenders to poetic knowledge:
'Others have no Ear for Verse, nor choice of Words; nor distinction
of Thoughts; but mingle Farthings with their Gold to make up the
Sum.' This swerve reminds Dryden, and his readers, of his earlier
career as a satirist: 'Here is a Field of Satire open'd to me: But since
the Revolution, I have wholly renounc'd that Talent. For who
wou'd give Physick to the Great when he is uncall'd: To do his
Patient no good, and indanger himself for his Prescription? . . . 'Tis
enough for me, if the Government will let me pass unquestion'd.'
Dryden clearly enough says that the times provide targets for satire
not just against literary pretenders but against the 'Great'. Once
again, as in the opening paragraph of his dedicatory letter to Lord
Clifford, Dryden ensures that his readers know where he stands
politically, and also reminds them of his well-known career as a

writer and a satirist. Close here to being on dangerous ground, Dryden promptly turns to thank those who gave the translation their support both in kind and as subscribers despite his political beliefs:

'Tis enough for me, if the Government will let me pass unquestion'd. In the mean time, I am oblig'd in gratitude, to return my Thanks to many of them, who have not only distinguish'd me from others of the same Party, by a particular exception of Grace, but without considering the Man, have been Bountiful to the Poet: Have encourag'd *Virgil* to speak such *English*, as I could teach him. . . . But how much more [gratitude do I owe] to those from whom I have receiv'd the Favours which they have offer'd to one of a different Perswasion: Amongst whom I cannot omit naming the Earls of *Darby* and of *Peterborough*. To the first of these, I have not the Honour to be known; and therefore his liberality was as much unexpected, as it was undeserv'd.[105]

The Earl of Derby is presented as a disinterested supporter of Dryden's translation, for whom poetry transcends politics and religion. This aesthetic trope is frequent in Dryden's three dedications and Postscript, and this passage indicates that he believed it to be a conviction shared by others. Dryden's translation of *Virgil* offered, at a time when society was politically fragmented, a unifying national artistic enterprise.

Lady Mary Chudleigh's commendatory poem on Dryden's *Virgil* (in the event not published in the second edition) voices exactly what the translator wished to hear. This isle's 'wretched State' was one of 'Chaos', 'Night', and 'Darkness'

> Till Chaucer came with his delusive Light
> And gave some transient Glimm'rings to the Night. . . .[106]

In this progress out of poetic nothingness, Chaucer is followed by 'kinder Spencer' (stanza 2), and then by Waller, Milton, and Cowley, who 'blest our Eyes'. But

> Dark Shadows still were intermix'd with Light:
> Those Shades the mighty Dryden chas'd away,
> And shew'd the Triumphs of refulgent Day . . .   (stanza 3)

[105] *Works*, vi. 808. The quotations in the previous two paragraphs are from ibid. 807–8.
[106] *Works*, vi. 1188–90 reprints the commendatory poem.

Dryden's 'Work' as a 'great Poet' has freed the nation from 'confinement', and, as a direct result of Dryden's achievements, the English can now see

> ... as if we stood on Magick Ground,
> Majestick Ghosts with verdant Laurels crown'd:
> Illustrious Heroes, ev'ry glorious Name,
> That can a Place in ancient Records claim:
> Among the rest, thy Virgil's awful Shade,
> Whom thou hast rais'd to bless our happy Land,
> Does circl'd round with radiant Honours stand:
> He's now the welcom Native of our Isle,
> And crowns our Hopes with an auspicious Smile ...   (stanza 4)

Dryden's pains, cares, and toils have cleansed the previously filthy Augean stables in which 'Our Language ... lay', and with a Herculean effort his intelligence has cleansed the language of English poetry from the 'ancient Rubbish of the Gothick Times' (stanza 5).

The outline of Lady Mary's account of Dryden's place and role in the development of English poetry reflects the canon which Dryden's critical writings since the 1660s had sought to establish (though without naming himself as the culmination of this gradual establishment of English poetry's linguistic and intellectual purity). Tonson too, in his careful acquisition of copyrights in English poetry from his earliest days as a publisher, had been concerned to turn Dryden's reading of literary history into a publisher's list which reflected his own commitment to the establishment of a canon of English poetry, as far as possible under his own imprint.

Lady Mary's poem can be used to gloss the frontispiece which Tonson had specially engraved for the translation (it is the only plate not taken from Ogilby's *Virgil*). As William Frost notes, Tonson paid Michiel Van Der Gucht to copy the illustrated title-page of an edition of Virgil published by the Imprimerie Royale in 1641.[107] This is based on an original design by Poussin, and shows Apollo, harp in hand, crowning Virgil, who wears a toga and holds a copy of his works in his right hand, with a wreath of bays. Above them a putto with pan-pipes in one hand supports an oval cartouche, which originally read 'Publii Virgilii Maronis Opera'. For the 1697 edition this is altered to '*Dryden's* | VIRGIL | *Printed* | *for* | Iacob Tonson'.

[107] *Works*, v. 889.

The neo-classical imagery and the cartouche claim Virgil for English, and suggest that Dryden's Virgil is a monumental and lasting achievement fully equal to its original. (That Tonson's name appears almost as prominently as Dryden's indicates the publisher's sense of his own importance to the project.)

But if the frontispiece proposes the timelessness of Dryden's translation, when the volume was published in 1697 it located itself very precisely in contemporary politics. As Steven Zwicker and William Frost have demonstrated, Dryden, like his contemporaries, read the *Aeneid* as a political poem, and his translation, dedications, Postscript, and some of the plates, make a clear, if oblique, statement about his politics and his own alienated position in the 1690s.[108] However, too heavy an emphasis on the expression of Dryden's Jacobite sympathies obscures the ways in which Dryden used his three dedications, the Postscript, and even the 'Notes and Observations', to establish his own cultural credentials and those of his translation, and to site his achievement within the cultural field made up of his friends, acquaintances, patrons, subscribers, and the contemporary reading public. All these prose pieces were written shortly before publication, and Tonson could have had no control over what Dryden wrote to his three chosen dedicatees or in the Postscript. The importance of that freedom, which allowed Dryden to say what he wanted, is shown by his decision, when pressed for time, to allow Knightly Chetwood to write the life of Virgil and the Preface to the *Pastorals*, and Addison to write the essay on the *Georgics*.

One function of these four prose pieces was to enable Dryden to give his own view of Virgil and to explain the way he had translated his works. Another important objective, particularly in the Postscript, was to acknowledge his indebtedness, and, in so doing, to emphasize the active support given his project. Indeed, he claims that he tried to make the final book of the *Aeneid* 'shine amongst its Fellows' in response to 'the Commands of Sir *William Trumball*, one of the Principal Secretaries of State, who recommended it, as his Favourite, to my Care: and for his sake particularly I have made it mine'. More personal thanks are given to his long-standing friend Gilbert Dolben for the 'Noble Present' of several editions of Virgil's

---

[108] Zwicker, *Politics and Language*, pp. 177–205; *Works*, vi. 870–6.

works along with commentaries. (It also seems that he was sent a copy of Fabrini's edition, first published in Venice in 1588.) Dryden thanks Sir William Bowyer, with whom he had been at Cambridge, for his friendly 'Entertainment' at Denham Court where he had translated the first Georgic and most of the final book of the *Aeneid*, and the Earl of Exeter, at whose Burleigh House he had translated Book VII of the *Aeneid*. The Duke of Shrewsbury went to the trouble of getting proofs of the *Pastorals*, *Georgics*, and the first six books of the *Aeneid* from Tonson, which he then read in the country with William Walsh, 'the best Critick of our Nation'. The duke's 'Commendation' is one which Dryden chooses 'not to insert' in his volume, but it 'has made me vain enough to boast of so great a favour, and to think I have succeeded beyond my hopes'. Shrewsbury's (and Walsh's) endorsement of Dryden's translation when he was about three-quarters through the task must in fact have been a considerable relief. Four previous translators of parts of Virgil whose success, he politely claims, made his task the more difficult (the anonymous translation of the third Georgic, Roscommon, Addison, and Cowley[109]) are praised. Finally, Dryden thanks his two physicians, Dr Gibbons and Dr Hobbs, for their help, and the whole faculty of physicians, who (with the exception of Sir Richard Blackmore) were always ready to oblige him, and gives his 'acknowledgments to all my Subscribers'.[110] The Postscript is at once dignified and personal, but is also carefully directed at its readers. It aligns on the side of Dryden's translation an influential body of powerful men, including the young critic William Walsh, who had all given their support in differing practical ways well before Tonson published the volume in summer 1697. The subscription venture involved a pre-publication faith in Dryden's abilities by a select body of patrons, whose reward was to have their names put before the immediately contemporary English public in 1697, preserved for posterity in the first and then in the second editions.

The implication of the Postscript, full as it is of Dryden's own sense of his translation's achievement, is that the *Virgil* is in important part the outcome of a collaboration between the translator, his patrons, his friends, and his public. And, together, they are helping

---

[109] See *Works*, vi. 1112 for the details of these translations.   [110] *Works*, vi. 809–10.

to establish the superiority of English poetry over that of the Continent, and the English poetry of the late seventeenth century over its national predecessors. In the Dedication to the *Aeneis* he writes to Mulgrave, his old patron, arguing that English poetry, unlike French, can encompass the heroic: 'What I have said, though it has the face of arrogance, yet is intended for the honour of my Country; and therefore I will boldly own, that this *English* Translation has more of *Virgil's* Spirit in it, than either the *French*, or the *Italian*.'[111] This reinforces Dryden's earlier assertion that he is 'pleas'd to have been born an *English* Man',[112] and he goes on to praise his English predecessors' translations—Mulgrave himself, Lord Roscommon, Denham, Waller, and Cowley, given in that order to give aristocracy apparent precedence over commoners. In keeping with his strategy throughout his Dedication in the *Virgil* and elsewhere, Dryden proclaims his modesty—''tis the utmost of my Ambition to be thought their Equal, or not to be much inferior to them, and some others of the Living'—before asserting his own superiority. The translation of episodes is one thing, but it is quite another 'to have the weight of a whole Author on [your] shoulders': 'They who believe the burthen light, let them attempt the Fourth, Sixth or Eighth *Pastoral*, the First or Fourth *Georgick*; and amongst the *Aeneids*, the Fourth, the Fifth, the Seventh, the Ninth, the Tenth, the Eleventh, or the Twelfth; for in these I think I have succeeded best.'[113]

A proper professional pride in his own work challenges both part-time writers and his critics (kept always just offstage, like Blackmore). Yet Dryden is generous to those who helped him, and creates the image of an ongoing scholarly discussion with friends about his translation and other topics. His analysis of the reasons for the 'sweetness' of Denham's famous couplet—'Tho' deep, yet clear; though gentle, yet not dull; | Strong without rage, without o'reflowing full'—is one he has given 'to some of my Friends in Conversation, and they have allow'd the Criticism to be just'.[114] In the 'Notes and Observations' Dryden recalls that 'some of my Friends were of Opinion that I mistook the Sense of *Virgil* in my Translation [of vi. 1221]', even though he still disagrees.

---

[111] *Works*, v. 325. [112] *Works*, v. 281.
[113] *Works*, v. 325–6. [114] *Works*, v. 321.

Or again, Dryden's translation of 'falsar' as 'falsify'd' (*Aeneis*, ix. 1094) was criticized. 'When I read this *Aeneid* to many of my Friends, in company together, most of them quarrel'd at the word *falsify'd*, as an Innovation in our Language.' Dryden agrees that it is, but justifies his coinage (from the Italian 'falsare') at length.[115] Earlier conversations with his brother-in-law, Sir Robert Howard, about Jupiter's inability to prevent the death of Turnus (*Aeneid*, x. 469–72) are reported at some length in the Dedication of the *Aeneis*.[116] Dryden also refers his reader to Sir Robert's notes on the sixth book of the *Aeneid* published, he says, in 1660 as 'the most Learned, and the most Judicious Observations on this Book, which are extant in our Language'—unfortunately for the compliment, Dryden's memory seems to have confused Howard's translation of the fourth book in *Poems* (1660), which had no notes, with the annotations to John Boys's elaborately annotated version, *Aeneas His Descent into Hell* (1661).[117]

Thanks are given to others who had helped Dryden. Elaborate acknowledgement is made of the help given by the late Earl of Lauderdale's manuscript translation of the *Aeneis*, which, had death not prevented him, he could have published two years before Dryden's, and William Frost has demonstrated the use Dryden made of Lauderdale's translation. In his anxiety to clear himself of any imputation of having plagiarized a translation made by an earl, Dryden claims that he sought his Lordship's permission to translate Virgil, after Lauderdale had sent him his translation: 'But some Proposals being afterwards made me by my Bookseller, I desir'd his Lordship's leave, that I might accept them, which he freely granted; and I have his Letter yet to shew, for that permission.'[118] Here Dryden, whose decision to translate Virgil must have been his own, hides behind his bookseller, while claiming to have the necessary proof of his entirely professional conduct. Others are thanked who had helped on even minor points. Walter Moyle, 'a young Gentleman, whom I can never sufficiently commend', informed him after the translation was completed that 'the Ancients accounted drowning an accursed Death';[119] his 'Ingenious Friend' Anthony Henley asked him to annotate *Pastorals*, iv. 72, and gave

---

[115] *Works*, vi. 824, 828.   [116] *Works*, v. 293–4.   [117] *Works*, vi. 821, 1120.
[118] *Works*, v. 336.   [119] *Works*, v. 292.

him information about Jewish superstitious practices in naming children;[120] his 'Honour'd Friend' Sir William Bowyer told Dryden that Virgil 'had shewn more of Poetry than Skill' in the account of grafting in the second *Pastoral*, 'at least in relation to our more northern Climates';[121] and Dryden's 'most Ingenious Friend' Sir Henry Sheeres provided his observations of bees' behaviour, gained by using a 'Glass-Hive', to gloss *Georgics*, iv. 270.[122] Congreve reviewed the whole of the *Aeneis*, comparing Dryden's version with the original: 'I shall never be asham'd to own, that this Excellent Young Man, has shew'd me many Faults, which I have endeavour'd to Correct. 'Tis true, he might have easily found more, and then my Translation had been more Perfect.'[123] Finally, two 'other Worthy Friends of mine' (in fact, Addison and Knightly Chetwood), 'seeing me strained in my time, took Pity on me' and wrote the 'Life of Virgil', the Prefaces to the *Pastorals* and *Georgics*, and the prose arguments for the whole translation.[124] All these acknowledgements further enforce the idea of his translation of Virgil being a collaborative enterprise between Dryden, his friends, and his patrons (all of the above, except for Addison, were first or second subscribers). Their honour was, therefore, involved in the translation's success even more directly than that of the other subscribers.

But if the *Virgil* was seen by author, publisher, and patrons as a unifying national achievement, Dryden's dedications make it quite clear that the unbound volume which his patrons eventually received was itself a site of contestation. Steven Zwicker's thesis that Dryden's poetry is an 'art of disguise', using allusion and obliquity to assert his own beliefs in dangerous times, has furthered the understanding of Dryden's later poetry. Yet Dryden so frames his translation that the contemporary reader in July 1697 was immediately made aware of the poet's own earlier career and present politics. After admiring the frontispiece and turning over the title-page, the first thing the reader came across was Dryden's dedicatory letter to Hugh Clifford, Baron Chudleigh. Clifford, son of Dryden's old patron, was, like Dryden, a Catholic and opposed to William III. The first paragraph of the Dedication immediately asks the reader to

---

[120] *Works*, vi. 812–13.   [121] *Works*, vi. 814.   [122] *Works*, vi. 815.
[123] *Works*, v. 337.   [124] Ibid.

contrast Dryden's present isolation with his earlier career during Charles II's rule. Although what Dryden says is carefully tailored to fit his dedicatee, and the genre is one which demands exaggeration, the opening sentences are remarkably explicit. It required no skill in decoding to realize that Dryden's nostalgia for the past is a criticism of the present:

I have found it not more difficult to Translate *Virgil*, than to find such Patrons as I desire for my Translation. For though *England* is not wanting in a Learned Nobility, yet such are my unhappy Circumstances, that they have confin'd me to a narrow choice. To the greater part, I have not the Honour to be known; and to some of them I cannot shew at present, by any publick Act, that grateful Respect which I shall ever bear them in my heart. Yet I have no reason to complain of Fortune, since in the midst of that abundance I could not possibly have chosen better, than the Worthy Son of so Illustrious a Father. He was the Patron of my Manhood, when I Flourish'd in the opinion of the World; though with small advantage to my Fortune, 'till he awaken'd the remembrance of my Royal Master. He was that *Pollio*, or that *Varus*, who introduc'd me to *Augustus*: And tho' he soon dismiss'd himself from State-Affairs, yet in the short time of his Administration he shone so powerfully upon me, that like the heat of a *Russian*-Summer, he ripen'd the Fruits of Poetry in a cold Clymate; and gave me wherewithal to subsist at least, in the long Winter which succeeded.[125]

Dryden makes careful use of the protocols of the dedicatory letter, a private letter from client to patron, but one written in the knowledge of its publication. The first three sentences are disingenuous. Dryden had dedicated his translation of Juvenal (1693) to Dorset, William III's Lord Chamberlain, and there is no reason why he should not (and every reason why he should) have approached a patron currently in power, otherwise Tonson could not have wanted William III as the main dedicatee. Dryden is in fact asserting his independence, and declaring his political and religious affiliations. Everything that Dryden then says is entirely appropriate to the son of his earlier patron, to whom he had dedicated *Amboyna* (1673) and who in 1672 and 1673 had ensured that Dryden's salary was paid despite the stop of the Exchequer (Dryden glosses over the fact that Clifford's Catholicism forced his resignation and that he hanged himself only two months later[126]). By reminding the son of his

---

[125] *Works*, v. 3.   [126] Winn, *John Dryden and his World*, pp. 232, 240–1.

father's past support, Dryden compares, explicitly for his contemporaries, though far less so for late twentieth-century readers, his present position, a Catholic deprived of the Laureateship, with a lost past in which a Clifford not only protected his salary, but introduced him to my Royal Master', Charles II, characterized as Augustus, in whose Rome Virgil had flourished. Dryden uses the dedication not only to remind his reader of his present allegiances but of his own earlier career, a matter of public record through his poems and his published dedications if nothing else. As well as claiming to be faithful to his own beliefs, Dryden compares William III's court unfavourably with that of Charles II. All this in the opening pages of a book being distributed to a remarkably representative, and therefore divided, group of subscribers. Through his dedicatory letter to Clifford, Dryden locates himself publicly in a position identical to his patron's own beliefs. Dryden's loyalty to the Stuart cause and his Catholicism are made immediately evident to his patrons, whether first or second subscribers. For all the claims that the translation was a patriotic work belonging to the permanent realm of art, a claim made by Dryden himself, by the complimentary poems which acclaimed his genius, and by Lady Chudleigh's unpublished verses, his *Virgil* spoke directly and absolutely clearly about his own situation in the summer of 1697. The dedications and Postscript are a sequence of supplementary texts which firmly place the timeless translation of Virgil's works within an immediately contemporary present.

Dryden's prose framework for his translation, the composition of which was wholly in his hands, sets up, then, a complex relationship with his contemporary readers. It is therefore worth asking what other functions are served by his dedications and Postscript.

In addressing Clifford, Dryden stresses his youth (aged 34, Clifford may or may not have been flattered by this), his knowledge of Virgil, the virtues of his retirement, and his ancient lineage, which proves his family's faithful adherence to their beliefs and, significantly in the 1690s, to their 'Party'. 'Your Forefathers have asserted the Party which they chose 'till death, and dy'd for its defence in the Fields of Battel.' Not only does Dryden insist on his right to Clifford's support as his father's son—'You are acquainted with the *Roman* History, and know without my information that Patronage and Clientship always descended from the

Fathers to the Sons'[127]—but describes Edmund Spenser as the third pastoral poet after Theocritus and Virgil, one descended from Chaucer, who is unmatched 'in any Modern Language' and is a 'Master of our Northern Dialect'. Dryden asserts that his own translation of the *Pastorals* and *Georgics* has a lineage as ancient as (indeed, more ancient than) Clifford's son. For all Dryden's gestures of modesty—'May you ever continue your esteem for *Virgil*; and not lessen it, for the faults of his Translatour'[128]—his Dedication makes clear that his own ambitions and sense of achievement make him the superior of Clifford as both poet and scholar, while yet remaining 'Your Lordship's most Humble, | and most Obedient Servant, | JOHN DRYDEN'.

Dryden's use of the panegyric conventions of the dedicatory letter allows him to assert his own status as poet and scholar. Indeed, Griffin uses this reminder to Clifford of the Roman practice of patronage descending from father to son as an example of how Dryden insists that Clifford is duty-bound to continue his family's support of the ageing, faithful, and patriotic poet.[129] Dryden's dedications after 1688 increasingly assert his power and authority within the client–patron relationship, in particular the poet's power to transmit the 'honour' of the individual and the nation to posterity.[130] In the case of the *Virgil*, Dryden takes the opportunity in the prose surrounds of his translation to further fashion his own self-image, giving a self-reflexive account within the folio itself of the work's gestation and progress. He also, once the protestations of inadequacy and carefully directed flattery to both dedicatees and patrons have been properly interpreted, gives a very clear rationale for the work, one which is surprisingly personal, even intimate. The dignity with which the out-of-favour, elderly poet describes his situation in the 1690s is possible only because of his own conviction of his superiority as poet and classicist, and his sense that his readers shared his own valuation of his whole career and of the importance of the *Virgil* itself (and which his 349 patrons and Tonson had made possible). Dryden is at once rhetorically calculating and honest. His three dedications and Postscript enable him to establish his own political, religious, social, and artistic beliefs with absolute clarity in

---

[127] *Works*, v. 7.   [128] *Works*, v. 6–8.
[129] Griffin, *Literary Patronage*, pp. 87–8.   [130] Ibid. 94–5.

a more than usually contentious period, yet, at the same time, allow his readers, of whatever persuasion, to relate to his (and his patrons' and publisher's) attempt to make a permanent contribution to English poetry, and to a newly developing English cultural identity. The whole drive of the dedications and Postscript is to be inclusive, while admitting to the multiple rifts in contemporary politics and society. Dryden's acknowledgement of the nation's generosity towards his and Tonson's unifying cultural project is balanced by the way his own prose additions to his translation point up the multiple divisions only too apparent among the names of the first and second subscribers.

APPENDIX I

Subscribers to *The Works of Virgil*

The subscribers' names are given in approximate order of precedence. The first column indicates whether they were first or second subscribers. The final column notes those subscribers who could not be identified ('Un.') or whose dates of birth could not be determined ('ND'). The names of two second subscribers who were also first subscribers are marked with a dagger.

The biographical information is drawn from the following sources: *The Dictionary of National Biography*; *The Complete Peerage*...by G. E. C. [Cokayne], ed. Vicary Gibbs *et al.* (London, 1910–40); *Complete Baronetage*, ed. G. E. C. [Cokayne] (Exeter, 1900–6); *Alumni Cantabrigienses* ...*Part I: From the Earliest Times to 1751*, comp. John and J. A. Venn (Cambridge, 1922–7); *Alumni Oxonienses*...*1500–1714*..., comp. Joseph Foster (Oxford and London, 1891); *The Record of Old Westminster*...*to 1927*, comp. G. F. Russell Barker and Alan H. Stenning (London, 1928); *Register of Admissions to the Honourable Society of the Middle Temple*...*to the Year 1944*, comp. Sir Henry F. MacGeach and H. A. C. Sturgess (London, 1949); *The History of Parliament: The House of Commons 1660–1690*, ed. Basil Duke Henning (London, 1983); *The History of Parliament: The House of Commons 1715–1754*, ed. Romney Sedgwick (London, 1970). A few additional sources are referred to in the notes.

In preparing this table, the spelling of a few names has been normalized, and some first names added in brackets.

Sub.	Name	Title	Profession	MP	Politics
I	Anne	Princess	royalty		
I	George	Prince	royalty		
I	William	Prince	royalty		
I	Beauclerk, Charles	D. of St Albans	soldier		Williamite
I	Butler, James	D. of Ormonde	soldier		Jacobite
I	Butler, Mary	Dss of Ormonde			
I	Lennox, Charles	D. of Richmond	soldier		Williamite
I	Seymour, Charles	D. of Somerset			Williamite
I	Talbot, Charles	D. of Shrewsbury	Secretary of State		Williamite
I	Cavendish, William	M. of Hartington		MP	Whig 96
I	Sheffield, John	M. of Normanby			Tory
I	Sheffield, Ursula	Mss of Normanby			
I	Bertie, James	E. of Abingdon			?Jacobite★
I	Boyle, Lionel	E. of Orrery		MP	Tory
I	Bruce, Thomas	E. of Aylesbury			Jacobite
I	Cecil, James	E. of Salisbury			Tory
I	Cecil, John	E. of Exeter			Tory
I	Cecil, Anne	Css of Exeter			
I	Compton, Mary	Css Dow. of Northampton			
I	Fielding, Basil	E. of Denbigh	soldier		Tory
I	Finch, Elizabeth	Css Dow. of Winchilsea			
I	Herbert, Arthur	E. of Torrington	sailor		
I	Herbert, Thomas	E. of Pembroke	Privy Seal		Tory
I	O'Brien, William	E. of Inchiquin			
I	Sackville, Charles	E. of Dorset	Lord Chamberlain		Williamite
I	Spencer, Robert	E. of Sunderland	Lord Chamberlain		
I	Stanhope, Philip	E. of Chesterfield			
I	Stanley, William	E. of Derby			Whig
I	Sydney, Henry	E. of Romney	soldier		Williamite
I	Cholmondley, Hugh	Viscount			Williamite
I	Constable, Robert	Viscount Dunbar			
I	Fitzharding, John	Viscount	soldier	MP	Whig 96
I	Berkeley, William	Bn of Stratton			Tory
I	Boyle, Charles	Bn of Lanesborough			
I	Clifford, Hugh	Bn of Chudleigh			Jacobite
I	Herbert, Henry	Bn of Cherbury			Whig
I	North, Francis	Bn of Guildford			Tory
I	Sackville, Lionel	Ld Buckhurst			
I	Somers, John	Bn of Evesham	Lord Chancellor	MP	Whig
I	Bruce, Robert	Hon.			
I	Granville, John	Hon.		MP	Tory 96
I	Montagu, Charles	Hon.	Chancellor of the Exchequer	MP	Whig 96
I	Noel, John	Hon.			
I	Sackville, Mary	Lady			
I	Crew, Nathaniel	Bp of Durham	cleric		
I	Hartstonge, John	Bp of Ossory	cleric		
I	Blount, Walter K.	Bt			
I	Bowyer, William	Bt			

★ James Bertie, Earl of Abingdon, initially welcomed William but seems soon to have become a kind of Jacobite fellow-traveller. See Anne Barbeau Gardiner, 'Dryden's Patrons', in Robert P. Maccubbin and Martha Hamilton-Phillips (eds.), *The Age of William III and Mary II: Power, Politics and Patronage 1688–1702* (Washington, DC, 1989), pp. 326–32, at p. 327.

Dates	Age	Westminster School	Oxford	Cambridge	Law	Un.
1665–1714	32					
1653–1710	44					
1689–1700	8					
1670–1726	27					
1665–1745	32		Christ Church 1679			
						ND
1672–1723	25					
1662–1748	35			Trinity		
1660–1718	37					
1673–1729	24	✓				
1648–1721	49					
d. 13 Aug. 1697						ND
1653–1699	44		Magdalen 1667			
1670–1703	27					
1656–1741	41					
1691–1728	6		Christ Church 1705			
1648–1700	49			St John's 1667		
1650–1703	47					
						ND
1668–1717	29		Christ Church 1685			
1661–1745	36					
1647–1716	50					
1656–1732	41		Christ Church 1673			
1666–1719	31					
1638–1706	59					
1641–1702	56					
1634–1714	63					
1655–1702	42					
1641–1704	56					
d. 1724			Christ Church 1678			ND
1651–1714	46					
1650–1712	47					
d. 1741						ND
1639–1704	58					
1663–1730	34					
1654–1709	43		Trinity 1670		Inner Temple 1671	
1673–1729	24		Trinity 1689			
1688–1765	9	✓				
1650–1716	47		Trinity 1667		Mid. Temple 1669	
1670–1729	27			Queens' 1684		
1665–1707	32					
1661–1715	36	✓		Trinity 1679		
						Un.
						ND
1633–1722	64		Lincoln 1652			
1654–1717	43					
1642–1717	55					
1660–1722	37			Trinity 1653	Inner Temple 1654	

Sub.	Name	Title	Profession	MP	Politics
I	Brownlowe, Dorothy	Lady			
I	Dyke, Thomas	Bt		MP	Tory 96
I	Giffard, Mary	Lady			
I	Isham, Justinian	Bt		MP	Tory 96
I	Leveson-Gower, John	Bt		MP	Tory 96
I	Orby, Charles	Bt			
I	Percival, John	Bt			
I	Sheppard, Fleetwood	Bt	Black Rod		Williamite
I	Hawles, John	Sir	Solicitor General	MP	Whig 96
I	Howard, Robert	Sir	Auditor of the Exchequer	MP	Whig 96
I	Kneller, Godfrey	Sir	painter		
I	Mompesson, Thomas	Sir		MP	Whig 96
I	Shower, Bartholomew	Sir	lawyer		Jacobite
I	Trevor, Thomas	Sir	Attorney General	MP	Whig 96
I	Trumbull, William	Sir	Secretary of State	MP	Uncertain
I	Fitzpatrick, Edward	Brig.	soldier		Williamite
I	Cholmondley, George	Col.	soldier		Williamite
I	Codrington Christopher	Col.	soldier		Williamite
I	Farringdon, Thomas	Col.	soldier		Williamite
I	Browne, Edward	Dr	physician		
I	Gibbons, William	Dr	physician		
I	Hobbs, Thomas	Dr	physician		
I	Montague, John	Dr	Master of Trinity College		
I	Waller, Stephen	Dr	lawyer		
I	Dobins, William	Esq.	lawyer	MP	Tory
I	Dolben, Gilbert	Esq.	lawyer	MP	Whig 96
I	Dormer, John	Esq.			
I	Foley, Thomas, Jnr.	Esq.		MP	Whig 96
I	Fox, Charles	Esq.		MP	Tory 96
I	Hammond, Anthony	Esq.	author	MP	Tory 96
I	Harcourt, Simon	Esq.	lawyer	MP	Tory 96
I	Harley, Robert	Esq.		MP	Tory 96
I	Henley, Anthony	Esq.		MP	Whig
I	Hopkins, Thomas	Esq.	lawyer		
I	Jekyll, Joseph	Esq.	lawyer	MP	Whig
I	Knight, Christopher	Esq.	of Chawton		
I	Lewknor, John	Esq.	author	MP	Uncertain
I	London, George	Esq.	gardener		
I	Loving, John	Esq.			
I	Mainwaring, Arthur	Esq.			Whig
I	Norton, Richard	Esq.		MP	
I	Pulteney, John	Esq.		MP	Whig 96
I	Rich, Christopher	Esq.	lawyer		
I	St John, Henry	Esq.		MP	Whig 96
I	Stepney, George	Esq.	diplomat	MP	Whig 96
I	Tasburgh, Henry	Esq.			
I	Tilney, Frederick	Esq.			
I	Vernon, Thomas	Esq.	lawyer		Whig
I	Waller, Edmund	Esq.	lawyer	MP	Tory 96
I	Walkaden, John	Esq.			
I	Walsh, William	Esq.	author	MP	Whig
I	Baynard, Ann	Mrs			
I	Closterman, John	Mr	artist		

Dates	Age	Westminster School	Oxford	Cambridge	Law	Un.
1665–1700	32					
1650–1706	47		Christ Church 1666		Mid. Temple 1667	
						ND
1658–1730	39		Christ Church 1674		Lincoln's Inn 1677	
1675–1709	22					
1640–1716	57					
1683–1748	14	✓	Magdalen 1699			
1634–1698	63		Magdalen Hall 1650		Gray's Inn 1657	
1645–1716	52		Queen's 1662		Lincoln's Inn 1670	
1626–1698	71			Magdalene		
1646–1723	51					
d. 1701						ND
1658–1701	39				Mid. Temple 1676	
1658–1730	39		Christ Church 1673		Mid. Temple 1672	
1639–1716	58		St John's 1655		Mid. Temple 1657	
d. 1696						ND
1664–1733	33	✓	Christ Church 1680		Inner Temple 1680	
1668–1710	29		Christ Church 1685		Mid. Temple 1687	
1664–1712	33					
1644–1708	53			Trinity 1657		
1649–1728	48		St John's 1668			
1647–1698	50					
1655–1728	42	✓		Trinity 1672		
1654–1707	43		New 1672		Lincoln's Inn	
1646–1709	51	✓		Christ's 1661	Lincoln's Inn 1663	
1658–1722	39	✓	Christ Church 1674		Inner Temple 1680	
1669–1719	28					
						ND
1660–1713	37					
1668–1738	29			St John's 1683	Gray's Inn 1684	
1661–1727	36		Pembroke 1677		Inner Temple 1683	
1661–1724	36					
1667–1741	30		Christ Church 1682		Mid. Temple 1684	
d. 1720					Mid. Temple 1679	ND
1663–1738	34				Mid. Temple 1680	
d. 1702						ND
1658–1707	39		Christ Church 1673		Mid. Temple 1675	
d. 1713						ND
						Un.
1668–1712	29		Christ Church 1683		Inner Temple 1683	
1667–	30		Christ Church 1682			
1661–1726	36	✓	Christ Church 1677			
d. 1714			Christ Church			ND
1652–1742	47			Caius 1669		
1663–1707	34	✓		Trinity 1682		
1674–1706	23					
1669–	28		Queen's 1669			
1654–1721	43				Mid. Temple 1672	
1651–1700	46		Christ Church 1664		Mid. Temple 1675	
						Un.
1663–1708	34		Wadham 1678			
1672–1697	25					
1656–1713	41					

Sub.	Name	Title	Profession	MP	Politics
2	Cavendish, Mary	Dss of Devonshire			
2	Lennox, Anne	Dss of Richmond			
2	Paulet, Charles	M. of Winchester		MP	Whig 96
2	Capel, Algernon	E. of Essex	soldier		
2	Hyde, Henry	E. of Clarendon			
2	Mordaunt, Charles	E. of Peterborough	Admiral		Whig
2	Paulet, St John	E. of Bolingbroke			
2	Robartes, Charles	E. of Radnor			Whig
2	Thynne, Thomas	E. of Weymouth			Tory
2	Jones, Richard	Visc. Ranelagh		MP	Whig 96
2	Clifford, Hugh†	Bn Clifford			
2	Cavendish, Henry	Lord		MP	Whig 96
2	Coningsby, Thomas	Bn Clanbrassis	Paymaster General		Williamite
2	Cooper, Anthony A.	Lord		MP	Whig 96
2	Cutts, John	Bn Cutts	soldier	MP	Whig 96
2	Hamilton, Archibald	Lord	navy		
2	Hyde, Henry	Lord		MP	Tory 96
2	Bertie, Montagu	Lord Norreys		MP	Tory
2	Spencer, Charles	Lord		MP	Whig 96
2	Boyle, Henry	Hon.	soldier	MP	Tory 96
2	Cheyne, William	Hon.		MP	Tory
2	Cornwallis, Charles	Hon.	soldier	MP	Whig 96
2	Fielding, William	Hon.			
2	Howard, Bernard	Hon.			Jacobite
2	Mordaunt, Henry	Hon.	Brigadier General	MP	Whig 96
2	Stanley, Thomas	Hon.	Colonel		
2	Andrews, Francis	Bt			
2	Ash, James	Bt			
2	Bettenson, Edward	Bt			
2	Blount, Thomas P.	Bt	author	MP	Whig 96
2	Bolles, John	Bt		MP	Tory
2	Chudleigh, Mary	Lady	author		
2	Clarges, Walter	Bt		MP	Tory
2	Cowper, William	Bt		MP	Whig 96
2	Cotton, Robert	Sir		MP	Whig 96
2	Ernle, Edward	Bt		MP	Tory 96
2	Fenwick, Mary	Lady			
2	Fettiplace, Edmund	Bt			
2	Granville, Bevil	Bt		MP	Whig 96
2	Hales, Christopher	Bt		MP	Tory
2	Hussey, Thomas	Bt		MP	Tory 96
2	Leveson-Gower, Jane	Lady			
2	Lucy, Berkeley	Bt			
2	Parsons, John	Bt		MP	Tory 96
2	Peachy, Henry	Bt			
2	Phillips, John	Bt		MP	Tory 96
2	Pickering, John	Bt			
2	Skipwith, Thomas	Bt		MP	
2	Trevillian, John	Bt		MP	Tory 96
2	Walter, John	Bt			
2	Windham, Francis	Bt		MP	Tory 96
2	Windham	Lady			
2	Woodhouse, John	Bt		MP	
2	Bowes, William	Sir		MP	Whig 96

Dates	Age	Westminster School	Oxford	Cambridge	Law	Un.
1646–1710	51					
d. 1722						ND
1630–1699	67					
1670–1726	27					
1638–1709	59					
1658–1709	39		Christ Church 1674			
d. 1711						ND
1660–1723	37					
1640–1714	57					
1641–1712	56					
1673–1700	24					
1656–1729	41					
1671–1713	26					
1661–1707	36			St Catharine's 1676	Mid. Temple 1678	
d. 1754						ND
1672–1753	25					
1673–1743	24		Christ Church 1685			
1674–1722	23					
d. 1725		✓		Trinity 1692		ND
1657–1728	40		Brasenose 1671			
1675–1722	22					
1656–1723	41		Queen's 1672			
d. 1717						ND
1663–1720	34	✓	Christ Church 1680			
1664–1736	33					
1641–1709	56					
1660–1733	37					
1668–1733	29			Clare 1686		
1649–1697	48				Lincoln's Inn 1668	
1669–1714	28		Christ Church 1683		Gray's Inn 1680	
1656–1710	41					
1654–1706	43		Merton 1671			
1643–1706	54					
1644–1717	53					
1661–1729	36					
d. 1708						ND
1654–1707	43		Queen's 1668			
1665–1706	32			Trinity 1677		
1671–1717	26		Christ Church 1689			
1639–1706	58					
1653–96	43					
1672–1759	25					
d. 1717						ND
1671–1737	26		Trinity 1689			
1666–1737	31			Trinity 1682	Lincoln's Inn 1684	
1660–1703	37					
1652–1710	45					
1670–1755	27		Wadham 1687			
1673–1722	24		Queen's 1691			
1654–1711	43		Merton 1670		Mid. Temple 1670	
						ND
1669–1754	28					
1657–1707	40			Trinity 1672	Gray's Inn 1675	

Sub.	Name	Title	Profession	MP	Politics
2	Forbys, James	Sir			
2	Forrester, William	Sir		MP	Whig 96
2	Haddock, Richard	Sir	Navy		
2	Seymour, John	Sir			
2	Skrimshire, Charles	Sir			
2	Turner, Edmund	Sir			
2	Erle, Thomas	Maj. Gen.	soldier	MP	Whig 96
2	Sackville, Edward	Maj. Gen.	soldier	MP	
2	Trelawney, —	Maj. Gen.	soldier		
2	Trelawney, Charles	Maj. Gen.	soldier	MP	Tory 96
2	Finch, Heneage	Col.	soldier	MP	Tory
2	Kendall, James	Col.	soldier	MP	Whig 96
2	Parsons, William	Col.	soldier		
2	Stanhope, James	Col.	soldier	MP	Whig
2	Strangways, (Thomas)	Col.	soldier	MP	Tory 96
2	Tidcomb, John	Col.	soldier		
2	Trelawney, (Henry)	Col.	soldier	MP	Tory 96
2	Wood, Cornelius	Col.	soldier		
2	Berkeley, John	Capt. (Col.)	army		Williamite
2	Conoway, James	Capt.	army/navy		
2	Phillips, —	Capt.	army/navy		
2	Pitts, —	Capt.	army/navy		
2	Finch, (Charles)	Dr			
2	Garth, (Samuel)	Dr	physician		
2	Knipe, (Thomas)	Dr	headmaster of Westminster		
2	Oliver, (William)	Dr	physician		Williamite
2	Bowes, John	Prebend	cleric		
2	Fuller, (Samuel)	Dean	cleric		
2	Pickering, Theophilus	Prebend	cleric		
2	Adderley, Charles	Esq.			
2	Ash, Edward	Esq.		MP	Whig 96
2	Atkins, Samuel	Esq.			
2	Austen, Robert	Esq.		MP	Whig 96
2	Austen, Thomas	Esq.			
2	Barlow, William	Esq.	soldier		Tory
2	Bertie, Peregrine	Esq.		MP	Tory 96
2	Blathwayt, William	Esq.	Secretary of State for War	MP	Whig 96
2	Bloodworth, Charles	Esq.	lawyer		
2	Boyle, Richard	Esq.	soldier		
2	Bridges, William	Esq.		MP	Tory 96
2	Bridgeman, Orlando	Esq.			
2	Bridgeman, William	Esq.	Secretary to the Admiralty		
2	Bromley, William	Esq.	Secretary of State	MP	Tory 96
2	Brook, Chidley	Esq.	excise		
2	Bulkley, Thomas	Esq.		MP	Tory
2	Butler, Theophilus	Esq.			
2	Calthorp, James	Esq.			
2	Chamberlayn, Charles	Esq.	banker		
2	Clifford, Edmund	Esq.			
2	Cocks, Charles	Esq.		MP	Whig 96
2	Coel, Thomas	Esq.			

Dates	Age	Westminster School	Oxford	Cambridge	Law	Un.
						Un.
1655–1718	42			Trinity 1673		
1629–1715	68					
						Un.
						Un.
1649–1707	48		Magdalen 1666		Mid. Temple 1661	
c.1650–1702	47					
c.1640–1714	57					
						Un.
1654–1731	43					
1656–1726	41					
1647–1708	50				Mid. Temple 1666	
1658–1725	39		Christ Church 1676			
1673–1721	24		Trinity 1688			
1643–1713	54					
1642–1713	55		Oriel 1661			
1658–1702	39					
d. 1712						ND
d. 1712						ND
						Un.
						Un.
						Un.
1659–1706	38		Christ Church 1676			
1661–1719	36			Peterhouse 1676		
1638–1711	59		Christ Church 1660			
1659–1716	38					
1662–1721	35			Trinity 1680		
1635–1700	62		St John's 1650			
1662–1711	35			Sidney Sussex 1677		
1642–1713	55		Corpus 1658		Mid. Temple 1658	
1674–1748	23		Wadham 1690			
						Un.
1645–96	51					
						Un.
1655–1733	42					
1663–1711	34				Mid. Temple 1679	
1649–1717	48				Mid. Temple 1665	
1666–	31		Christ Church 1682		Inner Temple 1687	
1674–1740	23					
d. 1714						ND
1649–1701	48	✓		Magdalene 1664	Inner Temple 1658	
1646–1699	51	✓	Queen's 1662			
1664–1732	33		Christ Church 1679			
						ND
1633–1708	64		Jesus 1652		Gray's Inn 1652	
						Un.
						Un.
d. 1705						ND
						Un.
1642–1727	55					
						Un.

Sub.	Name	Title	Profession	MP	Politics
2	Coke, Thomas	Esq.			
2	Colville, Hugh	Esq.	Steward of St Cecilia's Day		
2	Crawley, John	Esq.			
2	Crocker, Courtney	Esq.			
2	Curwyn, Henry	Esq.			
2	Docmenique, Paul	Esq.	merchant	MP	
2	Drake, Montague	Esq.		MP	Tory 96
2	Draper, William	Esq.			
2	Elson, William	Esq.		MP	Tory 96
2	Elyot, Thomas	Esq.	cleric		
2	Farmer, Henry	Esq.			
2	Ferguson, Charles	Esq.	Commissioner of the Navy		
2	Franklin, Richard	Esq.	Postmaster		
2	Frewin, Thomas	Esq.	lawyer	MP	Tory 96
2	Goulston, Richard	Esq.			
2	Graham, Richard	Esq.	author		
2	Grahme, Fergus	Esq.			
2	Grove, William	Esq.	cleric		
2	Harley, Robert†				
2	Henley, Robert	Esq.		MP	Whig 96
2	Heveningham, Henry	Esq.		MP	Whig 96
2	Hewer, William	Esq.	naval official		Tory
2	Hewett, Roger	Esq.			
2	Holdworthy, John	Esq.			
2	Holdworthy, Matthew	Esq.			
2	Hornby, Nathaniel	Esq.	Commissioner of the Excise		
2	Howard, Craven	Esq.		MP	Whig 96
2	Howe, Mansel	Esq.			
2	Hunter, Samuel	Esq.	cleric		
2	James, John	Esq.	merchant		
2	Jenkins, William	Esq.			
2	Jefferyes, Edward	Esq.			
2	Jones, Samuel	Esq.			
2	Keally, Joseph	Esq.	lawyer		
2	Lamb, Patrick	Esq.			
2	Langley, Thomas	Esq.			
2	Latton, William	Esq.	lawyer		
2	Long, James	Esq.			
2	Lowndes, William	Esq.	Secretary to the Treasury	MP	Whig 96
2	Lydal, Dennis	Esq.			
2	Mannours, Charles	Esq.			
2	Mansel, Bussy	Esq.		MP	Whig 96
2	Mansell, Thomas	Esq.		MP	Tory 96
2	Martyn, William	Esq.	cleric		
2	Maxwell, Henry	Esq.			
2	Mein, Charles	Esq.			
2	Minshul, Richard	Esq.	lawyer		
2	Molesworth, Robert	Esq.		MP	
2	Moult, George	Esq.	chemist		
2	Montagu, Christopher	Esq.		MP	Whig 96

Dates	Age	Westminster School	Oxford	Cambridge	Law	Un.
						Un.
						ND
1651–	46			Caius 1669	Gray's Inn 1671	
1664–	33				Mid. Temple 1680	
						Un.
1643–1735	54					
d. 1698						ND
						Un.
1637–1705	60					
1667–	30			Trinity 1682		
						Un.
						ND
						ND
1630–1702	67		St John's 1650		Inner Temple 1656	
						Un.
1664–1720	33			Trinity 1680	Mid. Temple 1682	
						Un.
1664–	33			St Catharine's 1680		
						ND
1651–1700	46			Pembroke 1667	Gray's Inn 1669	
1642–1715	55					
						Un.
						Un.
						Un.
						ND
						ND
						Un.
1666–	31		Brasenose 1683			
						ND
						Un.
						Un.
						Un.
1673–1713	24		Pembroke 1689		Mid. Temple 1693	
						Un.
1667–1723	30			Christ's 1684	Mid. Temple 1684	
1653–	44		Wadham 1670		Gray's Inn 1679	
1682–1729	15		Balliol 1699			
1652–1724	45					
						Un.
						Un.
1623–1699	74					
1667–1723	30		Jesus 1686			
1674–	23				Mid. Temple 1690	
1677–	20				Mid. Temple 1693	
d. 1713						ND
1658–	39		Trinity 1674		Inner Temple 1685	
1656–1725	41					
						ND
1655–1735	42				Mid. Temple 1682	

Sub.	Name	Title	Profession	MP	Politics
2	Moyle, Walter	Esq.	author	MP	Whig 96
2	Nevile, Henry	Esq.			
2	Norris, William	Esq.		MP	Whig 96
2	Orme, Robert	Esq.			
2	Parry, Benjamin	Esq.			
2	Palmer, Robert	Esq.			
2	Palmes, Guy	Esq.	Teller Exchequer		
2	Pepys, Samuel	Esq.	naval official		
2	Petre, James	Esq.			
2	Peysley, William	Esq.			
2	Peyton, Craven	Esq.			
2	Pitts, John	Esq.	cleric		
2	Plowden, William	Esq.			
2	Rawlins, Thomas	Esq.	lawyer		
2	Rider, William	Esq.			
2	Robartes, Francis	Esq.		MP	Whig 96
2	St George, Oliver	Esq.			
2	Scroop, John	Esq.			
2	Sheldon, Edward	Esq.			
2	Sheldon, Ralph	Esq.			
2	Smith, John	Esq.		MP	Whig 96
2	Sothern, James	Esq.			
2	Stopford, Ro.	Esq.			
2	Temple, Henry	Esq.			
2	Toll, Ashburnham	Esq.	Commissioner of Salt		
2	Travers, Samuel	Esq.	lawyer	MP	Whig 96
2	Tucker, John	Esq.			
2	Verney, John	Esq.	lawyer	MP	Tory 96
2	Vernon, Henry	Esq.			
2	Vernon, James	Esq.	Secretary of State	MP	Whig 96
2	Ward, James	Esq.	merchant		
2	Wardour, William	Esq.			
2	Welby, William	Esq.			
2	Weld, William	Esq.			
2	Whorwood, Thomas B.	Esq.			
2	Ash, Ann	Mrs			
2	Atterbury, Francis	Mr	cleric		Williamite
2	Ball, Jeremiah	Mr			
2	Ball, John	Mr	? merchant		
2	Banks, Richard	Mr	merchant		
2	Barry, Elizabeth	Mrs	actress		
2	Beckford, (Peter)	Mr	lawyer		
2	Betterton, Thomas	Mr	actor		
2	Blount, Catherine	Mrs			
2	Bond, —	Mr			
2	Bond, —	Mr			
2	Bracegirdle, Anne	Mrs	actress		
2	Brockenburgh, Samuel	Mr			
2	Brown, Elizabeth	Mrs			
2	Bruche, Moses	Mr			
2	Bruneau, Michael	Mr			
2	Burton, Lancelot	Mr	official		
2	Clancy, John	Mr			
2	Claret, William	Mr			

Dates	Age	Westminster School	Oxford	Cambridge	Law	Un.
1672–1721	25		Exeter 1689		Mid. Temple 1691	
1643–1728	54			Peterhouse 1660		
1657–1702	40	✓		Trinity 1675		
1672–	25			Trinity 1688		
						Un.
1675–	22		Magdalen Hall 1691		Mid. Temple 1691	
						ND
1633–1703	64			Trinity Hall 1650		
						Un.
						Un.
1664–1738	33		Exeter 1681		Lincoln's Inn 1680	
1657–1723	40		Pembroke 1674			
						Un.
1662–	35				Mid. Temple 1678	
						Un.
1650–1718	47			Christ's 1663		
						Un.
						Un.
1675–	22		Pembroke 1693			
						Un.
1656–1723	41		St John's 1672		Mid. Temple 1675	
						Un.
						Un.
1673–1757	24			King's 1693		
1668–	29		Christ Church 1685			
1655–1725	42		Exeter 1674		Mid. Temple 1679	
						Un.
1652–1707	45		Jesus 1668		Mid. Temple 1670	
1637–1711	60		Christ Church 1655		Inner Temple 1653	
1646–1727	51		Christ Church 1662			
						ND
1665–	32			Christ's 1681	Lincoln's Inn 1683	
1667–1726	30			Trinity 1683	Mid. Temple 1683	
						Un.
1667–	30			Trinity Hall 1683	Inner Temple 1684	
						Un.
1662–1732	35	✓	Christ Church 1686			
						Un.
						ND
						ND
1658–1713	39					
1674–1735	23		New 1689		Mid. Temple 1695	
1635–1710	62					
						Un.
						Un.
						Un.
1663–1748	34					
						Un.
						Un.
						Un.
						Un.
						ND
						Un.
						Un.

Sub.	Name	Title	Profession	MP	Politics
2	Congreve, William	Mr	author		Whig
2	Cook, Henry	Mr			
2	Cooper, William	Mr	? merchant		
2	Creed, Elizabeth	Mrs			
2	Dahl, Michael	Mr	artist		
2	Davenport, —	Mr			
2	Delawn, William	Mr	President of St John's		
2	Draycot, Dorothy	Mrs			
2	Dryden, Edward	Mr			
2	Finch, George	Mr	? merchant		
2	Finch, Thomas	Mr			
2	Gibbons, Grinling	Mr	wood carver		
2	Gifford, Thomas	Mr			
2	Goulding, George	Mr			
2	Haistwell, Edward	Mr	merchant		
2	Hawksmoor, Nicolas	Mr	architect		
2	Hayter, Whitfield	Mr	goldsmith/banker		
2	Henriques, Peter	Mr	jobber		
2	Huckwell, Robert	Mr			
2	Kinkead, Michael	Mr	? merchant		
2	Longueville, Charles	Mr			
2	Marbury, Charles	Mr			
2	Metcalf, Christopher	Mr			
2	Monneaux, —	Mrs			
2	Nicoll, William	Mr	author cleric		
2	Owen, Michael	Mr	gentleman		
2	Peck, Daniel	Mr	? merchant		
2	Rose, —	Mr			
2	Seamer, James	Mr			
2	Seeks, William	Mr			
2	Sherwood, Joseph	Mr			
2	Slaughter, Paris	Mr	merchant		
2	Smith, Lawrence	Mr			
2	Southern, Thomas	Mr	author		
2	Stepney, Lancelot	Mr			
2	Townsend, George	Mr			
2	Tyldesley, Thomas	Mr			
2	Tyndall, (William)	Mr	cleric		
2	Walter, Mary	Mrs			
2	Wessell, Leonard	Mr	? merchant		

Dates	Age	Westminster School	Oxford	Cambridge	Law	Un.
1670–1729	27				Mid. Temple 1691	
1665–1717	32			Clare 1681		
						ND
1642–1728	55					
1656–1743	41					
						Un.
1659–1728	38		St John's 1675			
						Un.
1665–	32					
						ND
						Un.
1648–1720	49					
						Un.
1670–1739	27			St John's 1687		
d. 1709						ND
1661–1736	36					
						ND
						ND
						Un.
						ND
1677–1750	20			Clare 1695	Inner Temple 1693	
						Un.
						Un.
						Un.
1664–1712	33		Magdalen Hall 1680			
						ND
1669–	28		Merton 1686			
						Un.
						Un.
						Un.
						Un.
						ND
						Un.
1660–1746	37				Mid. Temple 1680	
						Un.
						Un.
						Un.
1655–1712	42			Trinity Hall 1671		
						Un.
						ND

APPENDIX II

It is impossible to know what proportion of the potential purchasers of Dryden's *Virgil* actually chose to subscribe to or buy the book. Gregory King's estimate of England's population in 1696, arranged by class, profession, and annual income, allows some reasonable guesses to be made.[131] King counts the number of families in each of his categories. For these purposes it will be assumed that one family would buy only a single copy (though in fact some aristocratic families made more than one subscription to the *Virgil*). According to King there were 16,586 families of the rank of gentleman or above (making up 1.2 per cent of the total population), with incomes between £280 and £2,800 per year. On these figures a five-guinea subscription for a gentleman would represent a week's income, and a two-guinea subscription a third of a week's income. Dryden's 349 first and second subscribers represent 2.1 per cent of this category. If purchasers of the small-paper copies of the first edition and of Tonson's 1698 second edition are taken into account, up to 2,000 copies may have been sold by 1709.[132] If so, as many as 12.1 per cent of the genteel and aristocratic cohort may have had copies of Dryden's translation in their homes.

However, as the two subscription lists demonstrate, office-holders, merchants, lawyers, and soldiers all subscribed to the edition. These are ranked below 'Gentleman' by King, and their annual income ranged from £60 (military officers) and £400 ('Merchants and Traders by Sea'). Clearly, the pool of potential buyers extended beyond genteel and aristocratic families. Assuming that the small-paper copies cost only £1 (this figure is partly for ease of calculation, but also to arrive at a maximum figure) and that a family's head might be willing to spend half a week's income on a book, a purchaser would need a minimum annual income of £104. Only the groups in Table 1 fall into this category. This represents a constituency three times as large as that used in the earlier calculation (and excludes both clergymen and soldiers, who had incomes well below £100). Dryden's subscribers represent 0.75 per cent of this cohort of families, while the 2,000 sold by 1709 amounts to 4.3 per cent (or 0.15 per cent of the total number of families in the country).

By 1709, then, between 4.3 and 12.1 per cent of those families who could afford to spend more than £1 a week on a book could have possessed a copy of Dryden's translation of Virgil.

---

[131] *The Earliest Classics: John Graunt, Natural and Political Observations made upon the Bills of Mortality (1662): Gregory King, Natural and Political Observations and Conclusions made upon the State of England 1696 (1804)* . . ., introd. Peter Laslett (London, 1973), pp. 48–9.

[132] See 'Large- and Small-Paper Copies of Dryden's *The Works of Virgil* (1697)', p. 271.

Table 1

Category	Families	Income (£ p.a.)
Temporal Lords	160	2,800
Spiritual Lords	26	1,300
Baronets	800	880
Knights	600	650
Esquires	3,000	450
Gentlemen	12,000	280
Persons in Offices	5,000	240
Persons in Offices	5,000	120
Merchants and Traders by Sea	2,000	400
Merchants and Traders by Land	8,000	200
Persons in the Law	10,000	140
	46,586	

9

'THE LAST PARTING OF HECTOR AND ANDROMACHE'

ROBIN SOWERBY

I must not forget, that Mr. *Dryden* has formerly translated this admirable Episode, and with so much Success, as to leave me at least no hopes of improving or equalling it. The utmost I can pretend is to have avoided a few modern Phrases and Deviations from the Original, which have escaped that great Man.[1]

Such was Pope's tribute (in the notes that he appended to his own translation) to 'The Last Parting of Hector and Andromache', Dryden's version of an extract from Book VI of Homer's *Iliad*, published in *Examen Poeticum* in 1693. For a critical account of the beauties of the original which have made this episode one of the most famous in the whole of Homer Pope's own commentary can hardly be bettered, but to introduce Dryden's version it will perhaps be more fitting to suggest the appeal of the episode from two earlier testimonies. First, Erasmus in the *De Copia* of 1534:

Quis enim non cum voluptate legat, quomodo apud Homerum Andromache Hectori armato occurrit ad portam civitatis, qua proditurus erat in praelium, non sola (neque enim id decet pudicas matronas, sed comitabantur pedisequae), puerum in vlnis gestans Astyanactem, Hectoris filium, patri vnice charum, et (quod addit Homerus) pulchro sideri adsimilem, quo per hunc vxor expugnaret affectus mariti. Hector tacite arrisit conspecto puero. Andromache propius adstans dextram porrexit, ac nominatim compellauit. Dein, post afficatam vtrique congruentem orationem,

---

[1] *The Twickenham Edition of the Poems of Alexander Pope*, gen. ed. John Butt, 11 vols. (London, 1939–68), vii. 349.

quum Hector infantem appeteret osculaturus, ille territus armorum splendore ac crista e galeae fastigio minitante, clamans reflexit se in sinum nutricis. Hic risit vterque, pater et mater. At Hector sublatam e capite galeam humi deposuit, atque ita puerum amplexus osculatus est. Mox ei fausta precatus, traditit matri. Illa eum excepit in sinum bene olentem, δακρυόεν γέλασασα, id est lachrymabile ridens. Ea res Hectori mouit misericordiam, atque vxorem manu sustentens consolatur, nomine eam appellans. Mox reponit galeam. Illa marito obtemperans domum se recipit. Ibi muliebri fletu complentur omnia, quod crederent eum ex quo praelio non rediturum. Itaque spirantem adhuc pro mortuo deflent.[2]

(Who could read without pleasure Homer's description of Andromache meeting the armed Hector at the city gate through which he was about to go out to battle? Andromache is not alone, which would be inappropriate for a modest matron, but accompanied by her maids; in her arms she holds the baby Astyanax, Hector's son and his father's darling. Homer adds that he is 'like a beautiful star', so that the wife can appeal to her husband's feelings through the child. Hector smiles without speaking when he sees his son. Andromache comes up to him, reaches out her right hand and addresses him by name. Then, after an appropriate speech composed for both of them, Hector reaches out to kiss his son, but the child, terrified by the gleam of his armour and the crest waving threateningly from his helmet-top, cries and shrinks back into his mother's arms. At this point both his father and his mother laugh. Hector now takes his helmet off, puts it on the ground, and then takes the child and kisses him. Then he prays for the child's success and hands him over to his mother; she takes him in her fragrant bosom, 'laughing tearfully'. Hector is moved by this to pity and, supporting his wife with his hand, consoles her, speaking to her by name; then he replaces his helmet. She obeys her husband and returns home. And then the whole house becomes filled with the weeping of women, because they think he will not come back from that battle. And so they weep for him as though he were dead, while he is still breathing.)

Erasmus' summary highlights the simple actions and emotions in this family scene and the paradox of their laughter amid tears. This for Rapin in the comparison he made between Homer and Virgil in 1667 is evidence of 'nature':

L'entreveuë d'Hector & d'Andromaque sur la fin du sixiéme livre de l'Iliade, est un des endroits des plus delicats, & des plus achevez d'Homere:

---

[2] *De Copia Verborum ac Rerum*, ed. Betty I. Knott (Amsterdam, 1988), pp. 276–8; *Opera Omnia Desiderii Erasmi Roterodami* (Amsterdam, 1969–   ), i. 6. The translation is from *English Humanism: Wyatt to Cowley*, ed. Joanna Martindale (London, 1985), pp. 130–1.

tout y est touchant, tendre, naturel en ce qu'il fait dire à l'un à l'autre à l'occasion du petit Astianax, qui se trouve à cet entretien, dont il fait une partie: le peur qu'il a de son pere armé, fait un effet où la nature est bien peinte.[3]

(The interview between Hector and Andromache at the end of the sixth book of the *Iliad* is one of the most delicate and finished pieces in Homer; all there is touching, tender, and natural in what they say to one another on the occasion of the little Astyanax, who finds himself at this conversation of which he becomes a part; the fear which he has of his father in armour has an effect in which nature is beautifully painted.)

The tender familial aspects of the episode to which Erasmus and Rapin are drawn occasion similar praise in Pope as he remarks upon the incident involving the frightened child: 'All these are but small Circumstances, but so artfully chosen, that every reader immediately feels the force of them, and represents the whole in the utmost Liveliness to his Imagination.'[4] The domestic aspect of this scene involving an infant is unparalleled in epic poetry. It is difficult to imagine Virgil, Spenser, or Milton attempting anything like it, let alone succeeding in the attempt. But this is only part of the episode's appeal. Equally moving are Hector's foreboding of the future when Troy will fall and when Andromache will be sold into slavery, and his dignified prayer to the gods that his son Astyanax will excel his father, a prayer of great pathos and irony because of this foreboding of a future which the audience knows will come to be. Astyanax's very name, meaning 'lord of the city', contains irony and pathos for his fate is at one with the city. For modern audiences the tragic irony is intensified, for in later literature it is recorded that he was thrown off the battlements by Ulysses (see Ovid's *Metamorphoses*, xiii. 415). Whether this version of events was familiar to Homer's audience cannot be known; Homer is silent about his fate, though it is clear in the *Iliad* that it is Aeneas and his line upon whom the future of Troy is to depend (see xix. 305), not the son of Hector. In the present action of the poem, therefore, there is a balance between fear and hope, between laughter and tears, while over all hangs the future doom of the city.

Dryden had already included an interview between Hector and Andromache in his revision of Shakespeare's *Troilus and Cressida*[5] in

[3] René Rapin, *Les Comparaisons des grands hommes de l'antiquité*, 2 vols. (Amsterdam, 1686), i. 140.   [4] *The Twickenham Pope*, vii. 355–6.   [5] *Works*, xiii. 252–355.

1677. Brief consideration of this revision will make an appropriate entrée to the later translation and suggest that the challenge it represented had yet to be met.

Towards the end of Shakespeare's play, in a scene reminiscent of Calpurnia's attempt to dissuade Caesar from attending the Senate on the Ides of March, Andromache attempts to dissuade Hector from going into battle (v. iii). She tells Cassandra of her dreams of turbulence and slaughter. Cassandra then prophesies Hector's death and Andromache's grief. Hector, conscious of his honour and 'i' th' vein of chivalry' (v. iii. 32), shows no tenderness towards her; offended by her interference, he dismisses her brusquely and bids her go indoors. Shakespeare's handling of this encounter owes much to post-classical reworkings of the matter of Troy. Caxton,[6] for example, had recounted Andromache's night of bad dreams which were not in Homer.

In his revision, Dryden introduced an encounter between Hector and Andromache early in the play in which Andromache enters to tell Hector of Astyanax's request that Priam make him a knight; 'he longs to kill a Grecian' (ii. i. 83). The little boy, no longer an infant, fears that after his father has done with them there may be no Grecians left, and he wants to send a challenge to the leading Greeks. Hector, admiring 'the sparks of honour' in his son (ii. i. 90), takes up the idea, but Priam is fearful for his life and bids Andromache help him make Hector change his mind. She, however, asserting that she has the soul of a man, takes pride in his courage and urges him on. Towards the end of the play, when Hector is about to go to battle, Andromache, having dreamt of Hector's death, is in quite a different mood. There is a deliberate contrast with the earlier encounter between hero and wife. When she fails to encourage him as usual, he accuses her of cowardice. She goes to gird his sword and it falls: 'Heaven! The Gods avert this omen!' (v. i. 29). She recounts her dream to Hector, but he is unmoved. When she says directly that she fears that if he goes out to fight she will not see him again, he rejects her emotion:

> Thou excellently good, but oh too soft,
> Let me not scape the danger of this day.

---

[6] William Caxton, *The Recuyell of the Historyes of Troye*, ed. H. Oscar Sommer (London, 1894), pp. 610–12.

But I have struggling in my manly Soul
To see those modest tears, asham'd to fall,
And witness any part of woman in thee!
And now I fear, lest thou should'st think it fear,
If thus disswaded, I refuse to fight,
And stay inglorious in thy arms at home.   (v. i. 78–85)

Andromache is not rejected as brusquely as she is in Shakespeare; what the honourable Hector rejects is something in himself, the woman within. As he is so bound up in himself, there is none of the intimate human feeling that binds husband and wife in the Homeric narrative where, though he rejects her pleadings and bids her leave the fighting to the men, Hector is nevertheless at one with Andromache in his response to their child, and can look beyond his own fame and honour in unselfish concern for his wife's future. Dryden's revision of the play imposes upon it the ethos of his heroic plays with the result that a stiff honour code dominates in these family relations, precluding the kind of human intimacy that shines through Homer. Translation of the episode in Homer, therefore, presented a challenge for which his previous revision of Shakespeare had not prepared him.

Dryden's approach towards translation and his method of going about it were well established by the time he produced 'The Last Parting'. He wrote extensively about translation, but two quotations will suffice to suggest his general approach. 'A Noble Authour wou'd not be persu'd too close by a Translator. We lose his Spirit, when we think to take his Body',[7] he wrote in his introduction to his translation of Juvenal, and he used the following formula *à propos* of Juvenal as well as Virgil here: 'taking all the Materials of this divine Author I have endeavour'd to make *Virgil* speak such *English*, as he wou'd himself have spoken, if he had been born in *England*, and in this present Age'.[8] As to his method, detailed examination of 'The Last Parting' reveals an extraordinary amount of preparatory reading in previous translations, for there are borrowings from the English versions of Chapman (1608), Ogilby (1660 and 1669), Hobbes (1676), and Chetwood (1685), the French version of de la Valterie (1681), the Latin prose version of Laurentius Valla (1474),

---

[7] 'Discourse of Satire', *Works*, iv. 87.
[8] 'Dedication of the *Aeneis*', *Works*, v. 330–1; see also *Works*, iv. 89.

and the Latin verse translation of Eobanus Hessus (1540). He also consulted the Latin commentary of Johannes Spondanus (1606 and 1686) that accompanied the Greek text, together with a Latin version in this bilingual edition.[9] These constitute the main materials from which he constructed his own version. Such an approach and method, involving the fusion of traditional translation and interpretation and its distillation into a contemporary poetic style, necessarily resulted in a version of Homer greatly elaborated and sophisticated in both content and style. Anyone who expects to encounter Homeric simplicity in Dryden will be disappointed. What Dr Johnson said of Pope's *Iliad*, which he called 'a poetical wonder',[10] is also true of Dryden's Homeric translation: its grand style lacks the artless, unaffected simplicity of the original.

That is not to say, however, that Dryden, who as a translator was highly conscious of the need to maintain the individual poetical character of an author, did not seek to represent stylistic features of the original. He did not usually attempt to render the traditional epithets, the bane of Homeric translators and an archaic feature inappropriate to a modern poet, like 'white-armed Andromache', 'Hector of the shining helm', or the 'fair-girdled nurse', but he did respond to Homeric repetition to produce a more patterned style than was his wont. This may be illustrated in the following example from the beginning of the episode where Hector is trying to ascertain the whereabouts of his wife.

αἶψα δ' ἔπειθ' ἵκανε δόμους εὖ ναιετάοντας,
οὐδ' εὗρ' Ἀνδρομάχην λευκώλενον ἐν μεγάροισιν,
ἀλλ' ἥ γε ξὺν παιδὶ καὶ ἀμφιπόλῳ ἐυπέπλῳ
πύργῳ ἐφεστήκει γοόωσά τε μυρομένη τε.
Ἕκτωρ δ' ὡς οὐκ ἔνδον ἀμύμονα τέτμεν ἄκοιτιν,
ἔστη ἐπ' οὐδὸν ἰών, μετὰ δὲ δμῳῆσιν ἔειπεν·
"εἰ δ' ἄγε μοι, δμῳαί, νημερτέα μυθήσασθε·
πῇ ἔβη Ἀνδρομάχη λευκώλενος ἐκ μεγάροιο;
ἠέ πῃ ἐς γαλόων ἢ εἰνατέρων ἐυπέπλων,
ἦ ἐς Ἀθηναίης ἐξοίχεται, ἔνθα περ ἄλλαι
Τρῳαὶ ἐυπλόκαμοι δεινὴν θεὸν ἱλάσκονται;"

[9] For fuller explication and further details see my 'Dryden and Homer', unpublished Ph.D. thesis, University of Cambridge, 1975, pp. 235–8.
[10] 'Life of Pope', in *The Lives of the English Poets*, ed. George Birkbeck Hill, 3 vols. (Oxford, 1905), iii. 236.

Τὸν δ' αὖτ' ὀτρηρὴ ταμίη πρὸς μῦθον ἔειπεν·
"Ἕκτορ, ἐπεὶ μάλ' ἄνωγας ἀληθέα μυθήσασθαι,
οὔτε πη ἐς γαλόων οὔτ' εἰνατέρων εὐπέπλων
οὔτ' ἐς Ἀθηναίης ἐξοίχεται, ἔνθα περ ἄλλαι
Τρῳαὶ ἐυπλόκαμοι δεινὴν θεὸν ἱλάσκονται,
ἀλλ' ἐπὶ πύργον ἔβη μέγαν Ἰλίου, οὕνεκ' ἄκουσε
τείρεσθαι Τρῶας, μέγα δὲ κράτος εἶναι Ἀχαιῶν.
ἡ μὲν δὴ πρὸς τεῖχος ἐπειγομένη ἀφικάνει,
μαινομένη ἐικυῖα· φέρει δ' ἅμα παῖδα τιθήνη."[11]   (ll. 370–89)

When he saw no sign of his perfect wife within the house, Hektor
stopped in his way on the threshold and spoke among the handmaidens:
'Come then, tell me truthfully as you may, handmaidens:
where has Andromache of the white arms gone? Is she
with any of the sisters of her lord or the wives of his brothers?
Or has she gone to the house of Athene, where all the other
lovely-haired women of Troy propitiate the grim goddess?'
    Then in turn the hard-working housekeeper gave him an answer:
'Hektor, since you have urged me to tell you the truth, she is not
with any of the sisters of her lord or the wives of her brothers,
nor has she gone to the house of Athene, where all the other
lovely-haired women of Troy propitiate the grim goddess,
but she has gone to the great bastion of Ilion, because she heard that
the Trojans were losing, and great grew the strength of the Achaians.
Therefore she has gone in speed to the wall, like a woman
gone mad, and a nurse attending carries the baby.'[12]

> But he, who thought his peopled Palace bare,
> When she, his only Comfort, was not there;
> Stood in the Gate, and ask'd of ev'ry one,
> Which way she took, and whither she was gone:
> If to the Court, or with his Mother's Train,
> In long Procession to *Minerva*'s Fane?
> The Servants answer'd, neither to the Court
> Where *Priam's* Sons and Daughters did resort,
> Nor to the Temple was she gone, to move
> With Prayers the blew-ey'd Progeny of *Jove*;

[11] *Homer: The Iliad with an English Translation* by A. T. Murray, 2 vols. (London and Cambridge, Mass., 1924). The Greek text for this episode does not differ substantively from the seventeenth-century vulgate as exemplified in an edition consulted by Dryden: *Homeri quae extant omnia . . . cum Latina versione . . . J. Spondani . . . Commentariis*, etc. (Basle, 1583; Geneva, 1606; Basle, 1686).

[12] *The Iliad of Homer*, trans. Richmond Lattimore (Chicago, 1951), used here and also later in this chapter, providing a fair key to the sense of the Greek.

But, more solicitous for him alone,
Than all their safety, to the Tow'r was gone,
There to survey the Labours of the Field;
Where the *Greeks* conquer, and the *Trojans* yield.
Swiftly she pass'd, with Fear and Fury wild,
The Nurse went lagging after with the Child.[13] (ll. 10–25)

Dryden is quite free with the original. Although he has omitted most of the formulaic phrases, in 'blew-ey'd Progeny of *Jove*' (for Athene) he has introduced one of his own. The repetition in Hector's question and the maid's reply is retained but with variation. The phrase 'was gone', first occurring in line 3, is repeated three times here. 'There to survey the Labours of the Field' echoes with variation the earlier couplet 'From whence with heavy Heart she might survey | The bloody business of the dreadful Day' (ll. 6–7). The pattern and sense of the final couplet in the extract are repeated with variation a little later: 'Breathless she flew, with Joy and Passion wild, | The Nurse came lagging after with her Child' (ll. 36–7). This latter repetition is introduced by Dryden. The patterning of repetition with variation, particularly prominent at the opening of the translation but evident throughout, reproduces in a more elaborate form stylistic features of the original, and this patterning is peculiar to this translation.

Dryden's sophistication of the simpler original is apparent in the opening couplet. In Homer, Hector simply sees no sign of his wife in the house, whereas Dryden's Hector thinks his palace empty if Andromache is not there, even though it is full of people. There is a similar sophistication introduced in the description of Andromache as 'His Wife, who brought in Dow'r *Cilicia*'s Crown; | And, in her self, a greater Dow'r alone: | *Aetion*'s Heyr' (ll. 32–4). In Homer she comes simply with many gifts as 'the daughter of high-hearted Eetion', the lord of Cilicia; there is no mention of her being his heir or bringing a crown, or play on the word dowry. Perhaps the most daring witticism is the description of the smiling child 'Who, like the Morning Star, his beams display'd' (l. 39). In the original the child is simply likened to a beautiful star (with no mention of smiling). The translator may have recalled a line in Ogilby's Virgil 'Bright, like the Morning-star dispensing Beams'.[14] If so, his wit

---

[13] For 'The Last Parting', see *Works*, iv. 425–31.
[14] *The Works of Virgil*, trans. John Ogilby (London, 1684), p. 303.

transformed the borrowing, and might be said to produce in the reader the kind of pleasure that the sight of the child affords its parents. Andromache, after reminding Hector of the death of her family at the hands of Achilles, and telling him that he is now all her family, appeals to him not to go out to battle with a sophisticated thought not in Homer: 'O kill not all my Kindred o're again' (l. 84). She bids him not to leave his son an orphan and his wife a widow but to marshal his troops in order to defend the rampart from within: 'This is a Husband's and a Father's Post' (l. 88); this is another additional thought with a pleasing play on the literal and the figurative. There is a similar play in the conqueror's 'insulting Sword' (l. 126), not in Homer, and another when Hector envisages Andromache in captivity as 'A spectacle in *Argos*, at the Loom, | Gracing with *Trojan* Fights, a *Grecian* Room' (ll. 128–9). In the original she simply works at the loom of another; here Dryden has improved upon a sophistication he found in Chetwood's version: 'Perhaps some haughty Dame your hands shall doom | To weave *Troy*'s Downfall in a Grecian Loom'.[15] Chetwood fills out the Greek with a specific image neatly encapsulated in a fine antithesis. The pathos and irony are further intensified when Dryden's Andromache is made a 'spectacle', gracing the room both by the tapestries she is forced to weave and by her own graceful beauty that makes her something to be admired, a 'spectacle' in a positive as well as a negative meaning. Her captivity, in which she will also have to perform menial tasks like fetching water, is indeed strongly imagined; 'groaning under this laborious Life' (l. 132), another sophisticated importation, suggests both physical and mental torment.

Throughout, Dryden is much more figurative than Homer. This may be related in part to a tendency in all Dryden's translating activity: his instinct to render the sense of an original with absolute clarity. In a simple example of this tendency in literal explication, he glosses the name Scamandrius given by Hector to his child with the line 'From that fair Flood which *Ilion*'s Wall did lave' (l. 41). This both informs the reader not too familiar with Homer and underscores Hector's patriotism, implicit in the original. Other figurative additions may be explained as a way of clarifying nuances that are

---

[15] Quotations from Chetwood's version of this episode, 'The Parting of Hector with his Princess Andromache', are from the 1693 edition: see n. 22.

implicit in the Greek. Hector's helmet is simply a physical object in the original; in the translation, when Hector takes it off because its nodding plume is frightening his infant son, it is 'The Pride of Warriours and the Pomp of War' (l. 153). One of Hector's recurring epithets highlighting his warlike appearance is κορυθαίολος (with glancing helm). The figurative rendering serves to enhance Hector in the manner of the heroic epithets without producing the stilted effect they inevitably have in a literal version in modern English, and it is beautifully placed by Dryden at the tender familial moment when Hector physically takes off his helmet, with appropriate symbolism, as he lays aside for the moment his warrior's pomp and pride in this fatherly gesture. In another addition, the child becomes 'The Pledge of Love, and other hope of Troy' (l. 143). There is perhaps a reminiscence here of the moment in Racine when Andromaque, recalling her last interview with Hector, calls Astyanax 'Ce Fils que de sa flamme il me laissa pour gage'[16] (This son whom he left me as a pledge of his love), echoing Hector's last words to her: 'Je te laisse mon Fils, pour gage de ma foy' (I leave you my son as a pledge of my faith). Behind this lie the words of Creusa's shade to Aeneas on Troy's last night: *nati serva communis amorem*[17] (*Aeneid*, ii. 789) 'I trust our common Issue to your Care' (*Aeneis*, ii. 1074), and the later description of Ascanius as *magnae spes altera Romae* (*Aeneid*, xii. 168) 'The second Hope of *Rome*'s Immortal Race' (*Aeneis*, xii. 254). These figurative expressions draw out what could be said to be implicit in the Homeric text in the light of what subsequent handling of the episode has suggested. The additions are therefore the product of the translator's close imaginative engagement with the afterlife of the original text through his reading of what it has become through other translation and adaptation.

The connection with Virgil, though, goes beyond phrases or particular borrowings in two fundamental respects. In the first place, Virgil, in Roscommon's phrase 'the sacred *Founder* of *Our Rules*',[18] represented the poetic standard which the Augustan Dryden aspired

---

[16] Jean Racine, *Théâtre de 1664 à 1667: La Thébaïde, Alexandre, Andromaque*, ed. Gonzague Truc (Paris, 1953), III. viii (p. 196). Racine's play was translated by John Crowne: *Andromache, a Tragedy* (London, 1675).

[17] *Virgil with an English Translation by H. Rushton Fairclough*, 2 vols. (London and Cambridge, Mass., 1935).

[18] The Earl of Roscommon, *An Essay on Translated Verse*, 2nd edn. (London, 1685), p. 23.

to emulate in English. It might be said that he adapted the sophisticated and figured style he had already forged in his translations of Virgil to the simpler material of Homer, imposing the Roman Augustan aesthetic on the simpler Greek out of which it grew as he did so. The result in 'The Last Parting' is a denser text than its original in the more elaborate style of which Virgil was the great exemplar. Secondly, whether by accident or design, it seems clear from the translation itself that the subject-matter of this Homeric episode engaged the former Laureate in the kind of political interest that he had exhibited in his panegyrics and Laureate poems and that has sometimes been seen in his later translation of the *Aeneid*.[19]

The effort involved in making Homer speak as an Englishman of the late seventeenth century entails some modification in the setting and the description of characters, who are accommodated to contemporary circumstances. Hector lives in a 'Palace' (l. 10), Priam has a 'Court' (l. 16) and a 'Crown' (l. 113), the child is a '*Royal Babe*' (l. 38), Andromache is Hector's 'Consort' (l. 190). But the modification goes beyond details of this kind, affecting more fundamental aspects of the translation. This can be illustrated by examination of two of its central passages: Hector's motivation for the fight, and his prayer that Astyanax may outdo his father's achievement.

When Andromache has appealed to him to stay inside the city rather than risk his life on the battlefield, Hector in the original replies that he would feel shame before the Trojans if he did not fight, and that his spirit, his θυμός (glossed as 'vital strength', 'the life force', 'instinctive energy', or 'appetite' in Homeric dictionaries) impels him to go. This is a motivation that he shares with all the heroes, Greek and Trojan; they are not reluctant warriors but experience joy in battle, χάρμα. Later in the poem, when Hector goes into battle, he is likened to a horse who breaks loose from his stall to run freely over the plain (xv. 263–8). Even Andromache recognizes this motivation when at the end of her appeal to Hector she describes the leading Greeks attacking the wall at a vulnerable point (l. 439), though Dryden does not translate or provide an equivalent for θυμός here. His Greeks are there 'by Augury, or chance' (l. 98), not, like Homer's, because they may have been

---

[19] See William J. Cameron, 'John Dryden's Jacobitism', in Harold Love (ed.), *Restoration Literature: Critical Approaches* (London, 1972); Steven N. Zwicker, *Politics and Language in Dryden's Poetry: The Arts of Disguise* (Princeton, NJ, 1984).

prompted by their θυμός (l. 439). He does not translate the Greek word directly in this speech either:

"ἦ καὶ ἐμοὶ τάδε πάντα μέλει, γύναι· ἀλλὰ μάλ' αἰνῶς
αἰδέομαι Τρῶας καὶ Τρῳάδας ἑλκεσιπέπλους,
αἴ κε κακὸς ὣς νόσφιν ἀλυσκάζω πολέμοιο·
οὐδέ με θυμὸς ἄνωγεν, ἐπεὶ μάθον ἔμμεναι ἐσθλὸς
αἰεὶ καὶ πρώτοισι μετὰ Τρώεσσι μάχεσθαι,
ἀρνύμενος πατρός τε μέγα κλέος ἠδ' ἐμὸν αὐτοῦ." (ll. 441–6)

'All these
things are in my mind also, lady; yet I would feel deep shame
before the Trojans, and the Trojan women with trailing garments,
if like a coward I were to shrink aside from the fighting;
and the spirit will not let me, since I have learned to be valiant
and to fight always among the foremost ranks of the Trojans,
winning for my own self great glory, and for my father.'

(ll. 440–6)

Chapman recognized that this is a critical moment. Not to fight would be spiritual death:

But what a shame and feare it is to thinke how Troy would scorne
(Both in her husbands and her wives, whom long-trained gownes adorne)
That I should cowardly flie off! The spirit I first did breathe
Did never teach me that—much less since the contempt of death
Was settl'd in me and my mind knew what a Worthy was,
Whose office is to leade in fight and give no danger passe
Without improvement. In this fire must Hector's triall shine.
Here must his country, father, friends be in him made divine.[20]

(ll. 478–85)

Though θυμός is emphatically rendered, there is not much joy here, rather a strange mixture of Stoic contempt of death, a moralizing emphasis upon duty, and a sense that here is a test through which all may be transfigured. By contrast Dryden's honourable Hector does express his delight in battle, though the use of the past tense makes it distinctly less immediate: as a born warrior he would be betraying his birthright were he not to fight:

That and the rest are in my daily care;
But shou'd I shun the Dangers of the War,

[20] *Chapman's Homer*, ed. Allardyce Nicoll, 2 vols. (London, 1967), i. 150.

251

With scorn the *Trojans* wou'd reward my pains,
And their proud Ladies with their sweeping Trains.
The *Grecian* Swords and Lances I can bear:
But loss of Honour is my only Fear.
Shall *Hector*, born to War, his Birth-right yield,
Belie his Courage and forsake the Field?
Early in rugged Arms I took delight;
And still have been the foremost in the Fight:
With dangers dearly have I bought Renown,
And am the Champion of my Father's Crown.   (ll. 102–13)

Although there is no overt allusion to the contemporary world here, the question 'Shall *Hector*, born to War, his Birth-right yield?' must have reverberated suggestively to a readership that had recently seen the warlike King James forfeit his birthright. The rhetorical arrangement of the speech, marked by the change of tense in the final line, gives a very clear climax. Even if 'dearly' is taken to mean 'eagerly' rather than more naturally interpreted to mean 'at personal cost', Dryden's Hector is both more self-effacing than his Greek counterpart, who is ἀρνύμενος πατρός τε μέγα κλέος ἠδ' ἐμὸν αὐτοῦ (gaining great glory for his father and for himself), and more conscious of his key dynastic role.

There is an even greater transformation in his greatly expanded prayer for Astyanax:

"Ζεῦ ἄλλοι τε θεοί, δότε δὴ καὶ τόνδε γενέσθαι
παῖδ' ἐμόν, ὡς καὶ ἐγώ περ, ἀριπρεπέα Τρώεσσιν
ὧδε βίην τ' ἀγαθόν, καὶ Ἰλίου ἶφι ἀνάσσειν·
καί ποτέ τις εἴποι 'πατρός γ' ὅδε πολλὸν ἀμείνων'
ἐκ πολέμου ἀνιόντα· φέροι δ' ἔναρα βροτόεντα
κτείνας δήιον ἄνδρα, χαρείη δὲ φρένα μήτηρ."   (ll. 476–81)

'Zeus, and you other immortals, grant that this boy, who is my son, may be as I am, pre-eminent among the Trojans, great in strength, as I am, and rule strongly over Ilion; and some day let them say of him: "He is better far than his father", as he comes from the fighting; and let him kill his enemy and bring home the blooded spoils, and delight the heart of his mother.'

(ll. 476–81)

Parent of Gods, and Men, propitious *Jove*,
And you bright Synod of the Pow'rs above;

On this my Son your Gracious Gifts bestow;
Grant him to live, and great in Arms to grow:
To Reign in *Troy*; to Govern with Renown:
To shield the People, and assert the Crown:
That, when hereafter he from War shall come,
And bring his *Trojans* Peace and Triumph home,
Some aged Man, who lives this act to see,
And who in former times remember'd me,
May say the son in Fortitude and Fame
Out-goes the Mark; and drowns his Father's Name:
That at these words his Mother may rejoice:
And add her Suffrage to the publick Voice.   (ll. 156–69)

The Homeric phrase ἶφι ἀνάσσειν (to rule forcefully) is emphatically expanded. Any possible inappropriate associations (for a modern monarch) attaching to the word ἶφι (with might) are dissipated
in the verbs 'govern' and 'shield', which help to define the quality of
the reign that is to be asserted. Astyanax's mother is not to rejoice
over the bloody spoils of a defeated enemy which he has brought
home, but to take pleasure in a more abstract triumph which is a
prelude to peace, applauded not only by her but by the people
whom he has shielded. He is indeed to be the people's prince.
Hector's prayer in Homer is generous and spirited. As Dryden
translates it, it is still generous and spirited, but it is more obviously
akin to the later address given by Hector's cousin to Hector's
nephew Iulus:

> My son, from my Example learn the War,
> In Camps to suffer, and in Fields to dare:
> But happier Chance than mine attend thy Care.
> This Day my hand thy tender Age shall shield,
> And Crown with Honours of the conquer'd Field:
> Thou, when thy riper Years shall send thee forth
> To Toils of War, be mindful of my Worth;
> Assert thy birthright; and in Arms be known,
> For *Hector*'s Nephew, and *Aeneas* Son.
>
> (*Aeneis*, xii. 644–52)

In 'The Last Parting' Dryden was partly indebted to an earlier
version in his translation of this prayer:

> *Jove*, and you Heavenly Powers, whoever hear
> Hector's Request with a Propitious Ear,

Grant, this my Child in Honour and Renown
May equal me, wear, and deserve the Crown;
And when from some great Action he shall come
Laden with Hostile Spoils in Triumph home,
May *Trojans* say, Hector great things hath done,
But is surpass'd by his Illustrious Son.
This will rejoyce his tender Mothers Heart,
And sense of Joy to my pale Ghost impart.

Knightly Chetwood's version of the same episode appeared in *Poems by Several Hands*[21] collected by Nahum Tate in 1685. It was published subsequently with a few changes in *A Collection of Poems by Several Hands*[22] in 1693, where in the list of contents is the note: 'Writ in 1677'. Chetwood's motive in translating the episode may be surmised from verses that he wrote on the Earl of Roscommon's *Essay on Translated Verse* and which were prefixed to the first edition of 1684. Under Roscommon's presiding genius poets may

Make *Warlike James's peaceful* vertues known,
The *second Hope* and *Genius* of the Throne

. . . .

But what *blest* voice shall *your Maria* sing?

. . . .

It is your part, (*you* Poets can *divine*)
To prophecy how *she* by Heavens *design*
Shall give an *Heir* to the Great *British* Line,
Who over all the *Western* Isles shall reign,
Both aw the Continent, and *rule* the Main.[23]

Two events on the same day provided an occasion which might have seemed at the time to have made such a prophecy in 1684 unnecessary. On 7 November 1677, Mary, daughter of James then Duke of York, married Prince William of Orange, and Mary of Modena, wife of James, gave birth to her first son, Charles, Duke of Cambridge, heir to the Stuart line. In *Epithalamium in Desideratissimis Nuptiis Serenissimorum et Illustrissimorum Principum*[24] both events were celebrated, for they offered, in the words of one of the contributors, *imperii spes*:

[21] *Poems by Several Hands and on Several Occasions Collected by N. Tate* (London, 1685), pp. 324–32.
[22] *A Collection of Poems by Several Hands* (London, 1693), pp. 103–10.
[23] *An Essay on Translated Verse*, sig. aᵛ–a2ʳ.
[24] *Epithalamium* etc. (Cambridge, 1677), sig. E4ᵛ.

Aemula sed Phoebi surgit Lux orbe Britanno
Nec tamen imminuit, Diva Maria, Tuam,
Solstitium Angliacis laetum det parvus Iulus,
Phospera sis, Princeps, lumina amica creans.

(But a light that rivals the sun rises over the world of the British; it will not, however, diminish yours, godlike Mary. May the little Iulus provide a happy solstice for the English; O Prince, may you be our morning star, bringing forth friendly light.)

There can be little doubt that this was the occasion of Chetwood's translation. However, although Chetwood, as a Fellow of King's, was one of the *Musae Cantabrigienses*, it was clearly unsuitable for inclusion in the *Epithalamium*, not because it was in English—for one or two English poems were customarily appended at the end of such collections—but because the volume, as the title indicates, had obviously been planned in advance to congratulate William and Mary. The birth of a male heir on the same day was an unpredictable event that might have produced a separate volume had the child not died a few weeks later. In that event, publication by Chetwood would have been inappropriate. It is perhaps significant that, when he published the translation in 1693, Chetwood should draw attention to the date of its composition, since it was not usual practice to date individual poems within miscellanies, though many had obviously been written considerably earlier than their date of publication. It is as if he wished to make its occasion clear for attentive readers who might see its potential political significance.

In 1688 Mary produced James's second son, and this birth was the occasion of Dryden's poem *Britannia Rediviva*.[25] Specific verbal parallels suggest a relation between this panegyric and 'The Last Parting':

When humbly on the Royal Babe we gaze,   (l. 104)

Of which this Royal Babe may reap the Grain.   (l. 164)

Thy Father's Angel, and thy Father joyn
To keep Possession and secure the Line;   (ll. 45–6)

But with an open face, as on his Throne
Assures our Birthrights and assumes his own   (ll. 117–18)

---

[25] *Works*, iii. 210–21.

The link between Hector's prayer and this royal birth had already been made in a poem included in *Illustrissimi Principis Ducis Cornubiae Genethliacon* produced by the *Musae Cantabrigienses* in 1688:

Ζεύς, ἄλλοι τε θεοὶ δὴ καὶ τόνδε γενέσθαι
Παῖδα βίην τ' ἀγαθόν, Ἄγγλοισι τε ἶφι ἀνάσσειν·
Καί ποτέ τις εἴπησι ἰδών ἐς πλησίον ἄλλον
Ω πόποι ἡμετέρην γαίαν μέγα κύδος ἱκάνει.²⁶

(Zeus, and the other gods grant that this child may grow great in strength and rule strongly over the English; and may someone looking at the man next to him say 'My goodness, what great glory comes to our country.')

Like Chetwood ('But is surpass'd by his *Illustrious* Son') Dryden transfers the epithet of Hector φαίδιμος (l. 472) (*illustris* in the Latin version) to the child, not once but twice: 'Th' Illustrious Babe thus reconcil'd, he took' (l. 154) and 'Th' illustrious Infant to her fragrant Breast' (l. 174). Furthermore, while the child is simply likened to a beautiful star in Homer, Dryden's 'Royal Babe' (l. 38) is likened to the 'Morning Star' (l. 39). Commentators identify the star which signals the way to the surviving remnant on Troy's last night as the star of Venus, the morning star, which also has messianic associations:

> The Croud, (that still believe their Kings oppress)
> With lifted hands their young *Messiah* bless:
>
> .   .   .   .
>
> Fame runs before him, as the morning Star
> And shouts of Joy salute him from afar:
>
> (*Absalom and Achitophel*, ll. 727–8, 733–4)²⁷

Part of Dryden's interest in this episode, therefore, can be said to be political, less directly so than in *Britannia Rediviva* but of a similar nature.

As to what this political interest signifies, there can be no clear answer. Iulus, the progenitor of the Iulian line, is an unambiguous symbol; but the prayer of Hector for Astyanax in the context of Troy's imminent fall may only express an individual's hope in spite of the inner foreboding that the hope must be in vain. In the later Dedication of the *Aeneis*, although he does not hesitate to make a

---

²⁶ From a poem to Mary by Johan. Goode in *Genethliacon* etc. (Cambridge, 1688), p. 123.
²⁷ *Works*, ii. 27.

clear connection between the poet's fable and the historical circumstances prevailing at the time of composition, Dryden does so in a
way that recognizes that close correspondences between the idea
and an actual historical reality are futile. While recognizing that he
was in some measure imaginatively involved in the fate of the
English royal family who had lost their kingdom in 1688, it would
not necessarily be right to regard the translation as even a disguised
declaration of continuing loyalty. Its relation to the events of its time
is as problematical as that of the *Aeneid* to Augustan Rome.

It is perhaps because he saw the episode in the light of recent
history that there is such a pronounced tendency to present the
protagonists with the advantage of hindsight in the translation, for
Dryden intensifies their feelings of doom. His clarifying emphasis
produces powerful images of Andromache's life in captivity, first
from Andromache herself, who speaks 'Prophetically' (l. 47), and
then with greater emphasis in Hector's more extended vision (parts
of which are cited above) which follows his prophecy of the fall of
Troy:

> And yet my mind forebodes, with sure presage,
> That *Troy* shall perish by the *Grecian* Rage.
> The fatal Day draws on, when I must fall;
> And Universal Ruine cover all.
>
> .   .   .   .   .   .
>
> Not these, nor all their Fates which I foresee,
> Are half of that concern I have for thee.
> I see, I see thee in that fatal Hour,
> Subjected to the Victor's cruel Pow'r:
>
> .   .   .   .   .   .
>
> But I opprest with Iron Sleep before,
> Shall hear thy unavailing Cries no more.
>
> (ll. 114–17, 122–5, 139–40)

The Homeric Hector does say 'For I know this thing well in my
heart, and my mind knows it: | there will come a day when sacred
Ilion shall perish' (ll. 447–8), though he does not actually prophesy
his own death in so many words. He then expresses his fear for
Andromache's fate, and his wish that the earth may cover him
before he hears her cries as she is dragged off into captivity (l. 465).
The optative mood in the Greek becomes the future indicative in
English, and what is feared in Homer becomes prophetic certainty

in the translation. 'Iron Sleep' from Virgil's *ferreus somnus* (*Aeneid*, x. 745) is a formula that helps to import an oppressive sense of fate, and 'unavailing' suggests the Latin *inanis* used in many tearful Virgilian expressions.[28] The words 'fate' or 'fatal', so insistent in Virgil's epic of national destiny, occur eight times in the translation. Hector is fatalistic in Homer, 'No man is going to hurl me to Hades, unless it is fated, | but as for fate, I think no man has escaped it | once it has taken its first form, brave man or coward' (ll. 487–9). Dryden's Hector is emphatically so:

> Think not it lies in any *Grecian*'s Pow'r,
> To take my Life before the fatal Hour.
> When that arrives, nor good nor bad can fly
> Th' irrevocable Doom of Destiny.   (ll. 179–82)

Perhaps this expressed the resigned fatalism with which Dryden came to view the events of 1688 when he translated this episode some time later.

Given what has been said of his imaginative involvement in the episode and his interest in its historical or political affinities, it will follow that the attractiveness of it for Dryden was not quite what had attracted Erasmus and Rapin, for his child is not so much the human archetype as in Homer,[29] but, like Iulus in Virgil, a symbol, *spes haeredis*. His own remarks in the Dedication to *Examen Poeticum*, while giving no hint that the episode had any contemporary significance for him, do not help to suggest any other motive or affinity. Indeed these remarks are grudging in their praise of the Greek poet. Introducing his patron to his own translation and those of Congreve (who translated the lamentations of Priam, Hecuba, Andromache, and Helen over the body of Hector), he calls their subject 'pathetical' but immediately goes on to remark that Homer 'is much more capable of exciting the Manly Passions, than those of Grief and Pity'. He then criticizes Homer for being 'somewhat too Talkative, and more than somewhat too digressive', with flippant remarks at the expense of Andromache for telling Hector of her 'Pedigree' and the long story of the death of her relatives at the

---

[28] 'unavailing gift' (*Aeneis*, vi. 1226) is Dryden's translation of Virgil's *inani munere* (*Aeneid*, vi. 885–6); see *Works*, v. 568.

[29] See the discussion of this by H. A. Mason in his chapter 'Hector and Andromache', in *To Homer Through Pope* (London, 1972), p. 170.

hands of Achilles. '*Virgil*, I am confident, wou'd have omitted such a work of supererrogation.' Moving on to the episodes translated by Congreve, he continues with a judgement about the translation which will not commend itself to a disinterested reader:

> But if this last excite Compassion in you, as I doubt not but it will, you are more oblig'd to the Translatour than the Poet. For *Homer*, as I observ'd before, can move rage better than he can pity: He stirs up the irascible appetite . . . he forms and equips those ungodly Man-killers, whom we Poets, when we flatter them, call Heroes; a race of Men who can never enjoy quiet in themselves, 'till they have taken it from all the World. This is *Homer*'s Commendation, and such as it is, the Lovers of Peace, or at least of more moderate Heroism, will never Envy him.[30]

This is not the full-hearted praise of the Greek poet he later wrote in his Preface to *Fables* (1700) after he had translated 'The First Book of Homer's *Ilias*' where he pronounced the Greek poet more akin to his genius than Virgil.[31] These remarks, written after the translation with no mention of the sort of thing that had appealed to Erasmus and Rapin and would later appeal to Pope, might well suggest that Dryden was not attuned to Homer's wavelength in this first attempt at translating him. Certain ringing phrases in Johnson's judgement of him spring to mind: 'Dryden's was not one of the "gentle bosoms" . . . He is therefore, with all his variety of excellence, not often pathetick; and had so little sensibility of the power of effusions purely natural, that he did not esteem them in others. Simplicity gave him no pleasure'.[32]

What then did Dryden make of the simple emotions and the touching human dimension in the family relations in this scene: of its pathos? It cannot be denied that the elaboration of his style entails a loss of pathos. In general it may be said that in his sophisticated Augustan style emotional expression is more formal and highly wrought, though it is by no means muted and extinguished. At the beginning Andromache goes from the palace 'with Fear and Fury wild' (l. 24), which fairly reproduces the effect of 'like a woman gone mad' in the original (l. 388). The strength of her emotions is given due recognition in the translation when Andromache 'Flew

[30] *Works*, iv. 373–4.
[31] See *Poems*, ed. Kinsley, iv. 1448, and my discussion of the translation in 'The Freedom of Dryden's Homer', *Translation and Literature*, 5 (1996) 26–50.
[32] 'Life of Dryden', in *Lives*, i. 458.

to his *Arms*, to meet a dear Embrace' (l. 31), and again when 'Breathless she flew, with Joy and Passion wild' (l. 36). At the end Andromache sheds tears copiously (ll. 192–3), though only after she has returned to the palace, and not on the way home as in the original (l. 496). There is some restraint too when the parents who in Homer laugh out loud in response to the child's fright (l. 471) merely 'smil'd with silent Joy' (l. 150) in the translation. Yet the expression here is quite natural and the description of the child's fright whom his father subsequently 'Hugg'd in his *Arms*, and kiss'd' (l. 471) continues in this natural vein. In the interaction between husband and wife there is a mixture of tenderness and dignity:

> His tender wife stood weeping by, the while:
> Prest in her own, his Warlike hand she took,
> Then sigh'd, and thus Prophetically spoke.   (ll. 46–8)

The additional touches in 'Warlike' and 'Prophetically' serve to elevate the tone and give dignity, though they also put some distance between the principals and interrupt the natural emotional flow. After Hector's prayer the physical actions and emotions are effectively rendered in a style that has a straightforward, lucid dignity:

> He first with suppliant Hands the Gods ador'd:
> Then to the Mother's Arms the Child restor'd:
> With Tears and Smiles she took her Son, and press'd
> Th' illustrious Infant to her fragrant Breast.
> He wiping her fair Eyes, indulg'd her Grief,
> And eas'd her Sorrows with this last Relief.   (ll. 171–6)

Chetwood by contrast is complicated, abstract, and pompous. There is no physical contact between husband and wife; the moment becomes a test of Hector's courage from which he recovers to rebuke Andromache:

> Then in the Mothers Arms he puts the Child,
> *With troubl'd* Joy, in flowing *Tears* she *smil'd.*
> *Beauty* and *Grief* shew'd all their Pomp and Pride
> Whilst those soft Passions did her Looks divide.
> This Scene even *Hector's* Courage melted down,
> But soon recovering, with a *Lover's* Frown,
> *Madam* (says he) *these Fancies put away,*
> *I cannot Die before my fatal Day.*

But in the content and tone of what follows in Dryden, there are echoes of the conclusion to his earlier interview between Hector and Andromache in *Troilus and Cressida*:

> My Wife and Mistress, drive thy fears away;
> Nor give so bad an Omen to the Day:
>
> . . . .
>
> Return, and to divert thy thoughts at home,
> There task thy Maids, and exercise the Loom,
> Employ'd in Works that Womankind become.
>
> . . . .
>
> At this, for new Replies he did not stay,
> But lac'd his Crested Helm, and strode away.
>
> (ll. 177–8, 183–5, 188–9)

There is nothing to suggest the omen in the Greek where Hector says μή μοί τι λίην ἀκαχίζεο θυμῷ (l. 486) (do not distress yourself so much in your heart on my behalf). The feeling of this line, which Dryden may have misinterpreted, is not rendered at all. And the tone of the speech, together with Hector's action in not waiting for further replies and striding away (which is not in the original), recalls the brusqueness of the hero's dismissal of Andromache in the earlier play. The emphasis in the speech here on the irrevocable power of fate, its commanding tone stressing the differences between the sexes, and its avoidance of feeling impose a steely Stoicism on the Greek which, while not being unimpressive in itself, seems ill calculated to ease the sorrows of the suffering Andromache. If there is a commendable restraint there is also a loss of pathos here.

If 'The Last Parting' did not represent the achievement for Dryden that he was later to gain with 'The First Book of Homer's *Ilias*', it was nevertheless a great advance upon the stiff and haughty heroism of *Troilus and Cressida* and other such productions. And if there are moments when the simple emotions of the original are obscured by the elaborate style of the translation, we only have to put alongside it an example of Dryden in full Laureate mode to appreciate its excellence. Here is the moment in the *Threnodia Augustalis* when news reaches James of the demise of his brother Charles:

> Soon as th' ill omen'd Rumour reacht his Ear,
> (Ill News is wing'd with Fate, and flies apace)

Who can describe th'Amazement in his Face?
   Horrour in all his Pomp was there,
Mute and magnificent without a Tear:
And then the Hero first was seen to fear.
Half unarray'd he ran to his Relief,
So hasty and so artless was his Grief:
Approaching Greatness met him with her Charms
     Of Pow'r and future State;
But look'd so ghastly in a Brother's Fate,
   He shook her from his Armes.
Arriv'd within the mournfull Room, he saw
   A wild Distraction, void of Awe,
And arbitrary Grief unbounded by a Law.
   God's Image, God's Anointed lay
   Without Motion, Pulse or Breath,
   A senseless Lump of sacred Clay,
    An Image, now, of Death.
Amidst his sad Attendants Grones and Cryes,
The lines of that ador'd, forgiving Face,
   Distorted from their native grace;
An Iron Slumber sate on his Majestick Eyes.
The Pious Duke . . .

                       (ll. 48–71)[33]

The occasion demands an emotional expression, yet royal decorum cannot be violated. There is a rare quality in the *Threnodia Augustalis* which distinguishes it from similar threnodies, panegyrics, and birthday odes of the period. In this poem 'An Iron Slumber' (l. 70), derived from Virgil's *ferreus somnus*, is a sublime touch, but it hardly needs to be said that the Augustan sublime here is always teetering on the brink of absurdity. Dryden's talent is straining at an impossible task; matter and manner cannot be harmonized. The royal connection has brought to Dryden's conception of the heroic an inhibiting emotional censor. As a result, in Dr Johnson's words, 'It has neither tenderness nor dignity, it is neither magnificent nor pathetick. He seems to look round him for images which he cannot find, and what he has distorts by endeavouring to enlarge them. He is, he says, "petrified with grief", but the marble sometimes relents, and trickles in a joke.'[34]

---

[33] *Works*, iii. 93.   [34] 'Life of Dryden', in *Lives*, i. 438.

Homer's fable, on the contrary, afforded a detachment from current events through which Dryden was nevertheless able successfully to continue to write in elevated strains as a public poet indirectly fulfilling his Laureate office, offering in 'The Last Parting' perhaps his true Augustan threnody, restrained, dignified, and poignant. Though the events of 1688 were a grievous personal blow for the Laureate, in so far as they confirmed him in a new vocation as translator and saved us from more effusions like the *Threnodia Augustalis* and *Britannia Rediviva*, the gain for English literature was incalculable. And even if this first attempt at Homer did not satisfy him as had some of his earlier translations, it nevertheless prompted him to contemplate a challenge that he later met so splendidly in 'The First Book':

The Earl of *Mulgrave*, and Mr. *Waller*, two the best Judges of our Age, have assur'd me, that they cou'd never Read over the Translation of *Chapman*, without incredible Pleasure, and extreme Transport. This Admiration of theirs, must needs proceed from the Author himself: For the Translator has thrown him down as low, as harsh Numbers, improper *English*, and a monstrous length of Verse cou'd carry him. What then wou'd he appear in the Harmonious Version, of one of the best Writers, Living in a much better Age than was the last?[35]

[35] *Works*, iv. 374.

'ACCORDING TO MY GENIUS': DRYDEN'S TRANSLATION OF 'THE FIRST BOOK OF HOMER'S *ILIAS*'

JAMES A. WINN

The most important English classical translations of the long eighteenth century are John Dryden's *Aeneis* (1697) and Alexander Pope's *Iliad* (1715–20). Successful at the time of publication and virtually unchallenged for the next 150 years, these renderings of epic poetry into heroic couplets are important poems in their own right, and revealing documents in the history of the reception of classical epic. A nearly forgotten part of that history is Dryden's version of the first book of the *Iliad*, published a few months before his death in 1700, but intended as a trial balloon for a complete translation. Until very recently, scholars have either ignored or devalued this vigorous and lively work; according to one respected expert, it 'represents not only a change in tactics but a falling off in skill from his Virgil'.[1] Yet I shall contend here that Dryden's 'First Book' is more Homeric than Pope's—indeed, more Homeric than any translation into a European language before the twentieth century. Pope files the rough edges off Homer, producing not only a smoother and more

A shorter version of this essay was first read at the Euroclassica conference on 'Homer and European Literature' in Chios, Greece, in August 1997. My thanks to the organizers of that conference, and to Kelli Intzides and Angeliki Frangou, my hostesses on that beautiful island, traditionally regarded as the birthplace of Homer. References to *Fables Ancient and Modern* are to *Poems*, ed. Kinsley; volume and page numbers are given in the text.

[1] William Frost, *Dryden and the Art of Translation* (New Haven, 1955), p. 66.

decorous verbal surface than the original, but a paler, more *neo-classical* version of heroic struggle. Dryden, by contrast, replicates and extends some Homeric qualities not often recognized before our own times: the rapid and muscular character of Homer's verse, the range and strangeness of his vocabulary, the boldness of his metaphors, and the moral complexity of his perspective on heroism.

Not only did Dryden produce a translation that found ingenious English equivalents for these aspects of Homer, but he advertised it by claiming that his fundamental poetic personality was closer to Homer's than to Virgil's. From a man who had enjoyed the success of his *Virgil* just three years earlier, this was an astonishing assertion. As with other changes of heart (politics, rhyming plays, religion), Dryden did not shrink from expressing his new-found beliefs in strong and colourful rhetoric. In the Preface to *Fables Ancient and Modern*, the volume in which the 'First Book of Homer's *Ilias*' appears, he returns several times to the claim of poetic kinship with Homer:

I have found by Trial, *Homer* a more pleasing Task than *Virgil*, (though I say not the Translation will be less laborious.) For the *Grecian* is more according to my Genius, than the *Latin* Poet. . . . One warms you by Degrees; the other sets you on fire all at once, and never intermits his Heat. . . . This vehemence of [Homer's], I confess, is more suitable to my Temper: and therefore I have translated his First Book with greater Pleasure than any Part of *Virgil*: But it was not a Pleasure without Pains: The continual Agitations of the Spirits, must needs be a Weakning of any Constitution, especially in Age: and many Pauses are required for Refreshment betwixt the Heats; the *Iliad* of its self being a third part longer than all *Virgil*'s Works together. (*Poems*, iv. 1448–9)

As Robin Sowerby points out, 'a cynic might conclude that in claiming he found Homer more congenial than Virgil, Dryden had half an eye on the subscriptions that would have been necessary' to support a complete translation of the *Iliad*.[2] But such claims to personal identification with the authors he translated had long been a part of Dryden's critical discourse. In his Preface to *Sylvae* (1685),

---

[2] 'The Freedom of Dryden's Homer', *Translation and Literature*, 5 (1996) 26–50, here quoting p. 26. Dr Sowerby's excellent and appreciative essay is one sign that the reputation of Dryden's Homer may finally be improving. Although it came to my attention after I had delivered the first version of the present essay, I have been pleased to notice many general points of agreement between Dr Sowerby's essay and mine.

he acknowledged that his practice had drifted away from paraphrase towards imitation, defending himself in advance against critics who might notice his considerable additions to the texts he had translated for that volume:

> I desire the false Criticks wou'd not always think that those thoughts are wholly mine, but that either they are secretly in the Poet, or may be fairly deduc'd from him: or at least, if both those considerations should fail, that my own is of a piece with his, and that if he were living, and an *Englishman*, they are such, as he wou'd probably have written.[3]

In this passage we may observe Dryden beginning to develop the theory he would expound more fully in the Preface to *Fables*, the belief that a translating poet might achieve a psychological identification with an author from an earlier time. As the Preface to *Sylvae* acknowledges, he adopted this idea from Wentworth Dillon, Earl of Roscommon, whose poetic *Essay on Translated Verse* (1684) includes these lines:

> Examine how your *Humour* is inclin'd,
> And which the *Ruling Passion* of your Mind;
> Then, seek a *Poet* who *your* way do's bend,
> And chuse an *Author* as you chuse a *Friend*.
> United by this *Sympathetick Bond*,
> You grow *Familiar, Intimate* and *Fond*;
> Your *Thoughts*, your *Words*, your *Stiles*, your *Souls* agree,
> No Longer his *Interpreter*, but *He*.   (pp. 6–7)

In claiming that Homer's 'vehemence' was 'more suitable' to his own 'Temper' than Virgil's restraint, Dryden was evoking just such a 'Sympathetick Bond' with the Greek poet.

If we are therefore inclined to give some credence to Dryden's claims of identification with Homer, we must still wonder why he delayed his engagement with Homer for so long. By the time he began thinking about translating the *Iliad*, he had already translated all of Virgil, all of Persius, much of Juvenal, and substantial excerpts from Ovid, Horace, and Theocritus into English verse, but he had published only one short excerpt from Homer, Hector's farewell to Andromache in *Iliad* VI, which appeared in a miscellany in 1693.[4] He had not avoided Homer out of ignorance. One of his school-

---

[3] *Works*, iii. 4.
[4] This poem is discussed by Robin Sowerby in Chapter 9 above.

fellows from Westminster and Cambridge remembered that he had 'read over & very well understood all ye Greek & Latin Poets' as an undergraduate;[5] frequent allusions in his dramas and essays bespeak a writer at ease with Greek literature. Pope, who was largely self-taught, was vulnerable to the charge of being less than professional in his knowledge of Greek; Dryden was not. His readers, however, were much more familiar with Virgil than with Homer. Although Greek was a part of the curriculum in schools and universities, even well-educated men were more likely to remember their Latin than their Greek. In part because of the limitations of Chapman's *Iliad*, the most readily available English version, Homer seemed strange, primitive, even crude—especially when compared with the more polished and literary Virgil, who had been much more influential in shaping the European literature of the Middle Ages and the Renaissance. For centuries, comparing the two poets was a schoolboy exercise, in which Homer was duly credited with invention, fire, and originality, but Virgil was preferred for refinement, balance, and judgement.

In the Dedication to *Examen Poeticum* (1693), the volume for which he translated the excerpt from *Iliad* VI, Dryden rehearses these conventional notions. He describes Homer as 'much more capable of exciting the Manly Passions, than those of Grief and Pity', then moves from that apparent praise to a series of criticisms:

To cause Admiration, is indeed the proper and adequate design of an Epick Poem: And in that he has Excell'd even *Virgil*. Yet, without presuming to Arraign our Master, I may venture to affirm, that he is somewhat too Talkative, and more than somewhat too digressive. . . . *Andromache* in the midst of her Concernment, and Fright for *Hector*, runs off her Biass, to tell him a Story of her Pedigree, and of the lamentable Death of her Father, her Mother, and her Seven Brothers. The Devil was in *Hector*, if he knew not all this matter, as well as she who told it him; for she had been his Bed-fellow for many Years together: And if he knew it, then it must be confess'd, that *Homer* in this long digression, has rather given us his own Character, than that of the Fair Lady whom he Paints. . . . *Virgil*, I am confident, wou'd have omitted such a work of supererrogation. But *Virgil* had the Gift of expressing much in little, and sometimes in silence: For though he yielded much to *Homer* in Invention, he more Excell'd him in his Admirable Judgment.[6]

---

[5] Trinity College Muniments, 'Great Volume of Miscellany Papers III', no. 42.
[6] *Works*, iv. 373.

Here the praise of Homer for his invention and his capacity to 'cause Admiration' seems almost perfunctory, a rhetorical gesture preparing us for the witty description of the ancient poet as 'somewhat too Talkative, and more than somewhat too digressive', a man who 'give[s] us his own Character' in his digressions and fails in courtesy to 'the Fair Lady whom he Paints'. Dryden's wit depends upon self-conscious anachronism: Homer, one feels, is being judged by the standards of a Restoration drawing-room. In calling Homer 'our Master', a phrase he later used for Dr Richard Busby, his teacher at Westminster school some fifty years earlier, Dryden implies that Homer is like an old schoolmaster: learned, deserving of respect, but antiquated and out of fashion.[7] Yet in calling Homer 'Talkative' Dryden also shows his powers of literary intuition: though of course unaware of the oral–formulaic hypothesis, which was not devised until the 1930s,[8] he perceives the oral qualities of Homer's poetry. In his translation of the first book of the *Iliad*, he respects the oral patterns of repetition that he criticizes here. When Achilles tells his mother Thetis about the origins of his quarrel with Agamemnon, exactly repeating several lines of Homer's earlier narration, Dryden repeats his own translation of those lines exactly. When Pope reaches the same passage, he engages in elegant variation and writes a long footnote criticizing the original repetition as 'unnatural'.[9]

By the time he turned to the first book of the *Iliad*, Dryden himself was playing the role of a 'Talkative' poet, calling attention to his digressiveness, his age, and his need to stamp 'his own character' on his material. The Preface to *Fables* abounds in self-conscious gestures. Dryden begins by describing himself as 'a Poet [who] alters his Mind as the Work proceeds, and will have this or that Convenience more, of which he had not thought when he began' (*Poems*, iv. 1444). He frequently calls attention to his some-

---

[7] In a letter to Charles Montagu, who was also an Old Westminster, Dryden encloses a poem and writes, 'These verses had waited on you with the former, but then they wanted that Correction which I have since given them.... I fear that I have purged them out of their Spirit, as our Master Busby used to whip a Boy so long till he made him a confirmed Blockhead' (*Letters*, p. 120).

[8] The fundamental work here is that of Milman Parry, especially 'Studies in the Epic Technique of Oral Verse-Making', *Harvard Studies in Classical Philology*, 41 (1930) 73–147; 43 (1932) 1–50.

[9] *The Iliad of Homer*, ed. Maynard Mack *et al.*, vols. vii–viii of *The Twickenham Edition of the Works of Alexander Pope* (London, 1967), i. 478–90 and n. (vol. vii, pp. 110–11).

what improvised outline with rhetorical gestures acknowledging digression:

But to return . . . (iv. 1445)

In the mean time, to follow the Thrid of my Discourse (as Thoughts, according to Mr. *Hobbs*, have always some Connexion) . . . (iv. 1446)

I resume the Thrid of my Discourse . . . (iv. 1447)

Besides, the Nature of a Preface is rambling, never wholly out of the Way, nor in it . . . (iv. 1450)

As a Corollary to this Preface, in which I have done Justice to others, I owe somewhat to my self . . . (iv. 1461)

He emphasizes his age by comparing himself to 'an old Gentleman, who mounting on Horseback before some Ladies, when I was present, got up somewhat heavily, but desir'd of the Fair Spectators, that they would count Fourscore and eight before they judg'd him' (iv. 1446)—a story somewhat analogous to the earlier criticism of Homer for 'giv[ing] us his own Character, [rather] than that of the Fair Lady whom he Paints', but told with far more sympathy for the older figure. Despite his age, Dryden insists on his ease of invention: 'I think my self as vigorous as ever in the Faculties of my Soul, excepting only my Memory, which is not impair'd to any great degree. . . . Thoughts, such as they are, come crowding in so fast upon me, that my only Difficulty is to chuse or to reject' (iv. 1446). He frankly acknowledges choosing the works he has translated because of their personal appeal to him, and links some aspect of his own personality to each of the authors—Homer, Ovid, Boccaccio, and Chaucer—whom he has chosen to translate.

Yet Dryden's assertion that 'the *Grecian* [Homer] is more according to my Genius, than the *Latin* Poet [Virgil]' does not evoke orality, age, or digressiveness as common traits. As we have seen, it comes cloaked in Longinian language about Homer's violence, rapidity, and freedom:

In the Works of the two Authors we may read their Manners, and natural Inclinations, which are wholly different. *Virgil* was of a quiet, sedate Temper; *Homer* was violent, impetuous, and full of Fire. The chief Talent of *Virgil* was propriety of Thoughts, and Ornament of Words: *Homer* was rapid in his thoughts, and took all the Liberties both of Numbers, and of Expressions, which his Language, and the Age in which he liv'd allow'd him: *Homer*'s Invention was more copious, *Virgil*'s more confin'd. (iv. 1448)

Although the grounds of the comparison are essentially the same as those in the Dedication of 1693, the value judgements have changed. What was once called Homer's tendency to talkativeness and digression has become his copious invention; what was once Virgil's admirable talent for 'expressing much in little' has become his 'quiet, sedate Temper', his 'confin'd' invention. I do not believe Dryden himself had actually become more 'violent, impetuous, and full of Fire' between the ages of 61 and 68. I do believe he had become more tolerant of his own tendency towards digression, more appreciative of his own copious invention, and more than a little nostalgic about the vigour and originality that had characterized his works as a young man.

The desire for inspiration and youthful fancy is already apparent in the Dedication to *Eleonora* (1692):

We who are priests of *Apollo*, have not the Inspiration when we please; but must wait till the God comes rushing on us, and invades us with a fury, which we are not able to resist: which gives us double strength while the Fit continues, and leaves us languishing and spent, at its departure. Let me not seem to boast, my Lord; for I have really felt it on this Occasion, and prophecy'd beyond my natural power. Let me add, and hope to be believ'd, that the Excellency of the Subject contributed much to the Happiness of the Execution: And that the weight of thirty years was taken off me, while I was writing. I swom with the Tyde, and the Water under me was buoyant. The Reader will easily observe, that I was transported, by the multitude and variety of my Similitudes; which are generally the product of a luxuriant Fancy; and wantonness of Wit.[10]

In this passage, as in the remarks on Homer in the Preface to *Fables*, Dryden describes poetic composition as an intensely physical process: in one case, he swims with the tide; in the other, he experiences 'continual Agitations of the Spirits'; the fit of inspiration leaves him 'languishing and spent' on one occasion, needing 'many Pauses . . . for Refreshment' on the other. If we may believe his enemies, this bodily view of creation had been a part of Dryden's idea of himself for many years. Mr Bayes, the parodic version of Dryden in *The Rehearsal*, offers a comic example:

If I am to write familiar things, as Sonnets to *Armida*, and the like, I make use of Stew'd Prunes only; but, when I have a grand design in hand, I ever

---

[10] *Works*, iii. 231–2.

take Phisic, and let blood: for, when you would have pure swiftness of thought, and fiery flights of fancy, you must have a care of the pensive part. In fine, you must purge the Belly.[11]

Buckingham's caricature captures Dryden's actual tendency to think of 'fiery flights of fancy' and physical weakness in the same breath. The imagery of swimming in the Dedication to *Eleonora* applies not only to Dryden's metaphorical swimming on the tide of his invention, but also to a recent attack of the gout: 'I cannot say that I have escap'd from a Shipwreck; but have only gain'd a Rock by hard swimming; where I may pant a while and gather breath: For the Doctors give me a sad assurance, that my Disease never took its leave of any man, but with a purpose to return.'[12] The claim to rapidity and power of thought in the Preface to *Fables* comes immediately after a passage on frailty: 'By the Mercy of God, I am already come within Twenty Years of his Number [the 88 years of the 'old Gentleman'], a Cripple in my Limbs, but what Decays are in my Mind, the reader must determine' (*Poems*, iv. 1446).

What all this biographical evidence points towards is the possibility that Dryden undertook his translation of Homer as a stay against death, recognizing in Homer a life-force from which he might draw strength. If the work was exhausting, it was also exhilarating, providing a challenge unlike that posed by translating Virgil. When he first considered translating Homer, in a speculative passage at the conclusion of the Dedication to *Examen Poeticum*, he argued that Homer could produce pleasure and even 'Transport' despite bad translations, and imagined providing a more 'Harmonious' version than Chapman's:

The Earl of *Mulgrave*, and Mr. *Waller*, two the best Judges of our Age, have assur'd me, that they cou'd never Read over the Translation of *Chapman*, without incredible Pleasure, and extreme Transport. This Admiration of theirs, must needs proceed from the Author himself: For the Translator has thrown him down as low, as harsh Numbers, improper *English*, and a monstrous length of Verse cou'd carry him. What then wou'd he appear in the Harmonious Version, of one of the best Writers, Living in a much better Age than was the last? I mean for versification, and the Art of Numbers.[13]

---

[11] *The Rehearsal*, ed. D. E. L. Crane (Durham, 1976), II. i. 114–20.
[12] *Works*, iii. 321. [13] *Works*, iv. 374.

Perfectly aware that he was himself 'one of the best Writers' in an age he believed had advanced the art of versification, Dryden in 1693 was surely considering undertaking this task himself. In 1700, having completed his harmonious *Virgil* and looked more closely at Homer, he took a different view. He had consistently argued that poets demonstrated their personality and genius in the details of their versification, and once he recognized that Homer had taken 'all the Liberties both of Numbers, and of Expressions, which his Language, and the Age in which he liv'd allow'd him', he had to abandon the notion that he should give his version harmony and smoothness. Instead, he took his own liberties in metre and diction; the 'First Book' is palpably rougher than either Pope's later version or Dryden's own *Aeneis*. Although the normative verse form is heroic couplets, the metre of Dryden's rhymed plays and satires, he deliberately roughened the texture with metric variation and heavy alliteration, as in these lines describing the failed embassy of Chryses:

> For venerable *Chryses* came to buy,
> With Gold and Gifts of Price, his Daughter's Liberty.
> Suppliant before the *Grecian* Chiefs he stood,
> Awful, and arm'd with Ensigns of his God:
> Bare was his hoary Head; one holy Hand
> Held forth his Laurel Crown, and one his Sceptre of Command.

> (ll. 17–22)

The trochaic inversions at the beginnings of lines ('Bare was his hoary Head') give the effect of Homer's characteristic dactyl. Line 18 has six feet and twelve syllables; line 22, *seven* feet and fourteen syllables, the length Dryden had called 'monstrous' in Chapman, and indeed a syllable-count permissible in Homer's hexameter. By doing some violence to the accentuation of the final word, the line may be scanned as dactylic hexameter, thus:

$$- \smile \quad \smile \quad - \quad - \quad - \quad - \quad - \quad - \quad - \quad \smile \quad \smile \quad - \quad -$$

Held forth his | Laurel | Crown, and | one his | Sceptre of | Command |.

Pope's version, published in 1715, uses many of the same words, but is much smoother, and thus in my view much less Homeric:

> For *Chryses* sought with costly Gifts to gain
> His Captive Daughter from the Victor's Chain.

> Suppliant the Venerable Father stands,
> *Apollo's* awful Ensigns grace his Hands:
> By these he begs; and lowly bending down,
> Extends the Sceptre and the Laurel Crown.   (i. 15–20)

As this brief comparison may suggest, the refined and polished versification of Pope might actually have been better suited to the *Aeneid*. But Dryden, having discovered his own affinities with Homer, delighted in experimenting with long lines. Later in the book, he allowed himself two seven-foot lines in the space of only three lines. Achilles, sulking in his tent,

> ... wish'd for bloody Wars and mortal Wounds,
> And of the *Greeks* oppress'd in Fight, to hear the dying Sounds.
> Now, when twelve Days compleat had run their Race,
> The Gods bethought them of the Cares belonging to their place.
>
>   (ll. 665–8)

So, too, with the choice of words. Dryden's vocabulary is broad and inclusive, enriched by tough Saxon phrases that Pope and others might have thought too 'low' for epic. Thus ἐκηβόλος, the epithet describing Apollo as one who strikes from afar,[14] becomes 'the *Bowyer* King' (l. 138); Agamemnon, according to Achilles, is 'In Threats the foremost, but the *lag* in Fight' (l. 337); Vulcan, pouring wine for the gods in the final scene, is 'the rude *Skinker*' (l. 803). The combination of such Saxon language with the more conventional epic diction derived from Latin is often striking, as in these lines from Agamemnon's rebuke to the prophet Calchas:

> And now thou dost with Lies the Throne invade,
> By Practice harden'd in thy sland'ring Trade;
> Obtending Heav'n, for what e'er Ills befal,
> And sputtering under specious Names thy Gall.   (ll. 159–62)

Some later critics, influenced by the careful decorum of Pope's version, have found the range of Dryden's diction disturbing, but his practice here is again authentically Homeric. Homer drew freely on archaic forms and variants from different dialects in order to fill out his metre and achieve his rich range of sound-effects; Dryden

---

[14] *Iliad*, i. 96. This and all quotations from the Greek follow the text of the Loeb Classical Library.

pulls together *sputtering* and *specious* for the sake of an alliteration that
enacts the fury of the king.

It is no accident that many instances of extreme diction come
from angry exchanges. In all his discussions of Homer, Dryden links
the violence of Homer's characters to the violence of his invention.
In the Dedication to *Examen Poeticum*, this leads to a serious moral
criticism of Homer:

He stirs up the irascible appetite, as our Philosophers call it, he provokes to
Murther, and the destruction of God's Images; he forms and equips those
ungodly Man-killers, whom we Poets, when we flatter them, call Heroes;
a race of Men who can never enjoy quiet in themselves, 'till they have
taken it from all the World. This is *Homer's* Commendation, and such as it
is, the Lovers of Peace, or at least of more moderate Heroism, will never
Envy him.[15]

In the summer of 1693, when this Dedication was published, the
military campaigns of King William III were proving disastrous on
land and sea. Politically, the criticism of Homeric heroes was a
covert way for Dryden to criticize the king, who had been responsible for his losing his official positions after the Revolution of 1688.
Yet even in this harsh passage Dryden has the honesty to include
himself among those poets who flatter 'ungodly Man-killers'.
Although personally sceptical about warfare, he had made his share
of flattering gestures towards military heroes. *Annus Mirabilis* (1667),
his poem on the Second Dutch Naval War, treats a badly managed
naval campaign as an epic triumph; it assured his appointment as
Poet Laureate. And when James, Duke of York, succeeded to the
throne in 1685, Dryden dutifully predicted a military reign:

So *James* the drowsy *Genius* wakes
Of *Britain* long entranc'd in Charms,
Restiff and slumbring on its Arms:
'Tis rows'd, & with a new strung Nerve, the Spear already shakes.
No Neighing of the Warriour Steeds,
No Drum, or louder Trumpet needs
T' inspire the Coward, warm the Cold,
His Voice, his sole Appearance makes 'em bold.

(*Threnodia Augustalis*, ll. 470–7)

[15] *Works*, iv. 374.

The final line alludes to the moment in *Iliad* XVIII when Achilles appears unarmed at the ditch and rallies the Greeks with his war-cry.

Nor was this the first time Dryden linked his patron James with Achilles. In dedicating *The Conquest of Granada* to James in 1672, he specifically mentioned Achilles as a model for his excessive hero Almanzor, and encouraged the duke to think himself analogous to the rough Almanzor and the impetuous Achilles:

I have form'd a Heroe, I confess, not absolutely perfect, but of an excessive and overboyling courage: but *Homer* and *Tasso* are my precedents. Both the *Greek* and the *Italian* Poet had well consider'd that a tame Heroe who never transgresses the bounds of moral vertue, would shine but dimly in an Epick poem. . . . But a character of an excentrique vertue is the more exact Image of humane life, because he is not wholy exempted from its frailties. Such a person is *Almanzor*: whom I present, with all humility to the Patronage of your Royal Highness. I design'd in him a roughness of Character, impatient of injuries; and a confidence of himself, almost approaching to an arrogance.[16]

Here roughness, impatience, and self-confidence are appropriate for epic heroes and future kings, while 'a tame Heroe' like the pious and restrained Aeneas 'would shine but dimly'. Again, Dryden is fitting his rhetoric to his audience: as his brief kingship would prove, James was courageous but stupid, 'impatient of injuries' and unable to compromise.

'Excessive and overboyling courage', as Dryden evidently knew, is not only destructive but potentially comic. His rhymed heroic plays, acted between 1664 and 1675, feature violent, huffing heroes and a blustering rhetoric made more pointed by the rhymes. As Buckingham demonstrated in *The Rehearsal*, they were ripe for caricature, and some passages in them may be self-parodic. The relation these plays bear to the *Iliad*, and especially to the debate between Agamemnon and Achilles in Book I, is complex. In constructing exchanges between his heroic figures in the plays, Dryden doubtless drew upon his knowledge and memory of such exchanges in the *Iliad*, and when he finally undertook a translation of the *Iliad* he drew in turn on his own plays. Here, for example, is a typical scene between Boabdelin and Almanzor, first acted in 1671:

[16] *Works*, xi. 6.

> *Boabdelin.* The succor which thou bring'st me makes thee bold:
>   But know, without thy ayd, my Crown I'le hold.
>   Or, if I cannot, I will fire the place:
>   Of a full City make a naked space.
>   Hence, then, and from a Rival set me free:
>   I'le do; I'le suffer any thing, but thee.
> *Almanzor.* I wonnot goe; I'le not be forc'd away:
>   I came not for thy sake; nor do I stay.
>   It was the Queen who for my ayd did send;
>   And 'tis I only can the Queen defend:
>   I, for her sake thy Scepter will maintain;
>   And thou, by me, in spight of thee, shalt raign.

> (*The Conquest of Granada, Part II*, iii. i. 106–17)

Although filtered through the Renaissance sensibilities of chivalric
epic and romance, the tone is recognizably descended from the
scene that Dryden would finally translate nearly thirty years later:

> To this *Atrides* answer'd, Though thy Boast
> Assumes the foremost Name of all our Host,
> Pretend not, mighty Man, that what is mine
> Controll'd by thee, I tamely should resign.
> Shall I release the Prize I gain'd by Right,
> In taken Towns, and many a bloody Fight,
> While thou detain'st *Briseis* in thy Bands
> By priestly glossing on the god's Commands?
>
> .   .   .   .
>
> At this, *Achilles* roul'd his furious Eyes,
> Fixed on the King askant; and thus replies.
> O, Impudent, regardful of thy own,
> Whose Thoughts are center'd on thy self alone,
> Advanc'd to Sovereign Sway, for better Ends
> Than thus like abject Slaves to treat thy Friends.
> What *Greek* is he, that urg'd by thy Command,
> Against the *Trojan* Troops will lift his Hand?
> Not I. . . .

> (ll. 196–203, 223–31)

The situation, which pits a king against his most powerful warrior in
a debate complicated by sexual desire, is quite similar, as are the
blustering threats. Here and elsewhere, Dryden sees the anger of the
characters as a licence to indulge in striking imagery and diction.

Even in *Aureng-Zebe*, the last and most restrained of his rhyming plays, debates and arguments call for colourful expressions. Here, for example, is an exchange between two brothers, Morat and Aureng-Zebe, just after their father, the old emperor, has condemned Aureng-Zebe to death:

> *Morat.* Would I had been disposer of thy Stars;
> Thou shouldst have had thy wish, and di'd in Wars.
> 'Tis I, not thou, have reason to repine,
> That thou shouldst fall by any hand, but mine.
> *Aureng-Zebe.* When thou wert form'd, Heav'n did a Man begin;
> But the brute Soul, by chance, was shuffl'd in.
> In Woods and Wilds thy Monarchy maintain:
> Where valiant Beasts, by force and rapine, reign.
> In Life's next Scene, if Transmigration be,
> Some Bear or Lion is reserv'd for thee.
> *Morat.* Take heed thou com'st not in that Lion's way:
> I prophecy thou wilt thy Soul convey
> Into a Lamb, and be again my Prey.
> Hence with that dreaming Priest.

$$(\text{III. i. } 300–13)$$

The politics owes something to Hobbes, but the tone, which may prompt us to giggle, is close to that used by Achilles and Agamemnon in their quarrels in the *Iliad*. Some of the details of Dryden's *Iliad*, however, draw on his own earlier invention: Agamemnon's claim that Achilles has engaged in 'priestly glossing on the god's Commands', for which there is not the slightest pretext in the Greek, is a distant echo of Morat's dismissal of Aureng-Zebe as a 'dreaming Priest'.

Even when Dryden stays closer to the original, he pushes Homeric rant towards the extravagance of stage debate. Here is another of Achilles' angry rebukes to Agamemnon:

> Dastard and Drunkard, Mean and Insolent!
> Tongue-valiant Hero, Vaunter of thy Might,
> In Threats the foremost, but the lag in Fight!
> When did'st thou thrust amid the mingled Preace,
> Content to bide the War aloof in Peace?
> Arms are the Trade of each *Plebeyan* Soul;
> 'Tis Death to fight; but Kingly to control;

Lord-like at ease, with arbitrary Pow'r,
To peel the Chiefs, the People to devour.   (ll. 335–43)

As we know from the preface, Dryden admired and emulated the bold metaphorical language of Homer, here perhaps most vivid in Achilles' description of Agamemnon as δημοβόρος, devourer of his people (i. 231). But the translator makes that image even stronger by turning an adjective into a verb, and by adding a fresh image of his own—'To *peel* the Chiefs, the People to devour'. This kind of verbal excess on the part of the epic poet was strongly linked in Dryden's mind with passionate excess on the part of the epic hero. Almanzor often uses similarly grotesque imagery: 'The best and bravest Souls I can select', he boasts, 'And on their Conquer'd Necks my Throne erect' (Part I, IV. ii. 478–9).

To many readers, then and now, the rough, muscular, and extravagant qualities of Dryden's Homer, like the similar qualities of his heroic plays, will seem to risk unintentional comedy. According to one modern scholar, Dryden's version 'ventures off... toward the lowlands of burlesque'.[17] But Homer himself engages in burlesque: the comic and drunken feast of the gods that concludes Book I, which Dryden renders with wonderful verve, parodies the debates of the mortal heroes, whose excessive vaunting already borders on the comic. Dryden, who had observed the frailties of the Stuart monarchs and risked the comic in his own heroic dramas, knew that the anger Homer sings in the *Iliad* is both devastating and preposterous. In his wise and vivid translation, he shows us Agamemnon and Achilles as elevated figures—'*Atrides* Great, and *Thetis* God-like Son' (l. 8)—but also as 'ungodly Man-killers', cursing each other as cowards and drunks. Had he lived to complete his *Iliad*, English and European perceptions of Homer in the eighteenth century and beyond might have been more accurate.

In his essay 'Of Heroique Plays' (1672), Dryden explains that writing in a heroic mode gives the poet 'a farther liberty of Fancy, and of drawing all things as far above the ordinary proportion of the Stage, as that is beyond the common words and actions of humane life.'[18] In 'The Author's Apology for Heroique Poetry, and Poetic License' (1677), he specifically alludes to Homer and invokes

---

[17] Cedric D. Reverand II, *Dryden's Final Poetic Mode: The 'Fables'* (Philadelphia, Pa., 1988), p. 12.   [18] *Works*, xi. 10.

Longinus as an authority for 'preferr[ing] the sublime Genius that sometimes erres, to the midling or indifferent one which makes few faults, but seldome or never rises to any Excellence'.[19] The phrasing closely resembles his earlier remarks about preferring 'a character of an excentrique vertue' to 'a tame Heroe who never transgresses the bounds'. Evidently casting himself as a hero-poet, Dryden 'transgresses the bounds' of literalism in virtually every line of his translation, assuming his own 'liberty of Fancy' by adding new layers of imagery. When Achilles taunts Agamemnon by telling him that he rules over worthless men, οὐτιδανοῖσιν ἀνάσσεις (i. 231), Dryden constructs an entire couplet from those two words:

> Nor could'st thou thus have dar'd the common Hate,
> Were not their Souls as abject as their State. (ll. 346–7)

To modern ears, this rhetoric of parallelism and antithesis may seem quite unlike Homer's direct and simple style, but for Dryden's readers, whose expectations were shaped by the tight rhetoric of heroic drama, this was the way angry heroes were supposed to talk. If challenged, Dryden would surely have defended his additions not only along the lines laid out in his Preface to *Sylvae* ('those thoughts are . . . either . . . secretly in the Poet, or may be fairly deduc'd from him'), but also along the lines he developed in the 'Discourse Concerning Satire' prefixed to the *Satires of Juvenal and Persius* (1693):

If sometimes any of us (and 'tis but seldome) makes [Juvenal] express the Customs and Manners of our Native Country, rather than of *Rome*; 'tis, either when there was some kind of Analogy, betwixt their Customes and ours; or when, to make him more easy to Vulgar Understandings, we gave him those Manners which are familiar to us. . . . If this can neither be defended, nor excus'd, let it be pardon'd, at least, because it is acknowledg'd; and so much the more easily, as being a fault which is never committed without some Pleasure to the Reader.[20]

In some more complex passages, Dryden enacts his claim to kinship with Homer by adding material alluding to his own works. The alert reader, whether in 1700 or 2000, can experience the complex 'Pleasure' of considering how this material points us towards Dryden's idiosyncratic reading of Homer—and towards his

[19] *Works*, xii. 87.   [20] *Works*, iv. 89.

279

reading of himself. One of Agamemnon's speeches, for example, begins with a perfectly ordinary formula:

Τόν δ' ἠμείβετ' ἔπειτα ἄναξ ἀνδρῶν 'Αγαμέμνον...
(Then answered him in turn the lord of men Agamemnon...)[21]

With no excuse at all in the Greek, Dryden foists in both a physical detail and a psychological perception, both absent in Homer, both based on his own work:

> The King, whose Brows with shining Gold were bound;
> Who saw his Throne with scepter'd Slaves incompass'd round,
> Thus answer'd stern!...
>
> (ll. 257–9)

The politically ironic notion of 'scepter'd' subordinates comes from the final song in *King Arthur* (1691):

> Our Soveraign High, in Aweful State,
> His Honours shall bestow;
> And see his Scepter'd Subjects wait
> On his Commands below. (ll. 9–12)

In the song, Dryden wickedly appropriates the whiggish notion that power comes from the consent of the governed to undermine his apparent praise of William. For a reader who remembers that context, Agamemnon at this moment is a covert version of William, a king whose 'scepter'd Slaves' may yet rise up against him. This reading gains force when we remember Dryden's earlier and overt identification of James with Achilles. Alert readers of Dryden's *Aeneis* have noticed many similar moments where the translator slyly winks at contemporary politics. But most of the language in this invented passage, including the rhyming words, comes from further back in Dryden's career, from the closing lines of the poem 'To the Memory of Mr. Oldham' (1684):

> Thy Brows with Ivy, and with Laurels bound;
> But Fate and gloomy Night encompass thee around. (ll. 24–5)

Although the context could hardly be more different, there is a moral point: Oldham's brows are symbolically bound by the

---

[21] i. 172; the literal translation is from *The Iliad of Homer*, trans. Richmond Lattimore (Chicago, 1951).

wreaths that indicate his poetic talent, but his life is 'encompass[ed]'
by the fate of an early death; Agamemnon's brows are bound with
gold bands that indicate his power and wealth, but his throne is
'incompass'd' by rebellious subordinates. Neither poet nor hero can
be saved by the symbols of his status.

Those recognizing the allusion might also remember Dryden's
gentle criticism of Oldham's metrics:

> O early ripe! to thy abundant store
> What could advancing Age have added more?
> It might (what Nature never gives the young)
> Have taught the numbers of thy native Tongue.
> But Satyr needs not those, and Wit will shine
> Through the harsh cadence of a rugged line:
> A noble Error, and but seldom made,
> When Poets are by too much force betray'd.
> Thy generous fruits, though gather'd ere their prime
> Still shew'd a quickness; and maturing time
> But mellows what we write to the dull sweets of Rime.   (ll. 11–21)

The notion of Oldham's 'force' as a 'noble Error' should remind us
of Dryden's defences of heroic excess and Homeric fire. By taking
up the task of Homeric translation some fifteen years later, and by
finding some metrical equivalents for the 'harsh cadence' of
Homer's 'rugged line', Dryden was refusing to settle for the 'dull
sweets of Rime', attempting to regain the youthful 'force' he had
recognized in Oldham. Like his master Homer, he has 'rather given
us his own Character' than that of the poet he translates. But if we
credit in any measure his claim to have discovered that Homer was
'more according to my Genius' than Virgil, the sly political nudges
and personal allusions constitute a claim that Homer, 'if he were
living, and an *Englishman*', would have thought and written like
John Dryden.

THE FINAL 'MEMORIAL OF MY OWN PRINCIPLES': DRYDEN'S ALTER EGOS IN HIS LATER CAREER

Cedric D. Reverand II

With modern scholarship over the last thirty years or so being more attentive to what Thomas H. Fujimura has aptly called 'the personal element' in Dryden's poetry,[1] we have become more alert to the ways in which he used alter egos in his poems to help him work through his frustrations, defend himself, and express his values. We have also become more alert to a recurrent Dryden concern, which often appeared when he addressed other artists, namely the power of art, of particular interest to him because he regarded his role as a public poet in a classical sense, as *vates*, meaning both bard and prophet, empowered with special authority to comment and criticize. One of the most telling examinations of this issue occurs in his ode to Anne Killigrew (1686), where Dryden, having recently converted to Catholicism, takes stock of his career to this point and rebukes himself for stooping to write obscene plays when he might have had nobler poetic ambitions. Seeking a fresh start, he sees in Anne Killigrew an ideal artist figure whose death might serve as an atonement for the poetic failings of 'This lubrique and adult'rate age' (l. 63), and whose moral purity might inspire him to better, in this case more morally proper, poetry. As he discusses

---

[1] Thomas H. Fujimura, 'The Personal Element in Dryden's Poetry', *PMLA* 89 (1974) 1007–23.

this heaven-sent artist, Dryden employs imagery that endows Killigrew with immense power. At one point, she is depicted as a military conqueror annexing defenceless countries (i.e. moving from poetry into painting, ll. 88–105); then, when she paints a portrait of her king, we discover that, far from merely rendering a likeness, she remakes him, calling forth virtues in James II that are not there until the artist puts them there:

> His Warlike Mind, his Soul devoid of Fear,
> His High-designing thoughts, were figur'd there,
> As when, by Magick, Ghosts are made appear.   (ll. 131–3)

This is more, I think, than mere hyperbole. We should bear in mind that it had not been long since Dryden, in *Absalom and Achitophel* (1681), depicted Charles II as 'godlike David', overcoming his disposition towards mildness, his 'tenderness of Blood' (l. 947), and instead drawing 'the Sword of Justice' (l. 1002) and exerting the law, which the Almighty confirms with peals of thunder (ll. 1026–31). In a manner of speaking, Dryden had attempted to evoke Charles II's 'Warlike Mind' and 'High-designing thoughts', both advising the monarch how to behave and at the same time creating an image of the ideal king that he felt the divided nation required. Killigrew's power, however, goes even beyond that. At the end of her poem, we see her leading mankind to the kingdom of heaven at the Last Judgement (ll. 178–95), for poets will lead there, as they are morally responsible for leading here on earth, or so Dryden would like to believe. These are indeed extravagant claims for the artist's power, but they are also expressions of Dryden's own idealistic hopes of his ultimate efficacy as a public poet.

The personal elements in most of the poems from the earlier part of Dryden's career have been studied admirably by scholars,[2] but the

---

[2] On personal elements in celebratory poems involving fellow artists, see Fujimura, 'The Personal Element', which covers the poems to Oldham, Killigrew, and Congreve, as well as *Alexander's Feast*; on the Congreve and Kneller poems as well as *Mac Flecknoe*, see Earl Miner, 'The Poetics of the Critical Act: Dryden's Dealings with Rivals and Predecessors', in René Wellek and Alvaro Ribeiro (eds.), *Evidence in Literary Scholarship: Essays in Memory of James Marshall Osborn* (Oxford, 1979), pp. 45–62; on the poem to Oldham see also Dustin Griffin, 'Dryden's "Oldham" and the Perils of Writing', *Modern Language Quarterly*, 37 (1986) 133–50, and David B. Morris, 'Writing/Reading/Remembering: Dryden and the Poetics of Memory', in Christopher Fox (ed.), *Teaching Eighteenth-Century Poetry*, AMS Studies in the Eighteenth Century, 12 (New York, 1990), pp. 119–45; on the poem to Kneller, see Cedric D. Reverand II, 'Dryden on Dryden in *To Sir Godfrey Kneller*', *Papers on Language and Literature*,

self-examinations in poems from his final years, which are what I intend to explore in this essay, have received far less critical attention. I think there is a remarkable shift in Dryden's use of alter egos and his treatment of the theme of the power of poetry at the end of his life. Typically, Dryden had relied upon alter egos, usually fellow artists (e.g. Shadwell, Oldham, Anne Killigrew, Godfrey Kneller, Congreve), to define and celebrate his own art, sometimes by way of contrast, often by way of near parallel. But in his last years, just when we might expect the former Laureate to become more fervent in justifying his art in the face of a hostile age, he seems to do the opposite. He now criticizes and even undercuts the very power he had so long exalted; if, in the Killigrew ode, the artist was endowed with the moral authority to lead mankind, in those final years he seems to be all too capable of misleading mankind. I think we first detect this shift in *Alexander's Feast; Or the Power of Musique. An Ode in Honour of St. Cecilia's Day* (22 November 1697), which followed hard upon the publication, in July, of Dryden's Virgil. Having lost the Laureateship in 1689, after the arrival of William III, and with it the security of an annual pension, Dryden had turned to plays and translations in order to make a living, in 1694 committing himself to the ambitious project of translating all of Virgil. This took him three years, made the more difficult by frequent bouts of illness that sometimes delayed his progress, and frequent needs for money that frustrated him. Once his Virgil appeared, however, it was a triumph, requiring a second edition within a year, and going through at least twenty-four editions in the next century. As he tells his sons in a letter written that September, 'My Virgil succeeds in the World beyond its desert or my Expectations', and that success was confirmed when he was visited by the stewards of the St Cecilia's Day Feast, 'who came in a body' asking him to write the ode for the 1697 ceremony.[3] He had last written the official ode for that occasion back in 1687, before losing the Laureateship, and in the intervening decade had to watch as lesser authors, including the man who replaced him as Laureate, Thomas Shadwell, wrote the

17 (1981) 164–80. James Winn's definitive biography, *John Dryden and his World* (New Haven, 1987), can be considered a culmination of this trend, for he not only sets out the facts and details that constitute Dryden's life, but also remains sensitive to the ways in which his writing comments on that life.

[3] *Letters*, pp. 93–4.

annual ode. To have been asked again in the wake of his Virgil translation, to have been visited by a delegation of prominent Londoners, must have been gratifying, and Dryden, the deposed Laureate, may well have considered this as recognition by his countrymen that his poetic accomplishments had transcended political circumstance, that he had finally won out over the Shadwells of his world.

The completion of such a laborious project, the relief from tension and uncertainty, the receipt of payments from Tonson, the feeling of triumph because of its recognition, all contributed to the exuberance of *Alexander's Feast*, where we discover a powerful poet-musician, Timotheus, addressing Alexander, a usurping, warrior-king who had just invaded Persia and conquered Darius. Given that William had invaded England (albeit quietly) to usurp the throne from the Stuarts and had plunged England into an expensive and unpopular war against France, which was commonly, and pointedly, referred to as 'King William's War', it is easy to recognize the parallels. In the swaggering Alexander, we are seeing a comic version of William, and in the figure of Timotheus, we hear a confident, even ebullient, Dryden, revisiting a favourite theme, the power of the artist. When Timotheus tells the myth of Alexander's birth, from Jove's rape of Olympia, the great conqueror seems to be transformed on the spot:

> The list'ning Crowd admire the lofty Sound,
> A present Deity, they shout around:
> A present Deity the vaulted Roofs rebound.
> > With ravish'd Ears
> > The Monarch hears,
> > Assumes the God,
> > Affects to nod,
> And seems to shake the Spheres.　　(ll. 34–41)

The great conqueror also seems to be both passive and dense; he only 'Assumes the God' after the song is sung and after the crowd reacts, and he remains completely unaware of how the change has been effected. Also, his power is a fiction: he only 'seems to shake the Spheres'. The real power belongs to the myth-maker, who has swayed the crowd and bestowed divinity upon Alexander by turning '*Philip*'s Warlike Son' (l. 2) into the son of Jove. Alexander emerges as something of a buffoon, grand in his folly; in rendering him a fool, the poet-musician in effect controls and disarms the monarch, making what should be a threatening figure—Dryden clearly regarded William with apprehension and foreboding—into somebody whose outrageous behaviour we laugh at rather than fear. As a reshaper of reality, and remaker of kings, Timotheus is reminiscent of Anne Killigrew, who was able to evoke qualities in her monarch that were not there until her hand called them forth. But where Killigrew endowed her king with positive attributes, Timotheus is doing the opposite, not so much telling his monarch what he should be, as puffing him up preposterously, and at the same time making him the offspring of a rapacious Jove, 'Sov'raign of the World' (l. 33), who is not so much godlike—'A Dragon's fiery Form bely'd the God' (l. 28)—as he is monstrous. As Timotheus continues singing, he demonstrates the full range of his power, with Alexander responding helplessly and rather stupidly to each shift of mood. A boisterous song about Bacchus renders the monarch drunk (ll. 47–68); then a mournful song reduces him to tears over the death of '*Darius* Great and Good' (l. 75); then, choosing a different strain, Timotheus sings of love, which causes Alexander to gaze longingly on his mistress, Thais, until finally, 'with Love and Wine at once oppress'd, | The vanquish'd Victor sunk upon her Breast' (ll. 114–15). He may seem to be the victim of love and wine, 'but Musique won the Cause' (l. 108), and the supposedly great Alexander is now merely the 'vanquish'd Victor', drunk, lovesick, and asleep. The final victor is 'The Mighty Master' (l. 93) Timotheus.

While the theme of the artist's power is familiar, this time there is something amiss. This is not merely awesome power, but excessive power, and Timotheus is manipulating Alexander, not guiding him in a responsible manner. Towards the end of the poem, when the Mighty Master changes the tune once again to 'A lowder yet, and yet a lowder Strain' (l. 124), he rouses Alexander from his lovesick swoon by crying 'Revenge, Revenge' (l. 132), and provokes him, and the company, to action:

> The Princes applaud, with a furious Joy;
> And the King seyz'd a Flambeau, with Zeal to destroy;
>   *Thais* led the Way,
>   To light him to his Prey,
> And, like another *Hellen*, fir'd another *Troy*.　　　(ll. 146–50)

Off he goes to conquer Persepolis, because the poet exhorts him to do so. Timotheus has no particular reason for doing this. He can as easily urge the opposite, as he did earlier during the feast: 'War, he sung, is Toil and Trouble; | Honour but an empty Bubble' (ll. 99–100). It makes no difference to him what actions he inspires or what destruction might follow, so long as he can exercise his power over his king and his audience.

Can Dryden, who felt pangs of remorse over the immorality of his plays and who had once hoped that Anne Killigrew might, by virtue of her purity, serve as an atonement for his failings, possibly be identifying with an amoral, manipulative, poet-artist? Can Dryden, who throughout the last decade of the century persisted in condemning William's warlike spirit, possibly be identifying with a poet figure who so casually inspires bloodshed? I have long been intrigued by the fact that critics frequently comment on the parallel between the mighty Alexander and warlike William III, a parallel that was commonplace in political tracts at the time, and yet most of them have shied away from recognizing the next obvious parallel that follows. If Alexander is William, who could Timotheus represent? Some have gone so far as to see this poem as 'Dryden's assertion of his own values', but few have pursued the point and asked about the domineering figure asserting those values.[4] I think this is because the consequences of making the identification with Dryden are disturbing.[5] This is a radically different alter ego for Dryden, marking the beginning of a new strategy of self-expression in those final years. Where he had for his entire career unabashedly

[4] The phrase is Earl Miner's, from *Dryden's Poetry* (Bloomington, Ind., 1967), p. 273; similarly, Judith Sloman, in *Dryden: The Poetics of Translation* (Toronto, 1985), goes as far as to say that 'Timotheus is another of Dryden's masks' (p. 201), but she too does not pursue the point. Among those who have discussed Alexander as a William figure, but have pulled back from exploring the implications of linking Timotheus with Dryden, are: Bessie Proffitt, in 'Political Satire in Dryden's *Alexander's Feast*', *Texas Studies in Language and Literature*, 11 (1970) 1307–16, and Robert P. Maccubbin, in 'The Ironies of Dryden's *Alexander's Feast; or The Power of Musique*: Text and Contexts', *Mosaic*, 18/4 (1985) 33–47. One commentator who seems to have no trouble identifying Timotheus with Dryden is Pope, who ends his discussion of *Alexander's Feast* in *An Essay on Criticism* with: 'And what *Timotheus* was, is *Dryden* now' (l. 383). I have discussed this issue more extensively in *Dryden's Final Poetic Mode* (Philadelphia, Pa., 1988), pp. 126–38.

[5] Thomas H. Fujimura, one of those who faces the identification of Timotheus with Dryden head on, suggests why others have avoided that identification: 'Of course, it might be argued that Timotheus is irresponsible, and hence is not a wholly suitable analogue for Dryden' ('Personal Element', p. 1023).

revelled in the power of the artist, and confidently exercised that power as Laureate daring to criticize his king, Dryden is now depicting such power as dangerous, amoral, and irresponsible.[6]

Alexander's Feast was to be reprinted in Dryden's last major work, *Fables Ancient and Modern* (1700), which abounds with alter egos. Throughout the collection, we encounter this same unexpected change, with Dryden treating artist figures as dangerous, but there is another interesting change in strategy as well: in selecting vehicles for self-expression, Dryden now identifies himself with non-artists. This becomes most striking, perhaps, in what we would have to regard as the perfect alter ego, the other John Dryden, the featured figure of 'To my Honour'd Kinsman, John Driden of Chesterton in the County of Huntingdon, Esquire'. I give the complete title, because the location itself is significant. This is not just Dryden's honoured cousin, but his country cousin, and from the very opening, it is clear that Dryden is interested in praising his kinsman's rural life:

> How Bless'd is He, who leads a Country Life,
> Unvex'd with anxious Cares, and void of Strife!
> Who studying Peace, and shunning Civil Rage,
> Enjoy'd his Youth, and now enjoys his Age. (ll. 1–4)

He enjoys his age (he was 65 when the poem was published, Dryden 68) because, as everybody knows, and as urban dwellers still tend to believe, the country life is the healthy life. It is free from 'anxious Cares', and it provides the opportunity for wholesome, outdoor exercise, in the kinsman's case, by seeking 'the Champian-Sports, or Sylvan-Chace' (l. 51):

> By Chace our long-liv'd Fathers earn'd their Food;
> Toil strung the Nerves, and purifi'd the Blood:
> .   .   .   .
> Better to hunt in Fields, for Health unbought,
> Than fee the Doctor for a nauseous Draught.
> The Wise, for Cure, on exercise depend;
> God never made his Work, for Man to mend.
>
>   (ll. 88–9, 92–5)

Dryden's namesake exemplifies the classical ideal of the 'quiet

---

[6] James Winn also recognizes this different handling of this familiar theme, seeing Dryden as questioning 'the relationship between the artistic power to manipulate one's hearers and the moral imperative to instruct them' (*John Dryden and his World*, p. 495).

country life! | Discharg'd of business, void of strife' ('From Horace, Epod. 2d', ll. 3–4) that Dryden had celebrated elsewhere, notably in his translations of Horace and Virgil. Kinsman Driden's life is not terribly different from that of the happy swain in the second Georgic, who is 'Unvex'd with Quarrels, undisturb'd with Noise', and who in his 'secure Retreat' achieves 'A harmless Life' crowned with 'rural Pleasures' (from ll. 639–59).[7] But this is more than a mere gesture towards the traditional classical retreat. The surviving letters from Dryden's later years reveal frequent trips to the country—to Oundle, Cotterstock, Titchmarsh, Chesterton (to visit John Driden)—and from the warmth of his thank-you notes to his frequent hostess, Mrs Steward, it is clear that he enjoyed the opportunity of escaping the 'Civil Rage' of the city, even on occasion retiring to the country to get work done. Those same letters also reveal Dryden beset with 'many fitts of Sickness',[8] which he generally treats as the inescapable inconveniences of old age. Thus, Dryden has immediate personal reasons for appreciating his gentleman cousin's country life. It is the kind of life, a healthy, secure, self-sufficient old age in a rustic setting, that the beleaguered city poet, who on occasion referred to himself as an 'old decrepid Man',[9] would find appealing, and the kind of life he knew he could never hope to attain for himself.

In all kinsman Driden does, he is a bringer of peace and order. As a local Justice of the Peace, he reconciles contentious parties, so that those who were 'Foes before, return in Friendship home' (l. 9); his decrees are 'so design'd, | The Sanction leaves a lasting Peace behind' (ll. 14–15). Even when he hunts, he is bringing about a just order, serving 'the Common Good' (l. 53) by 'often' bringing 'the wily Fox | To suffer for the Firstlings of the Flocks' (ll. 54–5). He also serves the cause of peace as a Member of Parliament, but to do so, he must represent the people against the king:

> Some Overpoise of Sway, by Turns they share;
> In Peace the People, and the Prince in War:

[7] Jay Arnold Levine points out the echoes of Horace's second epode and explains that what in Horace is ironic—the speaker with the pastoral values turns out to be a moneylender—is straightforward in Dryden. Levine also discusses other elements Dryden incorporated from retirement poems, including poems by his contemporaries. See Levine, 'John Dryden's Epistle to John Driden', *Journal of English and Germanic Philology*, 63 (1964) 450–74.

[8] *Letters*, p. 114.   [9] *Letters*, p. 101.

.   .   .   .

> Patriots, in Peace, assert the Peoples Right;
> With noble Stubbornness resisting Might: (ll. 180–1, 184–5)

As a member of the parliaments of 1690, 1698, and 1700, all of which opposed William and his ministry, kinsman Driden seems to have been among those who resisted the king's attempts to secure funding for his Standing Army, thereby demonstrating that he was 'so tenacious of the Common Cause, | As not to lend the King against his Laws' (ll. 190–1).[10] After dwelling on his cousin's virtues and mentioning his 'noble Stubbornness', Dryden ends the poem by explicitly allying himself to his patriotic namesake:

> Two of a House, few Ages can afford;
> One to perform, another to record.
> Praise-worthy Actions are by thee embrac'd;
> And 'tis my Praise, to make thy Praises last.
> For ev'n when Death dissolves our Humane Frame,
> The Soul returns to Heav'n, from whence it came;
> Earth keeps the Body, Verse preserves the Fame.   (ll. 203–9)

Not only is the poet just as important as the man of action, but both depend upon one another, and they both trace their tradition of patriotic service to their 'gen'rous Grandsire' (l. 188), Erasmus Driden, who also had stubbornly resisted giving his king money (a mandatory loan Charles I levied on his subjects in 1626), and who was thrown in gaol for his defiance. When Dryden addresses his cousin as a 'true Descendent of a Patriot Line' (l. 195), the praise redounds to his own credit as well.

Later on, in a letter to Charles Montagu, Dryden referred to this poem as 'a Memorial of my own Principles to all Posterity',[11] which suggests how much he had invested himself in this portrait. But to achieve this memorial, Dryden had to do more than depict his cousin favourably; he had to negotiate the real disparities between himself and the other John Driden into a concord. Unlike the poet,

---

[10] The extant information about John Driden's political activity remains thin, but Levine argues that his willingness to allow these lines to stand, his known participation in the parliaments that opposed William, and his absence from the Parliament of 1695 that supported the king, together imply that he was among those who refused to lend the king money during peacetime (Levine, 'John Dryden's Epistle', pp. 452–3).

[11] *Letters*, p. 120.

kinsman Driden respected his king and did not seem troubled by the niceties of lineal succession. Dryden reports that upon seeing an earlier draft of this poem, which contained 'a Satire against the Dutch valour', his cousin 'desir'd me to omit it, (to use his Own words) out of the respect He had to his Soveraign', which is quite the contrary to the disrespect Dryden readily displayed at every opportunity. It is not unusual for Dryden to seek the approval of the person about whom he is writing (he was later to receive an appreciative donation from his cousin), but it is noteworthy that the man who admitted that 'Satire will have room, where e're I write' ('To Sir *Godfrey Kneller*', l. 94) not only willingly removed what might be construed as satire, but also took pains to consult his 'Unbyass'd friends', including sometime enemy as well as sometime friend Montagu, to make sure that his poem would not give offence. Dryden is uncharacteristically restraining himself, twisting the circumstances advantageously to make the suspected Catholic look more like a solid Anglican, the William-baiter and troublesome Jacobite outsider to appear basically similar to a member of the respectful opposition working from within the system.[12] Dryden has used the circumstances of his namesake's political and social position not to examine himself or his career, but rather to cast himself into the saintlike mould, as it were.

This is also what Dryden does in 'The Character of A Good Parson', which in many respects serves as a supplement to 'To my Honour'd Kinsman', a sacred memorial added to a secular one. We should note that, although this is based on the portrait of the parson in the General Prologue to *The Canterbury Tales*, Dryden's additions are considerable, expanding Chaucer's fifty-two lines to 140, so considerable that one can regard this as virtually an original poem. Again, the subject lives in the country, again he is both old—'Of Sixty Years he seem'd'—and apparently healthy—'and well might last | To Sixty more' (ll. 8–9: the remarks on age are Dryden's additions). Both characters concern themselves with distinguishing right from wrong, the Justice of the Peace locally, the parson eternally:

---

[12] Similarly, Elizabeth Duthie, '"A Memorial of My Own Principles": Dryden's "To my Honour'd Kinsman"', *ELH* 47 (1980) 682–704, observes that 'Dryden can appear a man of moderation and good sense, and ally himself with a country Whig' (p. 685).

He bore his great Commission in his Look:
But sweetly temper'd Awe; and soften'd all he spoke.
He preach'd the Joys of Heav'n, and Pains of Hell;
And warn'd the Sinner with becoming Zeal;
But on Eternal Mercy lov'd to dwell.   (ll. 25–9)

In a clever overlapping of metaphors, the kinsman, as hunter, avenged 'the Firstlings of the Flocks' by punishing 'the wily Fox' (ll. 54–5), while the parson, as pastor, 'duly watch'd his Flock' and 'hungry sent the wily Fox away' (ll. 72, 74). And like the kinsman, the parson also resists his king, but now that Dryden need not negotiate with a real person, he can design an analogy closer to his own situation: where his cousin only disagreed with his monarch, the fictitious good parson refuses to accept the imposition of a non-lineal king:

The Tempter saw him too, with envious Eye;
And, as on *Job*, demanded leave to try.
He took the time when *Richard* was depos'd:
And High and Low, with happy *Harry* clos'd.
This Prince, tho' great in Arms, the Priest withstood:
Near tho' he was, yet not the next of Blood.   (ll. 106–11)

Among the Job-like sufferings those who stay loyal to Richard II (like those who remain loyal to James II) have to endure is the loss of their positions:

He join'd not in their [the people's] Choice; because he knew
Worse might, and often did from Change ensue.
Much to himself he thought; but little spoke:
And, Undepriv'd, his Benefice forsook.

(ll. 123–6)

Just as Dryden lost the Laureateship, so did the parson lose his benefice, but using a bit of sleight of hand, Dryden makes his own loss appear more dignified than it actually was: he has the parson forsaking his benefice voluntarily, without complaint, carrying on his duties and responsibilities 'Still Chearful' (l. 129). Though by refusing to take the oaths Dryden may have technically abandoned the Laureateship rather than have it snatched away from him, he was scarcely cheerful, and, as his frequent protestations through the 1690s demonstrate, he did not proceed with the confidence and steadiness of the parson, who continues 'ever Constant to his Call' (l. 129).

Although Dryden claims that 'To my Honour'd Kinsman' serves as a memorial to his own principles, there is something hard-edged and distinctly cool about the character with whom he has decided to identify. His cousin is 'Just, Good, and Wise' (l. 7), in that order, assertive, nobly stubborn, and tenacious (ll. 184–90), but he is scarcely warm, and in one lengthy, misogynistic passage, he is praised for being 'uncumber'd with a Wife' (l. 18). With the parson, a fictitious character who can be more readily shaped to the poet's purposes, Dryden can in a way complete the memorial, can compensate for his kinsman's deficiencies by fashioning a complementary alter ego, equally noble, equally steadfast, but warm and outgoing. Indeed, Dryden seems to mitigate the character as he goes along, first mentioning a potential harshness, and then softening it away, as in the 'sweetly temper'd Awe' passage cited above. The parson

> Nothing reserv'd or sullen was to see:
> But sweet Regards; and pleasing Sanctity:
> Mild was his Accent, and his Action free.
> With Eloquence innate his Tongue was arm'd;
> Tho' harsh the Precept, yet the Preacher charm'd.   (ll. 14–18)

By doing this, Dryden not only attributes admirable qualities to a Drydenian figure, but also addresses an immediate problem. It had not been long since the Reverend Jeremy Collier, himself a nonjuring clergyman, had published his *Short View of the Immorality and Profaneness of the English Stage* (1697), in which he zealously attacked Dryden for being obscene and for perpetually abusing the clergy, a charge that was to be repeated by another clergyman, Luke Milbourne, in his cavilling *Notes on Dryden's Virgil* (1698). Dryden refrained from immediate counter-attacks, although he did eventually answer Collier's charges, both in his Preface to *Fables* and in the 'Poeta Loquitur' that precedes the last poem in the collection, 'Cymon and Iphigenia'. He responds to his critics here as well, indirectly but effectively. What better way to answer the charges that he abused the clergy than by depicting, and identifying with, an exemplary clergyman? I also think Dryden took a certain amount of pleasure in creating a non-juring clergyman who was warm, approachable, temperate, nurturing, because the very character serves as a critique of the impassioned, irascible, loose-cannon Collier, who, as Dryden describes him in his Preface, 'has not forgotten the old Rule, of calumniating strongly'.[13] To those aware of Collier's vituperative spirit, some of the praise of the softened parson sounds suspiciously like advice about what constitutes the most desirable and effective behaviour for would-be religious reformers:

> To Threats, the stubborn Sinner oft is hard:
> Wrap'd in his Crimes, against the Storm prepar'd;
> But, when the milder Beams of Mercy play,
> He melts, and throws the cumb'rous Cloak away.
> Lightnings and Thunder (Heav'ns Artillery)
> As Harbingers before th' Almighty fly:
> Those, but proclaim his Stile, and disappear;
> The stiller Sound succeeds; and God is there.   (ll. 34–41)

Dryden may be having the last word in his literary feud in another way as well. When Milbourne repeated Collier's charge that Dryden had 'fallen foul on Priesthood',[14] he also kept harping on the rumour that Dryden had originally intended a clerical career, referring to malicious inventions that would have seemed clever 'had *he* been unhappily *admitted in Holy Orders*', mentioning doctrines he might have propagated 'had he once crept into Orders', and so on.[15] The implication is that Dryden's supposed abuse of the clergy arose as revenge for his disappointed hopes: 'Mr. *Bays* has a spite to a *Country Parson*', Milbourne claims, 'because refus'd to be *one*'.[16] There is no way of knowing whether that last remark registered with Dryden, but there is poetic justice at work, perhaps achieved fortuitously, in Dryden's designing a poem that allows him, symbolically, to become a country parson after all.

That Dryden should want to leave some personal memorial in what was to be his final major work is understandable. But given his concern for his career and his fame as a poet, his perpetual interest in examining, and sometimes exulting in, the power of poetry, and his

---

[13] *Poems*, ed. Kinsley, iv. 1447.

[14] Preface to *Fables*, in *Poems*, ed. Kinsley, iv. 1461.

[15] [Luke] Milbourne, *Notes on Dryden's Virgil: In a Letter to a Friend. With an Essay on the Same Poet* (London, 1698), pp. 9, 17.

[16] Milbourne, *Notes on Dryden's Virgil*, p. 19.

practice of working out his values and beliefs by writing poems about fellow artists, I find it intriguing that in these two poems, his alter egos are not poets. Poetry is not even a major issue. Certainly, Dryden speaks in the kinsman poem as a poet, a calling he claims to be parallel to that of the responsible public servant, so that his family can boast two stellar members, 'One to perform [the kinsman], another to record [the poet]' (l. 204), but he is presenting himself as an Englishman first, a poet second, a man who serves his country as another 'Descendent of a Patriot Line' (l. 195), not a man who serves his art. And in the 'Character of a Good Parson', it is true that the alter ego has one of Dryden's most important attributes as part of his character, eloquence, but it is not a creative power. Instead, it is preaching, eloquence in the service of God, generously conveying the gospels to far-flung parishioners. I find nothing in the poem that suggests the speaker or his gift of eloquence have any power to reshape reality.

When we encounter figures in *Fables* who have the creative gift, the very kinds of characters that Dryden had so often used to make claims about the power of poetry, we discover that they tend to be, like Timotheus, suspect, unreliable, and potentially dangerous. For example, in 'The Cock and the Fox' (Dryden's version of the Nun's Priest's Tale), we encounter three silver-tongued characters, Chanticleer—'oh! what Joy it was to hear him sing' (l. 87)—Reynard the fox, and Chanticleer's father, who never actually appears, but who figures prominently in Reynard's temptation speech. I should think that Dryden, and Chaucer before him, might well have enjoyed the self-mockery entailed in writing a beast fable where the foolish victim is a renowned singer, undone by the pride he has in his own artistic skill. While the cock is pompous and proud in both versions, which is necessary to spring the moral of the tale, Dryden makes Chanticleer a bit more full of himself than the Chaucerian original. When the fox flatters him into singing,

> The Cock was pleas'd to hear him speak so fair,
> And proud beside, as solar People are:
> Nor cou'd the Treason from the Truth descry,
> So was he ravish'd with this Flattery:

That much is based, rather loosely, on Chaucer, but the lines immediately following are pure Dryden:

So much the more as from a little Elf,
He had a high Opinion of himself:
Though sickly, slender, and not large of Limb,
Concluding all the World was made for him.   (ll. 651–8)

It is difficult to avoid a smile upon reading such words from a man who was not inclined to be humble about his own poetic accomplishments, and whose small, plump figure once earned him the nickname 'Poet Squab'.

Some of Dryden's additions redefine the power of eloquence in interesting ways. After Reynard has praised Chanticleer for 'the sweetness of your Voice' (l. 600), he extends the praise to Chanticleer's father, and Dryden departs for a little excursion of his own:

But since I speak of Singing let me say,
As with an upright Heart I safely may,
That, save your self, there breaths not on the Ground,
One like your Father for a Silver sound.
So sweetly wou'd he wake the Winter-day,
That Matrons to the Church mistook their way,
And thought they heard the merry Organ play.
And he to raise his Voice with artful Care,
(What will not Beaux attempt to please the Fair?)
On Tiptoe stood to sing with greater Strength.   (ll. 616–25)

Chaucer alludes to the father and describes him stretching his neck and standing 'on his tiptoon'; the intervening lines (ll. 620–4), about the matrons and the organ, and about attempting to please the fair, are Dryden's additions. Now, the magical power of the singer becomes the power to deceive—they 'thought they heard the merry Organ play'—and to mislead matrons who are attempting to go to church. What would the good parson, whose eloquence is employed to lead people towards God, say about that? Where the original father was informed by 'discrecioun' and 'wisedom', attributes Dryden omits, this new version of the character is motivated instead by an attempt 'to please the Fair', which means his eloquence is ultimately self-serving: he flatters so that others will have a good opinion of him, which is also what poets who write dedicatory poems to patrons and their wives tend to do, and what Dryden just did in the dedicatory opening poem of *Fables*, where he praises the Duchess of Ormonde as 'The fairest Nymph' (l. 13).

Since Reynard is the villain, using his speech to entrap his intended victim, there is nothing unexpected in his admiration for a fellow artist who displays similarly deceptive skills. The expansions, then, are consistent with the alignment of characters in the tale. But it comes as something of a surprise when, after adding material to make the power of the singer more deceptive and fraudulent, Dryden also adds details that increase the similarities between himself and the suspect singers he is depicting. Reynard is still talking about Chanticleer's father:

> By this, in Song, he never had his Peer,
> From sweet *Cecilia* down to Chanticleer;
> Not *Maro*'s Muse who sung the mighty Man,
> Nor *Pindar*'s heav'nly Lyre, nor *Horace* when a Swan.
> Your Ancestors proceed from Race divine,   (ll. 631–5)

The first line is based on Chaucer, but all the examples that follow are invented, and we can hardly help noticing that the peerless cock is now associated with Cecilia, whom Dryden had celebrated in two odes, with Chanticleer, whom Dryden is celebrating right now, and with Virgil, whom Dryden had just translated. It seems that the ancient 'Race divine' from which Chanticleer descends includes Dryden. Since, metaphorically speaking, Chanticleer's father is also the poet who begets him, I cannot help thinking that Dryden may have inserted such references so as to highlight the ironies involved in being the poetical father writing about a poetical father.[17]

The most obvious Dryden interpolation occurs just when Chanticleer, 'ravish'd with this Flattery' (l. 654), opens his mouth to sing. It is time for the narrator to point out a moral:

> Ye Princes rais'd by Poets to the Gods,
> And *Alexander'd* up in lying Odes,
> Believe not ev'ry flatt'ring Knave's report,
> There's many a *Reynard* lurking in the Court;
> And he shall be receiv'd with more regard
> And list'ned to, than modest Truth is heard.   (ll. 659–64)

---

[17] For a discussion of poetic fatherhood as a favourite topic of Dryden's and of related topics, including inheritance, lineage, and succession, see Christopher Ricks, 'Allusion: The Poet as Heir', in R. F. Brissenden and J. C. Eade (eds.), *Studies in the Eighteenth Century, III* (Toronto, 1976), pp. 209–40.

Having emphasized similarities between himself and the proud, angel-voiced Chanticleer, himself and the deceptive, misleading father of Chanticleer, Dryden now aligns himself with the treacherous Reynard, the villain of the piece, 'th' Artificer of Lies' (l. 776), who is capable of lying up people in flattering odes.[18] Presumably, Dryden has in mind fawning pro-Williamite works that ridiculously inflated the monarch, but we cannot help but notice that *Alexander's Feast*, which is repeated later in this very volume, is also a lying ode. If I find *Alexander's Feast* bothersome because of what it implies about the artist's ability to manipulate, it appears that the narrator here shares my concern, but the narrator happens also to be the author of *Alexander's Feast*. Can Dryden be warning us all against such 'lying Odes', against dangerous poet-rhetoricians like Timotheus, who is also like Dryden?

If this is the comic treatment of the power of eloquence, Dryden also gives us a more serious treatment in 'The Speeches of Ajax and Ulysses' from Ovid's *Metamorphoses* XIII, a set rhetorical piece wherein the two heroic figures debate over who better deserves Achilles' armour. One could consider this poem as an extension of the issues addressed in *Alexander's Feast* for, once again, we find a man of action pitted against a man of words, and again, the powerful man of words, Timotheus there, Ulysses here, will demonstrate how easily he can sway the crowd. Ajax, who goes first and, of course, loses the argument, puts his finger on the problem:

> So much 'tis safer at the noisy Bar
> With Words to flourish than ingage in War.
> By different Methods we maintain our Right,
> Nor am I made to Talk, nor he to Fight.
> In bloody Fields I labour to be great;
> His Arms are a smooth Tongue; and soft Deceit.   (ll. 13–18)

He not only defines the nature of the contrast, arms vs. a smooth tongue, which Ulysses describes instead as brawn vs. brains (l. 553), but he also accuses Ulysses of being cowardly and deceptive, charging him with a number of shameful actions, including stranding Philoctetes on a bare island and framing Palamede for treason.

---

[18] To make matters worse, Reynard is consistently linked to Milton's Satan, 'th' Artificer of Lies' (l. 776) echoing the 'Artificer of fraud' (*Paradise Lost*, iv. 121), as Taylor Corse points out in 'Dryden and Milton in "The Cock and the Fox"', *Milton Quarterly*, 27 (1993) 109–18.

Ulysses rebuts Ajax with sufficient force to convince his audience, but he never quite exculpates himself from the basic charges. For instance, he does not deny deserting Philoctetes on Lemnos. Instead, he reminds everybody that leaving him 'Wounded, forlorn, of human Aid bereft' (l. 485) was a collective Greek decision: it 'Is not my Crime, or not my Crime alone' (l. 486). As for Palamede, 'If *Palamede* unjustly fell by me', it was not Ulysses' fault: 'I but accus'd, you doom'd' (ll. 478–80). Rather than defending himself, he cagily shifts the blame to others, who are now equally complicit. And throughout, he is the consummate actor, employing an intentional dramatic pause before starting, to allow his audience to settle down after Ajax's speech, feigning tears over the dead Achilles, and later employing the cheap, but effective, theatrical trick of baring his breast to show his battle scars. The victory for eloquence has a double cost. It results in the loss of the heroic, albeit slow-witted, Ajax, who falls upon his sword rather than accept defeat—'None but himself, himself cou'd overthrow' (l. 602), he declares—and it comes at the expense of the victor, because it is not sheer eloquence that wins the debate, but rather, as Ajax accurately explained, 'a smooth Tongue; and soft Deceit'. Ulysses may have won, but his ploys diminish his stature, just as Timotheus' amoral manipulations of Alexander make him appear ignoble. Ulysses' behaviour demonstrates the validity of an observation originally addressed to the Chanticleers of the world:

> There's many a *Reynard* lurking in the Court;
> And he shall be receiv'd with more regard
> And list'ned to, than modest Truth is heard.   (ll. 662–4)

Since 'The Cock and the Fox' is a beast fable, its characters comical exaggerations, its tone jocular, we should not take its warnings against the dangers of eloquence too seriously. And since there are no analogues in Dryden's life for the details of Ulysses' career as a warrior, nothing resembling cowardice in battle, desertion of Nestor in the field, and so forth, we should not regard Ulysses as another Dryden. Dryden does not invest himself in these lightweight characters or in the duplicitous, smooth-tongued Ulysses, as he does with his cousin or with the good parson; hence, these tales do not yield self-criticism, or introspection, or self-justification, but rather whimsical, sidelong self-parody in the one, and exploration of the power and deficiencies of eloquence in the other. Nonetheless, it is something of a surprise to find the major poet of his age producing a work wherein he represents his principles through non-poets, and then makes those with the creative gift either jokes, like the barnyard singers, or alarming manipulators, like crafty Ulysses.

There is another non-poet alter ego in *Fables*, namely Pythagoras from *Metamorphoses* XV, who may be the most significant of them all, which I infer from the care Dryden takes to emphasize this one tale; he both singles it out at the very beginning of his Preface as 'the Master-piece of the whole *Metamorphoses*',[19] and then adds a head-note to the tale itself, where he describes 'the Moral and Natural Philosophy of *Pythagoras*' as 'the most learned and beautiful Parts of the Whole Metamorphoses'. Once we encounter Pythagoras, we discover that, in many respects, he is a familiar Drydenian surrogate. He is introduced with the following description:

> Here dwelt the Man divine whom *Samos* bore,
> But now Self-banish'd from his Native Shore,
> Because he hated Tyrants, nor cou'd bear
> The Chains which none but servile Souls will wear: (ll. 77–80)

This sounds much like the parson, who surrendered his benefice because of his disapproval of the monarchical succession, with Dryden again making his loss of his court posts look like a voluntary action undertaken for a noble reason. This is one of those passages that, because of its applicability to Dryden's personal circumstances, looks like an interpolation, but in fact the voluntary exile and the hatred of tyranny appear in Ovid as well (Dryden adds the chains). Ovid, who was banished from Rome to Tomis on the Black Sea, may be engaging in the same kind of identification with his character as Dryden, and we may be in the middle of a historically regressing series of alter egos, each major author out of favour, one psychologically, the other literally an exile, identifying with the next banished figure. Dryden, alert to such similarities between himself and other authors, had employed this parallel before, explaining his delay in finishing *Eleonora* (1692) by likening himself to Ovid, who 'going to his Banishment, and Writing from on Ship-

---

[19] *Poems*, ed. Kinsley, iv. 1444.

bord to his Friends, excus'd the Faults of his Poetry by his Mis-fortunes'.[20] I believe one of the reasons Dryden was attracted to Ovid at this stage of his career—eight of the twenty-one tales of *Fables* are from Ovid—is because of this perceived similarity.[21]

Like several other alter egos, Pythagoras is a master of eloquence, and since the goal of rhetoric is to persuade, eloquence is best demonstrated by convincing an audience. When we first meet Pythagoras, we learn that he 'Lov'd in familiar Language' to explain the universe, and when he did so, 'The Crowd with silent Admiration stand | And heard him, as they heard their God's Command' (ll. 86–8). This brings to mind Timotheus ('The list'ning Crowd admire the lofty Sound', l. 34), the good parson ('He drew his Audience upward to the Sky', l. 20), and Ulysses, whose entire speech is a demonstration of how to sway a crowd. Pythagoras also acts as a prophet, ending his long account of continual change as the operating force throughout the universe by predicting the next change in civilizations, the replacement of destroyed civilizations with Rome:

> *Mycene, Sparta, Thebes*, of mighty Fame,
> Are vanish'd out of Substance into Name.
> And *Dardan Rome* that just begins to rise,
> On *Tiber's* Banks, in time shall mate the Skies. (ll. 635–8)

He amplifies this by next repeating the prophecy of Helenus to Aeneas, promising him that, even as Troy was 'in a sinking State', a new empire, 'Greater than what e'er was, or is, or e'er shall be', will spring up, and a new 'Race deriv'd from Thee' would extend until 'thy *Rome* shall rule the conquer'd Earth' (ll. 647–59). This kind of vatic pronouncement is typically Drydenian; we hear such pro-phetic strains in *Absalom and Achitophel*, the ode to Anne Killigrew, 'To Congreve', 'To the Dutchess of Ormond', and in *The Medall*, oddly enough in a passage that begins 'Without a Vision Poets can

---

[20] *Works*, iii. 231.

[21] As Earl Miner argues, Dryden may also have turned to Ovid at this point because of self-consciousness about his relationship to Milton. Just as Ovid, after Virgil's epic, had to write a different kind of epic, an episodic 'second epic', so did Dryden, following *Paradise Lost*, have to produce a similarly episodic second epic in *Fables*. This still involves identification with Ovid, but in a different manner, as a fellow author encumbered by the burden of the past. See Miner, 'Ovid Reformed: Fables, Morals, and the Second Epic', in Earl Miner and Jennifer Brady (eds.), *Literary Transmission and Authority: Dryden and Other Writers* (Cambridge, 1993), pp. 79–120.

fore-show' (l. 287).[22] Pythagoras plays another familiar role as well, that of adviser to the legendary Numa Pompilius, king of Rome during its supposed Golden Age, successor to Romulus. This would be of key importance to the one-time Laureate who considered it his duty to advise monarchs, and who in his post-Laureate years persisted in criticizing William and his 'stupid Military State' ('To Sir *Godfrey Kneller*', l. 51).

If we look more closely at Pythagoras as adviser, however, I think we discover something new about this counsellor. He is not merely an adviser to the king, but The Adviser to the king. Numa is no sooner chosen to 'guide the growing State', than, 'Urg'd by this Care, his Country he forsook', journeying to Crotona, becoming a disciple of Pythagoras in order 'To cultivate his Mind' (ll. 1–11). This is how Book XV starts; the basic purpose of the speech is to instruct the monarch, and the implication is that this instruction is necessary for Rome to grow, reach maturity, and achieve the glory Pythagoras predicts for it. In short, this particular counsellor to the king is all-important. However grandiose Dryden's claims may have been from time to time, and however often he availed himself of the opportunity of advising and warning monarchs, I do not think he ever conceived of himself as the tutor his monarchs specifically sought out for edification and direction. This is, to say the least, an idealistic view. And Numa, as it so happens, is an ideal king, distinctly unlike William III, in very specific ways. This is the final verse paragraph of the poem:

> These Precepts by the *Samian* Sage were taught,
> Which Godlike *Numa* to the *Sabines* brought,
> And thence transferr'd to *Rome*, by Gift his own:
> A willing People, and an offer'd Throne.
> O happy Monarch, sent by Heav'n to bless
> A Salvage Nation with soft Arts of Peace,
> To teach Religion, Rapine to restrain,
> Give Laws to Lust, and Sacrifice ordain:
> Himself a Saint, a Goddess was his Bride,
> And all the Muses o'er his Acts preside.   (ll. 711–20)

---

[22] I regard this as a typical Drydenian tongue-in-cheek strategy, pronouncing what appears to be a disclaimer, and then violating it immediately: he does the same thing in *Britannia Rediviva*, where right after announcing 'Tho' Poets are not Prophets' (l. 71), he proceeds to predict the future.

As one might guess, the idea that Numa was offered a throne by a willing people is a Drydenian addition and another stinging criticism of William. He was offered a throne by some willing people, but since Dryden and other Jacobites were not among them, we are led to read this as a sarcastic remark. And since, far from bringing peace, William plunged the nation into war, we discover, as the passage unfolds, that Numa emerges as everything usurping, warlike William was not. Since he is offered a throne, Numa sounds like Charles II, and Dryden had likened the monarch to Numa previously, in *Threnodia Augustalis* (ll. 465–9). But in fact Numa is more than Charles II; he seems instead to be a blend of virtues that would constitute an ideal monarch. He is appointed to the position by a willing people. He brings peace to a naturally savage nation (neither Ovid nor Dryden seems inclined to regard the common people as peaceful—one recalls Dryden's harsh comments on the crowd in *The Medall*). Numa also brings religion, which I think may vaguely reflect Dryden's Jacobite hopes, not that he at this point desired to bring back James II, having given that over as a lost cause, but rather that he would ideally like to have had a Catholic, 'a Saint', on the throne, instead of either an autocratic James or Protestant William. Numa also serves as a conspicuous opposite of Charles II, who could never be described as giving laws to lust, since he spent so much time giving in to lust instead.

Not only is Numa an expanded version of kingship, but the advice Pythagoras offers him is an expanded kind of advice, markedly different from what Dryden's narrators usually offer their kings. Consider this typical piece of Drydenian counsel, offered, uninvited, to James II in *Britannia Rediviva*:

> Enough of Ills our dire Rebellion wrought,
> When, to the Dregs, we drank the bitter draught;
> Then airy Atoms did in Plagues conspire,
> Nor did th' avenging Angel yet retire,
> But purg'd our still encreasing Crimes with Fire.
> Then perjur'd Plots, the still impending Test,
> And worse; but Charity conceals the Rest:
> Here stop the Current of the sanguine flood   (ll. 152–9)

from which, after several more 'enough' clauses, Dryden goes on to urge restraint, calmness, moderation, charity, a 'steady Hand' holding 'our Ballance' (ll. 360–1), and so on. The passage is cluttered with recent events, the bloodshed of the Civil War, the Great Plague and the Fire of London, the Popish and Rye House Plots, the Test Act, with Dryden piling on specific evidence gathered from over forty years of English history.

Pythagoras' advice, by contrast, is general; it is not even advice so much as it is an explanation of how the universe operates, from which certain principles can be derived. His main point is that change is the basic, informing principle of all things, of nature, elements, even time itself:

> This let me further add, that Nature knows
> No stedfast Station, but, or Ebbs, or Flows:
> Ever in motion; she destroys her old,
> And casts new Figures in another Mold.
> Ev'n Times are in perpetual Flux; and run
> Like Rivers from their Fountain rowling on.   (ll. 262–7)

Throughout, he views change as neither negative nor positive. It works both ways: if rivers disappear, they also spring up anew; if the sea wears away the earth, oceans also retreat and new land emerges; if civilizations die, new civilizations are born: 'Nations and Empires flourish, and decay, | By turns command, and in their turns obey' (ll. 626–7). Since, in the long-term view, change is neutral, endings can also be construed as beginnings—for example, the destruction of Troy is also the creation of Rome—which implies that death is not a termination, but merely a stage in a continuing process of decay and renewal:

> Then, Death, so call'd, is but old Matter dress'd
> In some new Figure, and a vary'd Vest:
> Thus all Things are but alter'd, nothing dies;
> And here and there th' unbodied Spirit flies,
> By Time, or Force, or Sickness dispossest,
> And lodges, where it lights, in Man or Beast.   (ll. 237–42)

In Pythagoras' view, souls do not disappear but migrate by metempsychosis, making it immoral and improper to kill any living creature, or for that matter, to eat any living creature. This leads Pythagoras at last to his one specific piece of advice, at the end of his long disquisition:

> Take not away the Life you cannot give:
> For all Things have an equal right to live.
> Kill noxious Creatures, where 'tis Sin to save;
> This only just Prerogative we have:
> But nourish Life with vegetable Food,
> And shun the sacrilegious tast of Blood.   (ll. 705–10)

Actually, excepting the injunction to vegetarianism, this advice is basically the same as that given in *Britannia Rediviva*: avoid killing people unnecessarily ('stop the Current of the sanguine flood'), and this, together with the supporting philosophy, constitutes the 'Precepts', as the next line explains, which will ultimately help Numa bring the 'soft Arts of Peace' to Rome. But notice, where the advice in *Britannia* arises from a survey of recent historical events, the advice here at the conclusion of the poem is not specific, not based upon political experience, not bounded by circumstances, and not directed towards an immediate situation. The advice is not the statement of a political position so much as it is a consequence of a comprehensive understanding of the universe.[23] This is a different sort of Drydenian pronouncement. The engaged poet who argued repeatedly about the relevance of his poetry to his world, his culture, his kings, is now linking himself to a philosopher, somebody who has stepped back for a broader view, and in so doing has abstracted himself from the world at large. What we get in this alter ego is an idealized, philosophical Dryden, just as, in Numa, we get, literally, a philosopher-king.

With the three non-poetic alter egos we might be tempted to think that, at the end of his career, Dryden is resolving the complexities he has raised by assuming a Prospero-like detachment. All these Dryden-like characters are removed from their worlds, the kinsman having retired to the country, the parson forsaking his benefice, Pythagoras self-banished, and together they reflect how the displaced Laureate might have felt, the once relevant commentator now off to the side, watching the times pass him by, and making

---

[23] This poem is not without its topical political allusions, of course, perhaps most notably in a passage Dryden added to Ovid where the principle of flux is applied pointedly to the recent departure of James II: 'For former Things | Are set aside, like abdicated Kings: | And every moment alters what is done, | And innovates some Act till then unknown' (ll. 274–7). But when Dryden gets to the conclusion of the poem, he is able to put aside such immediate concerns in favour of a more distanced, more philosophically detached view.

virtue of necessity by linking himself with outsiders whose distance from the world may give them a better perspective than that of ordinary men. Like Prospero, Dryden seems to be leaving his magical robe behind him, relinquishing his role as a poet in order to present himself as a patriotic, just, dutiful, moral, philosophically detached commentator.[24] But this is not quite the case. Dryden was always the poet. Even as he conscientiously links himself to non-poets, he is, quite obviously, using couplets. And although he appears to be in philosophical retreat, by collecting these fables, by translating into English Homer, Ovid, Boccaccio, and Chaucer, after having already Englished Virgil, he is not merely asserting his identity as a poet, but assuming the mantle of his great predecessors as well, contributing patriotically to England in his own poetic way, by subsuming other important literary cultures within his own poetry.

As in the past, Dryden uses alter egos both to examine and explore issues important to him as a poet, and to convey values and principles, making many of the alter egos in *Fables*, not just his kinsman, a memorial to himself, and that includes the suspect fiction-makers as well as the idealized figures. If we find the contradictory images of these eloquent characters bothersome, we should recall that it was typical of Dryden to examine an issue by presenting different sides of the case and then allowing the contrary positions to interact, as he did as early as 1667 in his essay *Of Dramatick Poesie*, where the central issues are addressed by four distinct characters

---

[24] Quoting both a passage from this tale (ll. 215–20), and one from Dryden's translation of Lucretius, David Hopkins points out that, like his classical antecedents, Dryden at times enjoyed writing 'about human life from a standpoint in some ways resembling that of a god, looking down on humanity with a broader, more comprehensive, view than human beings can ordinarily attain' (p. 179). Similarly, Steven N. Zwicker, relying on the 'Pythagorean Philosophy' as an index to all of *Fables*, sees Dryden transcending his losses and disappointments through the consolations of philosophy, thereby rising above the particulars of his age. Zwicker takes this idea a step further in his essay in the present volume, where he argues for a shift in Dryden's final years towards patterns of dissolution and incompleteness, sometimes employing a Lucretian view of 'perpetual flux', in the sense of life winding down. I think this dovetails with my own thesis about the change in Dryden's attitude. If the poet is now thinking in terms of lost rather than fulfilled successions, deferral rather than achievement, it makes sense that his previous endorsement of the power of his art would give way to a more critical, hedged view of that power. See Hopkins, 'Dryden and Ovid's "Wit Out of Season"', in Charles Martindale (ed.), *Ovid Renewed* (Cambridge, 1988), pp. 167–71; Zwicker, *Politics and Language in Dryden's Poetry* (Princeton, NJ, 1984), pp. 171–6; and Zwicker, 'Dryden and the Dissolution of Things', Ch. 12 below.

with conflicting viewpoints who debate with one another. By admitting, and at times laughing at, the deficiencies of creative artists and masters of eloquence, Dryden disarms his Puritanical opponents who regard fiction-makers as intrinsically dangerous. By derogating the silver-tongued, Dryden in effect joins Collier and Milbourne on their side of the argument. But by identifying with an unimpeachable patriot, a good parson, and a famed philosopher with a spacious and positive view of nature and humanity, Dryden raises himself above his pious detractors. Paradoxically, and shrewdly, Dryden's disparagement of creative artists and his identification with non-poets ultimately serve to defend himself as a poet.

12

DRYDEN AND THE DISSOLUTION OF THINGS: THE DECAY OF STRUCTURES IN DRYDEN'S LATER WRITING

STEVEN N. ZWICKER

In his last years, Dryden paused more than once to remark the digressive character of his writing, and to explain his casual and ruminative manner as a mere symptom of age. It may be tempting to take Dryden at his word, but digression in these years was more than physiology; it was also a structure of feeling and association that allowed him to brood over and accommodate a powerful set of personal disruptions and public dislocations. Of course, Dryden had begun to use digression early in his career: he points to his own digressive manner in the Preface to *Annus Mirabilis* (1667),[1] and thereafter he made a habit of noting his digressive moves. By the middle of his career, digression had become one of the most telling marks of Dryden's strongly purposeful style. Behind the veil of the casual and the digressive, Dryden constructed superbly shaped literary instruments; the occasional diffidence and self-consciousness of both prose and verse mask daring arguments and demolitions. Yet the inward turn of his prose in the 1690s and the ruminative and associative structures of his late verse were not merely habit. No one would mistake the circuitous length of the 'Discourse Concerning

References to *Fables Ancient and Modern* are to *Poems*, ed. Kinsley; volume and page number are given in the text.

[1] *Works*, i. 53.

the Original and Progress of Satire' (1693) for posture,[2] or the casual self-declaration and the prose harmonies of the Preface to *Fables* (1700) for merely one more rehearsal of a familiar repertoire of figures. The poet declares the ruminativeness of age—the pleasures of delay and dilation—and the prose he fashions is a superb emblem of lateness; but to understand the character of his late writing, and especially its increasing digressiveness, we need to allow that the style he forged in the 1690s was constituted not only of old habits and a more recent apprehension of corporeal change, but also of a politics, a psychology, even a philosophy that allowed Dryden to acknowledge—and then to embrace—in the very structures and gestures of his writing, the casual and inevitable drift of all things towards dissolution.

The Lucretian overtones of this mood are not difficult to hear, nor should they surprise us in a poet who had displayed an interest in Lucretius from his earliest work,[3] planned to translate Lucretius as early as the mid-1660s,[4] and returned to that project to produce a set of fragments from *De Rerum Natura*, published as part of *Sylvae* (1685). To one side of this miscellany stood the poet's moving tribute to John Oldham, with its elision of Christian consolation and its beautifully managed images of body and soul dispersed to 'Fate and gloomy Night'; to the other side of the collection we find *Threnodia Augustalis* (1685), Dryden's classicized funeral ode to Charles II. Between lay Dryden's translations from Lucretius, including 'Against the Fear of Death'. In his Preface to *Sylvae*, Dryden piously denies Lucretius' mortalism—'As for his Opinions concerning the mortality of the Soul, they are so absurd, that I cannot if I wou'd believe them'[5]—but the verse in which he renders the Latin poet suggests the force not only of Lucretius' style—what

---

[2] On digression in the 'Discourse Concerning the Original and Progress of Satires', see Anne Cotterill, 'The Politics and Aesthetics of Digression: Dryden's *Discourse of Satire*', *Studies in Philology*, 91/4 (Fall 1994) 464–95.

[3] See Dryden's reference to Lucretius' atomic theory in 'To My Honored Friend, Sir Robert Howard' (1660), l. 31 and n., *Works*, i. 209.

[4] See Dryden's Preface to *Sylvae* (1685), *Works*, iii. 14: 'What I have now perform'd, is no more than I intended above twenty years ago: The ways of our Translation are very different; he [Creech] follows him more closely than I have done; which became an Interpreter of the whole poem.'

[5] *Works*, iii. 11. James Winn notes the peculiar phrasing of Dryden's rejection of Lucretian mortalism; see Winn, *John Dryden and his World* (New Haven, 1987), p. 404.

Dryden calls Lucretius' 'sublime and daring Genius'[6]—but of the vision of his poems, the images of chance, and of jarring atoms, the casual and indifferent dispositions of the natural world. The materialism of these passages may have been softened,[7] but for Dryden Lucretius' mortalism had a powerfully seductive allure:

> Nay, tho' our Atoms shou'd revolve by chance,
> And matter leape into the former dance;
> Tho' time our Life and motion cou'd restore,
> And make our Bodies what they were before,
> What gain to us wou'd all this bustle bring,
> This new made man wou'd be another thing;
> When once an interrupting pause is made,
> That individual Being is decay'd.
>
> ('Lucretius: Against the Fear of Death', ll. 19–26)

By the 1690s that dance of revolving atoms and vision of the decay and transformation of the material body had deepened into a poetic stance, an attitude towards the structural properties of the natural world, and, perhaps most importantly, a way for Dryden to experience his own mortality. The most direct link between the translations of Lucretius from the 1680s and *Fables* is Dryden's translation 'Of the Pythagorean Philosophy' (in *Fables*, from Ovid's *Metamorphoses*, Book XV) with its own Lucretian counsel 'to think of Death, as but an idle Thing' (l. 222), and its images of time's 'perpetual Flux' (l. 266): the restless alteration of acts and forms, the transformation of bodies and transmigration of souls. The moving spirit of this meditation is cyclical renewal at Nature's 'innovating Hand', but the episodes and images of exhaustion and decay are sharply rendered in Dryden's translation. The poet's responsiveness to these themes is not, however, limited to the translation from Ovid; it distinguishes Dryden's late writing throughout.

Among the verse translations that Dryden published in *Fables* are to be found two original poems that provide a telling commentary

---

[6] *Works*, iii. 10.

[7] On Dryden's 'Christianizing' of Lucretius, see Norman Austin, 'Translation as Baptism: Dryden's Lucretius', *Arion*, 7 (1968) 576–602, and Austin's contribution to *Works*, iii. 277–81; but see, as well, Paul Hammond's challenge to Austin in 'The Integrity of Dryden's Lucretius', *Modern Language Review*, 78 (1983) 1–23, and, more generally, 'John Dryden: The Classicist as Sceptic', *The Seventeenth Century*, 4 (1989) 165–87. On the 'pagan' element in Dryden's translation of Horace, see H. A. Mason, 'Living in the Present: Is Dryden's "Horat. Ode 29. Book 3" an example of "Creative Translation"?', *Cambridge Quarterly*, 10 (1981) 91–129.

on literary digression and on Dryden's late style: a panegyric on the Duchess of Ormonde, and a poem in praise of the rural life and country virtues of John Driden of Chesterton. The panegyric is the first poem in the collection; it logically follows on and complements the prose dedication of the volume to James Butler, Duke of Ormonde, and it frames Dryden's translation of Chaucer's Knight's Tale. Dryden writes Chaucer into the opening lines of the panegyric, and out of the verse that directly follows Dryden fashions an elaborate compliment for the duchess, a metempsychosis from Chaucer's world to his own, an evocation of ancient and modern love and chivalry, devotion, and aristocratic ardour:

> O true *Plantagenet,* O Race Divine,
> (For Beauty still is fatal to the Line),
> Had *Chaucer* liv'd that Angel-Face to view,
> Sure he had drawn his *Emily* from You.
> Or had You liv'd, to judge the doubtful Right,
> Your Noble *Palamon* had been the Knight:
> And Conqu'ring *Theseus* from his Side had sent
> Your Gen'rous Lord, to guide the *Theban* Government.

('To the Dutchess of Ormond', ll. 30–7)

The interweaving of Chaucerian materials suggests a certain degree of design in the order of materials at the opening of *Fables*; but it is not clear why the poem to Driden of Chesterton should follow directly on 'Palamon and Arcite' or precede the first of the translations from *Metamorphoses*, 'Meleager and Atalanta'. There is of course more to be said about the design of the collection and the sense of structure and poetics conveyed by Dryden's Preface, but I want to begin with some observations on 'To my Honour'd Kinsman' because its qualities make the poem seem the very emblem of Dryden's late style, perhaps in ways that the poet intended— for he called the verse 'a Memorial of my own Principles to all Posterity'[8]—and in ways that he may not have consciously designed.

That the poem itself has something of a design, that Dryden was loosely indebted to or thinking about Jonson or Herrick, perhaps Marvell, and their classical models, as he composed this celebration of country life is as clear as the verse's topicality or its broad political

---

[8] *Letters*, p. 120.

argument.[9] None of this is in doubt, and suggests nothing to distinguish this poem from Dryden's earlier verse epistles or indeed his earlier verse. Nor do the topics and themes themselves surprise. The poem's hints of Jacobitism, its endorsement of a 'blue-waters' policy, the strenuous patriotism, the assertion of the poet's elevation above the partisan fray—all of this is familiar and transparent. Maybe Dryden's responsiveness to nature—and he seems utterly indifferent to this subject for most of his career—strikes a new note; but if so, it is singular for the 1690s since there is little else from the decade that suggests a feeling for nature. Nor is the misogyny, or the poem's veiled and not so veiled satire, or the fluent handling of scriptural and classical analogy something that would have struck Dryden's contemporaries as peculiar, or distinctive of his late writing, had anyone bothered to think about Dryden's post-revolutionary writing as a whole, or indeed to wonder at its inflection by age or fortune or principle. And yet there is something to pause over here, not in the poem's expected work, but in the surprises it holds.

The deep gravitational forces in 'To my Honour'd Kinsman' are the poem's simplest surprise. Cast in a literary mode given to projection, extension, and the celebration of reproductive continuity, the poem seems caught in a gravitational force field: the principal verbs are 'slide', 'encumber', 'dwindle', 'wander', and 'stray'; the directional vectors are downward; and everywhere the poem seems to discover diminution and exhaustion, weariness and decay. The culmination of the poem is not chaste fecundity or the celebration of futurity, but the dissolution of the human frame. Of course the confirmed bachelorhood of cousin Driden did not easily yield to images of reproductive plenty, but nothing in the genre demanded the condemnation of marriage as a snare, or the Marvellian refiguring of perfection in paradise as the single life. Even Marvell understood that the country house poem best figures paradise through the promise of futurity. What the conventions of the country house poem seem to demand, Dryden takes peculiar care to deny, as if working in and through the genre excited the particular pleasures of

---

[9] For an analysis of the politics of 'To my Honour'd Kinsman', see Elizabeth Duthie, ' "A Memorial of My Own Principles": Dryden's "To My Honour'd Kinsman" ', *ELH* 47 (1980) 682–704; J. A. Levine, 'John Dryden's Epistle to John Driden', *Journal of English and Germanic Philology*, 63 (1964) 450–74; and the contribution to the present volume by Cedric D. Reverand II.

disappointment. Indeed what emerges through Dryden's handling of the genre is an insistent pattern of counterpointing through denial: no great house, no classless embrace between the lord of the manor and the rural poor, no feasting, indeed no food, and no reproduction. The hunt at Chesterton produces nothing for the table; it yields only the pleasure of diminished expectations. Everywhere on this estate and in this verse death stalks his prey: in the sheepfold, on the plain, in the doctor's care, in the apothecary's shop, on the foreign battlefield, in the hollow victories of Alexander and Hannibal, and, perhaps most surprisingly, in the triplet that closes the poem, where the human frame is consigned to dust. From here Dryden wrests the conventional celebration of the eternity of verse, but it is the weight of the poem's embrace of death that can be felt in these figures of dust and dissolution.

Nor have we mentioned the structure of the poem, its proportions, and its manner of counterpointing conventional themes with digressive motions. The praise of the countryside and the topics of rural biography are familiar enough: Driden is first imagined as country Justice of the Peace, then as a generous patron to locals and relatives, and next as sporting gentleman; his broader embrace of public welfare is represented through his independence as a Member of Parliament; and a genealogy of the Dryden family near the close of the poem discovers in the cousins' shared ancestry a model for the public integrity of both poet and parliamentarian. What could be more conventional and less surprising? But this account fails to mention that nearly half the verse is occupied with materials that fall outside generic convention and panegyric commonplace. The praise of the solitary life turns into a diatribe against marriage and women; the pleasures of rural sport are fashioned into a satire against doctors and apothecaries; and the praise of political independence occasions an attack on William III's land war in Europe.

In each instance, it is possible to discern a hinge joining digression and praise, but these digressions serve less to expand the conventional topics than to darken their implication. Praise for the integrity of the single life might just allow caution against the insecurity of fate; but failing marriage and offspring, the future of the line would be hard to secure. Health and sport might well be contrasted with luxury and ease, but Dryden uses the hunt first to conjure the vanity of human life, then to invoke the theory of historical decay, and finally to depict the partnership of physician and apothecary in the prescription of suffering and the business of death. And while the praise of patriotism might include themes of martial daring, the digression on the land wars yields to a meditation on wary mortality, on belatedness and the uncertainty of fortune. Even in this schematic account we might suppose that digression serves to balance and generalize, but in fact these digressions seem harsh and pointed and unusually detailed. Rather than underpin the whole, they burden the verse with extraneous material that wanders away from topics at hand to suggest a poet at work on private matter. In his Dedication of the *Aeneis* (1697) Dryden imagined Virgil writing his own concerns into his epic poem, honouring the memory of local patrons in the funeral games, and figuring those who had 'disoblig'd' him as the men and families who lost the prizes in Book V.[10] Whether or not Virgil composed in this manner, there is no doubt that Dryden translated Virgil with such a model in mind, and that his own poetry in the 1690s was fashioned for such address. The allegorical mode of *Absalom and Achitophel* (1681) offered spectacular opportunities for such writing, but Dryden made this Horatian epistle work in a similar manner. Not that Dryden failed to distinguish between allegory and epistle, but rather that in his late writing he used the occasions of his verse, and in particular his poetry's digressive manner, across every genre, as a way of indulging private dramas and of blurring personal and public occasions. Indeed, the line that distinguishes the personal from the public had deteriorated to such a point that digression, even a kind of carelessness, has begun to hold sway over Dryden's earlier and quite powerful sense of design and propriety.

And the private drama of these years was to be discovered not only in the settling of personal scores—in smuggling Luke Milbourne or

---

[10] See *Works*, v. 282–3, 'And I could not but take notice, when I translated it, of some Favourite Families to which he gives the Victory, and awards the Prizes, in the Person of his Heroe, at the Funeral Games which were Celebrated in Honour of Anchises.... I likewise either found or form'd an Image to my self of the contrary kind; that those who lost the Prizes, were such as had disoblig'd the Poet, or were in disgrace with Augustus, or Enemies to Maecenas: And this was the Poetical Revenge he took. For *genus irritabile Vatum*, as Horace says. When a Poet is thoroughly provok'd, he will do himself justice, however dear it cost him, *Animamque, in Vulnere ponit*. I think these are not bare Imaginations of my own, though I find no trace of them in the Commentatours: But one Poet may judge of another by himself.'

Sir Richard Blackmore into poetry dedicated to Horatian solitude and parliamentarian integrity—but as importantly in those gravitational force fields of dissolution and decay. What Dryden seems to be yielding to in this verse are forces deforming and undoing formal structures and physical bodies. The pressures of such digression are quite palpable in 'To my Honour'd Kinsman', and they are equally striking in 'To Her Grace the Dutchess of Ormond', the verse panegyric that opens *Fables*. The poem bears an obvious and complementary relation to the prose Dedication of *Fables* to the Duke of Ormonde. Both are concerned with integrity and estate, with the privileges of aristocratic succession and the imperatives of lineal descent, and both I think are shadowed by a sense of the dangers and immanence of dissolution. In the Dedication endangered privilege is narrated by Dryden's little essay on gold and iron (*Poems*, iv. 1440), by his account of the duke's captivity which serves at once to compliment Ormonde's selfless generosity (a fitting theme for this client to elaborate) and to suggest the presence of suffering and misfortune (*Poems*, iv. 1442–3), and by the memory of untimely death. The Dedication opens as Dryden recalls his earlier commemoration of Thomas, Earl of Ossory (*Absalom and Achitophel*, ll. 830–59), and it closes with a figure of that same 'untimely Death of your Great Father [brought] into fresh remembrance', now compounded with a Virgilian tribute to Ossory that links his death with the vision of failed succession. Dryden's long patronage association with the Ormonde family surely rationalizes the presence of the Earl of Ossory in the Dedication, though the citation from Virgil, *Ostendunt terris hunc tantum fata, nec ultra | Esse sinunt* (in Dryden's translation, 'This youth (the blissful vision of a day) | Shall just be shown on earth, and snatch'd away' (vi. 1202–3)), which Dryden had earlier applied to Ossory, certainly darkens the mood of the tribute.[11] Yet more difficult to explain are the ways absence and disease darken the celebration of the duchess in the ode.

[11] The lines in Virgil refer specifically to Marcellus, Augustus' nephew and adopted son, who died an untimely death fighting for Rome; see Dryden's translation, vi. 1200–3: 'Seek not to know (the Ghost reply'd with Tears) | The Sorrows of thy Sons, in future Years...'. According to R. G. Austin, *Aeneidos, Liber Sextus* (Oxford, 1977), n. 268, Marcellus' 'early death in 23 BC shattered dynastic plans'. They might put us in mind as well of Dryden's earlier allusion to the death of youthful promise and hope for lineal succession in the elegy for Oldham ('farewel thou young, | But ah too short, *Marcellus* of our Tongue'). Both reinforce our sense that Dryden deeply shades the tribute to the Ormondes with the failure of lineal descent.

We sometimes fail to remember that many of the topics of such celebratory verse as Dryden's poem to his cousin or to the Duchess of Ormonde are simply the poet's choice. Of course the conventions of epideictic verse can be felt in all of Dryden's celebrations, but the merely topical and incidental matters of these poems are very much at his discretion. The opening forty lines of the poem to the Duchess of Ormonde announce the themes of aristocratic genealogy and the transmigration of souls: from Geoffrey Chaucer to John Dryden, and from Chaucer's Emily to Mary, Duchess of Ormonde. These themes are linked back to the celebration of family and estate in the Dedication, and they project forward into the verse of Chaucer that is placed after the poem to the Duchess of Ormonde: poetry and patronage are thus tied together in imaginative community. But what Dryden does in the rest of the poem does not have this topical and literary logic. At line 40 he begins to narrate what feels like the 'occasion' of the poem, the duchess's triumphal entry into Ireland and the ancestral seat of the Ormondes. If the poem were indeed occasional or commemorative, then the episode that occupies the centre of this verse might seem to have a rationale, but what Dryden makes of entry and retreat are not only triumph but also danger and seclusion. The brilliant progress of the duchess is interrupted and shrouded by illness, and when illness is removed, Dryden conducts an anatomy that allows him to expatiate on the very theme he would seem to have banished: 'Now past the Danger, let the Learn'd begin | Th' Enquiry, where Disease could enter in' (ll. 111–12). What the anatomy discovers is that the very material from which the duchess is wrought is the point of her vulnerability. The anatomy allows Dryden to cast a quarter of the poem in shadows near to mourning, indeed to imagine that what had begun as panegyric might well have ended as epitaph, 'Ev'n this had been Your Elegy, which now | Is offer'd for Your Health, the Table of my Vow' (ll. 129–30).

What is puzzling about this episode is its length, its gratuitousness, and the uses to which Dryden puts mortality. Nothing in the letters we have of the Ormondes during the 1690s mentions near-fatal illness,[12] nor does Dryden willingly leave the shadows into

[12] Though see Historical Manuscripts Commission, *Calendar of the Manuscripts of the Marquess of Ormonde*, viii, pp. xii–xxxiii, and especially p. xxx: 'Her journey [to Ireland] had been attended by more than one contretemps: delay in obtaining the man-of-war in

which he has cast the duchess. The poem's climax is the invocation of the duchess as that 'precious Mould, | Which all the future *Ormonds* was to hold' (ll. 142–3). But that image itself, oddly cast into the past tense (as if promise has already become failure), is boldly undercut, for the penultimate stanza, flush with admiration of genealogy and beauty, yields to absence and widowed tears and a poignant reminder of the very thing which this Penelope has failed to provide her Odysseus, and for which Dido yearns:

> All is Your Lord's alone; ev'n absent, He
> Employs the Care of Chaste Penelope.
> For him You waste in Tears Your Widow'd Hours,
> For him Your curious Needle paints the Flow'rs:
> Such Works of Old Imperial Dames were taught;
> Such for *Ascanius*, fair *Elisa* wrought.   (ll. 157–62)

A stanza that begins with admiration for chastity and constancy closes with the duchess as Aeneas' Dido. First the duke had mourned his loss like the 'young Vespasian' (l. 125), now the duchess is widowed by his absence, then the duchess becomes the weaving Penelope, and finally she is like Dido who weaves not for the lover who abandoned her, but for Ascanius, his son. Whatever else is narrated by this stanza, absence and longing, even betrayal, are its striking themes. The last stanza speaks of futurity, but futurity as debt, and a debt, the poem makes clear, as yet unpaid: 'You owe Your *Ormond* nothing but a Son: | To fill in future Times his Father's Place' (ll. 166–7).

What the complex geographies and chronologies of this poem make clear are distance and deferral. The poem's arrivals and departures are moments of attenuation and loneliness: the duchess arrives in Ireland without her lord; she recovers from near-fatal disease, but only to waste herself in tears; she preserves honour and is an exemplar of fortitude, but the references to Penelope and Dido underscore the absence of a male heir, an issue most poignant and most prominent in this celebration of an aristocratic family and

---

which she crossed, her own illness and finally a west wind which detained her for a fortnight at the waterside and for ten days on board ship.' Thomas D'Urfey, in his dedication of *The Comicall History of Don Quixote*, pt. 1 (London, 1694), sig. A1ᵛ, notes Ormonde's frequent absences from the duchess and her need for heavenly protection against 'the expected Hour of Trouble'.

fortune which takes its cue from the prose Dedication to the duke, where Dryden enumerates the three generations of Ormonde males: the 'excellent Grandfather', the 'Heroick Father', and the present duke himself. The Dedication announces genealogy and plays a series of variations on that theme whose text is the sanctity of lineal descent, but whose subtext is the contrast between this legitimate (but also fragile) aristocratic line and the broken promise of Stuart kingship. And now patrimony and succession have taken on even greater significance, for Dryden argues lineal descent as the integral and distinguishing feature of both landed and literary estate. That theme is beautifully played out in the Preface, which opens as Dryden toys with an image of the estate that he has built and proceeds through a set of figures of literary lineage and transmigration. Whether consciously or not, a host of values has come to inhabit lineal descent, and its pressure can be felt throughout the poem to the Duchess of Ormonde, especially in its failures and deformations.

In the middle of this poem the digression on the duchess's illness has remade a story that began as triumph and celebration into a narrative of frailty and failure. The externals may just match particulars of the Ormondes' lives and travels in the 1690s,[13] but why Dryden chose them for this panegyric is difficult to know. And here I would suggest that digression in this poem tells a story whose content and whose deforming of narrative line are similar to those in 'To my Honour'd Kinsman', and that both poems tell us of the flood of Dryden's own feelings, of the themes and preoccupations that have taken possession of the poet and have at various points been released by the mechanism of digression. Once digression has begun, Dryden allows his own apprehensions to subsume and transform the plot and the drama of the work under construction. The digressive materials assume outsized proportion within the finished work, and they manage simultaneously to stay proximate and to wander distantly from the forms and motives announced by the primary composition.

---

[13] See e.g. the duchess's letter to Benjamin Portlock (Historical Manuscripts Commission, *Calendar of the Manuscripts of the Marquess of Ormonde*, viii. 79), where she pines for word from the duke: 'Here are two packets come in to-night and a Sunday last, but not one letter from my Lord. Pray desire him to do me the favour but to write two words once in four posts, and I am satisfied.'

It would be too simple to say that Dryden is writing his own story whatever the occasion, that what is most on his mind crowds into and crowds out the work at hand. Such an account misleads because it gets the psychology wrong; when Dryden means to speak in his own person, and he does throughout his career, he has no trouble announcing his presence. But what happens in these poems is emblematic of Dryden's late writing when prose and poetry have become considerably looser in structure, more porous in character, and when the very looseness itself enables Dryden to house a group of related themes and materials in a diversity of works. The digressive impulse was hardly a new element of Dryden's style, but in his late work digression is an element transformed by experience, both internal and incidental, that in its turn transforms and makes at once casual and mysterious the whole of his late writing.

No work better exemplifies the late prose than Dryden's Preface to the collection of verse that we have been examining. While informal and digressive, the Preface exhibits a superb economy, and everywhere we feel the imprint of Dryden's mastery in its sentences. Writing of *Don Sebastian* in 1689, Dryden confessed to a certain excess; his long absence from the theatre meant that 1,200 lines had to be cut when preparing the play for the stage.[14] In the Preface to *Fables* not a sentence suggests the hand of revision. Yet the essay begins with the figure of miscalculation and loose improvisation. Surely that figure derived from Dryden's understanding of how exactly the prose performed the work at hand and how beautifully the theme of casual improvisation prepares the reader for the aesthetic of the collection that follows, in which the fragmentary and the digressive have such significant force:

'Tis with a Poet, as with a Man who designs to build, and is very exact, as he supposes, in casting up the Cost beforehand: But, generally speaking, he is mistaken in his Account, and reckons short of the Expence he first intended: He alters his Mind as the Work proceeds, and will have this or that Convenience more, of which he had not thought when he began. So has it hapned to me; I have built a House, where I intended but a Lodge: Yet with better Success than a certain Nobleman, who beginning with a Dog-kennel, never liv'd to finish the Palace he contriv'd. (*Poems*, iv. 1444)

[14] *Works*, xv. 66: 'Whatever fault I next commit, rest assur'd it shall not be that of too much length: Above twelve hunder'd lines have been cut off from this Tragedy, since it was first deliver'd to the Actors.'

Whatever else the images of literal and literary housing provide—and they allow Dryden his wonted and sly pleasures of topicality—they announce the themes both of impermanence and shelter and suggest that writing may provide the best place for poets to live. But even as the metaphor constructs, it takes away, for Dryden records here his understanding that the shelter of writing—of aristocratic patronage and public office—may be as transient as mere lodges or unfinished palaces.

With that uncertain emblem Dryden begins and then outlines the methods by which he has built. These seem logical enough at first—the translation of Book I of Homer's *Iliad* leads him to the twelfth book of Ovid's *Metamorphoses*, which contains elements of Homer's epic and compels him to translate the speeches of Ajax and Ulysses 'lying next in [my] way' (*Poems*, iv. 1444). But soon theme and topic have given way simply to pleasure, for Dryden writes that he next translated purely on the compulsion of desire: 'I was so taken with the former Part of the Fifteenth Book, (which is the Master-piece of the whole *Metamorphoses*) that I enjoyn'd my self the pleasing Task of rendering it into *English*' (*Poems*, iv. 1444–5). And literary pleasure then allows Dryden to proceed by association, 'There occur'd to me the Hunting of the Boar, *Cinyras* and *Myrrha*, the good-natur'd Story of *Baucis* and *Philemon*, with the rest' (*Poems*, iv. 1445). From Ovid Dryden is led to Chaucer, but by way of a digression on literary genealogy that suggests paths of literary affiliation and trans-migration and rationalizes the abundance of Chaucer in this collec-tion: the English poetic soul has migrated from Chaucer to Spenser, from Spenser to Milton; from Fairfax to Waller; and surely from Chaucer directly to this poet, literary genealogist, and translator. Now Dryden winds back, self-consciously picking up the thread of translation and composition, and, frequently over the rest of the Preface, calls himself away from his digressive moves: 'But to return . . . it came into my mind . . . In the mean time . . . I resume the Thrid of my Discourse . . .' (*Poems*, iv. 1445–7). At one point, perhaps conscious of the repeated moves and asides, Dryden inter-rupts a digression to observe that 'the Nature of a Preface is ram-bling, never wholly out of the Way, nor in it. This I have learn'd from the Practice of honest *Montaign*' (*Poems*, iv. 1450).

Whatever else Dryden may have learned from Montaigne, he needed no instruction on the digressive nature of the literary preface, and his performance here is masterly, a weaving together of literary history and appreciation, theories of poetry and translation, and, as always, the subtle and at times not so subtle gestures of personal vindication. Digression allowed Dryden at once to form a model for the collection that he had assembled, and to house in that introduction an assortment of its themes and preoccupations. The Preface both calls attention to the poetics of digression—its associative logic, its free, almost languid, sense of design, and the certainty that all thoughts are by some associative power connected—and acts on those principles. At one point Dryden seeks shelter in an analogy he draws between himself and an

old Gentleman, who mounting on Horseback before some Ladies, when I was present, got up somewhat heavily, but desir'd of the Fair Spectators, that they would count Fourscore and eight before they judg'd him. By the Mercy of God, I am already come within Twenty Years of his Number, a Cripple in my Limbs, but what Decays are in my Mind, the Reader must determine. (*Poems*, iv. 1446).

Witness to and subject of this scene, Dryden stands within and outside his own writing, objectively observing the character of his work but also caught within its pleasures and compulsions. The pleasures are amply demonstrated by Dryden's appreciation for the poets he translates; the compulsions are just as clear in digressions and diversions of the Preface. As Dryden moves towards the end of the essay, repeatedly admiring the depth of learning and the originality of the poets he translates, he suddenly turns to his own circumstance, 'As a corollary to this Preface, in which I have done Justice to others, I owe somewhat to my self: not that I think it worth my time to enter the Lists with one *M*——, or one *B*——, but barely to take notice, that such Men there are who have written scurrilously against me without any Provocation' (*Poems*, iv. 1461).

The bare notice-taking occupies the final hundred lines of the Preface, where Luke Milbourne and Sir Richard Blackmore are treated with Dryden's particular brand of contempt and feigned indifference. The veiling of identity by initial letters only heightens the provocation, for such letters hid nothing from view; the literary community knew very well of Milbourne's attack on Dryden's *Virgil*, of Milbourne's own translation of the *Georgics*, and of Blackmore's *Prince Arthur* with its scandalous portrait of Dryden as Laurus,

'An old, revolted, unbelieving Bard, | Who throng'd, and shov'd, and prest, and would be heard. | Distinguish'd by his louder craving Tone, | So well to all the Muses Patrons known, | He did the Voice of modest Poets drown.'[15] That Dryden saw the demolition of Milbourne and Blackmore as a corollary to his rehabilitation of Chaucer and consummate appreciations of Homer and Ovid might seem puzzling, but Dryden insists on its integrity. And here we can see how much Dryden's model of exposition has loosened from those brilliant prefaces he had written for *Absalom and Achitophel* and *The Medall*, or for *Religio Laici* and *The Hind and the Panther*.

From the beginning, Dryden used the preface both to lay out a sense of design and to indulge in strategic raids. He does so superbly in the prefaces to his Exclusion Crisis poems, but the conclusion to the Preface to *Fables* is more than a strategic raid. That the long and self-indulgent sentences of the Preface, the weaving together of literary portraits and poetics, should culminate in this extended attack suggests at the very least a loosening sense of structures and proprieties. What Dryden had once administered quickly and subtly— a half-sentence in the Preface to *Religio Laici* ('They may think themselves to be too roughly handled in this Paper; but I who know best how far I could have gone on this Subject, must be bold to tell them they are spar'd . . .');[16] a sentence in the Preface to *Absalom and Achitophel* ('They, who can Criticize so weakly, as to imagine I have done my Worst, may be Convinc'd, at their own Cost, that I can write Severely, with more ease, than I can Gently');[17] a few lines in the Preface to *The Medall* ('I have one onely favour to desire of you at parting, that when you think of answering this Poem, you wou'd employ the same Pens against it, who had combated with so much success against *Absalom and Achitophel*: for then you may assure your selves of a clear Victory, without the least reply')[18]—has now blossomed into a coda, a 'Corollary' to the Preface itself, but instead of admiring the ancients, Dryden now responds to his critics:

I contemn him [Milbourne] too much to enter into Competition with him. His own Translations of *Virgil* have answer'd his Criticisms on mine. If (as they say, he has declar'd in Print) he prefers the Version of *Ogilby* to mine, the World has made him the same Compliment: For 'tis agreed on

---

[15] Sir Richard Blackmore, *Prince Arthur* (London, 1695), p. 167.   [16] *Works*, ii. 108.
[17] *Works*, ii. 3.   [18] *Works*, ii. 411.

all hands, that he writes even below *Ogilby*: That, you will say, is not easily to be done; but what cannot *M*—— bring about? I am satisfy'd however, that while he and I live together, I shall not be thought the worst Poet of the Age. It looks as if I had desir'd him under-hand to write so ill against me: But upon my honest Word I have not brib'd him to do me this Service, and am wholly guiltless of his Pamphlet. 'Tis true I should be glad, if I could persuade him to continue his good Offices, and write such another Critique on any thing of mine: For I find by Experience he has a great Stroke with the Reader, when he condemns any of my Poems to make the World have a better opinion of them. . . . As for the City Bard, or Knight Physician . . . I will deal the more civilly with his two Poems, because nothing ill is to be spoken of the Dead. (*Poems*, iv. 1461–2)

Part of what we should register is the intricacy of moves, the complex dance of diminution and deferral in these sentences. The actions here seem all slights and denials; yet what emerges over the course of Dryden's engagement with Milbourne and Blackmore is more than humiliation. The coda beautifully illustrates how Dryden's management of ironies allows him at once to ventriloquize stupidity, to imply that the objects of his satiric attack are incapable of comprehending his slightest ironic move, and all the while to wink the reader into complicity with his satiric, even self-congratulatory strategies. And to the engagement with Milbourne and Blackmore, Dryden adds an address to Jeremy Collier, who had attacked him in the *Short View of the Immorality, and Profaneness of the English Stage* (1698).[19] Collier's presence in the coda is a slight disturbance, for the address to Collier begins with Dryden allowing the justness of Collier's attack and in a tone that suggests valediction, a final adjustment of the balance sheets: 'in many Things he has tax'd me justly; and I have pleaded Guilty. . . . It becomes me not to draw my Pen in the Defence of a bad Cause, when I have so often drawn it for a good one' (*Poems*, iv. 1462). But he cannot leave well enough alone; this model of recantation and leave-taking swerves back into satiric attack. From the figure of judicious moral critic, Dryden turns Collier into a fool who 'is too much given to Horse-play in his Raillery; and comes to Battel, like a Dictatour from the Plough' (*Poems*, iv. 1462); his manners are rude and he has exaggerated the

---

[19] In *A Short View of the Immorality, and Profaneness of the English Stage* (London, 1698), Collier had attacked, among others, Dryden's *Don Sebastian*, the 'Discourse Concerning the Original and Progress of Satire', *Love Triumphant*, *Cleomenes*, and *Amphitryon*.

condition of contemporary morals, pushing his case too far, 'like the Prince of *Condé* at the Battel of *Senneph*: From Immoral Plays, to No Plays' (*Poems*, iv. 1463). Finally, though Dryden claims to have finished with his critics, we are back in their midst: 'As for the rest of those who have written against me, they are such Scoundrels, that they deserve not the least Notice to be taken of them. *B*— and *M*— are only distinguish'd from the Crowd, by being remember'd to their Infamy' (*Poems*, iv. 1463). And with a tag from Horace's *Satires*, Dryden takes his leave of these fools.

It is tempting to think that the coda has simply gone astray, that Dryden lost control over his materials once he wandered into the temptation of arraigning villains and scoundrels, and perhaps this is pretty much what happened. But the odd analogy between Collier and the Prince of Condé complicates the close of the Preface, suggesting as well the mood of brooding battle. While Dryden may have let down his guard in the body of the Preface, in the coda he has rearmed. But if Collier is the Prince of Condé, for the moment Dryden has become the Prince of Orange. Perhaps identifying himself with the defeat of French aggression contains an element of Dryden's elaborate literary and civic patriotism in this essay—ever 'studious to promote the Honour of my Native Country' (*Poems*, iv. 1445)—but we ought also to recognize that the Prince of Orange at the battle of Seneffe turned out to be William III. This may be a momentary lapse, but it is tempting to think that Dryden wills a return, however brief, to the site of public authority he had so long occupied. Yet he closes not on this high civic note; the skirmishes of literary encounter recall his attention, for he would at once deny his enemies their identity and assure their fame: 'As for the rest of those who have written against me, they are such Scoundrels, that they deserve not the least Notice to be taken of them. *B*— and *M*— are only distinguish'd from the Crowd, by being remember'd to their Infamy' (*Poems*, iv. 1463)

On the very next page of *Fables*, Dryden turns up as Chaucer to the Duchess of Ormonde's Emily:

> Madam,
> The Bard who first adorn'd our Native Tongue
> Tun'd to his *British* Lyre this ancient Song:
> Which *Homer* might without a Blush reherse,
> And leaves a doubtful Palm to *Virgil*'s Verse:

He match'd their Beauties, where they most excell;
Of Love sung better, and of Arms as well.
  Vouchsafe, Illustrious *Ormond*, to behold
What Pow'r the Charms of Beauty had of old;
Nor wonder if such Deeds of Arms were done,
Inspir'd by two fair Eyes, that sparkled like your own.
('To the Dutchess of Ormond', ll. 1–10)

Perhaps the proximity of Milbourne and Blackmore to Dryden, Chaucer, and Virgil is adventitious, but it suggests how all the materials in this collection—Dedication, Preface, complimentary ode, translation, and verse epistle—are part of a more or less continuous script underwritten by Dryden's preoccupations—with mortality and immortality, with those whom he has been forced to acknowledge as his contemporaries and with those to whom he would assimilate the body of his work—and with the ways in which chance seems now to govern so much in this life, govern even the composition and disposition of this collection of verse.

We have followed a group of themes and preoccupations in the Dedication and Preface to *Fables* and in the poems to the Duchess of Ormonde and John Driden of Chesterton. I want finally to say something of the whole, which seems at once to raise and to disappoint expectations for order and design. Some of those expectations derive from our own critical practices, from notions of organic wholeness and strategic design, but Dryden himself suggests both order and imaginative coherence in his enterprise: he began with Homer and pursued heroic themes through Ovid and Chaucer; he turned to Boccaccio because the Italian was a contemporary of Chaucer and wrote in similar modes, and at some point he added original verse to the collection of translations. The Preface allows an order of chronology and mode, from antiquity to the present, from epic to romance.

But Dryden mixes other motives into this account; he insists on the associative and the imaginative in his project and, repeatedly, on the merely random connections among the threads of discourse which he seems casually to layer over one another. The collection may have begun with epic plans, but soon enough those ambitions gave way to less orderly impulses. What the Preface seems most to endorse is design by improvisation; whatever the poet may have thought of the enterprise before he began, the work contained its

325

own logic, suggested its own procedures. We are, if not in the grip, then in the vicinity of something like an organic account of the whole; and yet when we look at the order in which *Fables* was constituted as a published volume, a different plan seems to emerge.[20] The folio begins not with Homer and epic enterprise but with original verse, then with Chaucer and romance; the translation of Homer that Dryden claims as the originary event for the collection is tucked away between two very unheroic pieces— Ovid's tale of incest, 'Cinyras and Myrrha', and Chaucer's 'The Cock and the Fox'. The translations originally inspired by the rendering of Homer—Ovid's *Metamorphoses*, Books XIII and XV—are now separated from one another and from Homer. If we track Dryden's account of the origin of these translations against their published order, we quickly discover that the Preface does not describe the published volume. We cannot be certain whose hand was uppermost in the design of the published volume, Dryden's or Tonson's, but we might wonder if the volume has any design at all.

Despite repeated critical effort to discern its expression of order and coherence, what the *Fables* most expresses is its miscellaneousness. And miscellany is what Dryden and his publisher Jacob Tonson had been marketing since 1684 when they collaborated in the production of *Miscellany Poems*.[21] That collection was followed by several others, all of them mixing classical translation with original poetry. Nor were Dryden and Tonson alone in such a venture; their volumes competed with a number of other anthologies and miscellanies. Indeed, the last decades of the century witnessed a minor publishing boom in the verse miscellany, and that commercial and cultural order forms one of the contexts in which

---

[20] The idea that Dryden made argumentative or expressive use of the order of *Fables* is fundamentally put in doubt because we have no certain way of knowing whether it was Dryden or his publisher Jacob Tonson who determined the sequence of selections in the volume published in 1700. This has not, however, stopped a number of scholars from speculating about this intriguing question; see e.g. Cedric D. Reverand II, *Dryden's Final Poetic Mode: The 'Fables'* (Philadelphia, Pa., 1988); Judith Sloman, *Dryden: The Poetics of Translation* (Toronto, 1985); James Garrison, 'The Universe of Dryden's *Fables*', *Studies in English Literature*, 21 (1981) 409–23; and Earl Miner, *Dryden's Poetry* (Bloomington, Ind., 1967), ch. 8.

[21] On the seventeenth-century miscellany, see Barbara M. Benedict, *Making the Modern Reader: Cultural Mediation in Early Modern Literary Anthologies* (Princeton, NJ, 1996); the standard reference work is Arthur E. Case, *A Bibliography of English Poetical Miscellanies, 1521–1750* (Oxford, 1935).

Fables ought to be located. David Bywaters has argued that Dryden had thematic, indeed ideological, work to perform through the very disparateness of *Fables*, that the concourse of different voices from disparate moments expressed both an aesthetic and an argument: the random and timeless disposition of *Fables* allowed Dryden to take his own casual, but certain, position among ancient and modern, classical and vernacular voices.[22] Surely that is so; but I would also urge that the casual and the fragmentary character of the miscellany had a deep psychological force, that what *Fables* allowed, beyond self-presentation, was the luxury of the fragmentary and the dissolutive. These translations are pieces of other and larger wholes: selections from Ovid, a book of the *Iliad*, a scattering of Boccaccio. Could it be that Dryden celebrates in their assembly not a new order, but no order at all?

That a career devoted, from its beginnings, to the articulation of structure, and especially the structure of argument, should close in the fragmentary and overlapping modes of *Fables* has its own kind of logic. We have been exploring some of the thematic and psychological, even ideological, forces that might have compelled Dryden towards that logic: a sense of the decomposition of the body, of abandonment in public and political life, and a yielding to the notion of the chance disposition and dissolution of the material world. I want to add one more component to this discussion, something we might call the aesthetics of the late style. In a suggestive essay from some twenty years ago, Rudolf Arnheim proposed that the late style in the career of visual artists is often defined by a loosening of formal structures and an increasing attention to timbre and colour; the examples of late Titian, Rembrandt, and Monet come easily to mind.[23] Perhaps too the late style in Beethoven's career with its heavy chromaticism and its abandonment of familiar structural devices suggests a similar arc of development, a discarding of the forms and formal challenges worked through at earlier stages of the career and a yielding to the elements of the medium itself, to colour and sound. I want to suggest something like this trajectory for Dryden's writing in his last decade, that, in addition to the other

[22] David Bywaters, *Dryden in Revolutionary England* (Berkeley and Los Angeles, 1991), pp. 124–9.
[23] Arnheim, 'On the Late Style of Life and Art', *Michigan Quarterly Review*, 17 (1978) 148–56.

forces at work on the forms and preoccupations of his writing, we might think that the vector of career itself was turning Dryden's style inward and ruminative. He had triumphed over all the formal challenges that a literary career in the late seventeenth century might offer: poetry and prose; the theatre and literary theory; ode, epistle, and panegyric; contemplative verse and party polemic; he had even met the challenge of epic in his translation of Virgil. And having so brilliantly practised the varieties, and solved the problems, of literary form in so many genres, the poems and prose Dryden wrote at the end of his life display an indifference to form itself. The structural drama of such verse as *Absalom and Achitophel* or the argumentative grip of prose like that which prefaces *Religio Laici* posed no further mystery or challenge. The allure now was to be discovered in the digressive and ruminative work of writing.

Dryden cited with some pleasure the approval with which *Fables* had been greeted—'The Ladies of the Town . . . like my last Book of Poems, better than any thing they have formerly seen of mine'[24]— but I suspect that *Fables* also offered more private pleasures: an awareness of the casual, the incomplete, and the fragmentary nature of projects and institutions, and the seductive lure of all the dissolutive forces a writer might dare to indulge. The wandering prose and digressive, darkened verse of *Fables* brilliantly exemplifies those forces. Could it be that digression was a form of delaying closure altogether, that rumination felt like a forestalling of inevitabilities and finalities? Dryden wrote in the Dedication to *Examen Poeticum* (1693) (prose filled with extravagant delays): 'I will not give my self the liberty of going farther; for 'tis so sweet to wander in a pleasing way, that I shou'd never arrive at my Journeys end' (*Works*, iv. 369). That journey's immediate end was the close of an essay that was in part a fishing expedition for patronage. Perhaps Dryden wrote also of a different kind of imaginative space that digression allowed, and of a different end that might be delayed by the fragmentary, the incomplete, and the digressive forms of his late prose and verse.

Those who have written on the last part of Dryden's career are fond of quoting the Chorus from *The Secular Masque* to suggest the brisk indifference with which the poet contemplated the end of his century and what he must have known would be the end of his life:

---

[24] *Letters*, p. 135.

"'Tis well an Old Age is out, | And time to begin a New.' But there are other voices in *The Secular Masque*, including Chronos' lament: 'Weary, weary of my weight, | Let me, let me drop my Freight, | And leave the World behind. | I could not bear | Another Year | The Load of Human-kind' (ll. 7–12). I would not want wholly to assimilate Dryden either to the Chorus or to Chronos, and I would call attention to the complexity of Chronos' last line, which leaves us in some doubt as to whether it is simply the condition of humanity that cannot be borne, or the intolerable burden of humans under which Chronos groans. The distinction is subtle, nor must we choose between these two senses, and if we would hear Dryden in these lines we might allow how likely it is that both meanings conveyed Dryden's experience in the spring of 1700. We must also remember that Dryden could ventriloquize celebration as well as a sense of the heaviness of being in the world. Both these moods, and more, are orchestrated in *Fables*, with its miscellany of feelings and voices, its occasional tags of order and progressiveness, and its powerful sense of randomness and disorder. In the words that Dryden interpolated at the end of the translation positioned at the close of *Fables*, Boccaccio's 'Cymon and Iphigenia', he wrote of public life:

> What should the People do, when left alone?
> The Governor, and Government are gone.
> The publick Wealth to Foreign Parts convey'd;
> Some Troops disbanded, and the rest unpaid.
> *Rhodes* is the Soveraign of the Sea no more;
> Their Ships unrigg'd, and spent their Naval Store;
> They neither could defend, nor can pursue,
> But grind their Teeth, and cast a helpless view.   (ll. 615–22)

Dryden's interpolation may not represent the final vision of *Fables*, but these lines powerfully express an apprehension of the disorder into which the whole is so likely at any moment to fall, a sense, that is, of the drift of all things towards dissolution.

13

EDITING, AUTHENTICITY, AND TRANSLATION: RE-PRESENTING DRYDEN'S POETRY IN 2000

DAVID HOPKINS

I begin with two quotations. The first is from James McLaverty's paper 'The Concept of Authorial Intention in Textual Criticism':

Whereas some works of art (painting and sculpture, for example) are particulars, instanced by one unreproducible individual, other works of art, most clearly music, are types, instanced by any number of tokens. Those works of art which are types may have scores from which 'performances' of the work can be realized. If we accept that literature should be classed with music as an art in which works can be composed in the mind, can have any number of instances, and can be performed (as plays are and as poems used to be) we can say that the editor's concern is with the score. The score represents the work, it is not identical with it.[1]

My second quotation is from George Steiner's introduction to *The Penguin Book of Modern Verse Translation*:

We translate perpetually—this is often overlooked—when we read a classic in our own tongue, a poem written in the sixteenth century or a

Versions of this chapter were given as papers to the Literature and Theory seminar at the University of Bristol and to the Restoration to Reform seminar at the University of Cambridge. Audience responses on both occasions helped me to refine and reformulate a number of points. I am grateful to my colleagues Professor Charles Martindale and Dr Tom Mason, and to Mr Eric Southworth of St Peter's College, Oxford, for valuable comments on an earlier draft.

[1] *The Library*, 6th ser., 6 (1984) 127.

novel published in 1780. We seek to recapture, to revitalize in our consciousness the meanings of words used as we no longer use them, of imaginings that have behind them a contour of history, of manners, of religious or philosophical presumptions radically different from ours. Anyone reading Donne or Jane Austen today, or almost any poem or fiction composed before 1915 (at about which date the old order seems to recede from the immediate grasp of our sensibility), is trying to re-create by exercise of the historical, linguistic response; he is, in the full sense, translating. As is the player who acts Shakespeare or Congreve, making that which was conceived in a society, in a style of feeling, in an expressive convention sharply different from that of the modern, actual, active to the touch of our mind and nerve.[2]

In what follows, I offer some reflections on the implications of these two passages in the light of my recent work on the Longman Annotated English Poets edition of *The Poems of John Dryden*.[3] In what ways, I shall ask, might producing a modernized, annotated edition of a seventeenth-century poet resemble the preparation of an edition of an old composer's scores, designed to help contemporary performers to convey the meaning, significance, and artistry of those scores to best advantage? What kinds of fidelity or authenticity might such an edition seek or hope to attain or promote? And in what ways might presenting an old poet's text be usefully likened to 'translating' that poet's text for modern readers, or enabling them to translate it for themselves?

Such analogies have obvious dangers, which must be frankly acknowledged from the start. There are, for example, self-evident problems involved in positing too exact a parallel between literary and musical meaning, indispensable as the concept is to both arts. And, given the recognition by both scholars and composers of the imperfect and approximate nature of musical notation, one must concede at least some truth to Joseph Kerman's observation that 'a text is a much less complete record of a work of art in music than it is

---

[2] *The Penguin Book of Modern Verse Translation*, ed. George Steiner (Harmondsworth, 1966), p. 24.

[3] Volumes I (1649–81) and II (1682–5), edited by Paul Hammond, were published in 1995. The remaining volumes are being edited jointly by Paul Hammond and myself. Volumes III (1686–93) and IV (1693–6) are in press and due to be published in 2000. I am indebted at various points in this essay to Professor Hammond's introduction to Volume I, and, more generally, to conversations and exchanges with Professor Hammond over several years.

in literature'.[4] Moreover, to liken reading an older English text to translation from a foreign language may be to underestimate the degree to which a foreign literary work will always perhaps (except in the case of a few truly bilingual individuals) be more removed from readers' affective and cognitive experience than one in their mother tongue. It might also underestimate the degree to which, in reading imaginative literature in English (present and past) as much as texts in foreign languages, one is constantly expanding one's existing linguistic resources to encompass terms, and the forms of feeling and perception which they embody and allow, for which one has no ready equivalent in one's existing verbal and conceptual stock.

But both analogies nevertheless seem worth pursuing, for several reasons. To compare poetic texts with musical scores will serve to remind us of the important areas of common ground shared by what used to be called 'the sister arts'—a valuable corrective at a time when much literary commentary seems more concerned to stress affinities between (or even the identity of) poetic and other kinds of non-artistic verbal discourse: political, philosophical, psychoanalytic, economic. Both analogies also draw attention to the inescapably *transactional* nature of any attempt to re-present and re-experience, in the present, a work of art from the past: the subtle process of negotiation, dialogue, and exchange, in which both parties (artist and audience) move towards one another from their own highly complex historical contingencies and imaginative worlds, and meet in a conceptual, experiential, and aesthetic middle ground, neither purely present nor purely past. F. R. Leavis once famously characterized the way in which 'you cannot point to [a] poem; it is "there" only in the re-creative response of individual minds to the black marks on the page'. A poem, this formulation suggests, does not achieve its full ontological status as a poem without the collaboration of its readers. Its effective mode of existence is not as an object 'out there', but as a 'place' in which minds can meet, and

---

[4] Joseph Kerman, *Musicology* (London, 1985), p. 187. On musical scores as no more than an 'approximation' of the composer's 'exact thoughts', see Aaron Copland, *Music and Imagination* (Cambridge, Mass., 1952), pp. 49–50. On the limited indications provided in literary texts on how they are to be 'voiced', see Eric Griffiths, *The Printed Voice of Victorian Poetry* (Oxford, 1989), pp. 1–96, esp. pp. 17–18.

imaginings can be communicated and shared.[5] Leavis's sentiments are echoed, *mutatis mutandis*, by the testimony of many musicians, and are given support and extension by recent thinkers in several disciplines who have attempted to describe the complex dialogic and interactive processes by which past artworks and cultural forms are deciphered, understood, experienced, and reimagined in the present.[6]

There are clearly many viable and instructive ways of presenting both literary texts and musical scores, running the full gamut from photographic facsimiles to various kinds of creative editorial reconstruction. As the literary scholar G. Thomas Tanselle has argued, 'no one critical text can be the best one from everyone's point of view or for all purposes'.[7] The different circumstances in which different authors' works (and sometimes different works by the same author) were composed, transmitted, circulated, published, and revised means that no single set of editorial procedures or methods is likely to be appropriate to every case. But, equally importantly, editions will differ according to the kinds of user whose needs they are designed to meet. A scholarly specialist in medieval music will come to an edition of a medieval mass or motet with quite different needs and expectations from those of a working singer or instrumentalist wishing to perform the piece with ease in a modern concert hall. A twentieth-century actor or educated general reader will have quite different expectations of a modern edition of a Renaissance play or poem from those of a specialist student of Jacobean printing-house practices and conventions, or of the manuscript culture in which much Renaissance poetry circulated.

Any modern re-presentation of a musical or literary work must therefore not only be scrupulously attentive to the sources in which that work was originally encoded but also to the ways in which the modern re-presentation will be received by its target audience, in circumstances very different from those of the work's first

---

[5] F. R. Leavis, *Nor Shall My Sword: Discourses on Pluralism, Compassion and Social Hope* (London, 1972), p. 62. The quotation is from a lecture originally published in 1962.

[6] For an incisive discussion, focused on Roman literature, see Charles Martindale, *Redeeming the Text: Latin Poetry and the Hermeneutics of Reception* (Cambridge, 1993). For discussion of some of the analogous problems involved in the performance of early music, see the items cited in n. 8 below.

[7] Tanselle, 'Historicism and Critical Editing', *Studies in Bibliography*, 39 (1986) 1–46, at p. 36.

appearance. In an article published in 1983, Professor Laurence Dreyfus[8] described what he saw as a central confusion in some of the thinking of the early music movement—the body of scholars and performers devoted to the revival of pre-classical music and historical performance practices. A major claim of early music, Dreyfus argued, was that to reconstruct the sound of a musical work's early performances would, by itself, achieve an authenticity and fidelity to the composer's intentions unattainable in performances deploying more modern instruments and performance styles. But the success of the best early music performances, Dreyfus maintained, was, in fact, more attributable to the defamiliarizing challenge which they presented to modern audiences' expectations than to any authenticity to which they might have laid claim. The discrepancy between the early musicians' stated objectives and the actual effects of their endeavours was, Dreyfus argued, at least partly attributable to their espousal of an objectivist philosophy which made them insufficiently aware of the cultural environment in which their quest for authenticity was being conducted. Like all self-proclaimed objectivists, Dreyfus argued, they had failed to 'take stock ... of their own historicity'.[9]

Similar dangers, I would suggest, are potentially inherent in some well-established forms of literary editing and editorial theory. Implicit in much twentieth-century textual scholarship is the assumption that to reproduce early texts in a form as close as possible to the earliest manuscripts or printed texts—purged only of corruptions, obvious errors, and purely typographical archaisms—will ensure that those texts contain a uniquely authentic record of their authors' intentions, and will thus form the most authoritative basis for any modern reading or interpretation of the work in question. But such assumptions can, in a way which in some respects resembles the

---

[8] Laurence Dreyfus, 'Early Music Defended against its Devotees: A Theory of Historical Performance in the Twentieth Century', *The Musical Quarterly*, 69 (1983) 297–322. For a general account of the early music movement, see Harry Haskell, *The Early Music Revival: A History* (London, 1988). For discussion of some of the practical and theoretical issues raised by period performance, see Joseph Kerman, 'The Historical Performance Movement', in *Musicology*, pp. 182–217; Nicholas Kenyon (ed.), *Authenticity and Early Music* (Oxford, 1988); Bernard D. Sherman, *Inside Early Music: Conversations with Performers* (New York and Oxford, 1997).

[9] 'Early Music', p. 301. On the increasing wariness within the early music movement about the very use of the term 'authenticity', see Sherman, *Inside Early Music*, pp. 7–8.

practice of the early musicians discussed by Dreyfus, fail to pay sufficient attention to the ways in which literary editions will be approached and understood by many of their potential users.

***

The distinction drawn by James McLaverty between the score or text and the musical or literary work which it represents was central to the thinking of F. W. Bateson during the period when he was establishing the Longman Annotated English Poets.[10] The main *raison d'être* of the series was, Bateson wrote in his guidelines for prospective editors, 'to supply whatever information the adult reader (= approximately the undergraduate, English or American, specializing in English literature, upwards) may be expected to require if he is to appreciate the work's original impact and intention'.[11] The editions would be chronologically organized, since, according to Bateson, 'an essential clue to an author's intentions at any point is provided, on the one hand, by what he has already written, and, on the other hand, by what he will write later'.[12] They would provide, in headnotes to each poem, information on dates of composition and publication, sources, biographical and historical contexts, together with on-the-page annotation which glossed unfamiliar words, identified allusions and echoes, and provided information on such matters as puns and wordplay which could not be adequately signalled in the text itself. It was a central conviction of Bateson's that 'poetry *is* meaning'. Its 'proper function', he believed, is 'the communication of "thought" (using the word in the widest sense)'.[13] The prime function of his series, therefore, would be to counter what he saw as a massive academic fiddling while Rome burns, in which scholars had become increasingly preoccupied with bibliographical minutiae, such as the meticulous registering of textual variants of no authority or artistic significance,

---

[10] The publisher now prefers to be designated 'Longman', though it styled itself 'Longmans' when the Annotated Poets series was launched: I follow the current style throughout this essay.

[11] 'Longman Annotated English Poets: Policy and Stylesheet' (unpublished in-house Longman document, n.d.), p. 1. I return below to the problems attendant on Bateson's notion of a work's 'original impact'.

[12] 'Note by the General Editor', in *The Poems of Tennyson*, ed. Christopher Ricks (London, 1969), p. xv.

[13] F. W. Bateson, *English Poetry: A Critical Introduction* (London, 1950), pp. 39–40.

'which only one reader in a thousand ever looks at',[14] while the classics of English poetry were being widely misunderstood, or left to the mercies of 'the cult of poetic unintelligibility', for want of elucidatory help.

Bateson's commitment to annotation was accompanied by an equally powerful commitment to modernizing the so-called accidentals (spelling, punctuation, paragraphing, italicization, capitalization, etc.) of poetic texts. In this, he was adopting a stance which was deliberately opposed to the mainstream editorial orthodoxy of his day, according to which all scholarly texts, truly such, must be in 'old-spelling' format.[15] Bateson was convinced that a dogmatic commitment to old-spelling editing revealed a fundamental misunderstanding of 'the nature of the literary artifact'.[16] Editors of old-spelling texts, Bateson believed, regularly presuppose too simple an identity between literary works and the physical forms in which they are inscribed. A poem, he argued, is most aptly described as a 'temporal or oral artifact' ('its speech', he added in parenthesis, 'need only sound to the inner ear'), an 'oral drama in the mind' of the author, which is re-experienced, in the act of reading, in the mind of the reader or listener.[17] Poems, Bateson maintained, should thus not be thought of as (in New Critical parlance) 'structures' of 'words on the page' (phrasing which implies a static object which can be surveyed at a glance) but as communicative *processes*, tempor-

---

[14] *English Poetry*, p. 5.

[15] For this view, in Bateson's time and later, see the key statements by R. C. Bald and Fredson Bowers, repr. in Ronald Gottesman and Scott Bennett (eds.), *Art and Error: Modern Textual Editing* (London, 1970), pp. 42–3, 55; Tanselle, 'Historicism and Critical Editing', p. 26; Philip Gaskell, *From Writer to Reader: Studies in Editorial Method* (Oxford, 1978), p. 8 (cited below); Stanley Wells, *Re-Editing Shakespeare for the Modern Reader* (Oxford, 1984), p. 7.

[16] F. W. Bateson, *Essays in Critical Dissent* (London, 1972), p. 2. The spelling 'artifact' is Bateson's.

[17] Ibid. 10, 8. Bateson's thought here is similar to (and was perhaps influenced by) R. G. Collingwood's account of the 'imaginary' creation of works of art in *The Principles of Art* (Oxford, 1938), pp. 130–5. Bateson's stress on the primacy of the oral element in the conception and reception of poetry would doubtless be seen by an admirer of Jacques Derrida as evidence of a misguided faith in 'the metaphysics of presence'. But Bateson's argument, while stressing that an 'oral' artefact need not necessarily be literally vocalized, receives substantial historical support from accounts of the centrality of reading aloud in early modern culture. See e.g. Roger Chartier, 'Leisure and Sociability: Reading Aloud in Early Modern Europe', in Susan Zimmerman and Ronald F. E. Weissman (eds.), *Urban Life in the Renaissance* (Newark, NJ, 1989), pp. 103–20. Eric Griffiths offers a trenchant critique of Derrida's account of the relation between graphic signs and vocalization, and its metaphysical underpinning, in *The Printed Voice of Victorian Poetry*, pp. 48–59.

ally imagined (by the poet) and temporally received (by the reader).[18] The text which it is a literary editor's task to re-present, Bateson urged, should therefore not be confused with the 'black ink-shapes and white paper' in which it is recorded. These, he wrote, 'have no significance *in themselves*, because the written word is a *translation*, for storage purposes, as it were, of what has already been expressed orally and temporally into visual and spatial equivalents'.[19] 'An editor's duty', Bateson argued, 'is to establish his author's text, and since that text was originally oral and becomes oral again whenever it is properly read, what theory requires is a written text so spelled and punctuated that it can be translated back into an approximation of the oral original with the maximum certainty and the minimum difficulty or delay.'[20] The intention of the Longman editions would therefore be (in McLaverty's terms) to allow modern readers to 'perform' a poet's 'works', rather than to inspect a written document which closely resembles his original 'scores'. The 'oral artifact' which is the text, Bateson maintained, is a piece of public communication, rather than a reflection of the author's private idiolect or of the phonetic vagaries of his period. As common practice silently affirms, therefore, it is neither necessary nor desirable, even if it were possible, to simulate an author's own pronunciation (Tennysonian Lincolnshire, Keatsian or Blakeian Cockney) or that of his contemporaries (Richard III or Hamlet *à la* Burbage) in a modern reading of his texts.[21] In so far as they might claim to provide evidence of authorial or contemporary pronunciation, old-spelling texts are irrelevant, since such pronunciation will not be reproduced in a modern reading. They are, moreover, often downright misleading, since, in practice, most old-spelling texts do not embody the ideal famously described by W. W. Greg: 'the text . . . in the form in which we may suppose that it would have stood in a fair copy, made by the author himself, of the work as he finally intended it'.[22] They present, rather, an undifferentiated (and undifferentiatable) *mélange* of (possibly) authorially derived forms, and various kinds of modification and alteration of the author's manuscript imposed by scribes and printers:

[18] *Essays in Critical Dissent*, pp. 8–9.   [19] Ibid. 7.   [20] Ibid. 26.
[21] Ibid. 27–33; *The Scholar-Critic: An Introduction to Literary Research* (London, 1972), pp. 141–2.
[22] Greg's celebrated formula of 1951, quoted in *The Scholar-Critic*, p. 138.

The hodge-podge of some first-edition spellings (hardly ever including the long *s* for example), some authorial spellings, and some compositors' or printing-house spellings and punctuation—but with no serious attempt to distinguish between what is authorial, what is compositorial or a particular printing-house 'style'—is comparable with 'Ye Olde Tea-Shoppe' and similar monstrosities.[23]

To preserve the loosely rhetorical punctuation of a sixteenth- or seventeenth-century text may, Bateson conceded, serve to convey the ambiguities and the syntactical and conceptual fluidities of the poet's work. But it may also be to preserve illogical and meaningless pointing which is both unintelligible to a modern reader and incoherent and inconsistent on its own terms.[24]

❧

How do Bateson's principles stand up in the light of the particular experience of editing Dryden for the series which he instituted? In considering that question, I will return to the musical analogy, and consider some of the ways in which recent debates about musical editing and performance might illuminate the activity of preparing a modern reading edition of Dryden's poems.

A number of related questions have been repeatedly raised in recent discussions of the editing and performance of early music. Should it (as the early musicians discussed by Dreyfus supposed) be the ultimate aim of editors and performers to facilitate and deliver performances which reconstruct as closely as possible the sound of those heard in the composer's own day? Can a performance be considered authentic or faithful without any attempt to simulate the work's original sound? In either case, will performers' needs be best served by original, facsimile, or minimally edited texts, or by editions containing editorial interventions designed to mediate the unfamiliar notation and conventions of the sources in terms that will be more easily and rapidly accessible?

'Nowadays', the celebrated Dutch harpsichordist and conductor Gustav Leonhardt has remarked, 'it's no problem getting hold of a facsimile edition of early music. What else is there to add? When you've read what the composer has written, you don't really need

---

[23] *The Scholar-Critic*, p. 143.   [24] *Essays in Critical Dissent*, pp. 25–6.

anything else.'[25] And Margaret Bent has recently demonstrated the unique advantages to performers of fifteenth-century music of working directly from original notation. But the same scholar has also acknowledged that 'there should be no objection to fully edited prescriptive "phonetic" performance copies, in modern notation and in score, that will save expensive rehearsal and recording time, provided that they are recognized for what they are'.[26] And, for her, an understanding of the structure and grammar of medieval music is a far greater priority for prospective performers than any ambition to replicate its (largely irrecoverable) original sound.[27]

The reconstruction of a work's original sound is, to be sure, a more problematic concept than it might appear at first sight. For, as Roger Scruton has pointed out, the sounds heard by an original audience, even if replicated with exact fidelity, will have an inevitably different significance at a later historical moment:

How things sound depends upon who is listening, and upon the tacit comparisons that animate his perception. . . . [T]he same musical sounds will be received differently by someone who knows only the works of Bach and his predecessors and by someone who has been brought up on Brahms, Wagner, and Liszt. Even if we could reproduce exactly the vibrations in the air that Bach's choir and orchestra at Leipzig might have generated, there is no way of determining that we should hear those vibrations as he heard them, or that we should hear *in* them the musical life that *he* heard. Music is a living tradition, and we compare musical works in our hearing not only with works that are contemporary with them, but with works that came before and after. To us the 'Goldberg' Variations anticipate the Diabelli Variations—that is how they sound, and one reason why we wish to play them on the piano. For Bach they could not have sounded like that.[28]

For such reasons, Graham Bradshaw has argued, when we listen to a performance of Mozart's last symphony 'that corresponds—in the

<hr/>

[25] Leonhardt's remark (from an interview given in 1985) is quoted in Haskell, *The Early Music Revival*, p. 165.

[26] See Margaret Bent, 'Editing Early Music: The Dilemma of Translation', *Early Music* (Aug. 1994) 373–92 (quotation on p. 391).

[27] Dr Bent argued this case in her Loveday Lecture, 'Authenticity and Early Music: "Sound-Proof" Music and the "Face-Value" Fallacy', given at the University of Bristol on 4 May 1999. She has stressed the need to study the distinctive 'grammar' of medieval music as a necessary precondition for meaningful performance in 'The Grammar of Early Music: Preconditions for Analysis', in Cristle Collins Judd (ed.), *Tonal Structures in Early Music* (New York, 1998), pp. 15–59 (esp. pp. 39–54).

[28] Roger Scruton, *The Aesthetics of Music* (Oxford, 1997), p. 444.

size of the orchestra, the instruments used, and all the details of tempo, ornamentation and phrasing—to Mozart's expectations, we may be listening to, but will never *hear*, what Mozart's contemporaries heard'. In a similar vein, Charles Rosen has observed that

Every performance today is a translation; a reconstruction of the original sound is the most misleading translation because it pretends to be the original, while the significance of the old sounds have [*sic*] irrevocably changed . . . the basic philosophy of Early Music is indefensible, above all in its abstraction of original sound from everything that gave it meaning.[29]

And the philosopher Peter Kivy has recently employed similar arguments to conclude that a modern performance of a piece of early music which departs in many particulars from early instrumentation and performance practice may be more faithful to what he calls 'the sound-experience of the past musical listener' than one which reproduces exactly the air-vibration patterns of an early performance. 'Sonic' authenticity, Kivy maintains, is not necessarily the same as 'sensible' authenticity.[30]

'Sonic authenticity' is, of course, unattainable (even if it were thought to be desirable) in the reading of older literary texts. 'Old instruments', as Stanley Wells has observed, 'survive; old speakers do not.'[31] And even the most enthusiastic champion of Chaucer or Shakespeare in the original pronunciation is not likely to claim more than a very approximate exactitude for his efforts. As Bateson noted, the vast majority of modern readings of old texts, even by scholars of a markedly historicist bent, make no attempt whatever to simulate contemporary pronunciation.

'Sonic authenticity' aside, a reader of Dryden who attempts to reconstruct the poet's performance instructions—the ways in which he wished his verse to be emphasized, paced, and nuanced in reading—from the accidentals of the early printed texts of his work is faced with considerable difficulties. Dryden was not one of those authors like Blake, Ben Jonson, Congreve, or Pope, who took care over the presentation and physical appearance of their texts, and saw

---

[29] Graham Bradshaw, 'The Chimera of Authenticity', *The Literary Review*, 12 (21 Mar.–3 Apr. 1980) 37–9; Charles Rosen, 'The Shock of the Old', *The New York Review of Books* (19 July 1990) 46–52, at p. 52.

[30] Peter Kivy, *Authenticities: Philosophical Reflections on Musical Performance* (Ithaca, NY, and London, 1995), p. 78.

[31] *Re-Editing Shakespeare for the Modern Reader*, p. 21.

them as essential devices for conveying meaning.[32] Nor do the surviving records offer an editor any confidence that Dryden's own accidentals can be reconstructed with any certainty.

Only two very early poems, one a mere eight lines long, survive in Dryden's holograph, and careful study of the second of these, the *Heroique Stanza's* on the death of Cromwell, reveals that the spelling, punctuation, italics, and capitals used by Dryden were not closely followed by his compositors.[33] Moreover, some of Dryden's printed editions were set up not directly from an authorial manuscript, but from scribal copies which may have introduced their own stylings and modifications. We know, for example, that such a copy was made of *The Works of Virgil.*[34] Several pieces of evidence suggest that Dryden often had little say in, or was positively dissatisfied with, the printing of his work. In the Epistle Dedicatory to his play *The Kind Keeper* (1680) he remarks that the play was 'printed in [his] absence from the Town, this Summer, much against [his] expectation', so that he has not 'over-look'd the Press'. If the play goes into a second edition, he will, he says, 'faithfully perform what has been wanting in this'.[35] The first edition of *Annus Mirabilis* (1667) was seen through the press by Dryden's brother-in-law, Sir Robert Howard, who clearly missed a number of errors. In a note 'To the Readers', accompanied by a substantial list of errata, Dryden declared:

Notwithstanding the diligence which has been used in my absence, some faults have escap'd the Press: and I have so many of my own to answer for, that I am not willing to be charg'd with those of the Printer. I have onely noticed the grossest of them, not such as by false stops have confounded the sense, but such as by mistaken words have corrupted it.[36]

---

[32] On this topic, see e.g. David Foxon, 'Greg's "Rationale" and the Editing of Pope', *The Library*, 6th ser., 33 (1978) 119–24; id., *Pope and the Eighteenth-Century Book Trade*, ed. and rev. James McLaverty (Oxford, 1991); James McLaverty, 'The Mode of Existence of Literary Works of Art: The Case of the *Dunciad* Variorum', *Studies in Bibliography*, 36 (1984) 82–105; D. F. McKenzie, 'Typography and Meaning: The Case of William Congreve', in Giles Barber and Bernhard Fabian (eds.), *Buch und Buchhandel in Europa im achtzehnten Jahrhundert* (Hamburg, 1981) 81–125.

[33] See Paul Hammond, 'The Autograph Manuscript of Dryden's *Heroique Stanza's* and its Implications for Editors', *Publications of the Bibliographical Society of America*, 76 (1982) 457–70.

[34] See *Letters*, pp. 84–5.

[35] *Works*, xiv. 6. In accordance with the policy of the present volume, my quotations from Dryden are given (notwithstanding the argument of my essay) from 'old-spelling' editions.

[36] *Works*, i. 385.

And in the Preface to the miscellany *Sylvae* (1685) Dryden corrects a mistake of his own in the volume itself, which, he says, he 'will not lay to the Printers charge, who has enough to answer for in false pointings'.[37] Later, in a letter of December 1697, Dryden says that he has 'bestowd nine entire days' on correcting the first edition of the *Virgil*, and complains to Tonson that 'the Printer is a beast and understands nothing I can say to him of correcting the press'.[38] The poet's exasperation seems to have been justified. In the printed copy he had to insert an extensive errata list, to which he added a note: 'There are other Errata both in false pointing, and omissions of words, both in the Preface and the Poems, which the Reader will correct without my trouble. I omit them, because they only lame my *English*, not destroy my meaning.'[39] It is clear, then, that to reproduce the spelling and punctuation of Dryden's early editions would be to reproduce accidentals which are both far removed from those of Dryden's manuscripts and which were, even on their own terms, often inconsistently or incompetently executed. And similar arguments apply to the capitalization and italics of the early editions, which, close inspection reveals, are quite inconsistent, both within particular poems and from poem to poem, with italics sometimes being used conventionally and sparingly (e.g. for proper nouns) and sometimes (as in the 1682 text of *Religio Laici*) so profusely that a (surely unintentional) impression is given that almost every other word should be emphasized in a vocal rendering.

A striking example of the hazards attendant on an over-slavish reproduction of the physical forms of Dryden's early texts occurs in *Threnodia Augustalis*, Dryden's 'Funeral-Pindarique' on the death of King Charles II. This poem was rushed into print a month after the king's death in February 1685. The first edition was a handsome but carelessly printed quarto. A second edition, printed from the same setting of type, and incorporating many changes to both wording and accidentals, followed only a few days later. The substantive changes are almost certainly authorial; the accidental changes may derive from Dryden or from a printing-house proof-reader.[40] In both editions the poem occupies sigs. A2^r–D2^r.

---

[37] *Works*, iii. 13.   [38] *Letters*, p. 97.   [39] *Works*, v. 65.

[40] I here follow the arguments of the California and Longman editors, who suggest that the edition in smaller type also dated 1685 (item 20d in Hugh Macdonald, *John Dryden: A Bibliography* (Oxford, 1939)), and regarded by Kinsley as the first edition, is more likely to

Threnodia Augustalis is written in the so-called 'pindaric' form: irregular stanzas composed of lines of varying length and with varying patterns of rhyme. The customary convention for printing such verse was to indent lines to different degrees, broadly according to length, a procedure which mirrored the poem's rhythmical ebb and flow, thus providing important hints for the reader on how it might best be 'voiced', whether in an audible or silent reading. In the first two editions of *Threnodia Augustalis*, this convention is followed for the first three stanzas, which occur in sig. A. But from sig. B[r] onwards the indentation is abandoned, with all lines (apart from the opening lines of stanzas VIII–XVIII) beginning, thereafter, flush with the left-hand margin.[41] A new compositor, it seems, who was either unfamiliar with the conventions or was working at too great a speed to implement them, took over at this stage, and started to set the rest of the poem on entirely different principles.[42]

James Kinsley's Oxford English Texts edition of 1958 follows the 1685 indentation exactly, but, because of the way the poem's text is disposed in his edition, the abandonment of pindaric indentation occurs not at the foot, but in the middle, of a page.[43] Not only has the seventeenth-century printing-house error been preserved like a fly in amber for the bewilderment of readers three centuries later, but the means of recognizing it *as* a slip (the change of signature) has been obscured by the repagination.[44]

be a hasty reprint of the large-print edition (Macdonald 20a). Kinsley bases his text on Macdonald 20d, which has identical pagination to Macdonald 20a. There are minute differences between the indentation of the two editions, but none which affect the present argument. I am grateful to the Houghton Library, Harvard University, for supplying me with a photocopy of the (very rare) Macdonald 20d for consultation while preparing this essay.

[41] In the last stanza four lines (496–7, 504–5) are indented, in addition to the opening line, in what seems to be a partial reversion to the 'pindaric' method.

[42] The compositor responsible for sig. B had a 'foul case' (mixture of different types) which mixed italic and roman T (and sometimes A and P), but this problem did not affect the (?different) compositors of sigs. A, C, and D.

[43] *Poems*, ed. Kinsley, i. 445 (at the end of stanza III).

[44] The original mistake was perpetuated in the Dublin edition of 1685 (Macdonald 20c) and in the collected edition of Dryden's *Poems on Various Occasions*, published by Tonson in 1701, where the text seems to have been reprinted, without authorial revision, from the first edition. In Macdonald 20c and *Poems on Various Occasions* the disposition of the poem on the page ensures that (as in Kinsley) the pindaric indentation is abandoned mid-page (p. 131), to similarly baffling effect. The same confusion occurs in Volume I of Samuel Derrick's edition of *The Miscellaneous Works of John Dryden* (London, 1760), p. 368.

But, even if it is conceded that the early editions of Dryden's poems are faulty and have no status as an accurate record of Dryden's own accidentals, might it not be argued that they preserve, in their general tenor if not in specific details, a 'period flavour' which conveys the poems' historicity and 'otherness' more effectively than a 'falsely familiarizing' modernization?[45] Such a suggestion betrays confusions similar to those which Laurence Dreyfus identified in the thinking of some early music specialists. For seventeenth-century texts (with the exception of a few deliberately archaizing examples) did not have a 'period flavour' for those living in the period. And if old accidentals give a modern reader a sense of the historicity and otherness of old texts, they do so in less straightforward and more problematic ways than is often acknowledged.

The general case for the retention of period accidentals in editions of early texts has been conveniently summarized by Philip Gaskell in *From Writer to Reader* (1978). 'The deliberate modernization of the spelling, punctuation, etc. of an early text', Gaskell argues, 'is undesirable because it suggests that the modern meaning of the words of the text is what the author meant by them; because it conceals puns and rhymes; because it causes the editor to choose where the author was ambiguous; and because it deprives the work of the quality of belonging to its own period.'[46] But such arguments, as Stanley Wells and John Creaser have recently demonstrated, underestimate the ways in which the retention of old forms can be just as misleading for a modern reader as modernization.[47] We have already considered the question of an old text's 'period flavour'. Related problems are attendant on questions of spelling. Many words, as Wells and Creaser show, were spelt the same in the seventeenth century as they are today, but have subsequently changed their meaning significantly. Thus, to present a text in old spelling will not, by itself, guarantee that modern readers do not

[45] The terms are those of J. P. Sullivan and A. J. Boyle, in the 'Textual Note' prefixed to *Martial in English*, Penguin Poets in Translation (Harmondsworth, 1996), p. xxxviii.

[46] *From Writer to Reader*, p. 8. In Chapter 2 of the present collection, Howard Erskine-Hill argues the specific case for presenting Dryden's *Mac Flecknoe* 'in seventeenth-century printing style'.

[47] See Stanley Wells, 'Old and Modern Spelling', in *Re-Editing Shakespeare for the Modern Reader*; Stanley Wells, *Modernizing Shakespeare's Spelling*, with Gary Taylor, *Three Studies in the Text of 'Henry V'*, Oxford Shakespeare Studies (Oxford, 1979), pp. 1–36; John Creaser, 'Editorial Problems in Milton', *Review of English Studies*, NS 34 (1983) 279–303, at pp. 299–303.

interpose irrelevant modern meanings in their readings of old texts. Modern spelling may, Wells and Creaser concede, sometimes obscure rhymes, and such instances will need annotation. But old spelling itself does not always accord with rhyme or provide an eye-rhyme. Nor do modern readers pronounce old texts in ways which would produce perfect rhymes. An editor of Dryden, whether his text is old- or new-spelling, will therefore need to alert readers to the fact that, for Dryden, 'miracles'/'bees' and 'chronicles'/'ease' seem to have been full rhymes.[48] A modernizing editor may retain variant spellings if they are semantically significant, and convey important poetic colourings which might otherwise be overlooked. The non-specialist modern reader of Dryden stands only to be straightforwardly confused by such spellings as 'Cent'ry' (for 'sentry'), 'Bowsy' (for 'boozy'), 'Eugh' (for 'yew'), 'Oar' (for 'ore'), or 'Throws' (for 'throes'). But in a line like 'The Theatres are Berries for the fair' (*Ovid's Art of Love, Book 1*, l. 103), 'berries' should probably not be modernized (as it is in Sir Walter Scott's edition) to 'burrows', since (as the *OED* points out) it is uncertain whether this meaning or a slightly different one ('mounds, hillocks, or barrows') is intended. (The older spelling, moreover, might, in this instance, preserve a dialect usage from Dryden's native Northamptonshire.)[49] And the editor of 'Cinyras and Myrrha' (Dryden's translation from Book X of the *Metamorphoses*) will probably wish to preserve the spelling 'unsincere' at the moment when Myrrha is told that her incestuous passion for her father is to be consummated— '*Myrrha* was joy'd the welcom News to hear; | But clogg'd with Guilt, the Joy was unsincere' (ll. 258–9)—to suggest that the word is being used in the sense of 'not pure, adulterated, unsound' rather than, as the modern spelling might suggest, 'dissembling, disingenuous'.[50] If the word is modernized, a note is essential to clarify this point.

Old spellings, Wells and Creaser point out, can obscure puns for modern readers as much as reveal them, by preventing us from

---

[48] As noted in *The Poetical Works of John Dryden*, ed. W. D. Christie (London, 1873), pp. 18, 339.

[49] For the uncertainty about the word's meaning, see *OED*, s.v. *berry* (sb.$^{2-3}$). For the possibility of a dialect usage, see *The Poems of John Dryden*, ed. John Sargeaunt (Oxford, 1913), p. xviii.

[50] *OED*, s.v. *insincere* 2, notes that the quotations in Johnson and later dictionaries for the sense used by Dryden all have the spelling 'unsincere'.

seeing that the modern meaning of the word in question is one of those in play in the old poem. No edition, they make clear, can guarantee that readers will be alerted to double meanings merely by virtue of the way the words are spelt in the text. Problems arising from a common single-spelling form for words of different, or overlapping, meaning (e.g. 'loose/lose', 'human/humane') can only be resolved by a note, whether the text is in old or new spelling. Significant capitals and italics can be retained, or their significance explained—for example, in the case of clear personifications or references such as the description of Emily, the heroine of 'Palamon and Arcite', as 'A Virgin-Widow and a *Mourning Bride*', where a clear allusion seems intended to William Congreve's tragedy of 1697.

A few problems, to be sure, will remain insoluble for the modernizer. The most striking Drydenian example occurs in the 'Discourse Concerning Satire' (1693). Dryden has been supporting Isaac Casaubon and André Dacier in their dismissal of the older etymological association of 'satire' (the literary genre) with 'satyr' (the mythological personage). He then remarks:

In the Criticism of Spelling, it ought to be with an *i* and not with *y*; to distinguish its true derivation from *Satura*, not from *Satyrus*. And if this be so, then 'tis false spell'd throughout this Book: For here 'tis written Satyr. Which having not consider'd at the first, I thought it not worth Correcting afterwards.[51]

Here the modernizing editor is trapped, since his activities will have eliminated the very problem to which the poet is drawing attention: a footnote is the only way out.

But, it should be re-emphasized, a footnote is frequently the only way out, whether the text one is reading is in old or modern spelling. The necessary information for comprehension cannot be adequately signalled in the text alone. The footnote is an indispensable accompaniment to that text, and is integrally related to it in the reading experience.

The case for retaining old punctuation in a modern edition of Dryden might at first seem more compelling than the arguments for retaining old spelling, capitals, and italics. As we have seen,

---

[51] *The Satires of Decimus Junius Juvenalis. Translated into English Verse. By Mr. Dryden, and Several Other Eminent Hands* (London, 1693), p. xxviii.

F. W. Bateson was himself conscious of the risks of strait-jacketing the fluid syntactical relations of a seventeenth-century text.[52] Such are the dangers in this area that John Carey and Alastair Fowler, in their Longman *Milton* of 1968, modernized spelling, capitals, and italics, but followed the punctuation of their seventeenth-century copy-texts with diplomatic faithfulness, on the grounds that while spelling is designed primarily 'to enable the reader to make the right vocabulary selection', punctuation 'like word order, inflection and function words, is a class of grammatical symbols'. 'Consequently', they argued, 'we ought to be almost as reluctant to alter the punctuation of an old text as we would be, say, to alter its word order.'[53]

In a discussion of medieval punctuation, John Burrow has argued that 'punctuation-marks are "emic": their value depends, that is, upon their systematic relation to each other in any given text. Thus a comma has one value if you use a lot of semicolons, and another if you do not. This fact makes the *partial* retention of any system problematic.'[54] Carey and Fowler's decision to follow the punctuation of Milton's early texts depends on a conviction that this punctuation, though not necessarily Milton's own,[55] is consistent and intelligible in its own terms: that it constitutes, in Burrow's terms, a coherent 'system'. But, as we have seen, this is not the case with Dryden's texts, which are often carelessly, insensitively, and inconsistently punctuated—in short, anything but systematic.

Dryden was writing in a transitional period, when a predominately rhetorical system of punctuation (in which punctuation marks were used to indicate the pauses appropriate in a vocal rendering) was being replaced by a predominately grammatical one (in which punctuation marks indicated the logical relations between parts of a sentence).[56] On the scanty evidence available, it

[52] In the 'Policy and Stylesheet' (p. 4) he wrote that, though the Longman editions would have modernized punctuation, the editor's intention should be 'to create a text which makes immediate sense to the modern reader *not* to punctuate as a modern writer would'. 'The attempt to impose a modern system of punctuation upon earlier writers', he noted, 'frequently involves an editor in unnecessary and substantive interference with his text.'

[53] *The Poems of John Milton*, ed. John Carey and Alastair Fowler (London, 1968), p. x.

[54] 'Problems in Punctuation: *Sir Gawain and the Green Knight*, Lines 1–7', in D. M. Reeks (ed.), *Sentences: Essays Presented to Alan Ward on the Occasion of his Retirement from Wadham College, Oxford* (Southampton, 1988), p. 77.

[55] As they concede in *The Poems of John Milton*, p. xii.

[56] See Park Honan, 'Eighteenth- and Nineteenth-Century English Punctuation Theory', *English Studies*, 41 (1960) 92–101; Vivian Salmon, 'English Punctuation Theory, 1500–1800',

seems that Dryden preferred a lighter, rhetorical, punctuation, while his compositors tended to impose a rather heavier and more grammatical pointing.[57] It must be conceded that the early printed texts, imperfect as they are, often allow a flexibility that the full-dress imposition of modern punctuation would undoubtedly obscure. The seventeenth-century compositors' use of colons, for example, as a stop rather similar to the modern semicolon, allows the argumentative or narrative flow of extended passages to be nuanced in manageable units, without creating the jerkiness which would result from a wholesale substitution of full stops, or the shapelessness which would be created by replacing the colons with commas.

But modern punctuation systems are themselves less monolithic and prescriptive than might at first sight appear, and it is perfectly possible, as the example of D. H. Lawrence shows, for a twentieth-century writer and his editors to adapt modern punctuation marks (which will, for modern readers, have predominately grammatical associations) to serve a predominately rhetorical function, without misleading or baffling readers.[58] The modernizing editor of Dryden, therefore, has the option of adopting a compromise position—correcting the punctuation of the early texts in the many places where it seems incoherent, fussy, or misleading for a modern reader (for example where question marks are used, according to seventeenth-century convention, instead of exclamation marks), while following, and even enhancing, its rhetorical tendencies by lightening the pointing, and thus avoiding the dangers which would result from the blanket imposition of modern, grammatical punctuation. Such a process, of course, means that the reader will be experiencing a text whose punctuation includes a blend of rhetorical and grammatical effects, and which regularly, and silently, incorporates significant editorial interventions. But we should remember that, for reasons already given, there has never been a printed text of Dryden in which that has not been the case, nor—

Anglia, 106 (1988) 285–314; Malcolm Parkes, *Pause and Effect: An Introduction to the History of Punctuation in the West* (Aldershot, 1992), esp. pp. 87–92.

[57] *Poems*, ed. Hammond, vol. i, p. xx.

[58] See e.g. the editors' arguments for retaining Lawrence's manuscript punctuation in *D. H. Lawrence: Sons and Lovers*, ed. Helen Baron and Carl Baron (Cambridge, 1992), pp. lxxiii–lxxiv. I am grateful to Dr Helen Baron for allowing me sight of an unpublished conference paper, 'D. H. Lawrence: Mark My Words; The Relation of Lawrence's Punctuation to his Meaning', in which these arguments are further justified and illustrated.

unless a complete set of holograph manuscripts were to be discovered—could there ever be such an edition in the future. In this respect, the apparently greater editorial transparency of an old-spelling edition of Dryden is potentially very misleading.

There is, of course, a newer general line of argument which has been adduced in support of old-spelling editions. In a series of influential studies, from *A Critique of Modern Textual Criticism* (1983) to *The Textual Condition* (1991), Jerome J. McGann has argued that the physical aspects of books (typography, format, paper quality, etc.) are essential parts of texts as 'the locus of complex networks of communicative exchanges',[59] in which authorial intentions constitute only one part of the texts' meaning, and might be accompanied, or contradicted, by other elements in a holistic publication 'event'. Poems, McGann observes, have sometimes taken on markedly different significances in different physical incarnations: Byron's *Don Juan*, for example, seemed a more dangerously subversive work when printed in cheap editions circulating among the lower orders than it had when available in an edition affordable only by the gentry.[60] Such arguments have prompted the production of computer-readable hypertexts, by which numerous states of a particular work—each one of which is to be seen as the embodiment of a different publishing moment—can be made available at the touch of a button.

McGann's case has considerable weight, and it is difficult to imagine a world in which serious literary students would not wish to make regular reference to early editions, facsimiles, and (where available) hypertexts, as part of an attempt to discover as much as possible about the circumstances in which literary works were originally printed, circulated, and received. But McGann's approach cannot exempt one (or so it would seem to me) from acknowledging the necessarily transactional and dialogic nature of any modern engagement with past artworks—whether these are conceived of as the products of individual intentionalism, or of a concatenation of 'communicative exchanges'. For to read an old book, or a printed facsimile of an old book, *now* (let alone a computer-generated image, or a set of variant readings diffused

[59] *The Textual Condition* (Princeton, NJ, 1991), pp. 61–2.
[60] See Jerome J. McGann, *The Beauty of Inflections: Literary Investigations in Historical Method and Theory* (Oxford, 1988), p. 116.

through a scholarly apparatus criticus) is quite a different experience from reading the original *then*. No amount of information about the complex network of events which constituted the original moment of publication can cause us to inhabit that event in the same way that was available to readers at the time—even assuming that those readers themselves all inhabited the event in the same way. The questionable authenticity of 'the authorially intended text as it really was' is in danger of being displaced, in the McGannian model, by a multiple, but arguably no less chimerical, set of 'publication circumstances as they really were'.

To take the case discussed earlier. The erroneous indentation of the first edition of *Threnodia Augustalis* is quite a different phenomenon when encountered by modern readers who are unused to pindaric verse and for whom the death of Charles II is a remote historical event, than for a reader in 1685, accustomed to the normal pindaric conventions and the vagaries of seventeenth-century printing houses, and caught up in events of topical urgency. Only all-out time-travel could transport us into that moment. But even then we would be travelling *to* the event from our own, present, contingency. Once again, it can be seen that, as well as a sense of the historicity of the source-text, a sense of the historicity of the reader, the expectations, assumptions, experience, and knowledge which are brought to the text from the historical situation of its receivers, is vital in any full account of the process of reading and understanding.

The presence of on-the-page annotation in an edition like the Longman *Dryden* is bound up, in ways that might perhaps at first seem surprising, with important questions of canon-formation and aesthetic evaluation. When instructing prospective Longman editors on the amount of annotation to be devoted to each poem in their allotted volume, F. W. Bateson offered the following advice:

The density of annotation will vary from poem to poem, depending on its importance as poetry. Normally it will be very clear from the criticism and scholarship which poems are and are not important, but new evidence may lead an editor to feel it necessary to reveal the importance of hitherto neglected areas of a poet's work.[61]

[61] 'Policy and Stylesheet', p. 5.

Bateson's remarks reveal the potentially powerful contribution which an editor can make in determining, or confirming, the body of poems within a writer's *œuvre* to which the reader's attention is most regularly and intensively drawn—to pursue the musical analogy, the repertoire of works which is deemed to be most worthy of regular performance.

The point is of particular relevance to Dryden, since, as a study of the reception history of his work reveals, the repertoire of Dryden poems which has received most attention this century by no means exactly coincides with the body of work which was most admired in the century and a half after the poet's death, when his reputation was at its height. Nor does the twentieth-century description of Dryden's literary characteristics and qualities square at all readily with that which formerly obtained. From the late Victorian period until very recently, Dryden has been widely thought of as a conservative satirist and public poet, whose 'poetry of statement' was principally focused on the political, religious, and literary events and controversies of his day. But for Samuel Johnson, writing in the 1770s, Dryden was a boldly experimental poet, given to 'wild and daring sallies of sentiment' and 'the irregular and excentrick violence of wit', whose mind had been formed by 'comprehensive speculation' and whose works manifested 'the effects of a vigorous genius operating upon large materials'.[62] And critics of the eighteenth and early nineteenth centuries regularly assume that Dryden's poetic career, far from declining after the loss of his court offices after the 1688 Revolution, went from strength to strength, culminating in the works of his last years: *Alexander's Feast* and the *Fables Ancient and Modern*. It has been both cause and effect of the post-Victorian conception of Dryden that the vast bulk of academic commentary on his work this century has been devoted to explicating a handful of poems (*Annus Mirabilis*, *Mac Flecknoe*, *Absalom and Achitophel*, *The Medall*, *Religio Laici*, *The Hind and the Panther*) and that the discussion and presentation of his work has systematically privileged certain kinds of context (political, circumstantial, public) over others

[62] Samuel Johnson, *Lives of the English Poets*, ed. George Birkbeck Hill, 3 vols. (Oxford, 1905), i. 457, 460, iii. 222. For further discussion of the contrast between Johnson's view of Dryden and more modern estimates, see my 'A Poet's "World?"', *Cambridge Quarterly*, 19 (1990) 52–68.

(imaginative, poetic, philosophical), or has assimilated the latter to the former.

As is well known, Dryden's poems are densely referential to contemporary circumstance and discourse: political, literary, social, religious. An editor must not only illuminate obscure topical allusions (for example to numerous works by Shadwell and Flecknoe in *Mac Flecknoe*, or to contemporary political controversy in *Absalom and Achitophel*), but alert the reader to the powerful charge of political significance for Dryden and his contemporaries to be found in apparently simple terms: 'arbitrary', 'succession', 'exiled', 'faction', 'patriot', 'usurper'.

Contemporary allusions, moreover, are not restricted to Dryden's overtly political poems. When, for example, the poet remarks of the philosopher Democritus of Abdera (in his translation of 'The Tenth Satire of Juvenal') that

> a Land of Bogs
> With Ditches fenc'd, a Heaven Fat with Fogs,
> May form a Spirit fit to sway the State;
> And make the Neighb'ring Monarchs fear their Fate,   (ll. 75–8)

the reader needs to be alerted to the sly reference to William III and Holland (Juvenal makes no reference at this point to boggy lands or monarchical rule)—which may, in this instance, have been prompted by a cross-reference in the Delphin edition of Juvenal (used by Dryden) to a passage in Horace (*Epistles*, ii. i. 244), suggesting that the folly of Alexander the Great was such that one might have expected him to have been born in foggy Boeotia (William was frequently likened to Alexander in contemporary panegyric and satire, a connection which is exploited in *Alexander's Feast*).[63]

But Dryden's vocabulary and allusions also constantly resonate far beyond the immediately contemporary moment. A subtly interrelated set of larger, recurring, preoccupations (with their associated key words) concerning fortune, liberty and reason, human happiness, the flux of time, and man's place in the natural and inanimate world, pervade his work, and come into complex and perpetually changing interaction with his reflections on current personalities,

---

[63] See Howard Erskine-Hill, *Poetry of Opposition and Revolution: Dryden to Wordsworth* (Oxford, 1996), pp. 40–3.

events, and ideas.[64] The annotation of Dryden's topical and circumstantial references (reinforced by a chronological arrangement which tends to tie each poem precisely to the moment of its first appearance) therefore needs to be counterpointed with annotation which plots connections and affinities across the *œuvre*, drawing attention to Dryden's self-echoes and self-borrowings, to reveal the network of larger concerns which run like a set of subterranean passages beneath his work in all genres, surfacing recurrently in sometimes unlikely places.

Such concerns were often prompted by, or reveal, a subtly interconnected web of literary influences. In 'The Eleventh Book of the *Aeneis*', Diomedes tells the Latin embassy which has attempted to co-opt him in the fight against the Trojans:

> The Gods have envy'd me the sweets of life
> My much lov'd Country, and my more lov'd Wife. (ll. 117–18)

Dryden's phrasing imbues Diomedes' lament for the loss of his domestic happiness with resonance derived from Milton's evocation of the very different domestic bliss of prelapsarian humanity. For Dryden's key phrase ('the sweet[s] of life') had been used by Milton to characterize Adam and Eve's life together in Eden.[65] And when, in his translation of the Ovidian Pythagoras' speech on flux and the transmigration of souls from Book XV of the *Metamorphoses*, Dryden remarks that 'former Things | Are set aside, like abdicated Kings',[66] he combines an echo of the book of Revelation ('for the former things are passed away'[67]) with an ironic allusion to recent historical events (the supposed abdication of James II in 1688) to co-opt recent events in a vision of time's processes which embraces apocalyptic biblical vision and classical philosophy. Similarly, when translating Chaucer's Nun's Priest's Tale, Dryden combines allusions to ancient and modern history (Charles II, William III, the

---

[64] For a brief general description of these preoccupations, see the introduction to my edition of *John Dryden: Selected Poems* in the Everyman's Poetry series (London, 1998), pp. xviii–xxiii. On some of Dryden's recurrent key terms, see Paul Hammond, 'Dryden's Philosophy of Fortune', *Modern Language Review*, 80 (1985) 769–85.

[65] *Paradise Lost*, viii. 184: 'sweet' is one of the key adjectives with which Eden is evoked throughout the poem. By far the most extensive and searching account of Dryden's indebtedness to Milton is to be found in J. R. Mason, 'To Milton through Dryden and Pope', unpublished Ph.D. thesis, University of Cambridge, 1987.

[66] 'Of the Pythagorean Philosophy', ll. 274–5.

[67] Rev. 21: 4.

Habsburgs, Henry VIII, Louis XIV, the Ptolemies) with an elaborate pattern of allusion to Milton's *Paradise Lost*, to produce a poem which fuses political and literary commentary with a large, comic vision of human sexuality and self-deludedness.[68] And in the rhetorically patterned, yet moving speech in which Ovid's Myrrha meditates on her incestuous passion for her own father, Dryden deploys terms from his own religion ('sin', 'soul', 'sacred', 'piety') as part of an engagement in a long-standing cross-cultural debate about the conflicts and correspondences between 'natural' and 'human(e)' law, in which the classical, Renaissance, and modern ethical worlds are brought into various kinds of complex conjunction and disjunction.[69] In each of these instances, 'vocabulary', 'sources', 'allusions', 'implications', 'context', and 'stylistic devices' (the categories of poetic activity which, according to Bateson, an annotator needs to address[70]) are inextricably intertwined one with another, all combining in complex ways to create the meanings which it is incumbent on an editor to illuminate.

Dryden's chosen mode of translation was one in which his originals were accommodated within the idioms of the English language and the established forms of English poetry, so that his versions, as has often been observed, read and sound 'like original English poems'. In the Preface to *Sylvae*, the poet remarked, famously, of his expansions and enlargements of his originals:

I desire the false Criticks wou'd not always think that those thoughts are wholly mine, but that either they are secretly in the Poet, or may be fairly deduc'd from him: or at least, if both those considerations should fail, that my own is of a piece with his, and that if he were living, and an *Englishman*, they are such, as he wou'd probably have written.[71]

In a much-discussed recent book, Lawrence Venuti has attacked this way of translating, arguing that it represents a kind of poetic 'imperialism', a colonization, appropriation, or domestication of ori-

---

[68] See C. H. Hinnant, 'Dryden's Gallic Rooster', *Studies in Philology*, 65 (1968) 647–56; Tom Mason, 'Dryden's Chaucer', unpublished Ph.D. thesis, University of Cambridge, 1977, pp. 196–245; Peter Conrad, *The Everyman History of English Literature* (London, 1985), pp. 283–4; Taylor Corse, 'Dryden and Milton in "The Cock and the Fox"', *Milton Quarterly*, 27 (1993) 109–18.

[69] See my 'Nature's Laws and Man's: The Story of Cinyras and Myrrha in Ovid and Dryden', *Modern Language Review*, 80 (1985) 786–801.

[70] *The Poems of Tennyson*, p. xv.

[71] *Works*, iii. 4.

ginals, rather than a recognition of their true 'alterity'. Dryden's kind of translation, Venuti argues, is based on an imposition of pseudo-universal values (those of the translator's own culture) on an alien Other. Venuti consequently prefers the kind of 'foreignizing' translation which emphasizes, by various kinds of disruption, subversion, or bypassing of native literary norms, the source-texts' strangeness, their unsusceptibility to ready assimilation into the target culture.[72]

Such an argument, I believe, seriously underestimates the complex process of negotiation and dialogue which is visible in almost every line of Dryden's translations, where his source-texts (and the philosophical, aesthetic, and imaginative assumptions which they suggest and embody at any given moment) are continuously scrutinized, reimagined, and tested against Dryden's contemporary experience and literary memories, with the English poet's own art and imagination being modified and extended by his sources as much as those sources are assimilated to his own ways of thinking and feeling. In these versions, Dryden is not simply appropriating his originals, but (in T. S. Eliot's words) 'giving the original through himself and finding himself through the original'. His translating activity is, at one and the same time, self-expression and an escape from the self, an acknowledgement of 'a simultaneity of communion and difference'[73] between his originals and himself, an encounter between the historical and the transhistorical, the contingent and the timeless, experienced reality and imaginable possibility.

If little things with great we may compare, I would suggest that some interesting parallels might be drawn between Dryden's own activity as a translator and an editor's activity in modernizing and annotating Dryden's work for a modern reader. A large part of Dryden's artistic enterprise in the last fifteen years of his life was devoted to mediating past literature to his readers in the present—to convincing them that the works of Horace, Lucretius, Ovid, Virgil, Homer, Boccaccio, and Chaucer were at once venerably ancient and entirely modern. His intentions are clearest, and his methods most striking, in the case of Chaucer. Chaucer's name was frequently adduced in late seventeenth-century literary discussions,

---

[72] See Lawrence Venuti, *The Translator's Invisibility: A History of Translation* (London and New York, 1995).

[73] The phrase is Charles Martindale's, in *Redeeming the Text*, p. 106. For Eliot's remark, see his introduction to *Ezra Pound: Selected Poems* (London, 1928), p. 13.

but his works were little read outside specialist circles, and were only available in 'black-letter' editions[74] which signalled, in their very physical format, Chaucer's status as a relic of an alien, antique, culture. Dryden was convinced that Chaucer, like the great poets of classical antiquity, was a writer with one foot in his own age and one in eternity. For him, Chaucer's works provided crucial evidence of the paradox that 'Mankind is ever the same, and nothing lost out of Nature, though every thing is alter'd'.[75] Dryden supported this conviction in three principal ways. First, he made, in his Preface to *Fables Ancient and Modern* (1700), the critical claim—radical for its time—that Chaucer deserved to be set beside Ovid, Homer, and Virgil as a poet of classic status. Secondly, he attempted to substantiate that claim by composing, for the same volume, modern versions of several of Chaucer's tales which expanded and elucidated their implications and meanings for seventeenth-century readers; these versions were juxtaposed, in ways that cast further light on their potential meaning and significance, with translated episodes from Ovid, Homer, and Boccaccio. Finally, he encouraged comparison between his versions and Chaucer's originals by including texts of those originals in his own volume. (Dryden's *Fables* was the first occasion on which any of Chaucer's poems had been printed in a roman typeface.) Dryden's readers were thus able to move easily between a Chaucer who had been entirely rethought and re-presented in a modern idiom and a Chaucer who was presented, for the first time, in an intelligibly 'medieval' form. They were consequently encouraged to give equal weight to the alteration and continuity of words and things, to the cultural and linguistic conditions which joined, and those which separated, them from Chaucer.

In preparing a modernized edition of Dryden's works, an editor is constantly aware that he, too, is dealing with a document from a world (or, rather, as we have seen, several different worlds) quite different from his own. Both in his presentation of his author's text and in his annotations (the presence of which, on the same page as the text, signals the text's complex entanglement in a network of connections with events, real and imaginary, outside itself), those differences must be clearly, and multiply, signalled. But at the same

[74] Those of Thomas Speght (1598, 1603, 1687).   [75] *Poems*, ed. Kinsley, iv. 1455.

time, such an edition acknowledges that the only viable life that a literary text can have is in the re-creating imaginations of readers in the present. It is in the complex dialogue between present and past, the subtle, moment-by-moment negotiation or meeting (which is never simply a merging) with other centres of human consciousness, imagination, and meaning, that the process of reading an older literary text takes place. The aim of a modernized, annotated edition is both to enable that process, and to embody it in action.

APPENDIX

SOME CONTEMPORARY
REFERENCES TO DRYDEN

PAUL HAMMOND

Dryden's editors, biographers, and bibliographers have recorded many contemporary allusions to Dryden which help us to understand the complex and changing relations which he had with his readers, colleagues, rivals, and publishers. The purpose of the present appendix is to assemble some further references which have not been noted by modern Dryden scholars, and so to offer a supplement to the bibliography of Drydeniana compiled by Hugh Macdonald.[1] The allusions collected here are additional to those recorded in modern scholarship on Dryden and

[1] Hugh Macdonald, *John Dryden: A Bibliography of Early Editions and of Drydeniana* (Oxford, 1939). It should be noted that Macdonald's emphasis upon printed material results in a very incomplete presentation of the chronological development of contemporary commentary on Dryden, since some pieces which circulated in manuscript are recorded by him (if at all) only at the point when they reached print: this applies particularly to poems from the 1670s and 1680s which were printed after the Revolution in the various volumes of state poems listed on pp. 316–22. Other manuscript poems, and some very significant printed materials, are only alluded to unsystematically in footnotes to other items, and are therefore hard to evaluate. A comprehensive bibliography of Drydeniana, including manuscript works, remains a desideratum. Other principal sources of information about Dryden's contemporary reception are Hugh Macdonald, 'The Attacks on Dryden', *Essays and Studies*, 21 (1936) 41–74; *Poems on Affairs of State*, ed. George DeF. Lord *et al.*, 7 vols. (New Haven, 1963–75), hereafter cited as *POAS*; Stanley Archer, 'Some Early References to Dryden', *Notes and Queries*, 215 (1970) 417–18; *Dryden: The Critical Heritage*, ed. James and Helen Kinsley (London, 1971); the Garland facsimile series *Drydeniana*, 14 vols. (New York, 1974–6); *Court Satires of the Restoration*, ed. John Harold Wilson (Columbus, Oh., 1976); James Anderson Winn, *John Dryden and his World* (New Haven, 1987); and the commentaries in *Works* and in *Poems*, ed. Hammond. Recent articles on Dryden's contemporary reputation include an exchange on Dryden and Higden between Steven N. Zwicker and David Hopkins in the *TLS*, 24 Feb. 1995, p. 13, and 19 May 1995, p. 12; John Barnard, 'Early Expectations of Dryden's Translation of Virgil (1697) on the Continent', *Review of English Studies*, NS 50 (1999) 196–203; and David Hopkins, 'Charles Montague, George Stepney, and Dryden's *Metamorphoses*', *Review of English Studies*, NS 51 (2000) 83–9.

Restoration literature, except that brief entries are included for some published material which readers might otherwise overlook. In addition, some items which I noted in my edition of *The Poems of John Dryden*, Volumes I and II, are transcribed here. I have not included any of the speculative and malicious attributions to Dryden which are found in manuscripts of Restoration verse: these did contribute significantly to contemporary perceptions of Dryden's canon, but I hope to treat them separately in an appendix to the final volume of the Longman edition.[2]

The following material is significant particularly for documenting early responses to *Annus Mirabilis*, *Mac Flecknoe*, *Absalom and Achitophel*, *The Medall*, *Religio Laici*, *Threnodia Augustalis*, *The Hind and the Panther*, and Dryden's plays. It also establishes that Dryden enjoyed a reputation as a writer of prologues as early as 1669, adds to existing comments on his conversion to Catholicism, shows the popularity of his classical translations, and provides evidence that the musicality of his verse was much admired. There are also further examples of the common allegations that Dryden is a mercenary writer and a turncoat. While some allusions are derogatory and satirical, others indicate the high esteem in which Dryden was held by his contemporaries. Indeed, even the hostile comments and ironic imitations indicate the degree to which he influenced the rhetoric of public discourse in the late seventeenth century. Moreover, the vicious and scurrilous remarks which were circulated about him make one wonder anew at Dryden's ability to retain his equanimity and good humour in the face of such sustained and public character-assassination.[3] For as Congreve recorded: 'he was of a Nature exceedingly Humane and Compassionate; easily forgiving Injuries, and capable of a prompt and sincere Reconciliation with them who had offended him'.[4]

¶I 1667
J. G., ᾿Ακάματον Πῦρ, *Or, the Dreadful Burning of London: Described in a Poem* (London, 1667)
Wing[5] *G 31*

Dryden's *Annus Mirabilis* was published by Henry Herringman early in 1667: it was entered in the Stationers' Register on 21 January, and Pepys

---

[2] I have cited some principal examples in 'The Circulation of Dryden's Poetry', *Papers of the Bibliographical Society of America*, 86 (1992) 379–409, at pp. 382–4.

[3] For his responses to personal abuse see in particular 'To my Ingenious Friend, Mr. Henry Higden, Esq; On his Translation of the Tenth Satyr of Juvenal', and the 'Discourse Concerning Satire' (*Works*, iv. 70–1).

[4] William Congreve, 'Epistle Dedicatory' to *The Dramatick Works of John Dryden*, 6 vols. (1717), quoted from *Dryden: The Critical Heritage*, p. 264.

[5] Donald Wing, *Short-Title Catalogue of Books Printed in England, Scotland, Wales, and British*

bought his copy on 2 February. A few months later there appeared this other poem on the Fire of London by Joseph Guillim, which is clearly indebted to Dryden's work, and was also published by Herringman.[6] It was licensed by Sir Roger L'Estrange on 2 May 1667, which establishes that Guillim had about three months to absorb Dryden's poem before presenting his own for publication. Guillim's poem is written in couplets rather than the quatrains which Dryden used, but it has many verbal echoes of *Annus Mirabilis*.

The first borrowing comes in Guillim's description of the beginning of the fire:

> Which through some narrow room, did gently creep
> With a still foot, e're it abroad durst peep.
> Which will no longer now confined be.   (p. 1)

This echoes stanza 218 of Dryden's poem:

> Then, in some close-pent room it crept along,
>   And, smouldring as it went, in silence fed:
> Till th' infant monster, with devouring strong,
>   Walk'd boldly upright with exalted head.   (ll. 869–72)

This same stanza also provided Guillim with material for some lines on the next page:

> Weak at the first, it humbly crept along,
> Till higher it aspir'd, as it grew strong: (p. 2)

Dryden notes that 'Some cut the Pipes' (l. 915) to provide water to fight the fire, a detail also used by Guillim:

> The Pipes are cut, and all the Conduits flow.   (p. 3)

Dryden compares the fire to the Hydra:

> *Hydra*-like, the fire,
> Lifts up his hundred heads to aim his way.   (ll. 993–4)

and so does Guillim:

> Such ranks of Flames, the chief fire forward leads,
> Which Hydra-like lifts up a hundred heads.   (p. 3)

America, and of English Books Printed in Other Countries, 1641–1700, 2nd edn., 3 vols. (New York, 1982–94).

[6] The poem is reprinted with a brief introduction in *London in Flames, London in Glory: Poems on the Fire and Rebuilding of London 1666–1709*, ed. Robert Arnold Aubin (New Brunswick, NJ, 1943), pp. 31–45.

The image of the flames dividing like a rank of soldiers is found in both; Dryden writes:

> In parties now they straggle up and down,
>   As Armies, unoppos'd, for prey divide.   (ll. 939–40)

and Guillim has:

> But as those Flames in several ranks divide;
>   And as they march, stretch o're from side to side.   (p. 4)

Dryden recalls the account in *Iliad*, xxi. 305–82 of how the river Xanthus called on its tributary Simois for help and tried to drown Achilles, but was attacked by Hephaestus with fire:

> Old Father *Thames* rais'd up his reverend head,
>   But fear'd the fate of *Simoeis* would return: (ll. 925–6)

Guillim alludes to the same episode:

> So *Xanthus* boil'd, while the flames did destroy
>   The stately Palaces of ancient *Troy*.   (p. 7)

Dryden's play on the old name of London, 'Augusta', in the lines:

> More great then humane, now, and more *August*,
>   New deifi'd she from her fires does rise: (ll. 1177–8)

is echoed by Guillim:

> To see sprung up, a more august Exchange.   (p. 8)

Guillim's lines on the destruction of St Paul's cathedral also draw material from *Annus Mirabilis*. Guillim writes:

> When Horses thus *Pauls* Temple once defile,
> How soon becomes it then a flaming Pile?
> For which Profaneness, well might heaven be urg'd,
> To have it thus by Fire again be purg'd
>
> .   .   .   .
>
> Yet when they [the flames] lookt down, toward the awful Quire,
> And on the Altar spy'd more Sacred Fire,
> They fear'd as 'twere to spread unhallowed heat;
>
> > (pp. 10–11)

Compare Dryden:

> Nor could thy Fabrick, *Paul's*, defend thee long,
>
> .   .   .   .

The dareing flames peep't in and saw from far,
  The awful beauties of the Sacred Quire:
But, since it was prophan'd by Civil War,
  Heav'n thought it fit to have it purg'd by fire. (ll. 1097, 1101–4)

Guillim's description of the fire destroying Christ Church begins by echoing Dryden's line 1097 (just quoted above):

> Nor could the Buckets of its Sacred Quire,
>   Defend it now from this unhallow'd Fire. (p. 12)

and these lines also return to Dryden's stanza 229 for more details:

> Some run for Buckets to the hallow'd Quire: (l. 914)

Both writers describe the effects of the fire on Christ Church Hospital, an orphanage; Dryden says:

> The fugitive flames, chastis'd, went forth to prey
>   On pious Structures   (ll. 1089–90)

and Guillim says:

> No sooner doth this sacred Structure fall,
>   But th' agil Fire preys on the Hospital: (p. 12)

Guillim also has an extended passage on the King weeping (pp. 11–12), which may have been suggested by Dryden's stanzas on the same topic (ll. 957–64).

Taken altogether, these examples show that the two poems are related by more than the inevitable coincidence of subject-matter and vocabulary: Guillim evidently read *Annus Mirabilis* closely and profitably.

¶2 1669
Praelectio Musica

Leeds University Library Brotherton Collection, MS Lt 38, fos. 5ᵛ–14ʳ

The manuscript is dated 1670, and is a collection of material relating to the University of Oxford. This item, by Thomas Lawrence, is headed 'Praelectio Musica propalam | Apud Oxonienses habita | Die julij 11. Ano. dom. 1669.' (For the verses which conclude it see Crum A 1665A.[7]) In the English section of the speech, headed 'The ffirst addresse to ye Ladyes', there is the following comment, which shows that by 1669 Dryden had already acquired a reputation as a writer of witty prologues, and suggests

---

[7] *First-Line Index of English Poetry 1500–1800 in Manuscripts of the Bodleian Library Oxford*, ed. Margaret Crum, 2 vols. (Oxford, 1969), hereafter 'Crum'.

that these were particularly appreciated by female members of the audience. It is also an early indication of Dryden's popularity at Oxford. The first surviving prologue which is known to have been written specifically for delivery at Oxford is datable to 1673,[8] but there may have been earlier ones, or earlier Oxford performances of his plays.

> you hate a witlesse Gallant as bad as a sottish Husband, & you love to have your Imaginations tickled as well as your sides. This yor great (1) [*marginal note*: Dryden] Poet of y^e Age knows well & y^{re}fore is sure to hitt yor humour wth a brisk Prologue, wch hee often findes takes more wth yor fancyes, y^n y^e Repetition of five tedious after=Acts. (fo. 8^r)

¶3 1671–2
The Correspondence of Thomas Blount

Thomas Blount mentions Dryden in two letters to Anthony à Wood. Quotations are taken from *The Correspondence of Thomas Blount (1618–1679) A Recusant Antiquary*, ed. Theo Bongaerts (Amsterdam, 1978), pp. 123 and 125:

(i) 'The Thing [Blount's *Animadversions Upon Sir Richard Baker's Chronicle*] sells better then I could imagin, I gave Mr. Dryden one, who seemed to be wel pleasd with it.' (7 December 1671)

(ii) 'Mr. Dreydens Granada came out yesterday. the Postscript at least is worth your Reading—which som condemn, others admire, I am one of the last.' (6 February 1672)

This latter reference provides a more precise date than we have previously had for the publication of *The Conquest of Granada*, which Macdonald (p. 109) notes was entered in the Stationers' Register on 25 February, and in the Term Catalogues on 7 February.

¶4 c.1672
To the selfe-conceyted Authour of the Rehearsall
Bodleian Library Oxford, MS Don. b. 8, pp. 223–4. Crum T 2269

This attack on the Duke of Buckingham tells him: 'Other mens faults then lett alone' (p. 223), and observes:

> But yett we must lament thy Fate,
> That thou shouldst spend thy whole Estate,
> And not arriue att Laureate.   (p. 224)

---

[8] *Poems*, ed. Hammond, i. 277.

¶5 1677
Ecclesia Restaurata: A Votive Poem to the Rebuilding of St Paul's Cathedral (London, 1677)
Wing E 133

This poem by James Wright uses the same stanza as *Annus Mirabilis*.[9]

¶6 1678
Aphra Behn, *Sir Patient Fancy* (London, 1678)
Wing B 1766

The prologue to this play (Danchin 249),[10] of which the first recorded performance was on 17 January 1678, praises Dryden's comic writing and regrets the hostile reception which audiences accord it (ll. 5–14). But it is also possible[11] that lines later in the prologue on an 'elevated Poet' describe Dryden's equanimity in the face of ingratitude and disparagement in the theatre:

> I've seen an elevated Poet sit
> And hear the Audience laugh and clap, yet say,
> Gad after all 'tis a damn'd silly Play:
> He unconcern'd, crys onely——is it so?   (ll. 20–3)

¶7 1678
The Diary of Robert Hooke

In *The Diary of Robert Hooke 1672–1680*, ed. Henry W. Robinson and Walter Adams (London, 1935), in the entry for Saturday, 27 April 1678 (p. 355), Hooke records: 'talkd with Dryden of Burlington'.

¶8 *c*.1679
Procul este Prophani
Nottingham University Library, MS Portland PwV 39, pp. 93–9

Verses headed 'Procul este Prophani' (first line: 'Satyr is growne so dull that Fopps increase') include a reference to Dryden and his relationship with the Earl of Mulgrave. The implication seems to be that *An Essay upon Satire* (circulated in manuscript in 1679) was written by Dryden but passed

---

[9] See *London in Flames*, pp. 265–7 for an account of Wright and his four poems on St Paul's; *Ecclesia Restaurata* is reprinted on pp. 273–8.
[10] *The Prologues and Epilogues of the Restoration*, ed. Pierre Danchin, 7 vols. (Nancy, 1981–8).
[11] As Dr David Hopkins suggests to me.

off by Mulgrave as his. For the circumstances of the composition and circulation of the *Essay*, and the debate on its authorship, see *POAS* i. 396–401.

> The haughty Mul: they say does not want Witt
> I will beleive it yet he never writ
> 'Tis Dryden Scribbles & he bears the name
> The Poett for a Stipend quitts the Claime.   (p. 96)

¶9 1679

Troades: or the Royal Captives. A Tragedy. **Written Originally in Latin, By Lucius Annaeus Seneca, The Philosopher. English'd By Edward Sherburne Esq. (London, 1679)**

Wing S 2258

In the preface 'To the Reader' Sherburne quotes from Dryden's *Essay of Dramatick Poesie*:

> And one of the most Eminent Modern Masters of Dramatick Poesy among us, Mr. *Dryden*, in his Essay upon that Subject, hath declar'd it to be the Master Piece of *Seneca*; especially that Scene therein, where *Ulysses* is seeking for *Astyanax* to kill him. *There* (says he) *you have the Tenderness of a Mother so represented in* Andromache, *that it raises Compassion to a high Degree in the Reader, and bears the nearest Resemblance of any thing in the Antient Tragedies, to the excellent Scenes of Passion in* Shakespeare, *or in* Fletcher. (sig. A3ᵛ)

¶10 1679

Charles Blount, *Anima Mundi* (London, 1679)

Wing B 3298

On p. 86 Blount says: 'with the same Arguments a modern most ingenious Poet, brings in St. *Catharine* vindicating Christianity from Paganism', and then quotes from Dryden's *Tyrannick Love*, II. i. 211–20.

¶11 c.1680

The Saint turn'd Curtezan: Or, A New Plot discover'd by a precious Zealot, of an Assault and Battery design'd upon the Body of a Sanctify'd Sister **([London], n.d.)**

Wing S 359, dating it 1681

On p. 2 a cudgelling is described as 'A *Dryden*'s Salutation', an allusion to the attack on him in Rose Alley on 18 December 1679.

¶12 1680

Charles Blount, *Great is Diana of the Ephesians* (London, 1680)

Wing B 3303

On p. 13 Blount quotes Dryden's lines from *The Indian Emperour*, IV. ii. 78–9:

> Those who to Empire by dark paths aspire,
> Still plead a Call to what they most desire.

¶13 1680

The Miseries of Visitts

Leeds University Library Brotherton Collection, MS Lt 87, fos. 50ʳ–51ʳ

Verses entitled 'The Miseries of Visitts' refer to the Rose Alley attack on Dryden and the attribution to him of Mulgrave's *An Essay upon Satire*. This text is printed in Paul Hammond, 'The Miseries of Visits: An Addition to the Literature on Robert Julian, Secretary to the Muses', *The Seventeenth Century*, 8 (1993) 161–3; another text is printed by Harold Love in *Scribal Publication in Seventeenth-Century England* (Oxford, 1993), pp. 257–8.

¶14 1680

The Papers of John Aubrey

Bodleian Library Oxford, MS Ballard 14, fos. 127 and 131

These papers include notes that Aubrey was soliciting commendatory poems for his work on Hobbes:

(i) 'I doubt not but to get the honour and favour of the E. of Dorset (my good friend) to write some verses. Sr W. P. will speak to Mr Edm. Waller, (who was his old & good friend.) Fleetw: Shepard, and Mr J. Dryden.' (21 February 1680)

(ii) 'I have engaged the Earle of Dorset, my Ld John Vaughan to write verses, and they will engage my Ld Mowgrave, & the E. of Rochester. I [have *deleted*] first engaged Mr Dreyden, & Mr Waller who is willing he tells me (for they were old acquaintances) but he is something afrayd of the Ecclesiastiques.' (27 March 1680)

¶15 1681

***Amaryllis to Tityrus* (London, 1681)**

Wing S 2143

This volume, a translation from Madeleine de Scudéry, includes 'An Essay on Dramatick Poetry' which has praise of Dryden. It is printed and discussed by Arthur C. Kirsch in '"An Essay on Dramatick Poetry" (1681)', *Huntington Library Quarterly*, 28 (1964–5) 89–91.

¶16 1681
John Dryden, *Absalom and Achitophel* (London, 1681)
Wing D 2212; Macdonald 12a

Many copies of the poem are annotated by contemporaries with identifications of the persons signified by the biblical names. A copy in the Folger Shakespeare Library (call no. D 2212) has annotations which go beyond this, and amount to a hostile running commentary on Dryden and his poem. The following selected marginalia omit routine identifications.

To the Reader. *draws his pen*] Confesseth his drawing his pen for a Party.
Genius] Com[m]ends himselfe.
rebating] Let him write Sharper if he can.
l. 1 *In pious times*] The Poet an Atheist exceeding Lucretius.
l. 61 *Those very Jewes*] The Phanaticks as he calls them before.
l. 82 *The Good old Cause*] This blind Poet can not see ye Plot which 3 Parliam^{ts} did: and ye Judges haue hang'd so many for.
l. 99 *For Priests*] the poet an enemy to all Priests.
l. 108 *From hence began*] Sorry ye Plot was discouered and defeated.
l. 207 *behind the Laws*] The Laws ye Poets grieuance.
l. 215 *easie to Rebell*] Reproacheth the people as Rebells.
l. 299 *And Nobler is a limited Command*] His grief is Englands Governm^t is not absolute.
l. 495 *The Best*] The protesting Lords.
l. 501 *The next*] The Com[m]ons
l. 509 *with them*] The House of Com[m]ons
l. 569 *Titles and Names*] A low value of the Nobility.
l. 914 *These were the chief*] God help ye King if these be all.

Another annotated copy, this time of the fourth edition (1682; Wing D 2219; Macdonald 12g), is also worth recording. This belonged to Benjamin Godfrey, the younger brother of Sir Edmund Berry Godfrey whose murder marked the beginning of the Popish Plot. The volume containing the poem passed to his son John Godfrey. The annotations to *Absalom and Achitophel* are not in John's hand, so are quite probably Benjamin's commentary. The copy is now in the collection of Paul Hammond.

Apart from uncontroversial identifications of the principal characters, it is worth recording that the annotator interprets 'The *Jews*' (l. 45) as 'the Citizens of London' rather than the English people generally, thus emphasizing the metropolitan character of the crisis. When Dryden says that

Shaftesbury 'Usurp'd a Patriott's All-attoning Name' (l. 179) he comments: 'on[e] yᵗ pretends to stand up for the Liberty of the subject'. 'The Malecontents of all the *Israelites*' (l. 492) and 'Hot *Levites*' (l. 519) are both glossed 'fanaticks', while '*Aaron*'s Race' is labelled 'Tub: prechers'. The line 'Their *Belial* with their *Belzebub* will fight' (l. 1016) is glossed 'Their: Wittness', alluding to Oates's use of perjured and contradictory witnesses to secure convictions. Whether or not the annotator was the brother of the man who inadvertently became a Protestant martyr, he was himself no lover of extreme Protestants.

¶17 *c.*1682
Quem Natura Negat, &c.

British Library MS Harley 7317, pp. 6–14. First line: 'I who from drinking ne're could spare an hour'. There is another copy in BL MS Harley 7319, fos. 114ʳ–119ʳ

This poem dates from *c.*1682, since it alludes to Otway's *Venice Preserv'd*. It includes the following lines:

> I . . .
> Who hate all Satyrs whether sharp or dull
> From *Dryden* to the Governor of Hull . . .   (p. 6)

> Let *Dryden's* pen indulgent David blame,
> And brand his friend with hated Rebells name,
> He that could once call *Charles* a sauntring cully
> By *Portsmouth* sold & Jilted by Bitch *Nelly*:
> He that could once the Prince of Rebells praise,
> With the same hand the Tory cause may raise.
> A starving Muse, no Interest can advance,
> He writes, as Parson's preach, for Sustenance.
> A pamper'd Hero, for the Duke's applause,
> A Cudgell'd Martyr for the Whiggish cause.
> A Cur that fawns on him last gave him bread,
> And growles & snarles at the whole world besides.
> Ungratefull, mercenary, fearfull, mean,
> The best of Rhimers, and the worst of Men.   (pp. 9–10)

The reference to 'the Governor of Hull' may be to Andrew Marvell, who had been MP for Hull. The allusions to Dryden include comment on his treatment of Charles II in *Absalom and Achitophel*, and his earlier *Heroique Stanza's* on the death of Cromwell, but the reference to him calling Charles 'a sauntring cully' must be to some anonymous poem which is no longer associated with him. The reference to the Rose Alley attack interprets it as a politically motivated assault.

¶18 1682
Advice to yᵉ Satirical Poets. 1682

British Library MS Harley 7319, fos. 85ᵛ–86ʳ. First line: 'Satyr's depostick [i.e. despotic] now; none can withstand'

The poem describes the dangers incurred by poets such as Dryden, the 'wondrous *Mufti*' of the tyrannical realm of satire:

> Still Punishing, no pardons, no Rewards
> Makes Tyranny unsafe; You'l need new Guards.
> Your wondrous *Mufti* danger in't has found;
> That Head was broke, that was so justly Crown'd,
> By most Invective Scandalous Cudgel's Flayl'd,
> Without distinction just as he had Rail'd.
> Yet let's do Right, & proise [*sic*] him where 'tis fit;
> Some strain to Mimick, none can match his Wit;
> Save but his bones, he's well Secur'd of Fame;
> The Chancellours Epitaph must preserve his Name.
>   'At Barr, abusive; on the Bench, unable;
>   'Knave on the Woolsack; Fop at Council Table.
> Such Pregnant Sense & truths were never put
> In so small Room, Since *Homer* in the Nut.
> Too many times a far less meaning Text,
> Has Doctors, Schools, Ages, & Empires vext.
> Oh, cou'd my Muse but two such Lines afford,
> (If any Muse wou'd take a Poets word)
> I'de promise fair, nay Solemn Oaths I'de take,
> By all the Gods, & by their Stygian Lake,
> Ne're more to Stretch her on yᵉ Rhyming Rack.

The quoted couplet comes from *An Essay upon Satire*, ll. 164–5, and refers to Lord Chancellor Finch.[12]

¶19 1682
The Observator, no. 86, 4 Jan. 1681/2

This issue opens with the following exchange between 'Whig' and 'Tory', which is probably a reference to *Poetical Reflections on a Late Poem Entituled Absalom and Achitophel* (London, 1681; Macdonald 200), Luttrell's copy of which is dated 14 December 1681:

[12] I owe this identification to Dr Tom Mason.

WHIG. Well! But they are now more Outrageous then ever, I make no doubt but you have seen some Late *Poeticall Raptures* upon *Absalom* and *Achitophel*.

To[ry]. Yes, yes. The Devil ow'd them a shame and had no way to come out of their debt, but by making 'um *Poets*.

¶20 1682
Letters of Gilbert Burnet to Anne Wharton

Quotations are taken from *The Surviving Works of Anne Wharton*, edited by G. Greer and S. Hastings (Stump Cross, 1997), pp. 349, 351. In a letter to Anne Wharton dated 12 December 1682, Burnet comments on *Religio Laici*:

> Mr. Dryden's 'Religion of a Layman' is farre below what might have been expected of him on such a subject; and I wonder much to hear that the verses before it are my Lord Vaughan's, for I thought his strain was more exalted.

And on 19–20 December he writes about reactions to Mulgrave's *An Essay upon Poetry*:

> all the wits in the toun, not excepting *Dryden* for all his being ill used, are of my mind, that it is incomparable.

¶21 1682–4
The Papers of White Kennett
British Library MSS Lansdowne 936 and 937

These contain several references to Dryden:

(i) 'Sent into Kent...Dryden's Satyr ag[st] Sedition' (10 April 1682; MS Lansdowne 937, fo. 8[v]). The reference is to *The Medall*, which was published on or about 16 March 1682.

(ii) Kennett records a conversation with Mr Brome: 'In discourse contracted my judgment of our own late Poets in this censure. That Johnson and Dryden were Poeta[e] facti non Nati, Davenan[t] was Natus non factus, y[e] incomparable Cowly was both, & all y[e] rest were neither.' (17 January 1683; MS Lansdowne 937, fo. 31[r])

(iii) 'Plutarchs Lives translating out of Greek in 5 volumes 8[vo]. The first part already out[.] The Epistle dedicatory to y[e] d of Ormond & y[e] Life of Plutarch wrot by Mr Dryden' (3 May 1683; MS Lansdowne 937, fo. 39[v]). Macdonald (p. 168) notes that *Plutarchs Lives* was entered in the Stationers'

Register on 25 April 1683, and advertised in *The Observator* on 2 May and in *The London Gazette* in the issue for 30 April–3 May.

(iv) Kennett notes: 'Heard Mr Drydens dedication of ye 1st pt of Plutarch's Lives, to ye d of Ormond, commended for one of the best Essays of eloquent English that ever was wrot.' (17 May 1683; MS Lansdowne 937, fo. 40^v)

(v) 'A report that Mr Creeches late verses for ye entertainment of the Duke were great part stole out of Mr Dryden's Annus Mirabilis.' (24 May 1683; MS Lansdowne 937, fo. 41^v)

(vi) 'Miscellany Poems by severall hands ye best Translations those two of M^r. Dryden's' (9 February 1684; MS Lansdowne 937, fo. 54^v). Macdonald (p. 68) notes that Tonson's *Miscellany Poems* was entered in the Stationers' Register on 4 February 1684, and advertised in *The Observator* on 2 February. The two translations referred to by Kennett are probably the fourth and ninth eclogues of Virgil, though Dryden also translated 'Ovid's Elegy the Nineteenth, Book II' and 'Amaryllis, Or the Third Idyllium of Theocritus'.

¶22 1683
Thomas Shipman, *Carolina: or, Loyal Poems* (London, 1683)

Wing S 3440

Macdonald includes this as item no. 220, but omits a reference in Shipman's Preface to Dryden's plans to write an epic poem. After discussing Waller, he says:

> Another, [*margin*: M. D.] as eminent, calls them *Fumblers* who write after *forty*. But I hope he will fumble on still; having put us in expectation of an *Epick Poem*, which (like *Solomon*) must be the *Darling* of his Age, and out-wit his other *Brethren*. I see no cause but *Dotage* to make it be left off. (sig. A2^v)

The allusion to fumblers is to the Epilogue to *1 Conquest of Granada*, ll. 19–20.

¶23 1683
The Saints Liberty of Conscience in the New Kingdom of Poland **('Warsaw', 1683)**

Wing S 363

The Polish trope alludes to the report that the Earl of Shaftesbury had been a candidate for the throne of Poland (see *Poems*, ed. Hammond, ii. 9). There are two allusions to Dryden's work:

(i) On p. 2: the power of granting indulgences for liberty of conscience is vested in:

> Oggi Shadwelliski Poet Bayse of Poland.
> Doeggi Settleliski Casuist and Characterer

These are names for Shadwell and Settle from *Absalom and Achitophel: The Second Part.*

(ii) On p. 3: money is to be paid out:

> For a Whigg-Poet, in Pension, to Write against the Government, the Lawreat and Lent-Prologues, per annum. 050 00 00 . . .

> > For the Author of the Growth of Popery. 100 00 00
> > For the Lawreat, if he had undertaken it. 400 00 00.

¶24 1684
News from Tunbridge. 1684

Bodleian Library Oxford, MS Rawl. Poet. 159, fos. 170ʳ–174ʳ. Crum T 3355. There is another copy in British Library MS Harley 7319, fos. 178ʳ–182ᵛ

On fo. 173ʳ are the following lines on Dryden at Will's Coffee House:

> And now, you mighty Critics, Wits, and those
> That to true Poetry your Minds dispose,
> Tell me (if you can Judge) of my Defect,
> Or of the smallest fault can me detect:
> If aid you want, *Will's* Coffee-house convene,
> And *Dryden* too, who in Imperious Strain
> Pretends to the whole Province of the Brain.

¶25 1684
E: Phileroy, *A Satyrical Vision, or, Tragy-Comedy As it Was lately Acted in the City of Bristol, Discovered in a Dream* (London, 1684)
Wing P 1985[13]

This is a satire against dissenters. On p. 2 there is a mock dedicatory poem by 'Philo: Phileroy' which refers to Dryden being the victim of attacks from Nonconformists:

> The mighty *Laureat* (that darling of the Nine)
> Who in each Immortal Line,
> Doth wit and Judgment joyn,

[13] I owe this and the following item to Dr Paulina Kewes.

Whose muse alone boy's up the sinking stage
(Such is th' Ingratitude of th' unthinking Age)
    Is not beneath his Bays, free from their bruitish Rage
So senceless Curs (they say) are often known
To bark with fury 'gainst the Radiant *Moon.*

¶26 1685
W.C., *The Siege of Vienna, A Poem* (London, 1685)
Wing C 169

In his Preface the author laments the inadequate rewards which poets have received, and the enmity which they have attracted:

> I confess Poverty an epidemical Distemper amongst Poets, their Fortunes is a large Inheritance in fairy Ground. *Ben. Johnson*, the meritorious *Cowley*, and my incomparable Country-man Mr. *Marvell*, died poor... The illustrious *Cowley* and *Devanant* with the Sages of the Times, *Dryden, Duke, Creech*, have their Enemies. (sigs. A3^v–A4^r)

¶27 1685
The Quakers Elegy on the Death of Charles late King of England, written by W. P. a sincere Lover of Charles and James (Dublin, 1685)
Wing P 137A; another edition is P 137

This poem (printed on a single sheet) uses Dryden's names from *Absalom and Achitophel*, but nevertheless includes an allusion to Dryden's *Heroique Stanza's* on the death of Cromwell:

> We take not *Absalom*'s, but *David*'s part;
> Nor no *Achitophel* with his false art;
> Nay joyn'd with *Zimry*'s poyson, ever shall
> Like the disloyal *Corah*, make us fall
> .   .   .   .   .   .
> 'Twas Loyal Zeal made us presume thus far,
> We ne'r were Poets unto *Oliver.*

¶28 *c.*1685
Bays his Blind side
Bodleian Library Oxford, MS Firth c. 16, pp. 96–7, without title; the title and the first two stanzas occur again on pp. 101–2, but deleted; Crum F 686. The following text takes the title from p. 101 and the rest of the poem from pp. 96–7. It is a satire on the costly failure of Albion and Albanius

Bays his Blind side
or
Satyricall Remarks upon a late
Raree Show Vulgerly calld an Opera
And sett to the only tollerable good tune in
the whole worke.

From Father Hopkins whos V[e]ines did Inspire him
Bayes sends this Raree Show to Publique view[14]
Prentices Fops and their footmen Admire him
Thanks Patron painter and Mounseir Grabeu

Each Actor on the Staig his luck bewailing
Finds that his loss is Infallible trew
Smith Noakes and Lee, in a feauor with Railing
Curs Poett painter and Mounseir Grabeu

[*blank*] thy Decorations
And the Macheins were well written wee knew
But all the words are such stuff, wee want patience
And Little better is Mounsier Grabeu.

Damme Crys Underhill Im Out two hundred
Hoping that Rainbows and Peocoks woud doe
Who thought Intollerable Tom woud haue blunderd
Ah Plague Uppon him and Mounsier Grabue

Law thou hast had no Applauses for thy Capers
Tho all without thee woud make a Man Spew
And a Month hence will not pay for the Tapers
Spight of Jack Lawreat or Mounsier Grabeu

Bayes thou woudst haue thy skill thought Universall
Tho thy dull Eare be to Musick Untrue
Then whilst wee striue to Confute the Rehersall
Prethe learn thrashing of Mounsier Grabue

With thy dull prefaces still thou woudst treat us
Striuing to make thy dull bauble look fair
So the Hornd heard of the Citty do Cheat us
Still most Commending the worst of their wear

Leaue making Operaes and writing Lyricks
Till thou haist Eares and canst alter thy streine
Stick to thy talent of bould Panigericks
And still Remember the breathing the Veine[15]

[14] Emended from the text on p. 101; p. 96 has 'Rare' and 'publick to Vew'.
[15] A reference to *Heroique Stanza's*, l. 48.

Yett if thou thinks that the Towne does extoll em
Print thy dull Noutes but be thrifty and Wise
Instid of Angells subsc[r]ibd for thy Vollume
Take a Round shilling and thanke my Advise

[*blank*] the this may be charming
Gleaning from Laureats is no shame att all
And lett this song be sung the next performeing
Either ten to one the Prices will fall

The Hopkins of the opening line who is said to be Dryden's poetic father is John Hopkins, who with Thomas Sternhold was responsible for the metrical version of the Psalms.

¶29 c.1685
Uppon the Author of the Poem yᵉ Medall

Bodleian Library Oxford, MS Firth c. 16, pp. 50–1. Crum O 1138

An anonymous poem on *The Medall*. It must postdate Dryden's conversion (at least in its present form) which happened *c.*1685.

Uppon the Author of the Poem yᵉ Medall
Once more the Nedy Poett sells his Pen
And Barters all his honesty for gaine,
Once more perswasiue Gold Obtaines the feild
And mercenary hopes has made him Yeald
To ills his Conscience had so long declined
Soe far from what his former thoughts designed
When he with all watcht for the needfull hower
To stem the Torent of Impetuous Power
When Liberty braue Liberty was his Theame
And the bould truth flowed from his Silver Stream.
Nor patiently would see his countrymen betrayd
But sent his Genious to the Peoples Aid
Blest muse whose Witt with such a cause was Crownd
But curse the cause that made him quitt his Ground
Was itt his Pention or his baser feares
From Statesmans promise or a Strumpitts tears
May he rely on the and still depend
On the Kings purse, and his Court smiling freind
And may som subtle pimp still trump his card
Yett he hope on and starue for his Reward
Let me no longer wish for Virtues face
For tis a Scandall to pretend to Grace

If he be good or honest he that liues
On wrecks of Vertue and on slander thriues
That on Mankind with Vennom he does fall
And black distraction Ouerflows his Gall
That dares gainst Right & Justice too Ingage
And Glut on Mangled Innocence his Rage
His fury without all distinction sheds
On sacred freindship and his Patrons heads
To none but Rouges and Villains Gentle found
And hugs dear mischeiff when it giues the wound
Att Canting Magpye beast he Raild before
But now who pleads more strongly for the whore
Tis Sordid Intrest his Conscience draws
And his Religion Changes with his Cause
Whenere he writes tis heauen he makes his Jest
And layes his Nasty Load on euery Preist
Dares rally that most bright most blest aboad
And trespass on the Mercy of his God
Then Wonder not if now he turnes his Stile
And stabs the Noblest Patriot of this Ile
But Courage wants to Act the bloody part
For Nature durst not trust him with a heart
    To you his darling freinds I recommend
These truiths youl find em Gosple in the end
Tho he like wax haue your Impression Tane
The Next warm hand will Soften him againe
Beleiue him honest trust his Principle
Rely on him he'le deceiue you all
As Ratts the buildings quitt before they fall
One day this vermine may desert Whithall
And now great Berd the tribute I can Raise
Is Onely this, may Tyburn wear thy Bayes.

¶30 1685
A Letter to Julian from Tunbridge

British Library MS Harley 7319, fos. 204ʳ–207ᵛ. Crum D 82a

This poem includes a quotation from *Threnodia Augustalis* (1685): 'Our
Atlas fell indeed; But *Hercules* was near' (l. 35):

> Of all our Travel'd Youth, none dare
> With *Newburgh* vye for the *Belair*

He is so *French* in all his ways
Loves Dresses, sweares *al-a Francoise*
Sings to the Spinnet & Guitar
Those gentile ways to Charm ye Fair
And tho Sr *Edward Viller's* gone
Is able to support alone
Sr *Courtly Nice's* Character
Thus *Atlas* fell indeed, but *Hercules* was near   (fo. 206^{r-v})

¶31 1685
Julians farwell to the Muses

Bodleian Library Oxford, MS Firth c. 16, pp. 52–3. Crum M 380. There is another copy, dated 1685, in Bodleian Library MS Firth c. 15, p. 169

There is a brief reference to Dryden and Mulgrave:

Lett haughty Mul—ue One [*i.e.* own] the Lawrett rhimes
And Dreydens back answer for his Own Crymes.

¶32 1685
Nahum Tate (ed.), *Poems by Several Hands, and on Several Occasions* (London, 1685)

Wing T 210

On pp. 90–3 there is a poem by John Evelyn called 'The Immortalitie of Poesie' which has the following stanza on Dryden:

Dryden will last as long as Wit and Sense,
While Judgment is requir'd to Excellence,
While perfect Language charms an Audience.   (p. 92)

¶33 1685
The Laurel, A Poem on the Poet-Laureat (London, 1685)

Wing L 622

This poem on Dryden (Macdonald 234) also includes what seems to be an unrecorded reference to Milton on p. 15:

The Tuneful Smec, once left his hungry Prose,
In Doggrel twang'd his Calvin through the Nose.
Well may you teach his Renegado Priests,
When their dull Master aim'd so high as this.

¶34 1685
Matthew Taubman (ed.), *Loyal Poems and Satyrs Upon the Times*
(London, 1685)
Wing T 245

The title-page quotes 'Plots true or false are necessary things | To set up
Common-Wealths, and Ruin Kings' from *Absalom and Achitophel* (ll. 83–4)
as its epigraph. On p. 45 verses 'On Old Doctor Wild' allude to Dryden's
Mr Limberham:

> Just so *Sir Limber-ham* that scarce can crawl,
> Will on his *Venus*, and his *Cupids* call;
> And drains *Five hundred Pieces* from his Purse
> To keep a *Miss*, when more he wants a *Nurse*.

¶35 1685
Miscellany Poems and Translations By Oxford Hands **(London, 1685)**
Wing M 232

There are several poems which allude to Dryden:

(i) On p. 46 the anonymous poem 'Reason' includes a stanza which
echoes the opening lines of *Religio Laici*:

> At best, thou'rt but a glimmering Light,
> > Which serves not to direct our way,
> But like the Moon confounds our sight,
> > And only shews it is not day.

(ii) On pp. 82–3 the translation 'Out of MARTIAL Book the 3d Epig. 33d
imitated' includes the lines:

> Well Sir you say, if this thing does not hit,
> I'll Poetize and be a man of Wit;
> The lofty Verses which from me you hear
> With wonder you'll applaud your self, and swear
> That they as good as *L——s* or *D——s* are.
> Heav'ns Sir you rave, you talk so madly now:
> Those tatter'd things which out at Elbows go;
> Which wait for Scraps and Coach room at *White-hall*,
> Are *Spencers*, *Cowleys*, L——s and D——ns all.

The copy in the Brotherton Collection, Leeds University Library, has the
blanks expanded in manuscript to 'Lees' and 'Drydens'.

(iii) On pp. 91–2 is 'A Fragment out of P E T R O N I U S imitated, beginning Thus—*Quisquis habet nummos &c.*', which includes the lines:

> THE wealthy Lord thro Storms at Court may sail
>
> .   .   .   .
>
> He with nice Art the choicest Verse can write,
> Can baffle *D——* and the men of Wit:
> The Matchless *C——ly*, and great *W——ler* seem
> Rude, and unpolisht, when compar'd to him.
> If you have Wealth you may do what you please[.]

¶36 1686
An Epilogue Spoken to the University of Oxon

Danchin 355

The speaker, Mrs Sarah Cooke, says that one could not expect Dryden to write an Oxford prologue after his conversion to Rome.

¶37 1687
The Poets' Address to King James

Leeds University Library Brotherton Collection, MS Lt q 11 (3)

Dated 1687, this poem ironically compliments James II on his Declaration of Indulgence, and imagines a second part to *The Hind and the Panther*. It is a different work from the similarly titled *The Poets Address to King James II* (London, 1685; Macdonald 235).

> Only one stubborn part o' th Nation
> Would bind the power of Dispensation
> For which weel Rate ye Rogues again
> With Second part of Hind & Pan

¶38 *c.*1687
Upon the Hind and Panther

Nottingham University Library, MS Portland PwV 1212[16]

This is a single sheet of verses on *The Hind and the Panther* (1687); the points from the poem which it is refuting are quoted in the margin with page references to the first edition.

---

[16] Quoted by permission of the Department of Manuscripts and Special Collections, University of Nottingham.

Upon the Hind and Panther.

Tho nothing more irrationall appeares
Than to prick up predestinateing eares,
Predestination how can he deny,
Whose nimble Hind is fated not to dy?
But how can she who this received from fate, [5]
Of her owne Choice assume imortall state?
Yett in that faith it is not strange to see
Choice transubstantiated into decree:
Our poet's choice is meer Necessitie.
Since[?] vocal wants admonisht him to range, [10]
Methinks 'twere pitty he should starve & change.
The praise of that obtain'd no lasting boon,
Because his hated Memory stunk so soon:
Now sure he cannot fail of a supply,
ffrom a rich Mother fated not to dy [15]
But shall he be befriended by her Cowls
Who likend their beloved Nuns to Owls?
Or shall the soveraigns hand reward y^t tongue,
Which makes it his prerogative to wrong,
While he as factious do's the old Maxim name: [20]
The Lawyers Maxims he's allow'd to blame,
Whose old possession stands till older quitt ye plaine
W^{ch} since the Elder is not pleas'd to quitt,
That this should yeild unto its fate 'tis fitt
Like th' [*an illegible word here, and then the manuscript is torn*] [25]

Marginal notes:

l. 2] p. 10. And pricks up his predestinating eares.
l. 4] p. 2. And doom'd to death, tho fated not to dy.
l. 6] p. 2. Th' immortall part assum'd immortal state.
l. 9] p. 2. Whose vocal blood arose.
l. 16] p. 130. And sister Partlet with her hooded head
      Was hooted hence because she would not pray abed
ll. 19–20] p. 142. Such powers thay have as factious Lawyers long
      To Crowns ascrib'd, y^t kings can do no wrong.
l. 22] p. 46. And old possession stands till elder quitts ye claime.
l. 23] p. 5. Thy throne is darkness in th' abyss of light
      A Blaze of Glory, y^t forbids the [*manuscript torn*]

¶39 *c.*1687
The Dogg-Whigg and the Catt-Whigg

Bodleian Library Oxford, MS Rawl. Poet. 19, fos. 75ʳ–76ʳ. Crum Y 353

This poem is primarily a ballad on the Rye House Plot, and is therefore dated by Crum to 1683. But the first two stanzas (which may be a later addition to the ballad) refer to *The Hind and the Panther*.

> the Dogg-Whigg and the Catt-Whigg,
> A proper New-Ballad;
> Humbly dedicated
> To Colonel Bull and the rest of the Black Guard
> In Token of Gratitude for their Burning of New-markett
> And so Disappointing the Dogg Whigg's conspiracy at the Rye
>
> You sons of the panther spotted all ore,
> While a white Hind's Made of A scarlett Whore,
> By A Man that was made a Horn'd-Beast before,
> Which no Body can Deny;
>
> of Dogg-Whigg and Catt-Whigg Ile tell 'you A short story
> Shall Rival John Driden and Ravish John Dory,
> Then Mark my Rime-Doggrell both Whigg and Tory;
> Which no Body can Deny;

The remainder of the poem is rebarbative political doggerel.

¶40 1688
***On the Death of the Duke of Ormond. An Eclogue* (London, 1688)**

Wing O 309

This anonymous poem refers to Ormonde as Barzillai and Charles II as David, deploying the nomenclature of *Absalom and Achitophel*. For other poems which use the imagery of *Absalom and Achitophel* see *Poems*, ed. Hammond, i. 449.

¶41 1688
***Poems to the Memory of that Incomparable Poet Edmond Waller Esquire. By Several Hands* (London, 1688)**

Wing P 2724

On p. 24 an anonymous writer alludes disparagingly to *The Hind and the Panther*.

> Nor did *Old Age* damp the Poetick Flame,
> Loaded with *Fourscore* Years, 'twas still the same.

Some we may see, who in their Youth have writ
Good Sense, at *Fifty* take their leave of *Wit*,
Chimera's and incongruous Fables feign,
Tedious, Insipid, Impudent, and Vain:

¶42 1688
Satyr against the Poets

British Library MS Harley 7317, fos. 35ᵛ–37ᵛ. Crum W 2842. Also found in Leeds University Library, Brotherton Collection MS Lt q 52, fos. 69ʳ–70ʳ, where it is dated 1688

One passage reworks parts of *Mac Flecknoe*:

Hard by the fair Augusta's walls there stood
Of Yore, an Aged Cittadel of Wood
Which long the Attacques of pelting Boys had bore
And Prentice storming for Suburbian whore
Scene of lewd Nymphs & of polluted Swains,
Where now a Lordly Pile (so fate ordains)   —Bedlam
Stands, & surveys around the humble plains.
Goodly & great provided as a fence
'Against all the Batterys of thought or sense   (fo. 35ᵛ)

On fo. 36ᵛ Shadwell is referred to simply as 'Mac: Fleckno', and on fo. 37ʳ a passage on Rymer links him to Flecknoe, with further use of Dryden's poem:

Flecknoe & thou his Coleague in the War
The States against the Realm of Sence declare
Like Kings of Brentford hand in hand shall sit
The Target thou & he the Flail of Wit
Marcellus thus the sword of Rome did weild
Whilst his wise fellow Consull held the shield

¶43 1689
Mrs. A. M., *An Heroical Panegyrick, Humbly Dedicated to the Reverend Father in God, Gilbert, Lord Bishop of Salisbury* (London, 1689)

Wing M 2

On p. 1 the writer says to Burnet:

Who dar'st pretend to Write your Character?
Not *Dryden*, no; nor all the Muses dare:

Your Merits are too Great for *Cowley*'s Pen,
And what I aim at, wants a Nobler Strain.

¶44 1689
The Delusion

British Library MS Harley 7319, fos. 318ᵛ–319ᵛ. Crum S 497

Directed at various supporters of James II, the theme of the poem is that men 'Too oft [do] change their freedom for a Jail'. Lines on the Earl of Salisbury link him with Dryden, a connection which is also made in 'Song. By Mʳ Dryden; in the Person of My Lord Salisbury, then in the Tower'.[17] The passage on Salisbury runs thus:

> To close the Sence, Squab *Salisbury* begins
> Sinking beneath a load of Gutts & Sins
> That Shapeless Monster, indigested Lump
> Whose arms are Gammon, & whose Face is Rump
> With thy Gross Sence what Reason cou'd prevail
> That thou shou'd'st change Religion for a Jail
> Come over yet, if thou wou'd'st come in Play
> *Dryden*, & *Hayns* (thy Friends will show yᵉ way

Salisbury was a Roman Catholic, like Dryden; Jo Haines the actor had converted to Catholicism, but had announced his return to the Church of England in his 'Recantation Prologue' of April 1689 (Danchin 368).

¶45 1689
To Will: Richards. 1689

British Library MS Harley 7317, fos. 97ᵛ–98ᵛ

The author considers the plight of poets after the departure of James II and the arrival of William III, and in particular Dryden's imminent loss of the Laureateship:

And yet the *Muses* starve would they be merry
They must go hunt for Rats at Londonderry
One Crown might be among the Muses flung
By him who gets three Kingdoms for a song
The *Laureat* will e'er long forbidden, see   {John Dryden Esq.ʳ}
His Tun of Sack as French Commodity.   (fo. 98ᵛ)

---

[17] See Paul Hammond, 'A Song Attributed to Dryden', *The Library*, 6th ser., 21 (1999) 59–66. The song is found in Bodleian MS Firth e. 6, fo. 60ʳ⁻ᵛ; the same manuscript contains a text of 'The Delusion' on fo. 92ᵛ.

¶46 c.1689
An Ironical Panegyric; from Poet Bayes to King Phys

Bodleian Library Oxford, MS Firth e. 6, fos. 87ᵛ–92ᵛ. Crum T 2793

There is another copy in British Library MS Harley 7319, fos. 326ʳ–328ᵛ. This poem is mentioned by Macdonald (p. 215 n. 1) but its sustained usurpation of Dryden's persona, and its satire both on James II and on Dryden himself, make it worth transcribing.

An Ironical Panegyric;
from Poet Bayes to King Phys, in his
Irish Pilgrimage

Sir,
'Tis not in me your Miseries to redress,
I ne'r yet made my Neighbor's Sufferings less:
A natural Proness to be Doing Ill
Always attended my envenom'd Quill.
My greatest Patrons have not scap'd my spight,
And I remember they have done me right:
Now you at best were but a stingy Master,
And, since y'are fal'n under this sad Disaster,
I'l break your Head, let who will give y'a Plaister.
I ever triumph over him that's down,
Put on, with Fortune, both my Smile and Frown:
A Panegyric that's Ironical
Is at this Season most Emphatical.
To set your Scarlet Crimes before your Face
Wou'd bring an Ignominy on your Race;
And, tho' I Modesty do seldom use,
For once my Inclination I'l refuse:
Your lesser Faults, which in my Way do lye,
I'l onely open, and so pass 'em by.
 Your Charity I never shall forget,
Nor know I well how to remember it:
My Dedications no reward cou'd bring,
Tho', like a Rogue, I prais'd you 'bove my King;
Made him but as a Shade to sett you off,
A Cypher, or a mere John–hold–my–Staff,
Extol'd and flatter'd you in every Line;
Yet that Hook was too weak to catch your Coin:
My Praises to Hyperbole did rise,
While you were free of Gold as of your Eyes;

Against my Reason and my Inclination,
Abjur'd my Faith to be of your Perswasion,
And, in effect, my better Part did damn,
To gain your Gold; yet not one Guinney came.
    Your Conduct I ore Europe have diffus'd,
And publish this you may be disabus'd;
For, next to a Miracle, you've successfull been,
But most in gaining so renown'd a Queen:
Whose Birth and Parts had plac'd her far above
All other Monarchs, but your Princely Love;
Her Dowry, cause you doated upon Pelf,
Made her too Great for any but your self.
    Your Faithfulness was ever counted rare,
None ever trusted to't but bought it dear:
As Convert Coleman to the World made known,
When, to preserve your Life, he lost his own.
The Man, by all the World it is allow'd,
Was with Acquired and Natural Parts endow'd,
To which if you had had a just Pretence,
You'd never broke the Promise of a Prince;
When the last Words he spoke, as I can gather,
Were, *There's no Faith in Man, nor Princes neither.*
But to the Guilty let the Guilt remain,
As I can't cure, I won't augment your Pain.
    Your Building Chappels was a pious Cheat,
That made you Poor and Little to be Great:
Your cram'd Exchequer quickly did exhaust;
You trebly pay'd the Charge each Altar cost.
I laugh to think how you by th' Nose were led,
Peters had found the soft Place in your Head.
O, had I been but your Confessor made
(For I still coveted that gainful Trade)
I wou'd have lay'd a Tax on each loose Thought,
If Heav'n you'd purchase, 't shou'd be dearly bought:
Altars and Chappels had not don't alone,
Gold shou'd for your Ungodliness attone.
'Twas a good Work, that I must needs confess,
But your Attempts still meet the same success:
And, were I you, 'fore Heav'n, I'd sit me down,
You ne'r had Luck, since you attain'd the crown.
I'm of Opinion that you are bewitch'd,
Rid by a Hag, or by a Conjurer switch'd:

Such damn'd ill Fortune never did attend
A Man, thro' all the Courses he does bend;
For whatsoever side it is you own,
If you espouse it, it must needs go down.
Since you your self a Son o' th' Church declar'd,
I leave the World to judge how it has far'd:
And, tho' a Calm did for a while appear,
You see what Tempests follow'd in the Reer.

    Like one ore-loden with the Weight of Wit,
Your next Exploit I never shall forget;
When your Queen's Secrets you in Print expos'd,
Which to your self shou'd onely be disclos'd;
Proclaim'd she bore a Child you ne'r begot,
Became a Father to you knew not what:
For, tho' her Harvest-Season's not expir'd,
Your Generative Strength long since retir'd,
As to her Confessor she oft declar'd,
How from Conjugal Rights she was debar'd.

    Shou'd I proceed, the Time wou'd be too short,
To tell your Rambles since you broke up Court;
With what Attendance, and what Majesty,
What State and Grandeur, you did cross the Sea!
The just Reception you in France did meet,
The Salutations they return'd your Fleet!
The Roofs and Windows, in each Town you came,
Fill'd with Spectators, who had heard your Fame;
All coveting to see that Mighty Man,
Who, in such Gallantry, from three Nations ran!
How like John Dory you to Paris rid,
In the same Equipage that Heroe did!
Like Entertainment you did there obtain,
Your Tale was heard, and you sent back again.
Your Queen you left, because she cou'd not ride,
Tho' now, 'tis said, she practises astride;
For, since to Ireland you did hoise your Sails,
She's got with Child of a true Prince of Wales:
Which when to th' World her teeming Womb makes plain,
Faith, send the other to his Friends again.

¶47 1690s
Henry Hall, 'To Mr. Charles Hoskins upon my lending him Mr. Wallers Poems'

Leeds University Library Brotherton Collection, MS Lt q 5, p. 51 (the poems of Henry Hall the elder). There is another copy in MS Lt 6 fos. 13ᵛ–14ʳ

Hall's poem 'To Mr. Charles Hoskins upon my lending him Mr. Wallers Poems' includes these lines:

> Dryden, who now our great example is,
> Rose to that height by makeing Waller his.
> He first our native Language did refine,
> Rugged & Rough, like mettle in yᵉ. Mine,
> He purg'd the Dross & Stampt it into Coin.
> Dryden alone can equallize his Witt,
> But Dryden, well you know, is liveing yett.
> We to the Quick are spareing of that praise
> Whome dead it crowns with everlasting Bays.
> But when that Poett shall Imortall be
> And gett, what oft He gave Here, Imortallity;
> With how much wonder will his works be read!
> And then of Wallers selfe it will be say'd,
> He equal'd Liveing & Surpasses Dead.

¶48 1690s
To The Hon.ble Mʳˢ F——

Leeds University Library Brotherton Collection, MS Lt 82, fo. 157ᵛ

Anonymous lines headed 'To the Hon.ble Mʳˢ F—— under the name of Ardelia upon her incomparable Poems' are addressed to Anne Finch, Countess of Winchilsea, seeing her as Dryden's successor:

> . . . to you i'de give the Bayes,
> There yours of Right none can with you contend,
> Tho scribling Poetasters still pretend,
> Since Dryden did the Laureats Crown resign
> Take it Ardelia, it is onely thine.

¶49 1691
A Pastoral Dialogue. A Poem (London, 1690)
Wing T 202A

This poem in support of William III and the Revolution is attributed to

Nahum Tate; it quotes 'For common quiet is Mankinds Concern' from *Religio Laici* (sig. A2^v).

¶50 1691

Mr. Tutchin, *A Congratulatory Poem to the Reverend Dr. John Tillotson, upon his Promotion to the Arch-Episcopal-See of Canterbury* (1691)

Wing T 3372

For John Tutchin's career see Macdonald, p. 250. Tutchin uses language from *Absalom and Achitophel* (cf. ll. 45, 48) to characterize the non-juring priests:

> The Stubborn *Levites* are our Land's disgrace,
> A Haughty, Proud, and a Contentious Race;
> Byass'd in Judgment, Turbulent in Mind,
> No King can Please, nor Acts of Grace can Bind.   (p. 5)

¶51 1691

Mercurius Deformatus: Or the True Observator **(London, 1691)**

Wing M 1762

On p. 1 there is a satirical account of Dryden in a coffee-house, taking part in a philosophical discussion. There are various contemporary references to Dryden participating in coffee-house discussions of literature, but this provides evidence (albeit grotesquely distorted) of Dryden's interest in philosophical debate.

> ... Then, broke with grief, I did repair
> Unto a place, I know not where;
> Where *Athens Owls* stand round a Table,
> And speak as *Nature* makes them able:
> But *D——n* in the middle sits,
> As great *Apollo* of the Wits;
> With Leather Lugs, and Leather Jaws,
> With greasie Face and nasty Paws;
> Who, tho he be of Maggots full,
> Proves *Vacuum* by his empty Scull.
> Their *These*[18] it was an ill-look'd Monster,
> Whom every Fop and Fool dares conster;

[18] i.e. thesis.

Of *Ens*, and *Non-ens*, *Penetration*,
Of *Causa* and of *Ubication*;
But *D——n* was for *Generation*.

¶52 1691
An Account of the Late horrid Conspiracy to Depose Their Present Majesties K. William and Q. Mary (London, 1691)

Wing D 827A

Attributed to Daniel Defoe. An account of the trials of Lord Preston, Mr Aston, and Major Elliott, this includes the following observation:

> These Men had fairer play than Noble *Sidny*, &c. who were hanged by help of a *Marginal Note*, for controversial Papers of twenty years standing, to which they made both *Keys and Characters*, abused the *Court* as much as *Dryden*'s Poem, and by a rare new *Law-figure* (for 'twou'd puzzle one to find it in all *Vossius* his Rhetorick) called *Innuendo*, extreamly obliged the late King *Charles*, by turning him into a *Tarquin*. (pp. 29–30)

The reference to a poem by Dryden is probably to Arthur Mainwaring's *Tarquin and Tullia* (1689; *POAS* v. 46–54), which was sometimes attributed to Dryden (Macdonald, pp. 320–1).[19]

¶53 1691
John Dunton, *The Athenian Mercury*, vol. 5 no. 2 (Saturday, 5 December 1691)[20]

The answer to the question 'Whom do you think the best Dramatick Professor in this Age?' makes a case for Shadwell's skill in comedy, and then continues:

> As for his *Predecessor*, we doubt not but Mr. *Laureat* himself has the justice to own him his *Master* in many parts of *Poetry*, and the *numerousness* of his Verse among other things, we suppose hee'l scarce dispute with him, since 'tis really almost Musick but to hear a page of him read, and Mr. *Drydens* Heroic Verse is undoubtedly the sweetest in the World. As for the controversie between him and some great persons, we may without injury to his Poetical Fame, believe he was overmatch'd in't, having a stronger *Genius* than his own to struggle with, and besides odds against him as to number; and if he has bin dealt with

[19] As Dr David Hopkins suggested to me.
[20] I owe this reference to Dr Paulina Kewes.

by 'em a little severely, 'tis with so much Wit, that we dare believe Mr *Dryden* himself cou'd hardly ever see the *Rehearsal* without being pleas'd with't. And tho there might be some reason in what they there drive at, and he being then but a Young Poet, might begin to dictate too soon, and assume that as his right, which both *Experience* and *merit* now give him, yet none that pretends to judge must deny that his Plays are some of the best on the *English* Stage. His *Oedipus*, tho' its true another had a share in't, is indeed incomparable, and even in those which are most spoken against, his very *Faults* are so bright that there's few can imitate 'em, much less reach his *Beauties*. His Enemies must acknowledge that he has all the *ART of Poetry*, and whether or no his *Fancies* are his own, he dresses 'em so well, that [no] one else dares own 'em ... And then for his last Play, there needs no more to be said in its Commendation ... than that his *Enchanted Forrest* exceeds even *Tasso*'s himself, from whom 'tis copy'd. On the whole, we need say no more than as we did in the last *Mercury*, that in general Mr. *Dryden* is in our Judgment by far the most *compleat Dramatick Writer* not only of our Age, but of all the *English* Poets that went before him.

¶54 1692
The Gentleman's Journal (1692)

The Gentleman's Journal contains many references to Dryden's literary projects, not all of which have been collected by Macdonald, though some of those which he missed have been used by Dryden scholars. In addition, in the issue for January 1692 (p. 31) there is an imitation of Horace's *Carmina*, I. vi, which includes these lines:

> Dryden in Never-dying Verse,
> Your glorious Triumphs may rehearse,
> His lofty Muse for Panegyric fam'd,
> May sing the Rebel-Herd your Valor tam'd.

The poem is entitled 'To Lord de Ginkle, General of their Majesties forces in Ireland'.

¶55 1692
St Evremont, *Miscellaneous Essays* (London, 1692)
Wing S 305

Macdonald includes this item (no. 137) but omits to mention that the preface includes comments on Dryden, and is subsequently quoted by Thomas Blount in *De Re Poetica* (1694), p. 114.

¶56 1692
William Lowth, *A Vindication of the Divine Authority and Inspiration of the Writings of the Old and New Testament* (Oxford, 1692)
Wing L 3330

Lowth discusses Richard Simon's work on the text of the Bible, and the way in which this has been interpreted, by Dryden amongst others:

> many, to shew their good Will to the Bible, make him say much Worse things than he really does, and such as they would fain have him say, and would be glad if they could Vouch his Authority for. They are Industrious to make the world believe, that if we will take his Judgment, there have been so many Corruptions and Alterations made in the Text of the Bible, that 'tis impossible to tell which is the True and which is the False Reading. Mr. *Dryden* particularly in his *Religio Laici*, makes this Comment upon Mr. *Simon's Critick*, and tells us, as delivering that Author's sense, that the Jews have
>
> > Let in Gross Errors to corrupt the Text,
> > Omitted Paragraphs,—and
> >
> > With vain Traditions stop'd the Gaping Fence.
>
> Now one would think by this Account of his Work, that Mr. *Simon* had expressly asserted that the Jews had Wilfully and Designedly Corrupted the Original, by Adding to and Taking away from it as they thought fit. But in my Opinion 'tis taking a greater Liberty than *Poetry* it self will allow, to make a man speak quite contrary to his Sense and Meaning. For Mr. *Simon* makes it his Business to prove in several places of his Book, that the Jews have not corrupted the *Hebrew* Text, and answers the Arguments that are usually brought for that Opinion. All that he affirms as to this matter is, that the Bible has been obnoxious to the same Corruptions that other Books are, through the Ignorance or Negligence of Transcribers; and that such kind of Faults crept into the Text in those Ages chiefly that did not mind the Niceties of Criticism: and therefore the proper way to Reform those Errors is by Correcting the Suspected Places according to the Rules of that Art, and by diligent Comparing of Copies, as Criticks correct other Books, and the Massorets have already the *Hebrew* Text. And as for the Additions which are supposed by many to have been made to the Original Text, he supposes them inserted by Prophets, whereof there was a constant Succession, whose Business 'twas to take Care of the Publick Records. How true this *Hypothesis* is, 'tis not my Business to examine, 'tis sufficient to my present Purpose, that Mr. *Simon* does not represent these Additions as so many Corruptions of the Text. So that in this Case Mr. *D.* has Misrepresented Mr. *Simon's* Text,

aswell [*sic*] as that of the Bible: and put such a Gloss upon it, as it does not appear that he ever intended, as far as can be gathered from his Words. But I shall pursue this Matter no further, because Mr. *D.* may think it hard measure to urge any thing said in his *Religio Laici* against him at this time of day, when he has alter'd his Mind in so many Particulars since the Writing of that Poem, and has made Amends for his Former Incredulity by turning Advocate for *Implicite Faith.* (sigs. A8ᵛ–b2ʳ)

¶57 1693

An humble Remonstrance of the Batchelors, in and about London ([London], 1693)

Wing H 3616

On p. 1 the author alludes to Dryden as an '*Abdicating Poet*', probably referring to his verses 'To My Dear Friend Mr Congreve'.[21]

> They complain that the Holy State of Matrimony has of late years been very irreverently spoken of, that it has been rhymed to Death in Sonnet, and murdered *in Effigie* upon the Stage . . . However we are assured from all hands, that those Persons who have taken the greatest pains to expose that Holy State, were all of 'em married (to prove which we could name a famous *Abdicating Poet*, if we were minded).

¶58 1693

To Mʳ Nahum Tate upon his being made Poet Laureat. 1693.

Bodleian Library Oxford, MS Don. c. 55, fos. 19ʳ–20ʳ. Crum J 150

The poem includes the following passage on Shadwell, which reflects upon Dryden. It is notable that the writer's hostility to Dryden does not prevent him from admiring his translations, particularly his lucid versions of Persius, which are preferred to his original poems.

> His Predecessor too, tho still alive
> Deservedly his Lawrels do's survive.
> Tho none than he more charmingly appears,
> In flowing Number's and the Turn of Verse,
> Master of Measure and the softest Lays;
> So qualify'd, and could he loose the Bays?
> Look in the Statute, and you find the Doom
> Of him who reconcile's himself to Rome.
> ffrom a keen satyrist t'was a shamefull slip,
> To make himself the subject of the whip:

---

[21] See Paul Hammond, *Dryden and the Traces of Classical Rome* (Oxford, 1999), pp. 12–13.

Not Maevius, ffleckno, Withers, Wild nor all
That Tribe were capable of such a ffall.
But spare the lash[,] to be the Author off
The Hind and Panther's punishment enough:
An overt and sufficient Evidence,
How easily he could deviate from sense,
In those dark Times of popish ignorance.
When almost every thing his pen brought forth,
Look't still of a supposititious Birth.
But since our Day break, since—
The Sunshine of our Revolution drives
ffar off those ffogs, and to our senses gives,
Protection safe, as to our Goods and Lives.
His poetry recover's strength, he mends
Spite of himself, and all his Wayward freinds.
In his new smooth intelleagible Lines,
How clear the dark and clowdy Persius shines;
But if the whole composure be his own,
Dreggs of the Old Evil are strewd up and down.
Mix't with the unpleasant Leven of self praise
Which puffs up, and makes light his Prefaces.
His 'ffensive[?] pointing to his own Excellence,
Too much implys his Reader's want of sense,
Now shall the ffrench Bein Tourne so delicate,
To Works on worthless Subjects give a Date.
Boileau and he, had better both write ffarce,
Than choose such sort of Hero's for they'r verse
Whose Deeds must sully future Registers.
But if he be, to lasting Glory's born,
Heaven has design'd him yet another Turn.   (fos. 19ʳ–20ʳ)

¶59 After 1693
Manuscript quotations from Dryden's translation of Juvenal

In the margin of p. 316 of the Cambridge University Library copy (Syn. 4. 62. 10) of Thomas Heywood's Γυναικειον: or, *Nine Bookes of Various History Concerninge Women* (London, 1624), a late seventeenth-century hand has inserted a quotation from Dryden's translation of Juvenal's *Satires* III (ll. 75–88) at the point where Heywood quotes the lines. The annotator may have been Thomas Graver, who owned the book in the 1660s.[22]

---

[22] I owe this item to Dr Paulina Kewes.

¶60 1694
[Lawrence Echard], Preface to *Terence's Comedies: Made English* . . . By Several Hands (London, 1694)

Wing T 749. Edited by John Barnard for the Augustan Reprint Society (Los Angeles, 1968)

The Preface discusses on pp. vii–viii Dryden's objections in his *Essay of Dramatick Poesie* to Terence's handling of the unities of time and action in *The Eunuch*; then on p. xvi Echard turns to Dryden's own handling of the unities.

¶61 1696
Thomas Dogget, Epilogue to *The Country Wake* (London, 1696)

Wing D 1828. Danchin 459

Probably first acted *c.* April 1696. Arguing that only excellent playwrights are to be esteemed, Dogget says:

> And by the Orthodox none ought to be
> Admitted to this Sacred Ministry,
> Less then a *Dryden, Congreve, Wycherly*. (ll. 26–8)

¶62 1696
Mary de La Rivière Manley, Preface to *The Royal Mischief* (London, 1696)

Wing M 436. Danchin 460

Manley remarks that portions of *The Spanish Fryar* and *Aureng-Zebe* 'have touches as full of natural fire as possible' (A3^r).

¶63 1696
Basil Kennett, *Romae Antiquae Notitia* (London, 1696)

Wing K 298

This has numerous quotations from Dryden's translations of Persius, Juvenal, and Georgic III.

¶64 1697
Earl of Dorset, 'Pindaric Petition to the Lords in Council'

There is a reference to Dryden in the Earl of Dorset's 'Pindaric Petition to the Lords in Council', printed in *The Poems of Charles Sackville, Sixth Earl of Dorset*, ed. Brice Harris (New York, 1979), p. 99.

¶65 1697

Edward Filmer, *The Unnatural Brother* (London, 1697)

Wing F 907

In the Preface (sig. A2^r) Filmer records chancing upon a volume of Dryden's plays. This is quoted and discussed in Paulina Kewes, *Authorship and Appropriation: Writing for the Stage in England, 1660–1710* (Oxford, 1998), pp. 200–1.

¶66 1697

John Potter, *Archaeologiae Graecae: or, The Antiquities of Greece* (Oxford, 1697)

Wing P 3030

This has quotations from many of Dryden's classical translations.

¶67 1697

Charron, *De La Sagesse*

Leeds University Library Brotherton Collection, MS Lt 48, fos. 91^v–92^r (from the back of the volume)

Fourteen lines from Dryden's translation of Ovid's *Metamorphoses*, Book I (printed in *Examen Poeticum* (1693)) are used in George Stanhope's manuscript translation of Charron's *De La Sagesse*.

¶68 1698

***Examen Poeticum Duplex* (London, 1698)**

Wing E 3708

In addition to echoing the title of the Dryden–Tonson miscellany *Examen Poeticum* (1693), this anonymous volume of Latin verse includes a translation of Dryden's lines on Milton. Dryden's epigram was inscribed under the frontispiece portrait prefixed to the 1688 edition of *Paradise Lost*, and was itself a free adaptation of earlier Latin verses on Milton by Selvaggi. Though it is conceivable that the lines in *Examen Poeticum Duplex* are the original from which Dryden's poem was translated (which would require Dryden to have seen them in manuscript ten years before their publication) it is more likely that they are the translation and Dryden's lines the original. The Latin version of Dryden's lines is as follows:

In Miltonum Poetam.

Tres magnos vario florentes tempore vates
    Graecia cum *Latio*, & terra *Britanna* tulit.

Grandia *Maeoniden*; distinguit lenta *Maronem*
   Majestas; *noster* laude ab utraq[ue] nitet.
Tendere non ultra valuit natura; priores,
   Tertius ut fieret, junxerat ergo duos.   (p. 9)

The volume also has the following epitaph on Shadwell:

Epitaphium Sh—lli.

Conditur hoc tumulo Bavius; gravis esse memento,
   Terra Tuo Bavio, nam fuit ille Tibi.
Mors uni Bavio lucrum, nam jugera vates,
   Qui vivens habuit nulla, Sepultus habet.
Tam cito mireris Bavii faetere cadaver,
   Non erat in toto corpore mica salis.
Dicite, nam bene vos nostris, Gens Critica, Vates
   An fuerit Bavius pejor, an Historicus?

(second pagination, p. 20)

And a satirical 'Epitaphium Viventis. F. S.' (on Fleetwood Shepherd) ends
with these references to Dryden and Shadwell:

Anno publicae paupertatis,
Et, si poesis paupertati a tergo adhaereat,
Anno publicae poeseos restauratae tertio:
Cum de bicipiti certarent Parnasso
   Hinc bifrons *Drydenus*
   Hinc bicornis *Shadwellus*:
Quorum Hic de facto,
Ille de jure, *Archipoeta*.

(second pagination, p. 31)

¶69 1699
[John Toland], *The Life of John Milton* (London, 1699)
Wing T 1766

Toland writes of Milton's relationship to Homer and Virgil, and then turns
to Dryden as a judge of all three.

He [Milton] has incontestably exceeded the fecundity of HOMER,
whose two Poems he could almost repeat without book: nor did he
com much short of the correctness of VIRGIL; which is affirm'd by one
whose judgment in this Province will be acknowledg'd by every man
that is not willing to expose the defect of his own. I mean the famous
JOHN DRYDEN, the best *English* Poet alive, the present Glory of our

Stage, and the Model of the same to future Ages; for he (having absolutely master'd these three Originals by framing a Tragedy out of *Paradise Lost*, making the Charms of VIRGIL appear in the *English* Tongue, and studying HOMER for the same purpose) pronounces his Judgment in favour of MILTON by this incomparable and envy'd Epigram. (pp. 128–9)

Toland then quotes the lines on Milton prefixed to the 1688 edition of *Paradise Lost*. The lines were printed anonymously, and were hitherto thought to have been first attributed to Dryden in the 1716 edition of *Miscellany Poems*. Toland's text is unrecorded by editors of Dryden before Volume III of the Longman Annotated English Poets edition. There is one substantive variant from the 1688 text in l. 6: former *1688*, other *Toland*.

¶70 1699

***Twenty Select Colloquies out of Erasmus Roterodamus. By Sir Roger L'Estrange. To which are added, Seven New Colloquies, as also The Life of Erasmus. By Mr Brown* (London, 1699)**

Wing E 3212

Tom Brown's 'The Life of Erasmus' comments on Scaliger's attack on Erasmus, and then remarks:

> The same Man, (for with him like *Zimri* in *Absolon*, every one is either a God or a Devil, but generally speaking they are Devils) has said that all *Ovid*'s slippery[23] Stuff is not to be compared with that single *Epithalamium* of *Catullus* upon *Thetis*'s Marriage . . . and pretended to mend *Ovid*'s Poetry, which he has done to as much purpose as Parson *Milburn* has mended Mr. *Dryden*'s Translation of *Virgil*. (sig. c3^v)

¶71 1700

[John Toland], *Clito: A Poem on the Force of Eloquence* (London, 1700)

Wing T 1764

A passage on pp. 8–9 has several echoes of Dryden:

> Or if he's only but the World's great Soul;
> Or parts the Creatures are, and God the whole
> From whence all Beings their Existence have,
> And into which resolv'd they find a Grave;

---

[23] i.e. erotic.

How nothing's lost, tho all things change their Form,　　　[5]
As that's a Fly which was but now a Worm;
And Death' is only to begin to be
Som other thing, which endless change shall see;
(Then why should men to dy have so great fear?
Tho nought's Immortal, all Eternal are.)　　　　　[10]

Lines 5 and 7–9 of this extract are generally influenced by the vocabulary and thought of Dryden's 'Lucretius: Against the Fear of Death' (1685), while later on p. 12 Toland's description of William III as 'the thunderbolt of war' specifically echoes Dryden's use of the same phrase for Scipio in the same poem (l. 249). Moreover, l. 2 of this passage seems to echo Dryden's 'Parts of the Whole are we; but God the Whole' ('Palamon and Arcite', iii. 1042), with the same 'whole'/'soul' rhyme in both cases. 'Palamon and Arcite' was published in Dryden's *Fables Ancient and Modern* in 1700 (advertised 5–7 March); *Clito* was published in the same year, though it had apparently been circulating earlier in manuscript. Did Dryden read Toland in manuscript before publication, or vice versa? Or, as seems more likely, did Toland revise *Clito* after reading the *Fables*?

¶72 1700
Sir Charles Sedley, 'Prologue'

Printed in The Works of Sir Charles Sedley, *ed. Vivian de Sola Pinto, 2 vols.* *(1928), i. 47–8. Danchin 536c*

The prologue begins:

> Since glorious *Dryden* has withdrawn his Light,
> Some glimmering Stars relieve our gloomy Night;
> Poets of different Magnitudes advance,
> In humble Confidence of Song and Dance;

This prologue is assigned by Pinto to *The Reform'd Wife* by Charles Burnaby, which was performed *c.* March 1700. He suggests that the reference is to Dryden's abandonment of the stage after the performance of the *Secular Masque* on 25 March 1700. Danchin, however, thinks that the reference is to Dryden's death on 1 May 1700.

¶73 1700
'To Damon. 1700'

British Library MS Harley 7315, fos. 291ᵛ–293ᵛ

After a mostly satirical list of prominent writers and courtiers, the poem says:

Ingenious Pens immortalize the brave
Yet Rural Muses too their beautys have
For Virgils *Tityrus* has as many Charms   *Dryden
As when he rais'd his Voice to sing of Arms   (fo. 293^v)

¶74 1700
A New Session of the Poets, Occasion'd by the Death of Mr. Dryden (London, 1700)

Wing K 306A. Printed in the Garland Drydeniana *series*

Attributed to Daniel Kenrick. Apollo finds no one worthy to succeed Dryden.

INDEX

The Index covers the main text of the book and its Appendix. For a full listing of individual subscribers to *The Works of Virgil* (1697), and of the sources from which biographical information about them has been drawn, see Appendix 1 to Chapter 8 (pp. 223–37).

Index

Index

Index

Index

Index

Oldham, John 6, 14, 41, 284
Oldmixon, John 188
Ong, Walter J. 100
Ormond, On the Death of the Duke of (1688)
    382
Ormonde, James Butler, Duke of 184, 193,
    205, 315
Ormonde, Mary Butler, Duchess of 197,
    205, 296, 301, 311, 315–18
Orrery, Lionel Boyle, Third Earl of
    (1670–1703) 196, 205
Orrery, Roger Boyle, First Earl of
    (1621–79) 60, 65–6
Orrery, Roger Boyle, Second Earl
    of (1646–1682) 196
Ossory, John Hartstonge, Bishop of 193
Ossory, Thomas Butler, Earl of 315
Otway, Thomas 60, 74, 126; *History and Fall
    of Caius Marius, The* 71; *Venice Preserv'd*
    369
Oundle 289
Ovid (Publius Ovidius Naso) 5, 8, 10, 11,
    12, 54, 92, 97, 108, 269, 301, 306, 310,
    322, 325, 327, 355, 356, 398;
    Metamorphoses 11, 51, 54, 300–5
Owen, Susan J. 58, 73, 74, 75
Oxford Parliament 84
Oxford University 363–4

P., W.: *Quakers Elegy on the Death of Charles
    late King of England, The* (1685) 374
Palmer, Robert 195
Palmes, Guy 182
Parkes, Malcolm 348
Parnell, Thomas 159
Parry, Milman 268
Parsons, Sir John 187, 189
Pastoral Dialogue, A (1690) 388–9
Patterson, Annabel 124
Patrides, C. A. 35
Peacock, Thomas Love 159
Pembroke, Thomas Herbert, Earl of 181,
    184, 188
Penn, William 187
Pepys, Samuel 27, 182, 188, 360
Percival, Sir John 188
Persius (Aulus Persius Flaccus) 8, 92
Peterborough, Charles Mordaunt, Earl of
    213
Petitioning Movement 83
Petre, Thomas, Lord 181
Phileroy, E. 373–4

Phillips, John 170
Phillips, William 145
Pickering, Gilbert 195
Pickering, Sir John 195
Pickering, Theophilus 193
Pincus, Steven 44, 59, 69
Pinto, V. de Sola 399
Pix, Mary 199
Plato 12
Playford, Henry 97, 119
Playford, John 97
Plot, Robert 178
Poetical Dictionary, A (1761) 141
*Poetical Reflections on a Late Poem Entituled
    Absalom and Achitophel* (1681) 370–1
'Poets' Address to King James, The'
    (1687) 380
Polybius 91
Pope, Alexander 112, 141, 147, 208, 267,
    340; *Dunciad, The* 19; *Essay on Criticism,
    An* 104, 141–3, 149, 158, 169, 287; 'First
    Epistle of the Second Book of Horace
    Imitated, The' 92, 99; *Iliad of Homer,
    The* 123, 170–2, 192–3, 240, 242, 259,
    264, 268, 272–3; *Odyssey of Homer,
    The* 169, 170, 171
Popish Plot 28, 58, 59, 68, 71, 304, 368
Pordage, Samuel 83, 88
Portlock, Benjamin 318
Potter, John 396
Potter, Lois 68, 90
Poussin, Nicolas 7, 214
Praelectio Musica (1669) 363–4
Preston, Richard Graham, Viscount 177,
    195, 390
Prior, Matthew 44, 207
'Procul este Prophani' (*c.*1679) 365–6
Profitt, Bessie 143, 287
Prude, John 197
Ptolemies 354
Pulteney, John 203
Purcell, Henry 94–112 *passim*, 192; *Dido and
    Aeneas* 96; *Dioclesian* 96; *Fairy Queen,
    The* 101; *Orpheus Britannicus* 97
Pythagoras 300–5

Quem Natura Negat (*c.*1682) 369

Racine, Jean 93, 249
Radcliffe, Edward, Lord 115, 119, 122
Radnor, Charles Robartes, Earl of 188
Randall, Dale B. J. 68

Index

Index

413